THE JUNG–KIRSCH LETTERS

This book charts Carl Gustav Jung's 33-year (1928–1961) correspondence with James Kirsch, adding depth and complexity to the previously published record of the early Jungian movement. Kirsch was a German-Jewish psychiatrist and a first-generation follower of Jung, who founded Jungian communities in Berlin, Tel Aviv, London, and Los Angeles. Their letters tell of heroic survival, brilliant creativity, and the building of generative institutions; but these themes are darkened by personal and collective shadows.

The Nazi era looms over the first half of the book, shaping the story in ways that were fateful not only for Kirsch and his career but also for Jung and his. Kirsch trained with Jung and acted as a tutor in Jewish psychology and culture. In 1934, fearing that anti-Semitism had seized his teacher, Kirsch challenged Jung to explain some of his publications for the Nazi-influenced International Society for Psychotherapy. Jung's answer convinced Kirsch of his sincerity, and from then on Kirsch defended him fiercely against any allegation of anti-Semitism.

We also witness Kirsch's lifelong struggle with states of archetypal possession: his identification with the interior God-image on the one hand, and with unconscious feminine aspects of his psyche on the other. These complexes were expressed, for Kirsch, in physical symptoms and emotional dilemmas, and they led him into clinical boundary violations which were costly to his analysands, his family, and himself.

The text of these historical documents is translated with great attention to style and accuracy, and generous editorial scaffolding gives glimpses into the writers' world. Four appendices are included: two essays by Kirsch, a series of letters between Hilde Kirsch and Jung, and a brief, incisive essay on the Medical Society for Psychotherapy. This revised edition includes primary material that was unavailable when the book was first published, as well as updated footnotes and minor corrections to the translated letters.

Ann Conrad Lammers is a psychotherapist, writer, and teacher of theological ethics. She has degrees from Barnard, The General Theological Seminary, and Yale. Having worked in the San Francisco area for 20 years, she now lives and works in New England.

"The Jung and Kirsch letters offer an inner look at the ever-deepening exchange of thoughts, dreams and concepts of early Jungian psychology between these two influential and powerful men. As Kirsch journeys from Nazi Germany to Israel, to England, and finally to Los Angeles, California, we experience his seeking for a homeland, an outer and inner home for his brilliance and commitment to Jungian psychoanalysis, and his personal family. Kirsch's profound identity with his Jewish roots and his challenge to Jung to understand and integrate the philosophy and history of the Jewish people gives a deeply meaningful insight into the collective and individual struggle of that era, and is equally important today. Reading this book is crucial to our understanding of Jungian psychology." – Jacqueline Zeller Levine, Ph.D., Jungian analyst, The C.G. Jung Institute of Santa Fe, New Mexico, USA

"The Jung–Kirsch correspondence opens unique insights into their lifelong cooperation and their developing ideas about clinical and cultural issues. James Kirsch was one of the first who explained Jewish culture and identity to Jung. This edition of their letters is a milestone in the study of cultural complexes. It is eye-opening and fascinating to read." – Dr. Jörg Rasche, Psychoanalyst IAAP, ISST, C. G. Jung Institute Berlin, Germany

"*The Jung–Kirsch Letters* belongs to a category of literature where the thoughts and ideas of the psychoanalytic masters are revealed behind their more formal writings. We are here served an exceptional vista of ruminations, theoretical and clinical discussions, dreams and personal emotions, as they crystallize into meaningful ideas. Ann Lammers' skillful editing renders this correspondence between Jung and one of his most prominent Jewish disciples into a masterful volume of great interest for readers, both professional and lay, interested in depth psychology." – Erel Shalit, Ph.D., Jungian psychoanalyst and author, Tel Aviv, Israel

THE JUNG–KIRSCH LETTERS

The Correspondence of
C. G. Jung and James Kirsch

Revised Edition

Edited by Ann Conrad Lammers

Translated by Ursula Egli and Ann Conrad Lammers

Routledge
Taylor & Francis Group

LONDON AND NEW YORK

Revised edition published 2016
by Routledge
2 Park Square, Milton Park, Abingdon, Oxon OX14 4RN

and by Routledge
711 Third Avenue, New York, NY 10017

Routledge is an imprint of the Taylor & Francis Group, an informa business

British Library Cataloguing in Publication Data
A catalogue record for this book is available from the British Library

Library of Congress Cataloging in Publication Data
Jung, C. G. (Carl Gustav), 1875–1961, author.
[Correspondence. Selections. English]
The Jung-Kirsch letters : the correspondence of C.G. Jung and
James Kirsch / edited by Ann Conrad Lammers ; translated by Ursula Egli
and Ann Conrad Lammers. — Revised edition.
pages cm
Includes bibliographical references and index.
1. Jung, C. G. (Carl Gustav), 1875–1961—Correspondence.
2. Psychoanalysts—Correspondence. 3. Kirsch, James—Correspondence.
4. Psychiatrists—Correspondence. I. Lammers, Ann Conrad, editor. II. Title.
BF109.J8A4 2016
150.19′540922—dc23
[B]
2015033277

ISBN: 978-1-138-84348-6 (hbk)
ISBN: 978-1-138-84349-3 (pbk)
ISBN: 978-1-315-64040-2 (ebk)

Typeset in Times New Roman
by Swales & Willis Ltd, Exeter, Devon, UK

CONTENTS

CONTENTS

ILLUSTRATIONS

Many thanks to Riccardo Bernardini for his research proving the date and location of Margareta Fellerer's portrait of Jung (Figure 9.1), and to Andreas Jung for confirming the significance of Dr. Bernardini's evidence.

PREFACE

By Thomas B. Kirsch MD

Figure Pref. 1 **James Kirsch with grandson, 1967.** *Photo: ©1967, Thomas B. Kirsch. Courtesy Thomas B. Kirsch.*

As this revised edition of my father's correspondence with Jung approaches publication, it is now 26 years since my father died and 55 years since the death of C. G. Jung. I had known about the letters from Jung to my father for many years, and I knew that he valued them highly. About fifteen years ago I received a telephone call from Sasha Rosen, an American Jung-oriented sandplay therapist who had moved to southern England. She was doing research on the life of Margaret Lowenfeld, the original founder of sandplay therapy, at the ETH (Eidgenössische Technische Hochschule) in Zurich, and she came upon the complete correspondence of my father to Jung. This meant that both sides of the correspondence existed. In my father's archive I had already found 44 letters from Jung to my father. Yvonne Voegeli, responsible archivist of the C. G. Jung Papers Collection at the ETH-Bibliothek (the ETH Library), sent me copies of my father's letters in August 2004. I was eager to have the entire correspondence translated into English, so that I could have a deeper understanding of the relationship between the two. Initially there was little consideration to publishing the correspondence, but in studying it I realized there were some important themes which Jung discussed with my father which might have relevance for a larger audience.

The next question was, did I want to edit the letters myself? I did not. I felt that I had spent enough time and energy on my father both in real life and in analysis, and that at this stage of my life I did not want to devote myself to the absorbing task of editing the correspondence. However, I also did not want to completely let go of the correspondence and wanted to participate in some meaningful way. I looked for persons familiar with Jung who at the same time had established themselves as scholars. Ann Lammers seemed a perfect fit, because she was just finishing the Jung–White correspondence, so that she was familiar with the problems of editing a correspondence, knew Jung's oeuvre and had worked with the Jung heirs. And she was open to the project. As the careful researcher that she is, she found many other letters that Jung wrote to my father, both in my father's archive and in the Jung archive in Zurich. She also spent several weeks at our house going over my father's correspondence of 60 years, where she found much relevant information, which has been incorporated into the footnotes. In addition, she found a delightful Christmas card that Jung and others at the Psychological Club sent to my parents in 1958. Thus the correspondence became much larger and richer than had been originally planned.

The correspondence published here represents all the letters known to exist between the two men. No letters have been withheld, and no material from within any of the letters has been withheld (except as required to protect third party confidentiality), so one sees both the positive side and the shadow of the two men in this correspondence. The three most consistent themes are the Jewish/Christian issue, my father's relationship to his anima and to his women patients, and the hypothesis of synchronicity. Other topics mentioned are relationships to other Jungians, the development of the Jung Institute in Los Angeles and the promotion of Jung's ideas to the larger collective. Let me elaborate further on each of these themes:

1. The discussion of the Jewish/Christian question occurred during a time when European Jewry was being systematically stamped out. Jung was being labeled as an anti-Semite and a Nazi, and my father, writing from Tel Aviv, was questioning these rumors about Jung's anti-Jewish activities. After receiving Jung's reply, my father vigorously defended Jung, and enlisted other Jewish Jungians to defend him, especially in Zionist and psychological publications.

2. My father's relationship to his anima was a lifelong struggle. He had a tendency to become over-involved with his women patients, which led to sexual entanglements which should not have occurred. Although such boundary violations were common in those days, the extent to which my father got involved was unusual. I am sure his underlying insecurity with the anima was one of the issues which brought my father into analysis in the first place. From his earliest letters, Jung warned my father that he faced a serious challenge in confronting the anima, and that unconsciousness in this area could have dire consequences. In writing to Jung, my father presented his projections onto women patients in rather abstract terms. In one of his last letters to Jung he referred to his projections of the "Anthropos," the primordial God figure in the form of universal man. Jung, replying in kind, used archetypal language to defuse the intensity of some of these projections.

My father also saw Toni Wolff in analysis and consulted with her about his cases. She was a strong critic of my father's behavior towards his own anima and his women patients.

3. Synchronicity and other theoretical topics: Jung discussed with my father many of his psychological ideas, including alchemy, synchronicity, flying saucers, and other psychological and parapsychological phenomena.

What also becomes clear from this correspondence is the special place in Jung's heart occupied by my father, and one senses the care with which Jung dealt with him. So when my father appealed to this personal connection and called on Jung as an authority, Jung met him in a serious and concerned thera-peutic manner. The problem that I (and many others) had with my father was that he identified with Jung and saw himself as expressing the wisdom of Jung when he spoke to us. It would have been so much easier for my father, with his colleagues and his family, if he had been more secure in his own authority and leaned less on Jung's. As I was growing up, having Jung in the forefront of family life made us all uncomfortable, so my father's children pushed Jung into the background as much as possible. Even as a child, though, I responded positively to Jung, though ambivalently. I attribute my attraction to Jung to the positive and loving influence of my mother, whose sensitivity I attributed to her relationship to Jung.

Going through these letters later in my own life, I have come to realize that my father actually had an extremely close relationship to Jung, and furthermore (for reasons which are not completely clear to me even today), my father was an important colleague to Jung. For instance, in his introduction to *The Red*

Book,[1] Sonu Shamdasani notes that my father was one of very few outside Jung's immediate family to have seen the original text. Jung apparently showed him the Red Book in 1929, when my father first came to him for analysis. I think that Jung valued my father because he saw not only my father's troubled psyche, but also his sensitivity to the workings of the unconscious. Jung also sought understanding of Jewish culture and history, based on my father's vast knowledge of Judaism.

I would like to step back at this point to present the historical context from which my father sought analysis with Jung. My father came from an Orthodox Eastern European Jewish family who one generation previously had moved to Berlin from Poland. His father then did what many German Jewish men did at the time, which was to travel to the Americas and open up a business, usually a general store. My father's father opened up a button business in Guatemala City, Guatemala. As a result my father and his three older sisters and one younger brother were born in Guatemala City. James Kirsch was born on 21 July 1901. Realizing that his children would not get a proper education in Guatemala, his father sent them all back to Germany in 1907, visiting them every two years. My father was an excellent student. Against his family's wishes, he decided to study medicine at the University of Heidelberg. Meanwhile, my grandfather remained in Guatemala. The fact of the First World War meant that he did not visit his family in Berlin for nine years, between 1912 and 1921. According to my father, my grandfather may have had a second, Indian family in Guatemala. No members of a second family have ever surfaced.

When my father was in his teens he became a Zionist and joined a hiking club called the Blau-Weiss, one of many Zionist organizations which were developing all over Europe to promote Palestine as the homeland for the Jews. At the University of Heidelberg, my father made two lifelong friends in the Blau-Weiss Society: Erich Fromm, the psychoanalyst, and Ernst Simon, a close associate of Martin Buber. Fromm was in analysis with Frieda Reichmann, during which time they fell in love and married. The marriage did not last, but my father saw at close hand what could happen in an analytic relationship.

My father returned to Berlin after his medical studies and began working in a psychiatric hospital. He began a Freudian analysis, but was dissatisfied and ended it after two years. He then read Jung's *Psychological Types* and entered analysis with the Jungian lay analyst Toni Sussmann.[2] In late 1928 he wrote to

1   Sonu Shamdasani, Introduction, in C. G. Jung, *The Red Book: Liber Novus*, Sonu Shamdasani, ed. (translated by Mark Kyburz, John Peck, and Sonu Shamdasani, Philemon Series/Foundation of the Works of C. G. Jung, New York: W. W. Norton & Co., 2009), p. 215 (hereafter *Red Book*).

2   Jungian lay analyst and trainer of analysts, then working in Berlin, who had analyzed and trained with Jung. A Jewish convert to Catholicism, Sussmann fled Germany in 1938 and established herself in Oxford. Her determination to combine Indian theosophy with Jungian psychology raised concerns for Jung (cf. Jung, 19 August 1929, p. 6 and note, and 28 January 1933, p. 34) and led him in the 1940s to distance himself from her work (cf. Ann Conrad Lammers and Adrian Cunningham, eds, *The Jung–White Letters*, New York and London: Routledge, 2007, pp. 41–48, p. 77, p. 79; hereafter *Jung–White Letters*).

Jung asking to schedule appointments in Zurich. Jung wrote back, saying that it would be possible to meet the following May, and that exchange initiated a series of sixty analytical hours. My father's analysis with Jung also constituted his most important professional training as a Jungian analyst. In today's terms 60 hours doesn't seem like very much, but in those days 60 hours was considered a lengthy analysis. These hours were not consecutive, but my father would visit Zurich periodically, and he would also meet Jung for a chance hour or two when they were both attending a conference. In later life, when my father added up all his professional training, he listed his hours not only with Jung but also with Toni Sussmann, Toni Wolff, Liliane Frey-Rohn, and C. A. Meier.

It is important to locate Jung in his career trajectory at this time. After his "confrontation with the unconscious," the period lasting from 1913 to 1918, Jung's ideas had matured, and the psychology that he developed offered a completely different vision of the psyche to Freud's. Between the end of the First World War and the beginning of the Second World War in 1939, students from all over the world sought him out for analysis and analytic training. That was the time when Jung gave ongoing seminars in English at the Psychological Club, on dreams, visions, and Nietzsche's *Zarathustra*. He also gave lectures in German at the Eidgenössische Technische Hochschule (ETH), including his lectures on the Exercises of St. Ignatius of Loyola. And he gave seminars on children's dreams. Thus, individuals who came to Jung had the opportunity to attend seminars with him, in addition to having an individual analysis. They also would often see a second analyst, usually a woman, and that often turned out to be Toni Wolff. This was the training of most first-generation Jungian analysts.

Practically every member of the German Jewish group in Berlin whom my father had befriended (Erich Neumann, Gerhard Adler, Ernst Bernhard, Werner Engel, Heinz Westmann, and others) eventually ended up in analysis with Jung. With the rise of the Nazis, these new Jungian analysts spread to various corners of the globe. Given his earlier Zionist leanings, my father first emigrated to Palestine (the land which would later become the State of Israel). My mother, who was a patient of my father's at the time, was in deep mourning for her late husband, who had died in 1933. He had suffered fulminating multiple sclerosis and had committed suicide. Her transference to my father was intense, and she followed him to Palestine with her two young sons, even though he was married and had two small children of his own. They all ended up in Tel Aviv, where two years later my father divorced his first wife, Eva, who then returned to practice as a therapist in Berlin. In 1938 he helped Eva leave Berlin to settle in England.

During this time my father wrote to Jung about the rumors he had heard that Jung was anti-Semitic and even a Nazi. Their correspondence thus offers primary documentation about this thorny issue, which continues to haunt students of Jung to this day. I personally believe that this is the most important part of the lengthy correspondence, since Jung goes to great lengths to explain his views on Jews, Judaism, and Jewish mysticism. Hopefully, it will open some eyes to the complexity of Jung's relationship to Judaism.

In one of these letters, September 29, 1934, where he gives his views on Judaism, Jung switches in the last paragraph to offer a clinical consultation to my father. He describes the analytic process when the unconscious of both the patient and the analyst are activated, and interprets the patient's dream as the product of their unconscious relationship. It seems to me that Jung was exactly describing the position of what later has become the Relational School of Psychoanalysis, where the unconscious manifestation is always the product of what happens between the two psyches.

In 1935 my mother and father, now together, moved from Tel Aviv to London. They experienced the early Zionists as more fanatical than they were comfortable with. Living conditions in what was then called Palestine were also considered too primitive for those who were used to the modern conveniences of European life.

The family began anew in London, where my father again opened his analytic practice and where I was born. It was in London that my mother became an analyst as well. Jung sent to her a physician-analysand whom he could not see. This doctor had chosen my mother, a choice he checked out with Jung, who thought it was a good idea. That is the informal way that my mother became an analyst, even though she did not have a complete education, nor had she completed many hours of personal analysis with Jung and had had no supervision except from my father. Meanwhile, my father continued his correspondence with Jung from his new home in England.

When it appeared that the German war machine was ready to overrun the UK, my parents hurriedly made contact with relatives in San Francisco and got on the first boat which would take them to the United States. It was the good ship *Samaria* that carried us across the Atlantic in October 1940, accompanied by a destroyer convoy and air cover. Many such crossings were not as lucky as ours, and the *Samaria* was sunk two months later while attempting another crossing. My family settled in Los Angeles as the first Jungians, and they helped to build up a Jungian community there over the next 45 years. Although my parents wrote to Jung in 1944, there were no wartime letters from Jung to my parents between 1941 and 1945. The correspondence picked up after the war and continued until 1961. The topics they discussed were the religious and psychological differences between Christianity and Judaism, Jung's theory of synchronicity, further questions about my father's relationships with his women patients, and the political complications arising within the growing Jungian community in Los Angeles.

My father's continuing difficulties with his women patients were of great concern to Jung, and many of their letters allude to this problem. This was still a time when there were no legal ramifications for sexual contact with a patient. From Jung's responses one can tell that he was aware of the depth of the problem for my father. Jung continued to voice his concern about my father's behavior with women patients but seemed to realize that my father was painfully helpless in the face of it. He was not completely open with Jung about his behavior, and it was only in his last letters to Jung that the psychological roots of the problem were

Figure Pref. 2 **James and Hilde Kirsch, Israel, 1972.** *Photographer unknown. Courtesy Thomas B. Kirsch.*

revealed. Rather than discuss the problem in more depth here, I shall leave the reader to explore the development of this issue throughout the correspondence.

Meanwhile my mother and father, James and Hilde, along with Max Zeller, were working hard to build the Jungian community in Los Angeles. Most of the first members were German Jewish doctors and therapists (wartime refugees) who did not have the proper credentials to practice in California. In spite of this drawback, more and more people became interested in Jungian psychology. Starting in 1942 my father gave weekly seminars on Jung and Jungian material continuing until 1988, one year before his death. Both analysts and patients attended the weekly seminar, and while my mother was alive she prepared cookies, cake, coffee, and tea for the participants. There are literally hundreds of tapes of all the seminars and lectures which my father gave to various groups in Los Angeles. The Jung Institute in Los Angeles named the lecture room after him, and he was honored at the time. In addition to the weekly seminars, he wrote two books, *Shakespeare's Royal Self*[3] and *The Reluctant Prophet*,[4] a story of the late-nineteenth-century

---

3   James Kirsch, *Shakespeare's Royal Self* (Zürich: Daimon Verlag; and New York: C. G. Jung Foundation of New York, 1966).
4   James Kirsch, *The Reluctant Prophet: An exploration of prophecy and dreams* (Los Angeles: Sherbourne Press, Inc., 1973).

Rabbi Hile Wechsler, who dreamed that he and his flock should leave Germany and emigrate to Palestine. My father must have felt a strong affinity with Rabbi Wechsler when he was advising all his patients, friends, and family to leave Germany in 1933.

My mother and father continued to visit Jung until 1960 and continued to visit Zurich on an almost yearly basis up until their respective deaths in 1978 and 1989. Through them I had three occasions to meet with Jung, and these encounters strengthened my desire to become a Jungian analyst myself.

Unfortunately, because of his boundary violations with various woman patients and his arrogant attitude towards those who did not know Jung's psychology well enough to satisfy his high standards, James Kirsch has left a mixed legacy in Los Angeles.

This correspondence, translated from German into English by Ursula Egli and Ann Conrad Lammers and edited by Ann Conrad Lammers, should help to elucidate the long and complicated relationship between Jung and my father. I would also like to thank the Stiftung der Werke von C. G. Jung (formerly the Erbengemeinschaft C. G. Jung), especially Ulrich Hoerni and Peter Jung, for their permission to publish Jung's side of this important correspondence.

28 October 2015
Palo Alto, California

ACKNOWLEDGMENTS

This volume could not have been prepared without the generous help of many people, and the editor is deeply grateful to them all. I have done my best to include every name. If an oversight nonetheless occurs, I ask forgiveness and will correct the omission at the earliest opportunity.

There are two primary sources for the main text of this volume. First is the archive of the ETH-Bibliothek (Eidgenössische Technische Hochschule Zürich), C. G. Jung-Arbeitsarchiv, Archive und Nachlässe, Korrespondenz C. G. Jung–J. Kirsch (HS 1056, 1124): C. G. Jung Archive, Archives and Legacies, ETH [Swiss Federal Institute of Technology Zurich] Library, C. G. Jung–J. Kirsch correspondence. Other cited correspondences at the ETH Library archive include Jung's letters to and from Gerhard Adler, Gustav Bally, H. G. Baynes, E. A. Bennet, Eugen Bleuler, Walter Cimbal, Matthias Göring, Jakob Hauer, Gustav Heyer, Jolande Jacobi, Aniela Jaffé, Hilde Kirsch, Wolfgang Kranefeldt, C. A. Meier, J. H. Schultz and Toni Sussmann; also C. A. Meier's letters to and from Gerhard Adler, Kurt Binswanger, Walter Cimbal, Matthias Göring, Gustav Heyer, James Kirsch, Otto Körner, Wolfgang Kranefeldt, Ernst Kretschmer, Fritz Künkel, Toni Wolff and Heinrich Zimmer. Permission to receive copies of the Jung–Kirsch letters, and for access to the other cited correspondences, was given by Ulrich Hoerni and Peter Jung for the C. G. Jung Estate (now the Foundation of the Works of C. G. Jung), and by Rudolf Mumenthaler and Yvonne Voegeli for the C. G. Jung-Arbeitsarchiv and the ETH-Bibliothek.

The second primary source for this volume is the James Kirsch archive: C. G. Jung–James Kirsch Correspondence, Archive of James Isaac Kirsch (documents dating from 1928 to 1989), overseen by Dr. Thomas Kirsch, Palo Alto, California. Additional cited correspondences, located at the James Kirsch archive, include Kirsch's letters to and from Gerhard Adler, Ernst Bernhard, Chung-yuan Chang, Werner Engel, W. Y. Evans-Wentz, Heinrich Fierz, Michael Fordham, Liliane Frey-Rohn, Erich Fromm, Jess Groesbeck, R. F. C. Hull, Siegmund Hurwitz, Jolande Jacobi, Aniela Jaffé, Bruno Klopfer, Yechezkel Kluger, Akihisa Kondo, Wolfgang Kranefeldt, Fritz Künkel, C. A. Meier, Erich Neumann, John Sanford, Rivkah Schärf-Kluger, Gustav Schmaltz, Gershom Scholem, Ernst Simon, Toni Wolff, Marie-Louise von Franz, Max Zeller, and Heinrich Zimmer. Permission to receive copies of the Jung–Kirsch letters, and for access to these cited correspondences, was given by Thomas Kirsch for the James Kirsch Estate. Letters of Aniela Jaffé are printed with kind permission from her literary executor, Robert Hinshaw.

Background information about Jung and his family was generously supplied by Ulrich Hoerni and Peter Jung. Access to specific volumes in Jung's library, and information about others, was kindly provided by Andreas Jung. Permission to study in the private archive of James Kirsch was generously given by Thomas Kirsch. I am deeply grateful to Tom and Jean Kirsch for their warm hospitality during each of my extended visits, as they watched their dining room table disappear under James Kirsch's voluminous correspondence. In addition, Dr. James Silber and Ruth G. Kirsch provided essential information about the early histories of the Silber and Kirsch families.

I am grateful to the staffs of the following archives, libraries, and special collections, who welcomed me as a researcher and gave me the benefit of their learned consultation: The Cohen Center for Holocaust and Genocide Studies, Keene State College, Keene, New Hampshire, with special thanks to Henry Knight and Thomas White; the Flora Lamson Hewlett Library of the Graduate Theological Union, Berkeley, California; the Jewish Reading Room of the New York Public Library; the Kristine Mann Library of the Analytical Psychology Club of New York, with special thanks to Linda Seligman; the Virginia Allen Detloff Library of the C. G. Jung Institute of San Francisco, with special thanks to acting archivist Marianne Morgan; the C. G. Jung Institute of Los Angeles, with warm gratitude to archivist Deborah Wesley for finding and providing several original documents from the papers of James Kirsch.

The ETH Library archive is acknowledged above, but I cannot overlook the invaluable assistance of Yvonne Voegeli, responsible archivist of the C. G. Jung Papers Collection at the ETH-Bibliothek. I am grateful to Herr Huber and to everyone else on her staff. On each of my research trips to Zurich, and between times as well, Frau Voegeli – with kind permission from Ulrich Hoerni, for the Foundation of the Works of C. G. Jung – has gone out of her way to locate, organize, and make accessible a variety of primary and secondary documents for this volume.

In addition to allowing access to documents at the ETH Library archive, Ulrich Hoerni has repeatedly located valuable documents which either belong to the primary text or contribute to the "mosaic stones" of the annotations. He has graciously given access to rare and unpublished documents, provided bibliographic, historical and linguistic information, offered skilled advice on the translations, and given close, critical attention to the entire text. His support has been essential to the project from the beginning, and my appreciation would be hard to overstate.

Ursula Egli is thanked more than once in this volume, for good reason. In addition to working long and faithfully as the primary translator of the German-language portions of the volume, she has performed many tasks essential to preparing this complex project for publication. She typed transcriptions, edited my stylistic revisions of her initial translations, and proofread at every stage. She also independently researched linguistic and cultural questions and consulted with philologists. I am grateful for her skill, tact, and faithful partnership. Without her help this volume could not have been brought to publication.

Hundreds of annotations were made possible by the indefatigable research assistance of Luis Gutierrez. His creativity with internet tools and his unfailing encouragement added to the joy of researching. He also succeeded, through a combination of skill, persistence, and what appeared to be miraculous good luck, in locating several individuals whose scholarly assistance or legal permissions were needed.

Many other scholars assisted in specific areas. Richard Corney was most generous in translating Latin and Hebrew, untangling biblical citations, and offering his critical reading of parts of the scholarly apparatus. Steven Joseph kindly gave his learned advice on passages referring to the Kabbalah and other strands of Jewish literature. I am grateful to Alfred Ribi, who instructed me concerning many passages in the literature of alchemy. For our discussions of Jung's Berlin Seminar, and for information on the life and work of Ernst Bernhard, warm thanks to Giovanni Sorge. Günther Langwieler and Murray Stein provided guidance when I was searching through documents from the 1930s. For reviewing and correcting my discussion of Jung's historical relationship with the AAGP and IAAGP [the (International) General Medical Society for Psychotherapy], I am much indebted to Thomas Fischer for his careful consultation, and to Andrew Samuels for his critical perspective.

Martin Müller provided the text of a poem by Hans Sachs. Bryan Rennie advised me about Mircea Eliade's works. Diana Grace-Jones found historical information about Kathleen Kitchin and the Guild of Pastoral Psychology. Peg LeVine kindly informed me about the life and work of Akihisa Kondo. Jay Williams resolved some of the literary puzzles in Kirsch's lecture on Jack London. Jean Kirsch compared early versions of London's "The Red One" and carefully reviewed the whole text of Appendix C. Robert Segal was most generous with his scholarly advice and oversight as I was preparing the bibliography.

Copyright permissions to print the primary materials in this volume were kindly granted by the following. For the writings of James and Hilde Kirsch (Hildegard Silber), the Kirsch Estate, with special thanks to Thomas Kirsch, Ruth Kirsch, and Jim Silber. For the writings of C. G. Jung, the C. G. Jung Estate (Erbengemeinschaft C. G. Jung), later the Foundation of the Works of C. G. Jung (Stiftung der Werke von C. G. Jung), with special thanks to Ulrich Hoerni and Peter Jung. Thanks also to Peter Fritz, of the Paul and Peter Fritz Literary Agency, Zurich, for help and consultation concerning permissions matters, and for overseeing literary rights.

Other copyright permissions were sought and given by the following. The estate of Marianne Niehus-Jung; the estate of Marie-Jeanne Schmid-Boller; Hansueli Etter, Emmanuel Kennedy, and the Stiftung für Jung'sche Psychologie for the estates of Marie-Louise von Franz and Barbara Hannah; Robert Hinshaw for the estates of Aniela Jaffé and Liliane Frey-Rohn.

A summary of the letters published in this volume is provided in "List of Letters," pp. 318ff. Letters which have been previously published, in whole or in part, are identified there, together with the locations of their earlier publication.

Reprint permission for 11 previously published letters of C. G. Jung, in new translations for this edition, was kindly granted by Princeton University Press:

JUNG, C. G.; *C. G. JUNG LETTERS: Vol. 1.*
© 1973 Princeton University Press, 2001 renewed PUP
Reprinted by permission of Princeton University Press.

JUNG, C. G.; *SELECTED LETTERS OF C. G. JUNG, 1909–1961.*
© 1953, 1955, 1961, 1963, 1968, 1971, 1972, 1973, 1974, 1975, 1984
Princeton University Press
Reprinted by permission of Princeton University Press.

In addition, the present volume includes 29 letters by C. G. Jung and one by James Kirsch, previously published as "Letters to a Friend," edited and translated (with one exception) by James Kirsch, in *Psychological Perspectives,* Part I, Vol. 3, No. 1, The C. G. Jung Institute of Los Angeles, Spring 1972; and Part II, Vol. 3, No. 2, The C. G. Jung Institute of Los Angeles, Fall 1972. They are reprinted here, newly translated, with gracious support from the Editorial Board of *Psychological Perspectives*, Christophe Le Mouël, Executive Director of the Institute, and Gilda Frantz, Co-Editor-in-Chief.

Permission to reprint James Kirsch's lecture, "'The Red One': A psychological interpretation of a story by Jack London," reverting to its original version of 1954, was kindly granted by Christophe Le Mouël, Executive Director of the C. G. Jung Institute of Los Angeles, and Gilda Frantz, Co-Editor-in-Chief of *Psychological Perspectives*. The lecture was previously copyrighted:

James Kirsch, "Jack London's Quest: 'The Red One',"
Psychological Perspectives, Vol. 11, No. 2, pp. 137–54, Fall 1980,
© C. G. Jung Institute of Los Angeles.
Reprinted by permission of The C. G. Jung Institute of Los Angeles.

Various passages containing personal information are printed in their entirety in this edition, with generous permission from the following: Foundation of the Works of C. G. Jung; the Kirsch Estate; the Kollwitz Estate; the Estate of Mary Crile; the Estate of Toni Wolff.

Full credits for the volume's illustrations are listed in the List of Illustrations, pages vii–viii.

Funding for *The Jung–Kirsch Letters* was generously provided by several sources, including Jenny and Steve Chang, through the Taiwan Institute of

Psychotherapy; the Foundation C. G. Jung Institutes for Alumni, Supporters and Friends, Asheville, North Carolina; the Stiftung der Werke von C. G. Jung, Zurich; the Marie-Louise von Franz Stiftung, Zurich; the Stiftung für Jung'sche Psychologie, Zurich, the Forschungs und Ausbildungszentrum für Tiefenpsychologie nach C. G. Jung und Marie-Louise von Franz, Zurich; and the Stiftung C. G. Jung Küsnacht. In addition, six individual donors, including Judith Harris and Tony Woolfson, supported the project, some through repeated gifts. Profound thanks to all, especially those who gave so generously but asked to be unnamed, for the kindness and vision which carried this volume through to publication.

For their hospitality, I am deeply grateful to the deaconesses of the Baptistengemeinde, Zurich, at whose guest house in Fluntern I stayed for three weeks in the summer of 2008. For his support with the project's technical and practical requirements, I am much indebted to Edward Dell.

Finally, the editor wishes to express sincere gratitude to the publisher, Routledge, and especially to Kate Hawes, Sarah Gibson, Erasmis Kidd, Dawn Harris, and David Cradduck, for patiently seeing this project through its many stages of development, delivery, and production. Bringing out the revised edition has also proven a complex undertaking, during which I have been grateful to Susannah Frearson, editor at Routledge, for her dedicated and skillful oversight, to Tamsin Ballard for her expert copy-editing and to Caroline Watson at Swales and Willis.

Every effort has been made to trace copyright holders and to obtain permission to reproduce extracts from other sources. Any omissions brought to our attention will be remedied in future editions or reprints.

ABBREVIATIONS

AAGP   Allgemeine ärztliche Gesellschaft für Psychotherapie (General Medical Society for Psychotherapy), founded 1926. See also IAAGP.

Aion   C. G. Jung, *Aion: Researches into the Phenomenology of the Self.* Trans. R. F. C. Hull. PUP/Bollingen, 1959. CW 9.ii. (*Aion: Untersuchungen zur Symbolgeschichte,* Zürich: Rascher-Verlag, 1951.)

APC   Analytical Psychology Club (of Zurich, London, New York, Los Angeles, San Francisco, etc.)

Briefe I, II, III   *C. G. Jung Briefe. I, 1906–1945; II, 1946–1955; III, 1956–1961.* Herausgegeben von Aniela Jaffé, in Zusammenarbeit mit Gerhard Adler. Olten und Freiburg im Breisgau: Walter-Verlag, 1972/1980.

C. G. Jung Speaking   William McGuire and R. F. C. Hull, eds, *C. G. Jung Speaking: Interviews and Encounters.* PUP, 1977.

Club   Der psychologische Club [the Psychological Club], Zürich.

Countway Interview   Interview of James Kirsch by Gene Nameche, 15 December 1968, Los Angeles. Typescript, C. G. Jung Biographical Archive, Countway Library of Medicine, Harvard Medical School, Cambridge, MA.

CW   The Collected Works of C. G. Jung. 21 volumes. (Cf. Selected Bibliography, pp. 322f.)

EJ   *Eranos-Jahrbuch, -Jahrbücher* (annual collections of lectures from Eranos). Olga Fröbe-Kapteyn, ed., Zürich: Rhein-Verlag, 1933– .

ETH   Eidgenössische Technische Hochschule (Swiss Federal Institute of Technology), Zürich.

ETH Library archive   C. G. Jung-Arbeitsarchiv, Hauptabteilung Handschriften und Nachlässe des Archivs der ETH, Zürich (C. G. Jung Archive, Department of Manuscripts and Legacies, Archive of the Swiss Federal Institute of Technology, Zurich).

FJL	*The Freud/Jung Letters.* Ed. William McGuire, trans. R. Manheim & R. F. C. Hull. PUP/London: Hogarth Press, Routledge & Kegan Paul, 1974.
Göring Institute	Deutsches Institut für psychologische Forschung und Psychotherapie (German Institute for Psychological Research and Psychotherapy), Berlin. Founded 1937, under the direction of Dr. M. H. Göring.
GW	Die Gesammelten Werke von C. G. Jung (Collected Works, German-language edition), 21 volumes. (Cf. Selected Bibliography, pp. 323f.)
IAAGP	Internationale allgemeine ärztliche Gesellschaft für Psychotherapie (International General Medical Society for Psychotherapy). Founded 1933, through reorganization of the AAGP.
IAAP	International Association for Analytical Psychology.
IGS	Ann Conrad Lammers, *In God's Shadow: The Collaboration of Victor White and C. G. Jung.* Mahwah, NJ: Paulist Press, 1994.
Job	C. G. Jung, *Antwort auf Hiob.* Zürich: Rascher-Verlag, 1952. *Answer to Job.* Trans. R. F. C. Hull. London: Routledge & Kegan Paul, 1954. "Answer to Job", *Psychology and Religion,* CW 11, 1958/1969.
Jung–White Letters	Ann Conrad Lammers & Adrian Cunningham, eds, *The Jung–White Letters.* London & New York: Routledge, 2007.
Jungians	Thomas B. Kirsch, *The Jungians: A Comparative and Historical Perspective.* London & Philadelphia: Routledge, 2000.
Kirsch archive	Archive of James Isaac Kirsch: Private correspondences and papers, 1928 to 1989, overseen by Dr. Thomas Kirsch, Palo Alto, California.
KML archive	Archive of the Kristine Mann Library of the Analytical Psychology Club of New York.
Letters I, II	*C. G. Jung Letters. Vol. I: 1906–1950; Vol. II: 1951–1961.* Selected and edited by Gerhard Adler in collaboration with Aniela Jaffé, trans. R. F. C. Hull. PUP/London: Routledge, 1973, 1975.
Life & Work	Aniela Jaffé, *From the Life and Work of C. G. Jung.* Trans. R. F. C. Hull & Murray Stein. Einsiedeln: Daimon Verlag, 1989.
MDR	C. G. Jung, *Memories, Dreams, Reflections.* Recorded and edited by Aniela Jaffé, trans. Richard & Clara Winston, rev. ed. New York: Vintage Books, 1965.

MSAP — Medical Society of Analytical Psychology. Originally founded in London, 1936. Founded in San Francisco 1943; in New York 1946. As of 1947, MSAP (US) was a single organization, headquartered in New York and San Francisco.

Mysterium — C. G. Jung, *Mysterium Coniunctionis: Untersuchung über die Trennung und Zusammensetzung der seelischen Gegensätze in der Alchemie.* Unter Mitarbeit von Marie-Louise von Franz. GW 14, 1968. *Mysterium Coniunctionis: An Inquiry into the Separation and Synthesis of Psychic Opposites in Alchemy.* CW 14, 1963/1970.

PP — James Kirsch, ed. "Letters to a Friend," *Psychological Perspectives,* C. G. Jung Institute of Los Angeles; Part I, Vol. 3:1, Spring 1972; Part II, Vol. 3:2, Fall 1972. (Twenty-nine letters from Jung and one letter from Kirsch. Translations by Kirsch, except as noted.)

Psych & Alch — C. G. Jung, *Psychologie und Alchemie.* Zürich: Rascher-Verlag, 1944. *Psychology and Alchemy,* CW 12, trans. R. F. C. Hull. PUP/Bollingen; London: Routledge & Kegan Paul, 1953/1968.

Psych & Rel — C. G. Jung, *Psychology and Religion: West and East,* CW 11, 1958/1969.

PUP — Princeton, NJ: Princeton University Press.

"Reconsidering" — James Kirsch, "Reconsidering Jung's So-Called Anti-Semitism," *The Arms of the Windmill: Essays in Analytical Psychology in Honor of Werner H. Engel.* New York: The Jung Foundation, 1984.

Symbolik — C. G. Jung, *Die Symbolik des Geistes: Studien über psychische Phänomenologie,* Psychologische Abhandlungen 6. Zürich: Rascher, 1948; with contribution by Rivkah Schärf.

Symbols of — C. G. Jung, *Symbols of Transformation: An Analysis of Transformation the Prelude to a Case of Schizophrenia,* CW 5, 1956/ 1974. Cf. *Wandlungen.*

"Synchronicity" — C. G. Jung, "Synchronizität als ein Prinzip akausaler Zusammenhänge," in C. G. Jung and W. Pauli, *Naturerklärung und Psyche* (Studien aus dem C. G. Jung-Institut Zürich, 4). Zürich: Rascher-Verlag, 1952. In English, revised: "Synchronicity: An Acausal Connecting Principle," trans. R. F. C. Hull, in *The Interpretation of Nature and the Psyche.* New York: Pantheon; London: Routledge & Kegan Paul, 1955.

Transference	C. G. Jung, *Die Psychologie der Übertragung. Erläutert anhand einer alchemistischen Bilderserie. Für Ärzte und praktische Psychologen.* Zürich: Rascher-Verlag, 1946. "The Psychology of the Transference. Interpreted together with a series of alchemical images. For physicians and practical psychologists," in *The Practice of Psychotherapy,* CW 16, 1954/1966.
Types	C. G. Jung, *Psychological Types,* CW 6, 1971 (orig. pub. 1926).
VADL archive	Archive of the Virginia Allen Detloff Library of the C. G. Jung Insitute of San Francisco.
Wandlungen	C. G. Jung, *Wandlungen und Symbole der Libido: Beiträge zur Entwicklungsgeschichte des Denkens.* Leipzig und Vienna: Franz Deuticke, 1912.
Wirklichkeit	C. G. Jung, *Wirklichkeit der Seele: Anwendungen und Fortschritte der neueren Psychologie, mit Beiträgen von Hugo Rosenthal, Emma Jung, W. M. Kranefeldt.* Zürich: Rascher, 1934.
"Wotan"	C. G. Jung, "Wotan," CW 10 (orig. pub. *Neue Schweizer Rundschau,* Band III:11, March 1936).
Wurzeln	C. G. Jung, *Von den Wurzeln des Bewusstseins: Studien über den Archetypus* (Psychologische Abhandlungen 9). Zürich: Rascher-Verlag, 1954.
Zentralblatt	*Zentralblatt für Psychotherapie und ihre Grenzgebiete.* Leipzig: Hirzel Verlag, 1928– . Quarterly journal of the AAGP and IAAGP.

INTRODUCTION

By Ann Conrad Lammers, PhD

The Jung–Kirsch Letters

Volumes of Jung's published letters are now numerous enough to fill a modest bookshelf, *The Jung–Kirsch Letters* being the sixth major edition out of seven to date. First came the two-volume *C. G. Jung Letters,*[1] with its parallel in German, the three-volume *C. G. Jung Briefe.*[2] These comprise about 1200 of Jung's letters, written to hundreds of correspondents. Since their publication in 1972–73, five major correspondences have followed,[3] each reflecting Jung's dialogue with a significant colleague. The earliest of these, in content and date of publication, is his exchange with Sigmund Freud.[4] The second is based on his correspondence with an old friend, Hans Schmid-Guisan, with whom he worked on his theory of psychological types.[5] Three further, major editions have been published. One is Jung's far-reaching scientific exchange with the physicist Wolfgang Pauli;[6]

---

1   Gerhard Adler, ed. *C. G. Jung Letters, Vol. I: 1906–1950* and *Vol. II: 1951–1961* (selected and edited by Gerhard Adler in collaboration with Aniela Jaffé, trans. by R. F. C. Hull, Princeton, NJ: Princeton University Press/London: Routledge, 1973, 1975); hereafter *Letters I, II.* The original intention in selecting Jung's letters for publication was to include them in his Collected Works. For this reason, and for reasons of copyright, these volumes contain Jung's letters alone. They are edited and translated in a style consistent with the Collected Works.

2   Aniela Jaffé, ed., *C. G. Jung Briefe, Band I, 1906–1945; Band II, 1946–1955; Band III, 1956–1961* (herausgegeben von Aniela Jaffé in Zusammenarbeit mit Gerhard Adler, Olten und Freiburg im Breisgau: Walter-Verlag, 1972/1980); hereafter *Briefe I, II, III.* Translations of Jung's English-language letters are by Jaffé. The introduction and annotations vary somewhat from Adler's, but the same selection of letters is published in German as in English.

3   Four other correspondences, of varying weight, have also been published, containing Jung's exchanges with Sabina Spielrein, Emil Medtner, Ernst Bernhard, and Eugen Böhler. Further correspondences are now nearing publication through the Philemon Foundation, including Jung's exchanges with Mircea Eliade, Wilhelm Hauer, and Heinrich Zimmer (Giovanni Sorge, ed.) and Adolf Keller (Marianne Jehle, ed.).

4   William McGuire, ed., *The Freud/Jung Letters* (translated by Ralph Manheim and R. F. C. Hull, Princeton, NJ: Princeton University Press, 1974).

5   Hans Konrad Iselin, *Zur Entstehung von C. G. Jungs "Psychologische Typen": Der Briefwechsel zwischen C. G. Jung und Hans Schmid-Guisan im Lichte ihrer Freundschaft* (Verlag Sauerländer, 1982). The Jung–Schmid letters were also recently published in English: *The Question of Psychological Types: The Correspondence between C. G. Jung and Hans Schmid: 1915–1916,* edited by John Beebe and Ernst Falzeder, translated by Ernst Falzeder with Tony Woolfson (Princeton University Press, 2013).

6   C. A. Meier, ed., *Wolfgang Pauli und C. G. Jung, Ein Briefwechsel, 1932-1958* (herausgegeben von C. A. Meier, unter Mitarbeit von C. P. Enz und M. Fierz, Berlin & Heidelberg: Springer Verlag, 1992); *Atom and Archetype: The Pauli/Jung Letters 1932–1958* (trans. by David Roscoe, Princeton, NJ: Princeton University Press, 2001).

another records his profound psychological-theological debate with the English Catholic theologian Victor White.[7] Jung's correspondence with Erich Neumann has recently appeared,[8] a long-awaited volume, shedding new light on Jung's relationships with his Jewish disciples.

The present volume, Jung's correspondence with a first-generation follower, James Kirsch, brings a particular complexity into the record of his published letters. On the one hand, it tells a story of heroic survival, brilliant creativity, and the building of several generative communities. On the other hand, it tells a story with distinct personal and collective shadows. "Shadow" is Jung's term for that part of inner reality contrary to our individual and collective self-idealizations. This volume of letters compels us to contemplate certain difficult themes, personal to the two writers, which continue to resonate in the psychotherapeutic field, and especially in the Jungian world, down to the present day.

The timespan of the Jung–Kirsch correspondence is long, over 32 years. When the story begins, James Kirsch, a young Jewish psychiatrist in Berlin, has just written to Jung requesting analysis. At the time, Berlin still enjoyed the ferment and freedoms of the Weimar Republic, though these would soon disintegrate in waves of economic and political chaos. Hitler's movement was one of many competing parties in Germany in 1928, but its power was about to crest. Given this historical starting point, it will be no surprise if the Jung–Kirsch correspondence is deeply stamped by the events of the Nazi era. These loom over the first half of the volume, driving the story's plot and shaping some of its major themes – not only for Kirsch and his career, but also for Jung and his.

The dialogue of Kirsch and Jung exposes unconscious, unwanted dimensions of both writers. Jung struggles with the cultural shadow of anti-Semitism, and some of his writings in the early 1930s have troubling resonances with the emerging Nazi phenomenon. Personal and collective shadows also appear in Kirsch's decades-long struggle with recurrent states of archetypal possession – identification with the Self on the one hand, and with the inferior anima on the other. These unconscious complexes are expressed, for Kirsch, in recurring somatic symptoms and emotional dilemmas. They also lead him (in today's terms) into clinical boundary violations, at an inevitable cost to his analysands, his family, and himself. The impact of these themes is not confined, obviously, to the biographies of the two individual writers, but also have echoes in the writings and lives of successive generations of Jungians.

---

7   Ann Conrad Lammers and Adrian Cunningham, eds., *The Jung–White Letters* (London & New York: Routledge, 2007).

8   *Analytical Psychology in Exile: The correspondence of C. G. Jung and Erich Neumann*. Edited and introduced by Martin Liebscher. Philemon Series. (Trans. by Heather McCartney. Princeton, NJ: Princeton University Press, 2015.) Hereafter, *Analytical Psych in Exile*.

Nevertheless, along with these heavy qualities, another characteristic of the Jung–Kirsch correspondence is its buoyancy. A rising energy is mixed into these letters like yeast. It is compounded of passionate intelligence, humor, the instinct to survive, and the drive – shared by Kirsch and Jung – to honor the psyche in its depths and to give it symbolic form.

Biographical background

In 1928, when the 27-year-old psychiatrist James Isaac Kirsch (1901–1989) first contacted C. G. Jung, he had established a growing private practice in Berlin. Patients saw him at his apartment in Charlottenburg, the fashionable neighborhood where he lived with his wife, who was expecting their first child. Kirsch was part of a professional community centered in Berlin but extending to other cities, especially Heidelberg where he had done his medical training. In May and June of 1929 he had his first two months' work with Jung, which consisted of a combination of personal analysis and clinical training. Thereafter he traveled to Zurich as often as possible and stayed as long as he could, to continue the work he had started. He developed a professional community in Zurich, with which he would be connected for the rest of his life.

C. G. Jung (1875–1961) was 53 when he accepted Kirsch as his analysand and pupil. Fifteen years had passed since his break with Freud, in which time he had developed his school of analytical psychology and gathered a circle of followers. His reputation, already growing in the German-speaking parts of Europe, was beginning to take root in other parts of the world. He had stopped adding to the "Red Book," concentrating instead on the study of alchemy. He had begun offering English seminars on dream analysis at the Psychological Club in Zurich. His tower in Bollingen had been enlarged by one additional structure. He had recently begun to attend, and would soon join, an international association based in Germany, the Allgemeine ärztliche Gesellschaft für Psychotherapie [General Medical Society for Psychotherapy] (AAGP).[9]

Before Kirsch met with Jung, he had already spent four years in Jungian analysis. From 1922 to 1926 he saw Toni Sussmann, a lay analyst and trainer of analysts in Berlin, who had analyzed and trained with Jung a decade earlier. His first round of analysis in Zurich likely involved two to three hours a week with Jung, and almost as many with Jung's assistant, Toni Wolff.[10] Returning to Berlin

---

9 A historical overview of this organization, discussing Jung's participation and leadership during the political upheaval of the Hitler years, is provided as "A brief history of the AAGP / IAAGP," Appendix D, pp. 304ff.

10 In late 1929 or early 1930, Kirsch filled out a form for the *Berliner Arztregister* [Berlin Medical Registry], stating that he had been in a training analysis with C. G. Jung from 1 May to 30 June 1929 (Kirsch archive). Kirsch's whole analytic training, summarized in a questionnaire he filled out in 1953, seems to have been quite extensive: Toni Sussmann, Berlin, 1922–26 (300 hours); C. G. Jung (60 hours) and Toni Wolff (50 hours) in 1929, 1935, 1949, 1951 and 1952; and finally C. A. Meier (25 hours) and Liliane Frey (70 hours) in 1951 and 1952.

in July, he continued to consult with both Jung and Wolff about his analytic cases. In clinical emergencies he also turned, with Jung's approval, to Toni Sussmann. Between his visits to Zurich he did his own dream work with another Jungian colleague in Berlin, Wolfgang Kranefeldt. In 1931 he joined the AAGP, in which many of his colleagues were already members.

Many of Kirsch's Jungian colleagues in Berlin were, like himself, culturally assimilated Jews. In the pre-Hitler years, Jewish Jungians in Berlin included James and Eva Kirsch, Toni Sussmann, Hildegard Silber (later Hilde Kirsch), Werner Engel, Gerhard Adler, Ernst Bernhard, Erich and Julie Neumann, Erna Rosenbaum, Heinz Westmann, and Max and Lore Zeller.[11] All of these fled from Germany during the 1930s. Werner Engel, Kirsch's friend and analysand, emigrated to New York. The Neumanns settled in Tel Aviv. Bernhard went to Rome. Adler, Rosenbaum, and Sussmann moved to London. Westmann emigrated to London and thence to New York. Max and Lore Zeller first joined forces with James and Hilde Kirsch in London, and later came to work with them in Los Angeles.

As the first chapters of this volume make clear, the journey of the Kirsch family had several stages. As soon as Hitler took power, late in January 1933, Kirsch prepared to leave Germany. His family at that point included his wife, Eva, their four-year-old daughter, Gabi (later Ruth),[12] and their little son, Michael, born in May. They left Berlin in late July, accompanied by one of Kirsch's analytic patients, Hildegard Silber, who was newly widowed. With her came her sons, nine-year-old Rudi (later called Jim) and six-year-old Gerhardt (Jerry). Initially the Kirsches and Silbers took flats in the same apartment building in Ascona, where the adults attended Eranos. In late fall of 1933 the two families moved together to Palestine.

Kirsch lived in Tel Aviv for eighteen months and in London for five years, with occasional stays in Zurich. During this time, in addition to moving from place to place, his family also went through an internal realignment. In the spring of 1935 James and Eva Kirsch decided to divorce. Eva Kirsch returned with their children to Berlin, where she practiced as a psychotherapist until 1938, when she and Michael, then five, fled to Wales. James Kirsch joined Hildegard Silber in Zurich, where she had been living since March and working intensively with

---

11 Max and Lore Zeller became active Jungians only after they left Berlin. Max Zeller's connection with Hilde Kirsch began in 1932, however, when he rented a room from her during her first husband's illness. She later recalled that she and Max attended Jung's seminar in Berlin, in 1933, where they both met Jung (Hilde Kirsch, speech in honor of Max and Lore Zeller, 30 October 1970, Kirsch archive).

12 Until they moved to England, the Kirsch and Silber children went by their German names: Gabriele (Gabi) and Michael Kirsch; Rudolf (Rudi) and Gerhardt Silber. On arrival in London in September 1935, the three who lived with James and Hilde changed to the names they would keep thereafter: Gabi Kirsch took Ruth, her first name. Rudi Silber became Jim. Gerhardt Silber's name was anglicized to Gerald (Jerry). Michael Kirsch, who moved to Wales with his mother in 1938, changed his name only in pronunciation.

Jung and Wolff.[13] In September 1935 James and Hilde moved to London and were married. Her sons, then twelve and eight, moved with them. Kirsch's daughter, barely seven, no longer safe in Berlin and now forbidden to attend school there, came to live with them as well. The following summer their son Thomas was born. The Kirsches had become, as Hilde Kirsch liked to point out to Jung,[14] an enormous family.

To set up a practice in England, Kirsch – like several other Jewish refugees – relied on Jung's certificate stating his previous training and experience. Soon he was allowed to practice medicine in London with oversight from English doctors, and was also permitted to work as an analyst. At first, his letters show, he was barely able to support his family; but he persisted, and his practice filled. In 1936 Kirsch helped to found the Medical Society of Analytical Psychology (MSAP) in London, on which the MSAP of the United States would be modeled a decade later.[15] Also in 1936, while caring for her large household and nursing a new baby, Hilde Kirsch was surprised by Jung's referral of Michael Fordham, her first analysand.

As Thomas Kirsch describes,[16] in autumn 1940 his father once again moved the family, this time from England to the United States. Jim Silber, oldest of the children who made that trip, recalls that their entry into the United States was fraught with complications. Their papers were lost, and they were held as prisoners on Ellis Island until released, with the help of Kirsch's friend and former analysand, Werner Engel, who had, almost miraculously, learned their whereabouts.[17] A few months later the Kirsch family moved to Los Angeles, where they stayed. There, over the following years, James and Hilde Kirsch started the Jungian movement in southern California.

The Jung–Kirsch relationship

James Kirsch's unique importance to Jung, about which Thomas Kirsch comments, seems to have been related to a combination of factors. It was probably important, in the first place, that Kirsch was a Heidelberg-trained psychiatrist. More important to Jung, though, was the fact that Kirsch had a natural bent toward Jung's concept of the unconscious. It seems that Kirsch related immediately, with deep, religious

---

13 Hilde Kirsch later summarized her early analytic experience in Zurich as having entailed two or three hours a week with Jung and an equal number with Wolff, as was customary at the time (Hilde Kirsch to Marie-Jeanne Schmid, 30 September 1949, Kirsch archive).

14 Cf. "Letters of C. G. Jung and Hilde Kirsch," Appendix B, pp. 280f.

15 MSAP was founded in San Francisco in 1943, and in New York in 1946. In 1947 Jung approved "MSAP (U.S.)," headquartered in New York and San Francisco. Kirsch's letters of 1949 (e.g., Kirsch, 27 June 1949, p. 125) reflect a dispute which arose in the western section of MSAP concerning standards for membership.

16 Cf. Preface, p. xiv.

17 Cf. Kirsch, 19 November 1940, p. 95 and note.

feeling, to the symbolic dimension of the psyche. It is also evident that he was prepared, to an unusual degree, to face the dark aspects of the unconscious.

In a letter written close to the end of his life, Kirsch described what happened at his first session with Jung. His presenting dream showed that he was gripped, perhaps even more than Jung was at the time, by existential and theological issues:

> I remember the first dream I told him in 1929, in the first interview. The dream was very short. It simply said there is relative evil and there is absolute evil. And I remember how he got up from his chair, smoking the pipe and walking up and down. But I think, in the '20s, he did not suspect that, in a few years, absolute evil would be acted out on an unimaginable scale. [18]

Another gift which Kirsch brought to Jung was his increasingly conscious appropriation of his own religious and cultural identity. In 1933 Jung had serious doubts about Kirsch's decision to emigrate to Palestine; but this move arguably profited them both. Living in Tel Aviv, Kirsch embraced his Jewish tradition with fresh enthusiasm. He took the opportunity to improve his reading of Hebrew, studied biblical texts and commentaries in the original, and gathered cultural information which helped him, in the months and years that followed, to guide Jung toward a more accurate reading of certain aspects of Jewish history and experience.

Jung undoubtedly benefited from having Kirsch at his side while he gradually came to terms with the fact that, in certain writings of the early 1930s, he had borrowed words and phrases from the lexicon of anti-Semitism. In their letters of 1934 and 1935, as well as in later exchanges, Kirsch and Jung discuss specific passages which Jung published in the Hitler years. Whether or not he intended it, some of Jung's writings at the time had the potential to do harm, a fact which he came to recognize and – privately, at least – to confess. Jung always denied having had any anti-Semitic intentions, and Kirsch also denied it on his behalf.[19]

---

18 Kirsch to Heinrich Fierz, 3 January 1983, Kirsch archive. This three-page typed letter, originally in English, also discusses Jung's apology for his published statements in 1933–34 (cf. note 20 below).

19 Late in life Kirsch wrote to a Swiss colleague: "… when I saw Jung for the first time after World War II, that is in August of 1947,… he began the conversation by immediately apologizing to me. Again, I accepted this apology of a great man as an admission of mistaken advice and mis-understanding of the Nazis, but not as an admission of any guilt or of anti-Semitism" (Kirsch to Heinrich Fierz, 3 January 1983, Kirsch archive).

Nevertheless, Jung later apologized[20] for statements he had published, particularly for passages he wrote in late 1933 and early 1934, for the journal of the AAGP (which had now become the IAAGP), the *Zentralblatt für Psychotherapie und ihre Grenzgebiete*.[21]

Public reaction to these published statements came immediately, not only from those hostile to Jung but also from his friends. Soon after their publication, Kirsch drew Jung's attention to key passages, and also to the rumors that were circulating about Jung's supposed sympathies toward the Nazi regime. Kirsch asked how he, a Jew who was Jung's friend and follower, was supposed to understand what he had read and heard.[22] Jung's reply makes it clear that he is desperately serious about straightening out the record and that he urgently wants Kirsch on his side in the battle that has erupted. Kirsch accepts Jung's account and organizes public support for him. From then on he sends Jung every kind of educational help he can.[23] Starting in the early 1930s, Jung relies on Kirsch first as a tutor, then as a loyal critic, and finally as a staunch defender.[24]

Kirsch became a vigorous, lifelong promoter of Jung's psychology. He taught and built up communities of Jungians in every city where he resided, particularly in the one where he was at home from 1940 until his death. Led by the Kirsches and their colleagues, several of whom were likewise refugees from Germany, the Los Angeles Jungians kept strong ties with Jung's circle in Zurich. James and Hilde returned there often for additional analysis. Distinguished Zurich analysts visited Los Angeles to lecture to analytic candidates.

As a result, when the Jungians of Los Angeles and San Francisco began to have joint meetings, the "classical," or "Zurich-oriented" analysts of Los Angeles noticed differences between themselves and what they took to be the more

---

20 Jung's most often cited apology is something he reportedly said in 1946 in a private conversation with Rabbi Leo Baeck, formerly of Berlin, when he confessed to having made a bad mistake. Jung's reported phrase, *"Ich bin ausgerutscht"* (literally, "I slipped up") is idiomatic for an embarrassing public error. Baeck evidently told Gershom Scholem about the conversation, who repeated it later to Aniela Jaffé (cf. Jaffé, "Jung and National Socialism," *Life and Work,* pp. 99f). This exchange, about which we know only at second hand, is also discussed by Kirsch in his essay, "Reconsidering Jung's So-Called Anti-Semitism" (*The Arms of the Windmill: Essays in Analytical Psychology in Honor of Werner H. Engel,* New York: The Jung Foundation, 1984, pp. 5–27; hereafter "Reconsidering").

21 Cf. Appendix D, pp. 306ff.

22 The primary letters in which these discussions occur are Kirsch, 7 May 1934, pp. 40ff, and 8 June 1934, pp. 48ff; and Jung, 26 May 1934, pp. 44ff.

23 Kirsch's role as a tutor to Jung began before their 1934 exchange. His brief paper, "The Jewish Image of the World" (pp. 15f), is the first writing by Kirsch that Jung appears to have kept in his files. A longer lecture from spring 1934, titled (in Hebrew), "'Then He Will Open the Ears of Men'," is printed as Appendix A (pp. 267–77).

24 Aniela Jaffé, another of Jung's Jewish friends for many decades, also defends him, though not uncritically. She writes: "Over the years Jung revised and deepened his knowledge of Judaism. … The unlimited support he gave to Jews and non-Jews alike during the critical years of National Socialism, and his personality as a man, are the basis upon which his Jewish pupils have reconciled themselves to his mistakes" (*Life and Work,* pp. 98f).

"clinically" oriented Jungians of San Francisco.[25] Kirsch wrote to Jung about these philosophical and practical differences, which he thought would lead to inevitable tensions but also opportunities for learning. After their second joint meeting, he summarized the organizational challenge:

> If I may say it in somewhat simplified terms, what's essential for L.A. is the attitude to the unconscious, while S.F. hopes to be accepted someday as the Jungian group in the AMA (American Medical Association) and in the APA (American Psychological Association). These vastly divergent attitudes make it finally impossible, in my opinion, to unite the two groups organizationally. Nevertheless, here in Los Angeles we became aware of how inadequate our attitudes are to the local collective, e.g., medical and psychological organizations.[26]

It would be wrong to focus on Kirsch's institutional endeavors so much that one loses sight of the inner meaning the work had for him. Without an authentic connection to the unconscious, all his vigor and commitment would not have been enough to commend him to Jung or to build up the community of Jungians. At a certain point, however, the inner, symbolic meaning of the work becomes entangled in organizational-political disputes for the Jungians who do it, as we can see when Jung refers in 1959 to the "war" that Kirsch may start with his radio lectures.[27] It is clear, at any rate, that the Kirsches' loyalty to the Zurich community earned them lifelong friendship from Jung and his nearest followers. In late 1958, when the assembled Club members wrote their humorous, slightly tipsy Christmas greetings on the back of a dinner menu,[28] it was more than a coincidence that James and Hilde were the absent friends to whom these affectionate greetings were addressed.

Kirsch also remained close to Jung in terms of the personal, psychotherapeutic relationship that was their starting point. Caught up in inner struggles, he called repeatedly for Jung's help. Their letters make it clear that Kirsch suffered for decades from a religious complex, his identification with the Self. At the same time he was in the grips of an inferior and insecure anima – the internal feminine aspect of his psyche – which he projected onto women in his life. Readers will notice how often he asks Jung's help to deal with the painful human dilemmas which he both creates and undergoes through this combination of complexes.

---

25 A careful historical analysis, discouraging stereotyped comparisons, is found in a paper by Mel Kettner, "Orthodoxy, Heresy, and Shadow Projection: A brief history of the Los Angeles/San Francisco collaboration" (California Spring conference, Carmel, CA, 1993). This unpublished paper was kindly provided by Marianne Morgan, responsible archivist at the Virginia Allen Detloff Library archive, C. G. Jung Institute of San Francisco (hereafter VADL archive).
26 Kirsch to Jung, 7 June 1954, pp. 199f.
27 Jung to Kirsch, 12 November 1959, p. 250 and note.
28 "Greetings on a Christmas party menu from the Psychological Club, Zurich," pp. 241ff.

From the first, Jung warns Kirsch of the power of the anima, advising him to take the psychological risks seriously.

It was not until the end of Jung's life, however – in the last five minutes of the hour, as it were – that Kirsch directly asked for Jung's help with his most dangerous complex, his long-standing identification with the Self. The archetypal Anthropos had long been the focus of Kirsch's emotional and intellectual life. Now it thrust itself upon him in the dream-image of a hermaphroditic Christ. The two men's final letters, an unusually frank exchange, may be read as the final chapter in Kirsch's three-decade-long analysis with Jung. It contains, as it were, the key to many of the earlier letters in the correspondence.

By Kirsch's own account, his relationship to The Holy was extraordinarily close all his life. In old age he wrote an autobiographical piece[29] recounting his numinous experiences in childhood, including the mysterious voice he first heard at thirteen, predicting he would follow in the steps of Abraham and Moses (Kirsch 1986, p. 149). At the end of World War I, when he was barely seventeen, he reports that he heard the same voice, this time announcing: *"There was a man who should have been killed in the war but was not. He will try to kill all the Jews."* Three years later, Hitler's followers were in the headlines. At once, Kirsch writes, he recognized the man in the prophecy. Accordingly, the day after Hitler became Chancellor, Kirsch began preparing to leave the country (Kirsch 1986, p. 150).

Vicissitudes of the documents

As Thomas Kirsch points out, in his father's correspondence with Jung we see both the positive and shadow sides of the two men. In that sense, their relationship is complete. "Complete" is a relative term, however. This published correspondence includes every document of the Jung–Kirsch exchange that is available to date. Nevertheless, many of Kirsch's letters and a few of Jung's have proven impossible to find. Some of Jung's missing letters may surface in the future, as others have done in recent years. It is unlikely, however, that Kirsch's missing letters will be found, especially those written prior to 1931, when Jung's secretary began preserving Kirsch's letters. A number of Kirsch's letters from later years are unfortunately also lacking.

Jung's letters to Kirsch, in contrast, were preserved from the beginning, with few exceptions.[30] Kirsch evidently held everything from Jung with reverent

29 Kirsch, J. (1986) "Reflections at Age Eighty-Four," in *A Modern Jew in Search of a Soul,* J. Marvin Spiegelman and Abraham Jacobson, eds (Phoenix, AZ: Falcon Press, pp. 147–54). I am grateful to Aryeh Maidenbaum, who first brought this piece of writing to my attention in May 2011.

30 It should be mentioned that eleven of Jung's letters to Kirsch are previously published, in whole or in part, in Jung's *Letters* and *Briefe.* The originals of these letters (plus a few others that appear to have been considered for publication) were almost certainly lent to Adler and Jaffé during their editorial process. Perhaps not all of these were returned. One handwritten letter (Jung, 29 January 1953, pp. 157f), previously published in *PP, Briefe II and Letters II,* is now available only in its published versions.

respect, from the longest epistle to the smallest postcard. Even when traveling, in wartime, he treated Jung's letters with care. In one case, though, where a letter of Jung's is missing, one may guess it was intentionally destroyed: this missing letter is the first that Jung wrote to Kirsch after the death of Toni Wolff. Kirsch refers to it in the original draft of his 18 April 1953 reply: *"First I'd like to thank you most sincerely for your letter, written in such personal terms."*[31] This sentence does not appear in the final version of Kirsch's sent reply; and the letter from Jung, "written in such personal terms," is no longer extant.

No collection of historical letters can exist, it seems, without at least one close call affecting the physical survival of the documents. In mid-August 1982 James Kirsch wrote to Beat Glaus, then the scholar at the ETH Library with primary responsibility for the C. G. Jung Archive, to explain why he would not immediately send a batch of Jung's letters to the archive as planned. The reason, Kirsch said, was the car accident he and his wife had experienced two weeks before, when both the originals and the only existing copies of many of Jung's major letters to Kirsch were in the car. Kirsch writes:

> I had decided to send the larger portion of my Jung letters to you and decided on August the 4th to have copies made of them. My wife-secretary[32] had actually made the Xerox copies. I picked her up, and we were on the way home when I got involved in a very serious automobile accident. The car, a Volvo, was completely demolished and is beyond repair. My wife held on to the Jung letters. Both of us were saved by the strong seat belts.
>
> You may consider me as very superstitious, but I got the impression that fate is giving me a strong hint that I should not give away the letters of my great teacher before my death. I will keep the collection of letters that I intended to send to you in a special place and will instruct my executor to send the letters to you at the E.T.H. address. [33]

Around the time of his death, Kirsch's intention was carried out. Originals of 44 of Jung's letters, personally selected by Kirsch, were given to the ETH Library archive. The photocopies of these letters were then stored among James Kirsch's papers, at home. They were not returned, though, to the folders containing the bulk of Jung's original letters, those having been locked away long before at Kirsch's bank.

---

31 First draft of letter by Kirsch, 14 April 1953, p. 164.

32 Hilde Kirsch died of pancreatic cancer on 23 December 1978. The following June, after replacing a secretary who had been with him for 20 years, Kirsch married his new secretary. Seven years later this marriage ended in divorce.

33 Kirsch to Beat Glaus, 16 August 1982, Kirsch archive. Kirsch sent similar letters, written in a more dramatic tone, to Aniela Jaffé, Liliane Frey-Rohn, and C. A. Meier.

In a natural confusion, then, after James Kirsch's death, the 44 photocopies were mistaken for the total of what Jung had written to him. Thus in 2006, when I received raw documents for the present volume, these letters appeared to be the sum total of Jung's side of the correspondence. A year later, comparing my list of letters to the Jung–Kirsch documents at the ETH Library archive, I began to suspect that Jung had written many more letters to Kirsch than I had known. Before long, a search revealed all the previously uncounted Jung letters – originals – in a safe deposit box in Palo Alto, California. Once these documents were sorted and catalogued, the translator and editor faced a happy problem: Jung's side of the correspondence was nearly double what we had started with.

As time went by, even more documents came to light, though in smaller numbers. Some surfaced at the ETH Library archive, others at the Kirsch archive. Several of Aniela Jaffé's letters to Kirsch, written in her capacity as Jung's secretary, were found in a file that had been sent to Thomas Kirsch years before by Robert Hinshaw, Jaffé's literary executor in Switzerland. Letters that Jaffé wrote to Kirsch under Jung's supervision or at his behest are regarded as part of the Jung–Kirsch correspondence and are included here, with permission from her estate.

One more letter from Aniela Jaffé to James Kirsch surfaced seventeen months after *The Jung–Kirsch Letters* appeared. This letter adds crucial details to our picture of Jung's final days. It also illustrates what Jaffé felt to be his close friendships with a few of his Jewish followers – a circle that included, in addition to Jaffé herself, the Kirsches, the Hurwitzes, and the Klugers. This letter occupies a unique place in the Kirsch archive. I happened on it by accident in the fall of 2012 as one of several loose documents in a well-worn, unlabeled manila envelope filled with the telegrams, death notices, and newspaper articles that James Kirsch had evidently collected at the time of Jung's death.

Besides being Jung's secretary at the end of his life, Jaffé was a longtime friend of James and Hilde Kirsch and exchanged dozens of personal letters with them. These personal letters are full of human and historical interest but generally add little to our understanding of the relationship of Jung and Kirsch. So they are not printed as part of their correspondence. Jaffé's letter of 27 May 1961, however, is harder to categorize. Because of its historical importance, that letter is included[34] in this edition of *The Jung–Kirsch Letters*.

Translation and editing

Translation of the primary texts was a major undertaking for this correspondence. Fortunately, from the beginning, I did not have to worry about finding a translator. Thomas Kirsch told me about Ursula Egli as soon as we began discussing the publication of his father's letters. When we went to work, I soon knew why he

---

34 Cf. Jaffé, 27 May 1961, p. 266.

recommended her. We gradually evolved a collaborative process, in which – while Ursula did most of the transcriptions and initial translations – there were times when both of us transcribed, and both of us translated. We routinely checked each other's work. Ursula accepted almost all my stylistic corrections, but she never lost her eye for omissions and inaccuracies. At key points she offered linguistic research and well-documented cultural commentary. She proofread superbly. At every point she contributed, with flexibility and good humor, and her patient attention to detail helped me avert many errors. Some mistakes slipped past us, nevertheless, in the first edition, and were caught by careful readers. All of those have been corrected here. Any errors that remain are, of course, entirely my own.

Indeed, after publishing the first edition of this book I discovered that I had made at least one substantive error. Among Jung's letters of 1934, those of 16 August and 26 September were both handwritten on his professional letterhead. In the raw documents that originally came to me, I found a sheet of the same letterhead, undated but with the heading "II." It came to me with the letter of 16 August 1934. Despite discontinuities in content, I allowed this page to appear in the first edition of *The Jung–Kirsch Letters* as part of that letter. Later, however, prompted by the thoughtful queries of Robert Hinshaw and Thomas Fischer, I recognized that this "page II" must have been an addendum to Jung's letter of 26 September 1934. That sequence has been corrected for this edition, with associated small changes in the footnotes and index.

Recently, too, research by a colleague has produced yet one more correction. I am most grateful to Riccardo Bernardini for generously bringing forward evidence of the true date and location of Margareta Fellerer's black-and-white photograph of Jung (Figure 9.1, page 218). This portrait had commonly been dated to 1955, because it was published that year in the magazine *Du* on the occasion of Jung's 80th birthday. Further, it had been assumed that Fellerer took this picture in Ascona, where she did most of her work. In Olga Fröbe-Kapteyn's private photo albums, however, Dr. Bernardini has found a series of dated snapshots, to which the famous portrait obviously belongs, proving that Fellerer took the picture earlier, and in a different location, than previously believed. The year was 1944. The place was Jung's house in Küsnacht. Jung, who had recently recovered from a nearly fatal illness, was now evidently well enough to sit for a series of photographs. His age at the time was 69.

In preparing this book for publication I had the privilege of studying a vast amount of secondary material, mainly side-correspondences, located at the ETH Library archive in Zurich and the James Kirsch archive in Palo Alto. Many annotations are based on these unpublished documents, by which it was possible to map hidden corners in the correspondence and track down historical references. These textual discoveries proved endlessly fascinating to me, as the smallest increments of historical data (Ulrich Hoerni called them "mosaic stones") gave detail and color to the larger picture, revealing its texture in surprising ways. I should add, in this context, that I am profoundly grateful to all who have funded this project, many of whom are named in the Acknowledgments. Others, who asked not to be named, are very warmly remembered. Among other things, these gifts allowed me to spend days and weeks among otherwise inaccessible materials, in a process of education which led to many of the textual discoveries mentioned above.

Editing the documents of a historical correspondence, I have come to think, is a little like going to work on a photographic negative in the darkroom. The object is to bring out what is already there. In developing and printing, contrasts can be heightened. Missing pieces can be burned in. Parts of the image that were dark can be coaxed to emerge. There is a technique called dodging, in which a small square of cardboard is waved rapidly between the negative and the paper as if applying an eraser. Gradually the shadowed area lightens, and one begins to see that all along, behind the blackness, the camera knew the texture of the stones.

Ann Conrad Lammers, PhD
New Hampshire
November 2015

1928–1932

BERLIN

Figure 1.1 **C. G. Jung, October 1930**. *Photo: ©1930, Hans Meiner. Courtesy Andreas Jung.*

Dr. C. G. Jung
Küsnacht-Zürich
Seestrasse 228[1]

16 November 1928[2]

Dear Colleague!

I'm afraid it's quite impossible for me to reserve time for you in January, since my time is already fully accounted for. The earliest date when I could work with you in person[3] would be in early May, and if you decide on that I have to ask you to let me know as soon as possible, since I always have to book my appointments far in advance.

With collegial respect, Yours truly, C. G. JUNG

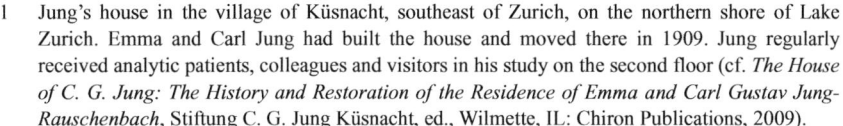

1 Jung's house in the village of Küsnacht, southeast of Zurich, on the northern shore of Lake Zurich. Emma and Carl Jung had built the house and moved there in 1909. Jung regularly received analytic patients, colleagues and visitors in his study on the second floor (cf. *The House of C. G. Jung: The History and Restoration of the Residence of Emma and Carl Gustav Jung-Rauschenbach*, Stiftung C. G. Jung Küsnacht, ed., Wilmette, IL: Chiron Publications, 2009).
2 Typewritten in German, on Jung's letterhead. As of this date, Jung's professional letterhead still shows only his medical title. His academic title (*Prof. Dr.*) first appears in this correspondence on his formal letter of recommendation for Kirsch, dated 7 June 1935 (cf. p. 69 and note).
3 Because of his busy schedule, Jung often referred new patients to his closest assistants, which at this date included Emma Jung and Toni Wolff. Kirsch later reported that his work with Jung began in May and June 1929 (Berliner Arztregister [Berlin Medical Registry], c. 1930, Kirsch archive; cf. Jung, 19 August 1929, p. 5, note 6).

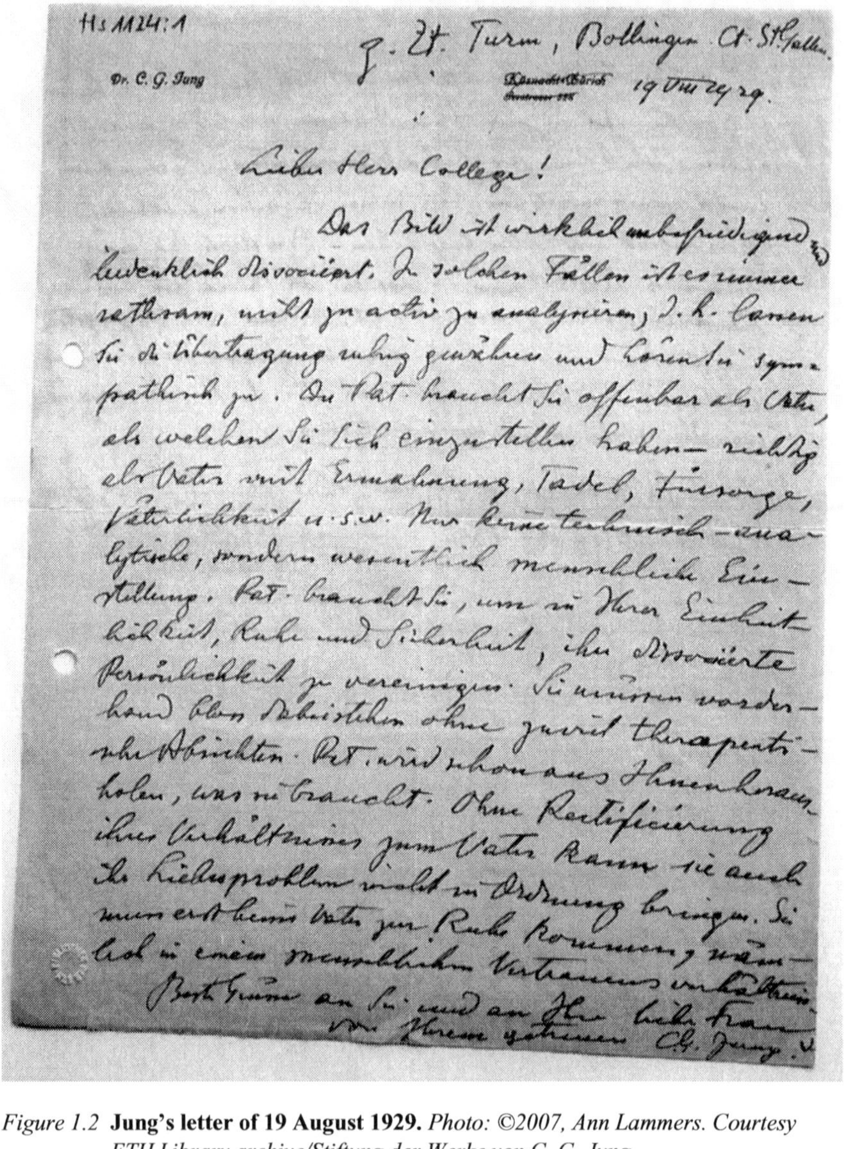

Hs 1124:1

z. Zt. Turm, Bollingen Ct. St. Gallen

Dr. C. G. Jung Küsnacht-Zürich 19 VIII 29.

Lieber Herr College!

Das Bild ist wirklich entsprechend bedenklich dissociiert. In solchen Fällen ist es immer ratsam, nicht zu activ zu analysieren, d. h. lassen Sie die Übertragung ruhig gewähren und hören Sie sympathisch zu. Die Pat. braucht Sie offenbar als Vater, als welchen Sie sich einzustellen haben – richtig als Vater mit Ermahnung, Tadel, Fürsorge, Väterlichkeit u. s. w. Nur keine technisch-analytische, sondern wesentlich menschliche Einstellung. Pat. braucht Sie, um in Ihrer Einheitlichkeit, Ruhe und Sicherheit, ihre dissociierte Persönlichkeit zu vereinigen. Sie müssen vorderhand bloss dabeistehen ohne zuviel therapeutische Absichten. Pat. wird schon aus Ihnen herausholen, was sie braucht. Ohne Rectificierung ihres Verhältnisses zum Vater kann sie auch ihr Liebesproblem nicht in Ordnung bringen. Sie muss erst beim Vater zur Ruhe kommen, nämlich in einem menschlichen Vertrauensverhältnis.

Beste Grüsse an Sie und an Ihre liebe Frau
von Ihrem ergebenen C. G. Jung.

Figure 1.2 **Jung's letter of 19 August 1929.** *Photo: ©2007, Ann Lammers. Courtesy ETH Library archive/Stiftung der Werke von C. G. Jung.*

Dr. C. G. Jung
pro tem. Tower[4]
Bollingen, Ct. St. Gallen

19 August 1929[5]

Dear Colleague!

The picture is really unsatisfactory and seriously dissociated.[6] In such cases it is always advisable not to analyze too actively, i.e. let the transference calmly run its course and listen sympathetically. Evidently, the patient needs you as a father, which is how you have to present yourself – properly as a father, with admonition, scolding, caring, fatherliness, etc. Not a technical-analytical attitude at all, but an essentially human one. The patient needs you so that she can unify her dissociated personality in your consistency, calm and security. For now, you must just stand by, without too many therapeutic intentions. The patient will surely take from you what she needs. Without rectifying her relationship with her father, she also cannot bring her love problem into order. She must first achieve peace with her father, that is, in a human trust relationship.

Best greetings to you and your dear[7] wife[8] from your faithful C. G. JUNG

---

4 Jung's retreat on Upper Lake Zurich in the village of Bollingen, Canton St. Gallen. Deliberately primitive, the tower gave Jung a secluded place for work and rest. The development and significance of Jung's tower are described in Ch. VIII of *Memories, Dreams, Reflections,* recorded and edited by Aniela Jaffé, trans. Richard and Clara Winston, New York: Vintage Books, 1965 (hereafter *MDR*).

5 Handwritten in German, on Jung's professional letterhead (address crossed out). This letter is previously published, twice, in English translations by James Kirsch and R. F. C. Hull (cf. Jung, 28 November 1952, p. 150, note 72). It is the first of 29 letters from Jung which Kirsch translated and published, with permission from Princeton University Press and Routledge, under the title "Letters to a Friend", in two issues of *Psychological Perspectives,* the journal of the Los Angeles C. G. Jung Institute (Part I, Vol. 3.1, Spring 1972; Part II, Vol. 3.2, Fall 1972) (hereafter *PP*). Eleven of these letters were also published, translated by R. F. C. Hull, in *C. G. Jung Letters, Vol. I: 1906–1950* and *Vol. II: 1951–1961* selected and edited by Gerhard Adler in collaboration with Aniela Jaffé, trans. R. F. C. Hull. Princeton, NJ: Princeton University Press (PUP)/London: Routledge, 1973, 1975 (hereafter *Letters I* and *II*).

6 Kirsch's letters to Jung before 1931 are not preserved, but he had evidently sought consultation with Jung about his treatment of a woman patient. As was common at the time, Kirsch's work with Jung combined personal analysis with professional training. On an official questionnaire from about this time in Kirsch's career, he lists all his post-licensure training, including his first two months' study with Jung: "1.V.1929–30.VI.1929" (Berliner Arztregister [Berlin Medical Registry], c. 1930, Kirsch archive).

7 Jung's phrase, *Ihre liebe Frau* (lit. "your dear wife") is one of several set phrases used by German-language writers of the period. Some of these phrases, such as *Ihre Frau* [your wife] and *Ihre liebe Frau* [your dear wife], can be easily rendered in English. Others, such as *Ihre verehrte Frau* [your esteemed wife] and *Ihre Frau Gemahlin* [your lady spouse], have no good English equivalents. For simplicity, we render most of these formulas simply as "your wife."

8 Eva Kirsch (1901–1999): German-born physical trainer, later a psychotherapist; married to James Kirsch from 1926 to 1935. Before their marriage she underwent a Freudian analysis; later she

P.S. Unfortunately I could not answer your earlier letters, since you didn't send me your address. I cannot quite understand the behavior of Frau Sussmann.[9] I must see if I can discuss it with her personally. It can't be done in a letter. However, the fact that she has recently somewhat changed her behavior or technique could be the symptom of an influence.[10] I view the subsequent discussion of Ifs and Buts as *essential* for the resolution of relationships.

    Please never forget to include your address. I had to ask Frau Sussmann for it.

Dr. C. G. Jung
Küsnacht-Zürich
Seestrasse 228

9 November 1929[11]

Dear Colleague!

A tangible difficulty in the case with your patient is obviously located in the identity of his masturbation-complex with your so-called ear-masturbation. The ears are connected with feelings, and you are not hearing feelings perceptively enough.[12] That could be a not insignificant problem in relation to this patient. It is possible that he's not reaching you properly on the feeling side. Masturbation is an expression of being isolated. The fantasy describes his transition to a feeling attitude in which he then meets the young girl who expresses feelings for him.

analyzed with various Jungians, then with Jung himself. She practiced for four years as an analyst under her husband's supervision (Eva Kirsch to C. A. Meier, 9 June 1935, ETH Library archive). In 1933, with James and their two small children, she emigrated to Palestine. In 1935, when the marriage ended, she and the children returned to Berlin, where she opened a private practice (C. A. Meier to Eva Kirsch, 22 June 1935, ETH Library archive). In 1938, bearing Jung's documentation of her professional competence (Certificate for Eva Kirsch, 25 March 1938, paper collection of the Foundation of the Works of C. G. Jung), she emigrated to Wales. There she worked as a physical therapist and psychotherapist and eventually remarried. (Many of these details were kindly provided by Ruth G. Kirsch, daughter of James and Eva Kirsch.)

9 Toni Fanny Sussmann (1883–1967): German-Jewish lay analyst and trainer of analysts, at this time living and working in Berlin. Kirsch had analyzed with Sussmann during his psychiatric training (cf. Introduction, p. xxix and note). Later, after beginning to work with Jung and Wolff, he continued to turn to Sussmann, with Jung's approval, for emergency consultation. Cf. Preface, p. xii and note; cf. also Jung, 13 December 1930, p. 13 and note.

10 *Wirkung:* practical effect. Lacking Kirsch's previous letter, we do not know what change may have been noticed in Sussmann's behavior, nor whose intervention Jung credits for it.

11 Typewritten in German, on letterhead.

12 *Sie hören die Gefühle ungenügend heraus.*

Around the 14th of January I'll be coming to Berlin[13] and hope to be able to see you there. We'll have an opportunity then to discuss all sorts of things.

With best greetings,[14] In haste, Yours, C. G. JUNG·

Dr. C. G. Jung
Seestrasse 228
Küsnacht-Zürich

17 March 1930[15]

Dear Colleague!

Dr. Körner[16] wanted to start making preparations for such a seminar right away. But I have the feeling it's still too early, and we could not bring enough of the right people together. So I think it's better if we let it go this year.

My work on "American psychology"[17] is already translated and will appear in a Swiss journal.[18]

I have a crazy amount to do, which prevented me from writing you and thanking you for your extremely kind reception.

Please give your wife my best thanks for her friendly letter. It's unfortunately not possible for me to thank her myself, since I hardly have time for the most urgent letters.

---

13 In letters exchanged at the turn of 1930, Toni Wolff asked advice from James Kirsch about suitable hotel accommodations for Jung and herself, close to the women's college where Jung was to lecture in Berlin (Wolff to Kirsch, 28 December 1929, Kirsch archive). She added that Jung would lecture in Frankfurt on 11 January and "visit Prof. Wilhelm, who is sick again" (Wolff to Kirsch, 8 January 1930, Kirsch archive).

14 Remainder of closing added in Jung's handwriting.

15 Typewritten in German, on letterhead.

16 Otto Körner, MD: German psychiatrist and psychotherapist, practicing at a sanatorium in Kipsdorf near Dresden. He attended Jung's lectures and seminars in Zurich (Körner to Jung, 3 June 1932, ETH Library archive). He was a member of the Allgemeine ärztliche Gesellschaft für Psychotherapie [General Medical Society for Psychotherapy], hereafter AAGP (cf. Jung, 26 May 1934, p. 44 and notes; cf. also Appendix D, pp. 304–12). Körner and Jung corresponded on AAGP business from the late 1920s until the mid 1930s. They resumed contact after the war, when Körner sent Jung an essay on psychology and religion (Körner to Jung, 18 July 1957, ETH Library archive).

17 "The Complications of American Psychology," originally written in English, was first published in a New York journal under the title, "Your Negroid and Indian Behavior" (*Forum*, Vol. 83, No. 4, New York, April 1930, pp. 193–99). In German translation (typescript, ETH Library archive), Jung's original title, "Die Compliciertheit der Amerikanischen Psyche," is struck through by hand, replaced by "Americana." In Jung's Collected Works (hereafter CW), this essay is "slightly revised stylistically" (CW 10, p. 502). Cf. "The Complications of American Psychology," *Civilization in Transition,* CW 10, ¶946–80.

18 No record has been found of the paper's publication in German in 1930.

I hope very much to see you in Baden-Baden.[19]

With best greetings, Yours very truly, C. G. JUNG

Dr. C. G. Jung
Küsnacht-Zürich
Seestrasse 228

14 April 1930[20]

Dear Colleague!

I regret very much that you weren't able to get through to me by telephone. Right now I'm on vacation, where I'm inaccessible except by letter. Could you perhaps give me some orientation[21] in writing before the Congress? At the Congress, of course, we'll have an opportunity for an exchange of views.

Meanwhile, with best greetings also to your wife,

Ever faithfully yours, C. G. JUNG

19 Baden-Baden, Germany: location of the first (1926), third (1928), and fifth (1930) annual Congresses of the AAGP (cf. Appendix D, p. 310). Jung became Vice-President of the AAGP in 1930 (cf. Jung, 26 May 1934, p. 44, note 46) and served as President of the reorganized society, the Internationale allgemeine ärztliche Gesellschaft für Psychotherapie (hereafter IAAGP), from 1933 to 1940. Although not yet a member in 1929 or 1930, Kirsch attended these AAGP congresses, meeting Jung at the Congress in Bad Nauheim, April 1929. He joined the AAGP in 1931 (cf. Figure 14.1, p. 305) and presented a paper that year at the Congress in Dresden (Cimbal to Jung, 16 October 1930, ETH Library archive).
20 Typewritten in German, on letterhead.
21 Jung's request for "orientation" apparently refers to Kirsch's urgent request for advice about a patient. Urgency is suggested also by the fact that Kirsch had tried to contact Jung by a long-distance phone call.

Dr. C. G. Jung
Küsnacht-Zürich
Seestrasse 228

2 June 1930[22]

Dear Colleague,

Your suggestion[23] suits me very well. Please let Dr. Cimbal[24] know about it right away.

Unfortunately I do not have access to any offprints of my American article.[25] It should be published in German, though, at which point I hope to be able to send you a copy.

With best greetings, Yours truly, C. G. JUNG

Dr. C. G. Jung
Küsnacht-Zürich
Seestrasse 228

15 August 1930[26]

My dear Kirsch!

I hope you won't think badly of me that I haven't gone into your letter[27] in detail. It was simply too much for me. But you can write to me any time. In urgent cases I'll respond, too.

It goes without saying that the anima problem[28] is always present, and the anima always comes forward with very absolute demands, so absolute that it

---

22 Typewritten in German, on letterhead.

23 Probably referring to Kirsch's proposal for a paper, "Darstellung somatischer Phänomene im Traum" [Dream representation of somatic phenomena], which he presented at the next AAGP Congress (*Bericht über den VI. Allgemeinen ärztlichen Kongress für Psychotherapie in Dresden 14. bis 17. April 1931*, Leipzig: Verlag von S. Hirzel, 1931, pp. 157–62). Years later he revised and published this paper in English (cf. Kirsch, 21 September 1948, p. 117, note 24).

24 Walter Julius Otto Cimbal, Dr. med. (1877–1964): German psychiatrist and psychotherapist with a specialty in child psychiatry, at this time located in Altona near Hamburg. As General Secretary of the AAGP (cf. Jung, 26 May 1934, p. 44 and note), he oversaw the list of Congress lectures. Cimbal later embraced Hitler's rise with quasi-religious conviction. He joined the Nazi party but quickly came under attack, owing to his wife's anti-Nazi activity (Cimbal to Jung, 27 July 1947, ETH Library archive) and was forced from his teaching position and from his office in the German section of the IAAGP. In 1935 he resigned from the IAAGP entirely. He and his wife moved to a small town, and in 1943 fled to western Poland (ibid.). In 1947 Cimbal returned to Hamburg and resumed a correspondence with Jung which continued, with occasional friendly responses, until June 1957.

25 Cf. Jung, 17 March 1930, p. 7 and notes.

26 Handwritten in German, on letterhead. Most of second paragraph prev. pub. in *PP*.

27 Kirsch's letter, which is missing, evidently concerned the clinical dilemma about which he had tried to reach Jung by phone (cf. Jung, 14 April 1930, p. 8, note 21).

28 In early 1930 a woman had entered analysis with Kirsch in Berlin, her treatment subsidized by the Psychological Club in Zurich (hereafter the Club). In July 1930 Toni Wolff wrote to Kirsch about

always signifies a kind of self-sacrifice (in the Christian sense) not to consent to them. First of all the anima must be put back in place, quite energetically, because every solution to the problem has *social consequences*. There are no "individual" solutions. Therefore the first question is always that of social appropriateness. The anima problem is always a problem of one's own social inferiority; in other words, on the edge of a glacial crevasse it's better not to make trial jumps, but rather to bring inner conditions into harmony with outer. In treating the anima, nothing is more dangerous than unworldly naïveté. You can measure your anima's social inferiority by your wife's resistances. So be careful!

With best greetings, Yours, JUNG

23 September 1930[29]

Dr. James Kirsch
Olivaer Platz 3[30]
Berlin W.15

My dear Kirsch!

We will surely (your wife[31] included) be able to talk together.[32] But a regularly scheduled series of sessions is impossible for me, since I'm drowning[33] in work.

Meanwhile best greetings from

Ever yours truly, C. G. JUNG

---

the Club's financial involvement in this case and about Kirsch's countertransference difficulties. She adds, *"Ihren Brief an Dr. Jung habe ich gelesen"* ["I have read your letter to Dr. Jung"] (Wolff to Kirsch, 13 July 1930, Kirsch archive). Jung's references to "anima" concern the feminine component in Kirsch's psyche.

29 Handwritten in German, on undated postcard. Date of mailing shown by postal stamp: *23.IX.30.*

30 Kirsch's office was at his home, Olivaer Platz 3, in an apartment overlooking a small square in a desirable neighborhood, where he lived and practiced from November 1926 until August 1933. The building is no longer standing, but the Olivaer Platz of today, near the fashionable Kurfürstendamm, is still an attractive square surrounded by apartment buildings, some with shops on the ground floor (T. Kirsch).

31 *Ihre Frau Gemahlin:* i.e. Eva Kirsch (Cf. Jung, 19 August 1929, pp. 5f and notes).

32 At the invitation of the Club, Kirsch delivered a lecture in Zurich on 4 October 1930: "Das Problem des modernen Juden" ["The Problem of the Modern Jew"] (Wolff to Kirsch, 12 September 1930, Kirsch archive). The original typescript of this lecture may be found at the Club library. Due to high interest, he gave the lecture a second time and received an honorarium (Wolff to Kirsch, 11 October 1930, ibid.). Its theme is discussed in letters exchanged by Kirsch and a colleague from Heidelberg, Dr. Gustav Schmaltz, who was present. In his lecture Kirsch affirmed the mutual psychological assimilation of Jews and Christians living in a shared culture, a view with which Schmaltz took issue (Schmaltz to Kirsch, 9 December 1930 and 23 December 1930, Kirsch archive). Jung later requested a copy of the lecture (Jung, 20 July 1931, p. 17), and suggested corrections (Jung, 12 August 1931, pp. 20f and notes).

33 *ich ersaufe* (a common, somewhat coarse alternate for *ich ertrinke*).

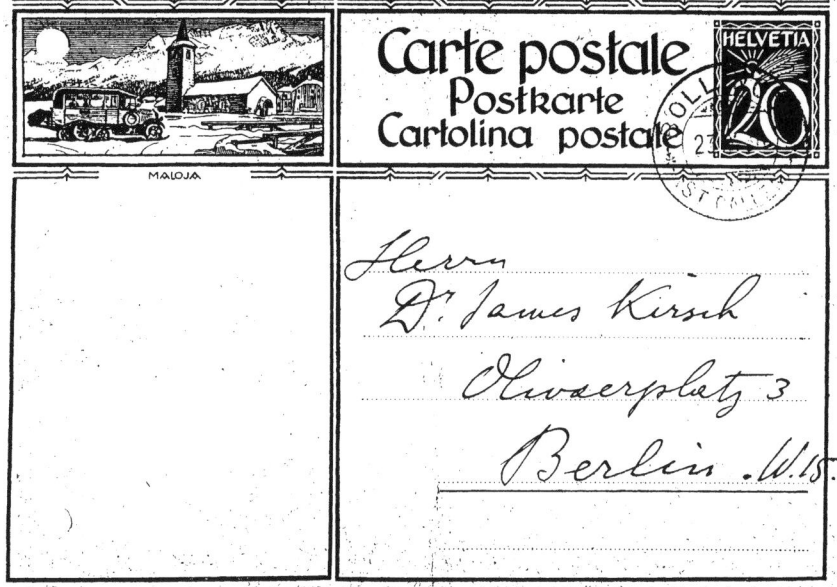

Figure 1.3 **Jung's postcard of 23 September 1930.** *Photocopy: ©2007, Ursula Egli. Courtesy Kirsch archive/Stiftung der Werke von C. G. Jung.*

Dr. C. G. Jung
Küsnacht-Zürich
Seestrasse 228

27 October 1930[34]

Dr. James Kirsch
Olivaer Platz 3
Berlin W.15

Dear Colleague,

I've referred a Herr von K[…] to you, a student at the Institute of Technology in Charlottenburg.[35] You will receive a letter from the patient's mother, in which she will send you, as I have recommended, a sketch of our consultation. Of course, you must read this communication with a critical eye. He seems to me to have caught a light case of theosophy,[36] and he cannot bring the spiritual world into connection with his technical profession. A Dementia Praecox appears to be

---

34 Typewritten in German, on letterhead.

35 A fashionable Berlin district. Patient's name is concealed to respect privacy.

36 *Er ist, wie mir scheint, theosophisch angekränkelt*: Jung's slightly derisive turn of phrase compares theosophy to an illness, like a cold, which the young man has picked up somewhere.

not entirely ruled out. He seems to have a great respect for analysis. Therefore I recommend that first you simply give him a chance to express himself, whereby you'll soon see what's needed, provided he really comes.

Best greetings to you and your wife, from yours truly, JUNG

From Marianne Jung:[37]

Küsnacht, 17 November 1930[38]

Dear Doctor,

I really haven't forgotten my promise, even though you seem to be firmly convinced of it. I just didn't know what I should be sending you, since the writings are mostly older and you may already know them, or even own them. First I'll send you a list of the offprints.[39] If you'd be good enough to put a cross or something next to the ones you don't know yet and are interested in, and send the whole thing back to me, I'll be glad to send you a whole shipment of offprints! To show my good intentions, I'm enclosing one herewith. The next thing to be published will be the third volume of the Psychologische Abhandlungen.[40] It contains 12 lectures and essays. I think it's being published by Rascher & Co. in Zurich. When, I'm not yet certain.

Next Sunday we travel to Darmstadt.[41] I'm looking forward to it, as it will probably be interesting. But I'm also afraid of all the brilliant people!

Cordial greetings to you and your wife[42] from MARIANNE JUNG

---

37 Marianne Jung (1910–1965): Jung's fourth child, later known by her married name, Niehus-Jung. Early in his career, before he hired Marie-Jeanne Schmid (cf. letter presumably from M.-J. Schmid, 21 October 1947, p. 110 and note), Jung turned to his own family for secretarial help. His sister Gertrud assisted him, 1909–26, then Emma Jung took over, until 1930, when Marianne stepped in for two years. It was she who first systematically filed her father's letters. At the end of her life, Marianne Niehus-Jung played an important role in the publication of Jung's works. From 1956 until her death she was one of the co-editors for Jung's Gesammelte Werke (Collected Works, German-language edition; hereafter GW). From 1958 she was also on the sub-committee for publication of the *C. G. Jung Briefe* (German-language edition of Jung's *Letters*; hereafter *Briefe*). Thanks to Ulrich Hoerni and the Estate of Marianne Niehus-Jung. Cf. also Aniela Jaffé, "Vorwort," *Briefe I,* p. 8.

38 Handwritten in German, on plain paper.

39 *Separata:* separately reprinted essays or chapters, originally part of a larger publication. Many of Jung's important early essays were reprinted in this way and made available as pamphlets.

40 "Psychological Treatises": series title for Jung's theoretical papers published in the 1930s. The third volume is titled *Seelenprobleme der Gegenwart* [Present-day mental problems], Psychologische Abhandlungen 3, Zürich: Rascher, 1931. No English edition exists. Translations of papers in this collection appear in several volumes of the CW (Cf. Kirsch, "The Jewish Image of the World," summer 1931, p. 16, note 59).

41 Conference held at Hermann Keyserling's Schule der Weisheit [School of Wisdom], Darmstadt, November 1930. Cf. Jung, 12 August 1931, p. 21 and notes.

42 *Ihrer Frau Gemahlin* (cf. Jung, 19 August 1929, p. 5, note 7.)

From Marianne Jung:

28 November 1930[43]

Dear Doctor,

Enclosed are the desired offprints. Don't you already have "Die Bedeutung von Constitution und Vererbung?"[44] In any case, it's already on your list.

On Wednesday we came back from Darmstadt. I found it quite interesting to have a chance to see what happens there. Since I like to meet new people and get to know them, and at the same time feel a certain curiosity about them, it was *gefundenes Fressen*[45] for me, as we like to say here.

I look forward to hearing from you from time to time.

With cordial greetings to you and your wife, MARIANNE JUNG

Dr. C. G. Jung
Küsnacht-Zürich
Seestrasse 228

13 December 1930[46]

Dr. J. Kirsch
Olivaer Platz 3
Berlin W.15

Dear Colleague!

I grasp your situation completely. It's quite right for you to go to Frau Sussmann. She told me everything necessary in Darmstadt.[47]

Please give the enclosed letter to your wife.[48]

With best greetings, Yours, C. G. JUNG

43 Handwritten in German, on plain paper.
44 Originally published in a Berlin medical weekly: "Die Bedeutung von Konstitution und Vererbung für die Psychologie" ["The Significance of Constitution and Heredity for Psychology"] (*Die Medizinische Welt,* III, No. 47. Berlin: November 1929, pp. 1677–79). Cf. "The Significance of Constitution and Heredity in Psychology," CW 8, *The Structure and Dynamics of the Psyche*, ¶220–31.
45 lit. "food found by chance": Swiss saying for "a lucky find" or "a gift from the gods."
46 Typewritten in German, on half-sheet letterhead.
47 In a clinical emergency, Kirsch had turned to Toni Sussmann, who presented his questions to both Jung and Toni Wolff when they were together at the School of Wisdom in November. Wolff then sent Kirsch a detailed letter about the case (Wolff to Kirsch, 13 December 1930, Kirsch archive).
48 No enclosure found.

13

Küsnacht, 6 February 1931[49]

Dr. J. Kirsch
Olivaer Platz 3
Berlin W.15
Deutschland

My dear Kirsch,

Best of thanks for your friendly notification. I'm glad if things are finally taking a turn for the better.

With best greetings, Yours truly, C. G. JUNG

Küsnacht, 13 February 1931[50]

Dr. J. Kirsch
Olivaer Platz 3
Berlin W.15

My dear Kirsch,

If you don't mean the Sermones,[51] then at best the rumor could relate to a short English address that I gave at the request of the relatives at the funeral of an American patient.[52] I do not know whether that address is still around. I'll look for it though. Cordial greetings to your wife. Give her my best thanks for her friendly letter.

Cordial greetings, from yours truly, C. G. JUNG

---

49 Typewritten in German, on plain postcard.
50 Typewritten in German, on plain postcard.
51 C. G. Jung, *VII Sermones ad Mortuos. Die Sieben Belehrungen der Toten. Geschrieben von Basilides in Alexandria, der Stadt, wo der Osten den Westen berührt. Übersetzt aus dem griechischen Urtext in die deutsche Sprache* [Seven Sermons to the Dead. Written by Basilides in Alexandria, the city where East touches West. Translated from the original Greek into the German language]. This brief writing by Jung was printed for private circulation in 1916. It was published first in English translation by H. G. Baynes: *VII Sermones ad Mortuos. The Seven Sermons to the Dead Written by Basilides in Alexandria, the City Where the East Toucheth the West* (trans. H. G. Baynes. Edinburgh: Neill, 1925). Later the Baynes translation was added as Appendix V to the US paperback edition of *MDR* (New York: Vintage, 1965, pp. 378–90).
52 Jung's eulogy for this patient, Jerome Schloss, appears in CW 18, *The Symbolic Life*, ¶1705–10.

Dr. med. James Kirsch
Olivaer Platz 3
Berlin W.15

[Summer 1931]

The Jewish Image of the World[53]

Since time immemorial primitive peoples have commonly believed that it is impossible to conquer a foreign land, because those who occupy a foreign land will then be taken over by the gods of that land. The settlement of America by white people provides ample evidence that the primitives' belief is true. Even though the whites in America did not absorb Indian blood to any extent worth mentioning, specific Indian traits are evident in the appearance, bearing, and physiognomy of present-day Americans.[54] Just as one and the same plant has different characteristics, depending on its habitat, so with human beings. Thus, we would do better to say, not that the inhabitants of North America exhibit Indian traits, but that when the Europeans were transplanted to America, the change of habitat bestowed on them a different physiognomy. Just as with physique, the psychology of the white population of North America shows a specifically American-Indian character. Their concept of excellence, their heroic ideal, is emphatically Indian. Only think of their rough training combats and boxing, the songs of a Walt Whitman, and more besides – unimaginable for Europeans. The gods of that country have taken possession of them.

This has been the experience of every conquering people, every people which has had to live on foreign soil for extended periods. Only one people proves to be an exception to this rule: *the Jews*. Through all lands they took their god with them, the god they conceived in the desert. The desert is a vast, desolate region, without plants, with very few animals. In rare and isolated places, oases exist. To experience the desert is to know its vastness, its distant horizon, with the *fata morgana*, the wind, the storm. Israel's god is a god of the wind, not originating from the earth, and from the very beginning he was grasped in spiritual form, as the Everlasting: I will be who I will be![55] As the Everlasting in Becoming, or as

---

53 Typewritten in German, on letterhead. Undated essay; probably early summer 1931 (cf. Jung, 20 July 1931, p. 17). Handwritten at top: *Beantwortet* [answered]. Kirsch's earliest writing to be preserved by Jung.

54 Cf. C. G. Jung, "The Complications of American Psychology," CW 10, ¶948f, 968–70; also "Mind and Earth," CW 10, ¶94.

55 In the Book of Exodus, Moses asks what name he should give to the divine presence whose voice he hears from a burning bush. The mysterious reply (Exodus 3:14) can be translated in either the present or the future tense. Most English translations use the present tense: "I am who I am."

Becoming in the Everlasting,[56] God, detached from all qualities, is the creative principle, in contrast to the gods of the earth, the material principle. They[57] had to be plural, if the divine showed itself as subject to quality of any kind. For the Jewish people, God is the energetic principle before it divides into its polarities.

The soul of the Jew was bound up with this single-singular principle;[58] his soul was not permitted to open itself to the land where he traveled. The Jew's bride, the Jew's anima was Israel, the Jewish people, the Sabbath, the Torah. His emotional character, his psychic disposition was defined by the Sabbath. The Jew's homeland is the Torah, and the only content of his soul is God.

And yet deep in every Jew is the yearning for oasis, for the earth. He longs to be like all other peoples, yet this cannot be. Therein lies the paradox of Jewish psychology. It is a human being's eternally impossible attempt to direct the soul away from the earth, to adapt collective energy and its specific formation to his soul, and to turn the Eternally Becoming into the only content of this soul. Such attempts must almost always fail. Then if money, socialism, or the belly take the place of God, the Jew turns away from his eternal task; he becomes inauthentic and his psychology a fraud. It is then that the earth-born peoples[59] perceive him as harboring hand-grenades in his unconscious. This is the deepest ground for anti-Semitism. On the other hand, if the Jew lives according to his proper dynamic psychology, he is the salt of the earth. Theocracy is the basis of his endurance.

---

56 *Als das Ewig-Seiende im Werden, oder das Werden im Ewig-Seienden.* Kirsch's punctuation has been corrected, substituting a comma for his period at the end of this phrase. It is unusual for him to use a sentence fragment in formal writing. In typing the essay, he left a space after each period but none after a comma; no space appears after this period in the original.

57 i.e. the gods of polytheistic cultures.

58 *mit diesem einig-einzigen Prinzip*: the phrase could equally be translated "unitary-unique." Consistent with the monotheism central to the Hebrew Bible, Kirsch emphasizes both the oneness of God and the exclusive claim of this one God upon the Jewish people.

59 Kirsch here modifies the concept of *Erdgebundenheit* [earth-boundness], which Jung had developed in his paper "Erdbedingtheit der Psyche" [The Psyche's Determination by Earth] (*Mensch und Erde* [Man and Earth], Keyserling, ed., Darmstadt: Otto Reichl Verlag, 1927), and discussed again in "Seele und Erde" [Mind and Earth] (CW 10, ¶49–103) (*Seelenprobleme der Gegenwart*; cf. M. Jung, 17 November 1930, p. 12 and note). Whereas Jung posits that the soul is naturally earth-bound, i.e. influenced by the land, and warns that the absence of "earth-boundness" makes the soul rootless ("Mind and Earth," CW 10, ¶93ff), Kirsch grants only that the non-Jewish peoples are "earth-born," while maintaining that psychic rootedness for Jews is found in the God-relationship.

Dr. C. G. Jung
Küsnacht-Zürich
Seestrasse 228

20 July 1931[60]

My dear Colleague,

Best thanks for sending your meaty lecture. I think you've hit something quite essential with it. The other lecture you delivered would interest me very much.[61] I'd have more time to read it now, rather than later.[62] I haven't read the work of Fräulein Geitel[63] yet; it is lying hidden under a mountain of manuscripts – but this mountain is unfortunately not like the great cake-mountain, three weeks after Christmas;[64] rather it towers physically before my eyes.

I have no objection to Dr. Lipschitz.[65] But whether I'll have the necessary time then remains unclear this far in advance. Please remind me about it again later.

With cordial greetings, Yours faithfully C. G. JUNG

Best wishes also to your wife.[66]

---

60 Typewritten in German, on letterhead.
61 Probably Kirsch's Club lecture, "Das Problem des modernen Juden," delivered twice in October 1930 (cf. Jung, 23 September 1930, p. 10, note 32).
62 Perhaps a reference to Jung's preparations for his "German seminar" of 1931 (cf. Jung, 28 January 1933, p. 34 and note).
63 Charlotte Geitel: elementary school teacher and Jungian analyst, practicing in Berlin. Her 1931 paper was titled "Psychische Bilder bei Kindern" ["Psychic Images in Children"] (cf. Kirsch, 20 August 1931, p. 22 and note). In 1937 she contributed a paper, "Das introvertierte Kind" ["The Introverted Child"], to the second volume of a series, *Reich der Seele: Arbeiten aus dem Münchener psychologischen Arbeitskreis* (G. R. Heyer and F. Seifert, eds, München/Berlin: Lehmanns Verlag, 1937, pp. 90–118). In a review by Toni Wolff, critical of the volume as a whole, Geitel's essay is singled out for praise (*Zentralblatt für Psychotherapie 1937/38*, pp. 239–78). (Cf. also Jung, 12 March 1932, p. 25, note 104).
64 "*der grosse Kuchenberg drei Wochen hinter Weihnachten*": Direct allusion to a fable in verse by the poet Hans Sachs (Nuremberg, 1494–1576). "Das Schlaraffenland" (1539) begins: *Eine Gegend heißt Schlaraffenland,/ Den faulen Leuten ist sie gut bekannt. / Sie liegt drei Meilen hinter Weihnachten. / Und wer dahin gelangen möchte, / der muss sich große Dinge zutrauen: / Er muss sich durch einen Berg aus Hirsebrei essen, / Der ist gut drei Meilen breit...* ["There is a place called the Land of Milk and Honey, / well known to lazy people. / It lies three miles behind Christmas, / And those who want to go there / Must dare great challenges / And eat through a mountain of millet gruel / Which is a good three miles wide ..."] With thanks to Ursula Egli and Dr. phil. Martin Müller, who located this literary source.
65 An obscure reference, apparently a Berlin colleague whom Kirsch had referred to Jung. A cryptic note in Kirsch's handwriting – "Lipschitz!" – appears on the back of a 1931 letter from a psychiatrist in Ascona, Dr. G. Kastein, who asks Kirsch for case materials concerning the "Jesus-complex," and says he hopes to talk with other Jewish psychiatrists on this topic (Kastein to Kirsch, 21 April 1931, Kirsch archive).
66 Handwritten postscript.

Berlin W.15
Olivaer Pl. 3

28 July 1931[67]

Dear, very honored Dr. Jung![68]

Please accept my most heartfelt thanks for your letter, which I enjoyed very much. If at all possible I'll avoid making demands on your time. I'm working through my dreams, fantasies, etc. on a regular basis with Kranefeld.[69] I'm doing quite well and – to the extent I can – have found my way back into life and am enjoying life. I would like to ask your fatherly and analytical advice, though, about a few things.

I. H. Schultz[70] presented a series of lectures here to the Berlin Psychotherapists on the subject of "self-relaxation,"[71] which I attended with great interest, despite the doubts which I. H. Schultz as a human being instills in me. His method amounts to a primitive form of Hatha Yoga. By it one learns to regulate one's inner organs at will. There is no doubt that this kind of "training" produces deep

---

67 Handwritten in German, on plain paper.
68 *Lieber, sehr verehrter Herr Dr. Jung!* In his earliest letters to Jung, Kirsch uses deeply honorific forms of address. Such formulas are now only rarely used in German-language correspondence. They are translated literally here, to convey the feeling in these initial letters from journeyman to master.
69 (= Kranefeldt) Wolfgang Müller Kranefeldt, Dr. med. (1892–1950): German psychiatrist and Jungian analyst in Berlin. He had analyzed with Jung, who wrote the introduction to his first book, *Psychoanalyse: Psychoanalytische Psychologie* (Berlin, Leipzig: de Gruyter, 1930; trans. Ralph M. Eaton, *Secret Ways of the Mind: A Survey of the Psychological Principles of Freud, Adler and Jung*). Jung included two essays by Kranefeldt in his own *Wirklichkeit der Seele* (cf. Jung, 20 February. 1934, p. 39 and notes). Active in the AAGP and IAAGP in the 1930s, Kranefeldt assisted in editing the *Zentralblatt für Psychotherapie* [Journal of Psychotherapy] (hereafter *Zentralblatt*). In 1936 he joined the faculty of the Göring Institute, Berlin (cf. Jung, 17 February. 1935, p. 67, note 4). In 1938 he was invited, as Jung's "leading pupil in Germany," to lecture beside Jung at the tenth Congress of the IAAGP (Meier to Kranefeldt, 26 June 1938, ETH Library archive). Kirsch, who later described Kranefeldt as having become "psychologically" a Nazi, nevertheless exchanged friendly letters with him after the war (Kirsch-Kranefeldt correspondence, Kirsch archive).
70 Johannes Heinrich Schultz, Dr. med. (1884–1970): German psychiatrist and psychotherapist. (His initials are published alternatively as J. H. or I. H.). Schultz opened a practice in Berlin in 1924 and became famous for teaching his technique of self-hypnosis, which he had been developing since the First World War. His major work *Das Autogene Training: Konzentrative Selbstentspannung* [Autogenic Training: Concentrational Self-Relaxation] (Leipzig: Thieme, 1932) went through many editions. He was a founder and director of the AAGP, 1926 to 1933, then served on the board of the German section of the IAAGP (cf. Appendix D, pp. 306f). From 1936 on, as a director at the Göring Institute, he promoted diagnostic and treatment modalities related to Nazi ideology. After the war he continued to practice and teach in Berlin.
71 *"autogenes Training"* (lit. "self-training"). At the second Congress of the AAGP, Bad Nauheim, April 1927, Schultz's lecture was titled, "Über rationalisiertes autosuggestives Training (Autogene Organübungen)" ["On rationalized self-relaxation (autogenic organ exercises)"].

relaxation. What's disturbing is just his insolent way of alluding to "well-trained circus horses," and that sort of thing. For me there's a real question here whether the appropriate training is in the hands of the appropriate man. For he uses this training to cause people to see images under deep self-hypnosis, and to use them analytically. For me these images appeared of their own accord. In fact, about three weeks ago I saw the following:

A rotating car wheel with M[…]'s[72] sleeping face looking out of it.
Then a blonde girl hiding behind a pillar.
Then a number of girls climbing the little stair into a bus, pushing each other, one of them pressing forward.

Then, with alarm:

A woman, covered with snow; snow continues to fall on her, and she seems to rise in a veil of snow, like a goddess, an archaic Greek goddess with an archaic smile.

At that moment I heard a ringing and came out of this state of absorption, feeling a slight tension. It felt as if someone had tightened a ring around my forehead. This tension grew stronger over the next few days. I began to have a fever of 38° and also a nasty cold, followed by a sinus infection, which gave me pain in exactly the place where I concentrated during Schultz's exercises, following his instructions. Since then I've abstained from these exercises.

Frau Sussmann, with whom I discussed Schultz's training superficially, told me that the yogi breaks off yoga exercises immediately if images come up, because he's afraid of the danger of physical or psychic illness, and because images mean desecration. What the Indians regard as a danger may have a far different meaning for us. After the dread the goddess instilled in me, there can be no question of a desecration. But in any case, the snow-covered goddess – the cold – is a powerful warning to me for the time being. I've also wondered whether this training may not to some degree be an avoidance of analysis. But I must admit, I've never before experienced my dreams and fantasies as realities in the way I do now – after the events of the past year. It's clear to me that analysis is very close to black magic, and I certainly don't wish to get into that.

***

---

72 Name of female patient who had committed suicide the previous year (Wolff to Kirsch, 27 January 1931, Kirsch archive).

Dear Dr. Jung, a few days ago, I took the liberty of sending you a small volume of poems by Lothar Schreyer[73] for your birthday. I hope that you'll find some time during your vacation to glance into the small volume. Lothar Schreyer is a well-known lawyer in Hamburg (Prof. Dr. ...) and has published several excellent books about German culture and German mysticism. Since he's familiar with all your works and is one of "die Stillen im Lande"[74] – those who also understand you – he was very pleased to know that this private edition is going to you. Belatedly, please accept my heartiest congratulations for your birthday.

With cordial greetings, Very truly and gratefully yours, JAMES KIRSCH

Dr. C. G. Jung
pro tem. Bollingen,
Canton St. Gallen

12 August 1931[75]

My dear Colleague!

Best thanks for your ms,[76] which I send back herewith! I read it with interest. It's essentially clear and may have instructed the public in some measure, insofar as they were willing to accept new ideas.

73 Lothar Schreyer (1896–1966): German Expressionist painter, writer, and poet. After studying law in Heidelberg, Schreyer worked as a dramaturg in Hamburg (1911–18). In later years he turned to Christian mysticism, art and iconography. The "small volume," privately published, is unlisted among his works. Jung's next letter calls it "das Marienbuch" (the Mary book) (cf. Jung, 12 August 1931, p. 21 and note).

74 "the silent in the land" (Psalm 35:20), i.e. the faithful, assailed by the ungodly. In Luther's version: *Denn sie trachten Schaden zu tun und suchen falsche Anklagen wider die Stillen im Lande.* ["For they plot to do harm and seek false accusations against the silent in the land"]. Jung had recently used this expression, twice, in a book review which Kirsch would have read: "Der Aufgang einer neuen Welt" (*Neue Zürcher Zeitung,* 7 December 1930, Bücher-Beilage, p. 6), which praises Keyserling's *Amerika: Der Aufgang einer neuen Welt* [America: The Rise of a New World] (Stuttgart und Berlin: Deutsche Verlagsanstalt, 1930). Cf. CW 10, ¶925–54, esp. ¶953f.

75 Handwritten in German, on letterhead with address deleted. Final paragraph prev. pub. in *PP.*

76 Probably Kirsch's lecture, "Das Problem des modernen Juden" (cf. Jung, 23 September 1930, p. 10, note 32).

N.B.: The parallel between subjective modern fantasy and papyrus-text is found in Wandl. u. Symb. der Lib.[77] (index: "Sun phallus"!).[78] The patient is not a Negro but a Swiss. I discussed the case again extensively in Keyserling's[79] *Mensch und Erde*[80] (earth-boundness).[81] By the way, my collected lectures have now appeared with Rascher, I hear.[82]

Intuition does not say what things "mean" but sniffs out their possibilities. *"Meaning"* is given by thinking.

With warm regards to you and your wife, Ever faithfully yours, JUNG

By the way – almost forgot! – my most sincere thanks for the book on Mary![83]

---

77 C. G. Jung, *Wandlungen und Symbole der Libido: Beiträge zur Entwicklungsgeschichte des Denkens* [lit: Transformations and Symbols of Libido: Contributions to the developmental history of thought], Leipzig and Vienna: Franz Deuticke, 1912 (hereafter *Wandlungen*). This groundbreaking work precipitated Jung's break with Freud (cf. Kirsch, 7 May 1934, p. 41, note 33). An early English translation, widely regarded as poor, was titled *The Psychology of the Unconscious: A Study of the Transformation and Symbolisms of the Libido* (trans. by Beatrice M. Hinkle, New York: Moffat Yard, 1916, 1919; London: Kegan Paul, Trench, Trubner, 1917, 1921). Jung later revised this work extensively as GW 5, *Symbole der Wandlung: Analyse des Vorspiels zu einer Schizophrenie* (1973); CW 5, *Symbols of Transformation:An Analysis of the Prelude to a Case of Schizophrenia* (1956/1974) (hereafter *Symbols of Transformation*).

78 Jung's patient at the Burghölzli Clinic, 1906, talked of seeing the sun's phallus, which he said was "where the wind came from" (CW 5, *Symbols of Transformation*, ¶150, p. 101). When Jung discovered the same image in a Mithraic liturgy, he concluded that an archetypal source underlay the idea in both cases.

79 Graf Hermann Keyserling (1880–1946): German historical philosopher and cultural psychologist from an aristocratic Prussian family. His main theme was the unity of spirit and life, psyche and intellect. In his early work, *Reisetagebuch eines Philosophen* [Travel Diary of a Philosopher] (1919), he suggests that Eastern cultures can be enriched through encounters with the West. In 1920 Keyserling founded the Schule der Weisheit [School of Wisdom] in Darmstadt, where he invited groups of intellectuals to explore themes of self-realization and cultural renewal (cf. Marianne Jung, 17 November 1930, p. 12 and note).

80 Hermann Keyserling, ed., *Mensch und Erde* [Man and Earth] (Darmstadt: Otto Reichl Verlag, 1927). A collection of papers from the 1927 conference of the Gesellschaft für freie Philosophie (Schule der Weisheit), Darmstadt. In addition to Jung and Keyserling, contributors to the collection include Frobenius, Much, Prinzhorn, Roeder von Diersburg, Salomon, Scheler, von Ungern-Sternberg, Welkisch, and Wilhelm.

81 *Erdgebundenheit*. Jung's contribution to *Mensch und Erde* is titled, "Die Erdbedingtheit der Psyche" ["The Psyche's Determination by Earth"]. Published in English in two parts, separately: "The Structure of the Psyche," CW 8, *Structure and Dynamics of the Psyche*, ¶283–342; and "Mind and Earth," CW 10, *Civilization in Transition*, ¶49–103. In the first part, Jung describes the collective unconscious as rooted in the deepest layers of animal existence, a position he demonstrates by reference to his previouly published case study (CW 8, ¶317ff). Cf. also Kirsch, "The Jewish Image of the World," p. 16 and note.

82 Cf. Marianne Jung, 17 November. 1930, p. 12, note 40.

83 *das Marienbuch*: book of poems by Lothar Schreyer (cf. Kirsch, 28 July 1931, p. 20 and note).

Dr. med. James Kirsch
Berlin W.15
Olivaer Pl. 3

20 August 1931[84]

Dear Dr. Jung!

Please accept my heartiest thanks for your letter with the corrections of my blunders.[85] I was very pleased that you were able to read my lecture so quickly, and would be equally delighted if you would retrieve Fräulein Geitel's essay on "Psychic Images in Children" from the mountain of manuscripts.[86] By the way, I collaborated extensively on that essay. I'd also be most grateful if you would say something briefly about the Schultz exercises that I recently wrote you about.[87]

From various sources I've heard that you won't accept any patients this fall, so you can dedicate yourself to your projects. All of us look forward very much to your new book.[88] Despite the heavy work load, would you be willing to arrange for a German Seminar again this year?

With cordial greetings also from my wife,
Very truly and gratefully yours, JAMES KIRSCH

Dr. C. G. Jung
Küsnacht-Zürich
Seestrasse 228

20 February 1932[89]

Herrn Dr. J. Kirsch
Olivaer Platz 3,
Berlin W.15

My dear Kirsch,

I'm truly sorry I didn't get around to answering your late November letter[90] until now. I'm not caught up with my correspondence in any way, even though I devoted over half my vacation to writing letters.

---

84 Handwritten in German, on letterhead.
85 Kirsch had wrongly identified Jung's Burghölzli patient (cf. Jung, 12 August 1931, p. 21, note 77).
86 Cf. Jung, 20 July 1931, p. 17 and note.
87 Cf. Kirsch, 28 July 1931, pp. 18f and notes.
88 Probably referring to *Seelenprobleme der Gegenwart* (cf. M. Jung, 17 November 1930, p. 12, note 40; also Jung, 12 August 1931, p. 21 and note).
89 Typewritten in German, on letterhead. Two versions exist for this letter – a signed original and an unsigned carbon copy. The carbon copy, found at the ETH Library archive, is apparently Jung's first draft. Its second page consists of three paragraphs (shown below in italics) and the closing. The shorter version, which was signed and sent to Kirsch, is found in the Kirsch archive. Its second page consists of only two sentences and the closing. That version appears here first.
90 Kirsch's letter of November 1931 is missing.

But in a certain sense, the failure to answer your letter is also right; for your dream about "passive homosexuality" and "mental weakness" says clearly enough that you absolutely have to stand on your own feet, or you'll be blown over by every wind (wind = animus).[91] So your animus-case[92] fits the picture perfectly. Even if I could give you the perfectly right answer in a particular case, a worse case would come by return mail, putting you to the same test again. The error, as you yourself suspect, is due to the fact that you get blown into the anima by every animus, which is only possible if you're too much identified with the anima.[93] This identity, in turn, comes about because you're not connected enough with your own foundation, and as a result there is nothing unshakable in your soul. Naturally you cannot release any woman from the animus, as long as you yourself are falling into the anima. One falls most easily into the anima when one is overrun by one's feelings,[94] because one fails to question them sufficiently. Anima-feelings, however, are symbols, or conditions, created by the anima when it commands psychic contents that it refuses to share with consciousness. In fact these anima-conditions could be taken as starting-points for fantasies, which would then lead you to the essential contents. A woman falls too much into the animus when the analyst is behaving in a too womanly manner towards himself and failing to keep his feelings objectively in hand.

What you write about Frau Sussmann interested me very much.[95] But it would be necessary to know more.

Please give your wife my best greetings. Yours truly, C. G. JUNG

---

91 The Latin word *animus* (spirit, soul) is related to *anima* (wind, air, breath, soul, life). The linguistic connection is even stronger in other ancient languages: in Hebrew (*ruach*) and Greek (*pneuma*), a single word carries both meanings. In Jung's psychology, the terms "animus" and "anima" have an important place, related but not identical to their original Latin definitions.

92 Evidently Kirsch had asked advice about working with a woman patient whose intra-psychic masculine aspect (animus) was dominant.

93 In Jung's psychology, the feminine aspect of a man's psyche.

94 *wenn man seinen Gefühlen verfällt*: In this construction, the verb *verfallen* means "succumb," "become possessed," or "be defeated."

95 Kirsch had evidently received advice about the case from Toni Sussmann. (This sentence concludes the first page of Jung's letter.)

[Page two of the unsigned carbon copy reads as follows:]

Perhaps these comments will be enough to explain to you my attitude toward K.'s book.[96] At present I could add nothing to this preliminary expression of my opinion. To do that, I'd need to know how things continue to unfold.

Now, concerning your friendly invitation to write a short book for your publisher about the rebuilding of the German Spirit,[97] I believe that such an assignment exceeds my ability. Since the Spirit[98] is not made but fulfils its own laws of life as a living entity, superordinate to the human being,[99] so the human being also cannot build it up or point the way for it. To me, the human being seems purely instrumental in this process. He must be in the same boat as Keyserling: grabbed by experience, he becomes the Spirit's obedient means of expression.

Nevertheless, if something appropriate should unexpectedly occur to me, I shall remember your friendly offer.

With greatest respect, Yours truly, [carbon copy unsigned]

---

96 Lacking Kirsch's letter, reference uncertain. "K's book" may be a reference to Keyserling's *Mensch und Erde* (cf. Jung, 12 August 1931, p. 21 and notes). Or "my attitude toward K's book" may refer to the fact that in 1930 Jung wrote an approving introduction to Wolfgang Kranefeldt's book, *Die Psychoanalyse* (cf. Kirsch, 28 July 1931, p. 18 and note). Kranefeldt's effort to find common ground among Freud, Adler and Jung may have provoked Kirsch, whose stark rejection of Freudian theory and practice sometimes led to harsh assessments of fellow Jungians (e.g. Kirsch, 5 August 1949, p. 128; also 18 October 1953, pp. 179f).

97 or "spirit." *Geist* has deep roots in German philosophical, religious, and psychological literature, making it sometimes difficult to capture the word's meaning precisely in English. In this context, it could also be rendered "Mind" (or "mind"). In association with his reference to Keyserling, "Spirit" is arguably Jung's intended meaning.

98 *Geist* (underlined by hand).

99 *Mensch:* the word could also be rendered as "individual," "person," or "man" (collectively).

Dr. C. G. Jung
Küsnacht-Zürich
Seestrasse 228

12 March 1932[100]

Dr. J. Kirsch
Olivaer Platz 3
Berlin W.15

My dear Kirsch,

Best thanks for your detailed letter.[101] The Kollwitz case[102] is really quite remarkable. I suspected as much. I had to wean another patient of Frau S.[103] away from similar magic. These Indian breathing exercises are psychological poison for Europeans.

It interested me to learn that you've spoken at the Social Institute,[104] because I recently received an inquiry from that Institute, whether I would give a lecture in Berlin. Could you please tell me something about this Institute? I have no idea what it is. Since I am turning down practically all lectures this year, with very few exceptions, to make time for my own work, I had to turn down this request, too. I'm experiencing the urgent need to return to my own scientific work and not to exhaust myself in public lecturing.

---

100 Typewritten in German, on letterhead. First paragraph prev. pub. in *PP.*
101 Kirsch's previous letter has not been found.
102 *Der Fall Kollwitz:* In Kirsch's 1972 translation, rendered as "The case of Dr. K...." Kirsch's attached footnote provides sufficient information to identify the patient as Dr. Hans Kollwitz (1892–1971). The elder son of renowned artist Käthe Kollwitz (1867–1945), Hans Kollwitz practiced medicine in Berlin. In 1945, after his mother's death, he retired to devote himself to her artistic legacy. Kirsch's footnote to this passage (originally written in English) reads in full: *"Dr. K. was a thirty-eight-year-old physician who had done Yoga and breathing exercises, and then developed a general septicemia, a condition in which bacteria are carried in the blood, causing infections anywhere in the body. The dreams made it very clear that in doing these breathing exercises, in exerting* tapas, *he had heated up the contents of his unconscious, which to a certain degree were pathological. This was the time before we had sulfonamides or antibiotics. After intensive psychological treatment the patient recovered. He lived to be seventy-eight –* post hoc, ergo propter hoc? *– J. K."* Permission to publish the name of Hans Kollwitz, together with Kirsch's comment on the case, was kindly given by the Kollwitz Estate.
103 Mrs. Toni Sussmann (cf. Jung, 19 August 1929, p. 6 and note).
104 Das Soziale Institut, Charlottenburg, Berlin. According to a typewritten newspaper of the Berlin Social Democratic Party, May 1932, one focus of the Social Institute was the education of family caregivers, school teachers and youth counselors. In this connection, several Jungian analysts from Berlin – Geitel, Kirsch, Kranefeldt, Sussmann, and Weizsäcker – lectured to an audience of Social Democrats at the Social Institute on 7–8 May 1932 (E. M.-R., "Kühne Psychologen!" [Daring Psychologists!], "Die Sozialistische Frau," *Sozialdemokratischer Pressedienst,* Berlin, 9 Mai 1932).

Please give your wife my best greetings and accept cordial greetings yourself from

Yours truly, C. G. JUNG

Dr. C. G. Jung
Küsnacht-Zürich
Seestrasse 228

6 April 1932[105]

Herrn Dr. Kirsch
Olivaer Platz 3
Berlin W.15

My dear Kirsch,

For the time being it's truly impossible for me to come to Berlin.[106] I will make a note of the matter, though. What would attract me most would be the thought of a smaller collegial working group. I expect nothing to come of a big lecture at the Auditorium Maximum.[107] Besides, I would have to spend precious time writing an appropriate general lecture. At present I have neither any ideas nor any desire for that. The other suggestion,[108] however, I will keep in mind. Perhaps I could give a week to it.

With cordial greetings, Yours C. G. JUNG

105 Typewritten in German, on half-sheet letterhead.
106 Kirsch's previous letter is missing. Possibly he had urged Jung to come to Berlin to lecture at the Social Institute, as Kirsch himself planned to do in May (cf. Jung, 12 March 1932, p. 25 and note).
107 Cf. Jung, 6 May 1933, p. 37 and note. According to Kirsch's later recollection, in 1933 Jung lectured to a very large general audience in Berlin, as well as meeting with a smaller group two hours a day for a week (Kirsch, interview with Gene Nameche, Countway Library, Harvard University, 1978, p. 18; hereafter Countway Interview).
108 Lacking Kirsch's previous letter, the other suggestion is unclear.

Dr. C. G. Jung
Küsnacht-Zürich
Seestrasse 228

23 May 1932[109]

Herrn Dr. Kirsch
Olivaer Platz 3
Berlin W.15

My dear Kirsch,

I'm sorry that I'm only now getting around to answering your letter. Up to now I haven't had time even to read all the mail, let alone answer it.

I'm aware from the particulars of your wife's letter[110] that a more than usually detailed certificate will be required. For that, however, I lack essential data. I need to ask you for an exact statement of the time you've spent here,[111] so I can write you the most persuasive possible certificate.

Your dreams are very interesting. Schmid[112] died of a streptococcal infection, which he got from a small cut caused by a car accident. It was the fourth bad accident in half a year. Sadly, he ignored this warning.

Please give my best greetings to your wife, and cordial greetings to yourself from

Yours faithfully, JUNG

---

109 Typewritten in German, on half-sheet letterhead.
110 This letter from Eva Kirsch has not been found.
111 Cf. Kirsch, 28 May 1935, p. 68 and note.
112 Hans Schmid-Guisan (1881–1932): Swiss psychiatrist, based in Basel. Schmid met Jung in 1911 and studied the practice of psychotherapy with him. For 15 years they were colleagues and friends, and their correspondence in 1915–16 laid the groundwork for one of Jung's influential early works, *Psychologische Typen* (Zürich: Rascher, 1921). In English, trans. R. F. C. Hull, *Psychological Types,* CW 6, 1971 (hereafter *Types*). Cf. Hans Konrad Iselin, *Zur Entstehung von C. G. Jungs "Psychologische Typen": Der Briefwechsel zwischen C. G. Jung und Hans Schmid-Guisan im Lichte ihrer Freundschaft* (Verlag Sauerländer, 1982). Jung wrote the foreword to Schmid's book, *Tag und Nacht* (1931), and published a memorial to Schmid in the *Basler Nachrichten,* 23 April 1932. After Schmid's death, his daughter, Marie-Jeanne, became Jung's secretary and continued in that role for 20 years (cf. secretary's letter, apparently by M.-J. Schmid, 21 October 1947, p. 110 and note).

Dr. C. G. Jung
Küsnacht-Zürich
Seestrasse 228

6 June 1932[113]

Certificate

I can confirm that Dr. James Kirsch worked with me for two months in the year 1929. At that time he brought with him a very good psychological training, and he further completed his training as a psychotherapist by attending my English seminars[114] as well as two vacation courses. He is continuously active in this field as a practicing psychotherapist as well as scientifically. I might also mention that, working collaboratively,[115] he has made very useful contributions to the field of psychotherapy and mental health through numerous lectures.

DR. C. G. JUNG

Küsnacht, 25 June 1932[116]

Dr. med. James Kirsch
Olivaer Platz 3
Berlin W.15

Dear Colleague,

Congratulations on your canonization as a specialist. I have registered you for the seminar week, but you should not have exaggerated expectations, because most likely I'll be besieged by all sorts of people. I shall participate in the Hauer

---

113 Typewritten in German, on letterhead.
114 Jung's "English Seminars," offered at the Club, were also available at the time as typewritten, mimeographed transcriptions, based on listeners' handwritten notes, which circulated privately in Zurich. All have since been published by PUP. As of 1932, Kirsch had attended Jung's English seminars of 1929 and 1932: "Dream Analysis, 1928–30" (PUP 1984); and "The Kundalini Yoga, 1932" (PUP 1996). Cf. Kirsch, 28 May 1935, p. 68; cf. also Kirsch, 17 March 1953, p. 161 and note.
115 *in Arbeitsgemeinschaft.* At the time of this certificate, Kirsch belonged to a collegial organization, the AAGP (cf. Jung, 17 March 1930, p. 8 and note). The specific reference is unclear.
116 Typewritten in German, on pre-stamped postcard.

seminar,[117] of course. The Indologist, Prof. Zimmer[118] of Heidelberg, will likewise be there, which promises to be quite interesting.

Best compliments to your wife, and warm regards to you,

Yours ever, C. G. JUNG

Küsnacht, 26 September 1932[119]

Dr. med J. Kirsch
Olivaer Platz 3
Berlin W.15

My dear Kirsch,

On Friday I'll be coming home late myself and won't be able to see you then. But I'll expect you on Saturday afternoon at four.

With best greetings, Faithfully yours, JUNG

---

117 Jakob Wilhelm Hauer (1881–1962): German Indologist, earlier a missionary to India. He had earned his doctorate at Oxford, and since 1927 had been professor of religious studies at Tübingen. In 1932 he published *Yoga als Heilweg, nach den indischen Quellen dargestellt* [Yoga as a Path of Healing, according to Indian sources]. His week-long seminar at the Club in Zurich, 5–8 October. 1932, drew a large audience (cf. *The Psychology of Kundalini Yoga*, Sonu Shamdasani, ed., PUP, 1996). After this, as Hitler's power grew, Hauer shaped his career around Nazi principles. In 1933 he founded the Deutsche Glaubensbewegung [German Faith Movement], a nationalist and racist substitute for Christian practice. Gaining status as an intellectual spokesman for Nazism, he published works such as *Deutsche Gottschau* [German View of God] (1935), *Glaube und Blut* [Belief and Blood] and *Religion und Rasse* [Religion and Race] (1941). When Hauer declared his Nazi affiliation, Jung broke with him, and in 1936 he attacked Hauer's *Deutsche Gottschau* in his essay "Wotan" (cf. CW 10, esp. ¶397f). Interned by the Allies after the war, Hauer was judged to be only a fellow traveler and freed. He died in Tübingen at the age of 80.

118 Heinrich Zimmer, Dr. phil. (1890–1943): German Indologist and historian of South Asian art. Holding a doctorate in Sanskrit from Berlin, he became Professor of Indian Philology at the University of Heidelberg in 1924. After their meeting in 1932, Jung and Zimmer quickly became colleagues and friends. Zimmer gave the opening lecture at Jung's 1933 Berlin Seminar. He attended Eranos meetings and congresses of the IAAGP (Zimmer to Kirsch, 2 April 1935, Kirsch archive). Jung wrote the introduction to Zimmer's *Der Weg zum Selbst* [Path to the Self] (Zurich: Rascher, 1944) (cf. CW 11, ¶950–63). Zimmer, whose wife was Jewish, was dismissed from his university position in 1938. He emigrated to England and taught at Oxford until 1940, when he moved to New York to become Visiting Lecturer in Philsophy at Columbia University. While living in New York, Zimmer lectured often at the New York Analytical Psychology Club (hereafter APC) (Zimmer to Kirsch, November 1940, Kirsch archive). He died of pneumonia in 1943.

119 Typewritten in German, on pre-stamped postcard.

29

Dr. med. James Kirsch
Berlin W.15
Olivaer Pl. 3

28 November 1932[120]

Dear Dr. Jung!

My wife and I would like to congratulate you most sincerely on the great honor bestowed on you with the Literaturpreis der Stadt Zürich.[121] We are particularly pleased that your compatriots have found their way to you and that they recognize something that is easily overlooked, i.e. the creatively evolved form of your work and teaching.[122]

With cordial greetings, Yours, JAMES KIRSCH

---

120 Handwritten in German, on letterhead.
121 Literature Prize of the City of Zurich. Jung commented, in a letter to an American friend: "There are great news happening here. Last week I got the 'Literaturpreis der Stadt Zürich,' which means that I'm no longer a prophet in my own country. A sad end to a hopeful young prophet's career. It is always sad when one loses a perfectly good reason for grumbling" (Jung to Mrs. N., 28 November 1932, *Letters I,* p 109).
122 *die schöpferisch gewachsene Form Ihres Werkes und Wirkens*: Kirsch's diction is at a high stylistic level.

1933–1934

TEL AVIV

Dr. C. G. Jung
Küsnacht-Zürich
Seestrasse 228

20 January 1933[1]

Dr. James Kirsch
Olivaer Platz 3
Berlin W.15

My dear Kirsch,

About Frau Sch.[2] unfortunately I have no information, so in this matter[3] I cannot advise you either for or against.

Concerning Frau S.,[4] however, your dream gives a very good critique. I recognize the individual necessity which leads Frau S. towards Indian practices, and I myself have advised her to do so. In principle of course I'm not at all in favor of imitating Indian methods, and consider it as mistaken as the Europeanization of Eastern civilization. My urging you to attend the seminar has nothing to do with your own psychology, but arose only from my personal wish to have an observer there who could determine objectively what sort of spirit was at work in the thinking there. I wouldn't like to see the subjective conditions of Frau S. outweighing the spirit of analysis and ultimately even falsifying it into a theosophy. For us the Indian way never leads to the unconscious, but rather to an Indian substitute system. To have this, we don't need to go to India; it would be much simpler to become Catholic.

If I should get to Berlin this summer, I certainly will not fail to spend an evening with you.

With best greetings and compliments also to your wife,

Ever faithfully yours, C. G. JUNG

1   Typewritten in German, on letterhead. Part of letter prev. pub. in *PP*.
2   Name abbreviated in original text. Reference unclear.
3   Kirsch's previous letter is missing.
4   From context, "Frau S." is Toni Sussmann (cf. Jung, 19 August 1929, p. 6 and note).

Dr. C. G. Jung
Küsnacht-Zürich
Seestrasse 228

28 January 1933[5]

Dr. James Kirsch
Olivaer Platz 3
Berlin W.15

My dear Kirsch,

Best thanks for your news. I feel that someone in your circle should enlighten Frau Sussmann somewhat about the currents that exist against her. In doing this, one would have to rely exclusively on facts, not on interpretations or opinions. I have the impression that Frau S. really doesn't know why others keep their distance from her endeavors.

I'm afraid I cannot lend you my picture material, since I'll be using it myself in the near future. Maybe you could use what's in the German seminar report.[6] When I'm in Berlin, perhaps I myself could speak about the Collective Unconscious, though I don't want to upstage you in doing that. I feel it's entirely right for you yourself to lecture about it.

With best greetings, Ever faithfully yours, C. G. JUNG

Dr. C. G. Jung
Küsnacht-Zürich
Seestrasse 228

3 February 1933[7]

Dr. James Kirsch
Olivaer Platz 3
Berlin W.15

My dear Kirsch,

Of course I wouldn't expect you personally to assume the role of the submarine that tries to torpedo Frau S. because, as you may correctly suspect, such a shot

5 Typewritten in German, on letterhead.
6 The "German Seminars," held in Küsnacht, 1930–31, were so called because, whereas seminars at the Club were usually in English, these were conducted in German. The contemporaneous report, which has not been published, contains images from the dreams and active imaginations of Jung's analysands. Ulrich Hoerni kindly provided the titles of the seminar typescripts, as collected by Olga von Koenig-Fachsenfeld: "Bericht über das deutsche Seminar von Dr. C. G. Jung, 6.–11. Oktober 1930 in Küsnacht-Zürich" and "Bericht über das deutsche Seminar von Dr. C. G. Jung, 5.–10. Oktober 1931 in Küsnacht-Zürich."
7 Typewritten in German, on letterhead.

could easily backfire. Your assessment of Frau S.[8] is undoubtedly accurate in every respect; but this complicates the situation considerably, because in the end the issue isn't only a purely personal working through,[9] but the larger question of her relationship to the unconscious. Of course, this affects her profession as much as her animus and could easily give rise to a ruinous mix-up of objective and personal goals[10] during the discussion. It would certainly be important to proceed in this matter with great tact. In reality, a good deal of analysis would be involved here, which I'd presumably have to take on. But I'm at a great disadvantage, lacking all the personal material on the basis of which her personal attitude could be criticized. On the other hand, the people in Berlin have these materials, so it would need to be someone in Berlin who would shoulder the responsibility of openly discussing these particular points with Frau S., and running the risk of being completely misunderstood. I am pretty certain that the personal issues are intimately intertwined with the Indian substitute system. However, I cannot tackle the Indian question unless Frau S. has first dealt with the necessary reactions on a personal level. But I could certainly clarify the subsequent confusion with her. I have always thought that this Indian interest absolutely cannot be challenged, as far as I am concerned, unless something happens in Frau S's environment which would become an insurmountable obstacle for her. Only in the face of such an obstacle can she realize that something is also not right with the Indian business.

I would be prepared to give Frau S. a first signal, if someone on your side will promise to stand ready with the necessary personal information. But if no one is willing to do that, it makes no sense for me to alarm Frau S. Therefore I would like to ask you to discuss the matter with the others and relate to them my assessment of the situation. Frankly speaking, I would not consider it fair to criticize her personally unless someone has the courage to talk to her openly about it. And I'm absolutely unwilling to take on something for which I completely lack the relevant details.

With best greetings, also to your wife, Ever faithfully yours, C. G. JUNG

---

8 Kirsch's previous letter is missing. From context, he has appealed to Jung, who is planning a trip to Berlin (cf. Jung, 6 May 1933, p. 37), to intervene personally with Toni Sussmann while he is there.

9 *Auseinandersetzung:* working through, confrontation, sorting out. The connotation is of struggling, successfully, to master a challenge.

10 *Momente* (plural of *Moment*, lit. "moment"): viewpoints, intentions, motivations.

Küsnacht, 17 February 1933[11]

Dr. J. Kirsch
Olivaer Platz 3
Berlin W.15

My dear Kirsch,

The case you report to me is certainly serious and may qualify as more or less conclusive evidence.[12] I shall certainly be hearing about further developments.

I am, it seems, on the way to recovery.[13]

With best greetings, Ever faithfully yours, C. G. JUNG

Dr. C. G. Jung
Küsnacht-Zürich
Seestrasse 228

28 February 1933[14]

Dr. James Kirsch
Olivaer Platz 3
Berlin W.15

My dear Kirsch,

Many thanks for your note regarding the battle of Jacob with the angel.[15] To be sure, I was of the opinion that this interpretation was somewhat far-fetched. So much the better if it's not; then it fits much better mythologically.

What disturbs you most in your dream, the sinking of the anima, corresponds to Faust's words, "Go down then, I could also say, rise up!" It's simply an enantiodromia, which is necessary because height consists of pure beauty, dead minerals, and coldness. Correspondingly, fire rises from the ground.

Tobacco in any form means a material for making fantasies (= clouds of smoke). The southern Slavs are part of a warmer, southern zone = realm of sensation.

With best greetings, Ever faithfully yours, C. G. JUNG

---

11 Typewritten in German, on pre-stamped postcard.
12 Lacking Kirsch's previous letter, the reference is unclear.
13 Obscure reference to Jung's state of health.
14 Typewritten in German, on letterhead.
15 Kirsch's previous letter is missing. Biblical reference: Gen. 32:22–30.

Dr. C. G. Jung
Küsnacht-Zürich
Seestrasse 228

6 May 1933[16]

Dr. James Kirsch
Olivaer Platz 3
Berlin W.15

My dear Kirsch,

Please accept my best wishes on the happy arrival of your offspring.[17] I had no idea that this joyous event was on the way.

Despite everything, it seems as though the Berlin seminar will take place.[18] But I'll still be happy to welcome you here before your departure, of which I've already heard.

With best greetings and wishes, Faithfully yours, JUNG

Küsnacht-Zürich, 31 August 1933[19]

Dr. James Kirsch
Casa Abondio
ASCONA[20]
Tessin

Dear Colleague,

Accept my best thanks for your kind gift of the small photo.[21] I also believe it's right to act according to the maxim: "What you will do, do soon."

16 Typewritten in German, on letterhead.
17 Birth announcement missing. The son of James and Eva Kirsch, Michael Bernhardt Kirsch, was born on 3 May 1933. Their daughter, Ruth Gabriele Kirsch, was born on 16 September 1928.
18 The following month Jung did go to Berlin, where he gave a radio interview, followed by a seminar on dream analysis. A contemporaneous typescript of these events, titled "Berliner Seminar," includes Heinrich Zimmer's lecture, "Zur Psychologie des Yoga" (25 June); Jung's interview on Radio Berlin with Adolf von Weizsäcker (26 June) (cf. Kirsch, 7 May 1934, p. 41 and note); and his six-day seminar on dream analysis (26 June–1 July). The seminar, covering roughly the first half of Jung's 1928–30 dream seminar (C. G. Jung, *Dream Analysis: Notes of the Seminar Given in 1928–1930*, William McGuire, ed., PUP, 1984), is now in process toward publication (Giovanni Sorge, ed., Philemon Series).
19 Typewritten in German, on pre-stamped postcard.
20 For two months in the late summer of 1933, Kirsch and his family lived in Ascona. He attended the Eranos *Tagung* of 1933, as did his wife, Eva. Also present was his patient Hildegard Silber (later Hilde Kirsch, cf. Jung, 11 June 1934, p. 57 and note; also Appendix B, p. 278). Hildegard Silber, who had been widowed in June 1933, fled Berlin soon after with her two sons, aged nine and six. The two families took flats in the same apartment building in Ascona and prepared to move on to Palestine (cf. Introduction, p. xxx).
21 Possibly a photo of Jung at Eranos. No enclosure found.

My best wishes will accompany you and your wife over the sea.[22]

With warm regards, Ever yours truly, C. G. JUNG

Figure 2.1 **Rudi and Gerhardt Silber, Ascona, mid August 1933.** Sons of Hildegard
Silber, on their way to Palestine. After moving to London in 1935, Rudi
Silber was known as Jim and Gerhardt as Jerry. *Photographer unknown.
Courtesy Jim Silber.*

22 Certificates in the Kirsch archive show that the Kirsch children, five years old and four-and-a-half
months old, were vaccinated against smallpox in Ascona on or before 21 September 1933. In early
October both families – Kirsches and Silbers – moved to Portofino, Italy, and in November took
ship to Haifa, settling in Tel Aviv. Details of their 1933 itinerary were provided by Jim Silber. (Cf.
also Jung, 11 June 1934, p. 57.)

Dr. C. G. Jung
Küsnacht-Zürich
Seestrasse 228

20 February 1934[23]

Dr. James Kirsch
Pension Aszodi
Abbessynianstreet[24]
Jerusalem

Dear Colleague,

Your first dream about Kranefeldt[25] gives extensive and accurate information regarding the situation. There's nothing to be concerned about on my side. In Ascona[26] I just felt very clearly that it was necessary for you to stand on your own, and that it would be wrong to encourage you in any way to depend on my support. All your libido was required to realize the change, undoubtedly enormous, which Palestine represents for you. I sensed in you, as well as in your wife, the weight of a significant destiny. It moved me to show the utmost restraint. Nothing has changed in our deeper relationship, but in the upper layers you must find your way to yourself as much as possible. Your dreams are pointing in this direction. The anima always takes possession of the ground one lives on. Therefore you are confronted with special tasks. Too much Europe isn't good for you right now. Later, when you are more deeply rooted not only in Palestine but also in your inner life, everything you need will fall into place of its own accord.

Indeed, Frau Sussmann was in a serious car accident: bad breaks to the collarbone and four ribs, as well as a large scalp wound to the forehead close to the hair line. She has now returned to Berlin. She was not run over in this case, but her chauffeur skidded into another automobile (a Zurich car!). India cannot have been completely without a role in this incident, and I have also communicated this to Frau Sussmann. But much is still dark to me there.

Otherwise there is little to report, except the fact that a new collection of my lectures and essays will be published soon, under the title "Wirklichkeit der Seele."[27]

With best wishes, Ever faithfully yours, C. G. JUNG

23 Typewritten in German, on letterhead. Part of first paragraph prev. pub. in *PP*.
24 Address is typed thus by Jung's secretary, confusing English and German usage.
25 Wolfgang Kranefeldt, MD (cf. Kirsch, 28 July 1931, p. 18 and note). Lacking Kirsch's previous letter, the dream reference is unclear.
26 Cf. Jung, 31 August 1933, p. 37 and note.
27 C. G. Jung, *Wirklichkeit der Seele: Anwendungen und Fortschritte der neueren Psychologie, mit Beiträgen von Hugo Rosenthal, Emma Jung, W. M. Kranefeldt* [Reality of the Soul: Applications and advances in the latest psychology, with contributions by...], Zürich: Rascher, 1934 (hereafter *Wirklichkeit*). The book comprises nine of Jung's lectures and essays, originating between 1929 and 1934; also two essays by Kranefeldt, one by Emma Jung, and one by Hugo Rosenthal. The

Dr. med. James Kirsch
Hayarkon str. 101[28]
Tel-Aviv

7 May 1934[29]

Dear Dr. Jung!

For many months I've avoided writing to you in detail. As much as I enjoyed your letter, and as much as I know that on deeper levels there is no misunderstanding of any sort between us, I also know that on a superficial level I have to be completely detached from you. All this makes your attitude toward me – especially as I experienced you in Ascona – incomprehensible. It would have been very good if we'd had a discussion at that time. But perhaps it's even better that we can have it now, after I've had a chance to read several of your publications.

First of all, I have to tell you that in Ascona, as well as here in Palestine, I've heard reports about some of your remarks which did not present you as a friend of the Jews. At this distance, of course, I was unable to verify what you actually said. For instance, it appears that you said Jews are not honest in analysis. Then Mr. Bally[30] appeared in this country, visited with all our colleagues, and stated publicly that you had openly crossed over to Hitler, that you had been received by him, and thus that you are an anti-Semite. His essay in the *Zürcher Zeitung* titled "Deutschstämmige Psychotherapie"[31] was read by a great many people. The result

volume as a whole was not translated into English, but Jung's essays appear in various volumes of the CW: CW 8, parts 13, 17; CW 10, part 7; CW 15, parts 1, 3, 8, 9; CW 16, part 12; CW 17, part 7; CW 18, part 113. Cf. Jung, 26 May 1934, p. 47, note 64.

28 Kirsch's letterhead, hand-stamped in the upper left corner of the page, gives the sender's name, professional title, and street address in Hebrew first, then in German. A minor German spelling error may have been made in manufacturing the stamp. The German abbreviation *str.* (for *Strasse*, street) should either follow the street name without a break (*Hayarkonstr.*) or else be capitalized (*Hayarkon Str.*). In Jung's letters to Kirsch in Tel Aviv, this incorrect spelling (*Hayarkon str.*) is often adopted unchanged.

29 Handwritten in German, on plain paper, with return address stamped.

30 Gustav Bally (b. 1893): Swiss psychiatrist and Freudian psychoanalyst, who had been forced to leave Germany "because of 'anti-state activities'" (Geoffrey Cocks, *Psychotherapy in the Third Reich, The Göring Institute*, 2nd ed., New Brunswick and London: Transaction Publishers, 1997, p. 140). Despite his initial suspicion of Jung, Bally later came to respect and admire him. Surviving correspondence between Jung and Bally reflects their increasing collegiality (Jung–Bally corresp. 1939–1951, ETH Library archive).

31 Bally's outraged letter to the editor, titled *"'Deutschstämmige' Psychotherapie?"* ("'German-born' Psychotherapy?") (*Neue Zürcher Zeitung*, 27 February 1934), was prompted by Jung's "Geleitwort des Herausgebers" [Editor's Comment] in the December 1933 *Zentralblatt* (Band VI.3, pp. 139f), in which he contrasted "Germanic" with "Jewish" psychology (cf. CW 10, ¶1014ff). Jung's position at this time came under suspicion even more because, contrary to the principle of neutrality governing the newly organized IAAGP and its journal, the same issue of the *Zentralblatt* featured a manifesto of Nazi principles by the president of the German section, M. H. Göring (cf. Jung, 17 February 1935, p. 67 and note; cf. also Appendix D, p. 307).

was that your books, which had been displayed in many bookstores, disappeared from the shop windows, and your name was placed on the boycott list. Your detailed reply[32] was not read. This general feeling against you was, of course, fabulously exploited by the Freudians in an effort to silence you totally, at least here.

Because of these events the entire field of psychotherapy is now in a difficult situation here. It is a fact that Freud[33] is also being rejected here. Adler's[34] students have generally not made any headway because of their shallowness. If you are also silenced, what then? For instance, Freud had personally proposed a student for the position of lecturer at the Hebrew University in Jerusalem. During the meeting to discuss the appointment, an essay by the Freudian in question was read, wherein the Sabbath was traced back to sexuality in an obscene way – and the lectureship was history. One of these days a situation may very well arise when we Jews will have to ask for your help for the sake of our soul!

Well, dear Doctor, the rumors about your being anti-Semitic do not appear to be dying down. In a letter I received from Germany last week someone wrote me that you had expressed on the radio,[35] via German broadcasting stations, your gratitude for and recognition of Hitler's reforms at the German universities. If that is a fact, I do not understand you as a Swiss. Please don't interpret my letter as being aggressive; I am merely attempting to understand you in this respect and hope that you will grant me the privilege of reaching such an understanding. On the other hand, I don't feel understood by you in this matter.

---

32 "Zeitgenössisches," *Neue Zürcher Zeitung* CLV: 437.1, 433.1, 457, March 1934. Cf. CW 10, ¶1016ff.

33 Sigmund Freud (1856–1939): Austrian-Jewish physician and psychologist, founder of the twenti-eth-century psychoanalytic movement. In 1906 Jung became Freud's disciple and was soon hailed by Freud as the next leader ("son and heir") of the movement. They parted ways bitterly in 1913, after Jung's *Wandlungen* (cf. Jung, 12 August 1931, p. 21 and note) challenged Freud's theory of sexuality. Freud felt personally betrayed, and some of his followers asserted that Jung's defection was a sign of anti-Semitism. When Jung was later troubled by repeated accusations of Nazi sympathies, he accused Freud's followers of stirring up the old rumor against him. (Cf. Ernest Jones, *The Life and Work of Sigmund Freud*, esp. *Vol. II: 1901–1919: Years of Maturity,* New York: Basic Books, 1955. Cf. also *The Freud–Jung Letters*, ed. William McGuire, trans. Ralph Manheim and R. F. C. Hull, PUP, 1974.)

34 Alfred Adler (1870–1937): Austrian-Jewish physician and psychologist, an early collaborator with Freud and core member of the Vienna Psychoanalytic Society. Adler separated from Freud in 1911 on account of their theoretical differences and founded his School of Individual Psychology. His theory of personality differs from Freud's in its emphasis on the social aspects of development (power-relationships, birth-order), in addition to intrapsychic factors.

35 On 26 June 1933 Jung was interviewed on Radio Berlin by Adolf Weizsäcker, a psychiatrist from Heidelberg who had analyzed with Jung and now served on the board of the Berlin Jung Society. The text of the interview is published: cf. William McGuire and R. F. C. Hull, eds, *C. G. Jung Speaking: Interviews and Encounters*, Princeton University Press, 1977 (hereafter *C. G. Jung Speaking*), pp. 59–66.

You know that I know and love German youth and can only subscribe, on the basis of profound experience, to what you are saying about the German people and also about the youthful Germanic spirit.[36] But, on the basis of many experiences, I know that the current leaders are abusing the young and misrepresenting their goals. You would be correct in stating that I am biased,[37] since I belonged to the defeated party. I don't know if that is an objection. Sometimes one sees more clearly from the outside. What is unbearable and incomprehensible to me is why you should be taking sides in this matter. And for an important reason: You've always rejected the "making" of things and "organizing." Why should you say "yes" to this? In China, an emperor is respected as a good leader when his rule goes unnoticed. In Germany's Third Reich one senses the "totality" of the state everywhere.

About the Jews you write: "The Jew ..., as far as one can see, will never create his own form of culture, because all his instincts and talents presuppose a more or less civilized host-people for their development."[38] I am dumbfounded to hear an anticipation from you. But even the premises to this prejudice seem incorrect to me. What you are writing certainly is true for the Galut[39] Jew. It seems to me that you received your image of the Jew essentially from Freud, who of course is an excellent example of this Galut psychology.[40] This Galut psychology was rejected by a few Jews at first, by many today, and in a not too distant future perhaps it will be rejected by all.

36 In the radio interview Jung spoke of the "youthfulness of the German nation" as the chief way Germany was to be distinguished from other European nations (*C. G. Jung Speaking*, p. 61). He described recent changes in Germany as "the assurance of German youth in pursuit of their goal" and referred to their natural "daring and drive and sense of adventure" (ibid., p. 62). Cf. Jung, 6 May 1933, p. 37 and note. In his 1936 essay "Wotan" (cf. Kirsch, 4 August 1936, p. 90 and note), Jung describes the German youth movement in darker terms (CW 10, ¶373–75).

37 *Sie können mit Recht sagen, ich sei darin Partei, gehörte zur Partei der Unterlegenen.* The reference may be to a private exchange Kirsch had with Jung in June 1933. Many years later he wrote to a colleague, "As you know, I tried to talk to Jung in 1933. I took him to the railway station, after he had given the seminar in Berlin, to tell him something about the Nazis. But he rejected it because he thought I was not impartial" (Kirsch to Jess Groesbeck, 28 December 1982, Kirsch archive).

38 Quoting from a passage in Jung's recent *Zentralblatt* essay, "Zur gegenwärtigen Lage der Psychotherapie" (*Zentralblatt* VII.1, 1934, pp. 1–16. Cf. "The State of Psychotherapy Today," CW 10, ¶333–70): *"Der Jude als relativer Nomade hat nie und wird voraussichtlich auch nie eine eigene Kulturform schaffen, da alle seine Instinkte und Begabungen ein mehr oder weniger zivilisiertes Wirtsvolk zu ihrer Entfaltung voraussetzen."* ["The Jew as a relative nomad has never and, as far as one can see, will never create his own form of culture ..."] (*Zentralblatt* VII.1, p. 9; trans. ACL). A single passage within the essay prompts several of Kirsch's statements in this letter. Cf. Jung, 26 May 1934, p. 45.

39 *Galut* (Hebrew): exile, exilic; implying banishment, as distinct from voluntary emigration. In this letter and in the essay by Kirsch that follows ("Conclusion," pp. 55ff), as well as in his longer paper of spring 1934 (cf. Appendix A, pp. 267ff), his use of *Galut* has both historical and psychological connotations.

40 Cf. Appendix A, "Then he will open the ears of men," p. 270 and note. Kirsch had recently sent Jung this paper on the shortcomings of Freud's psychology and the benefits of Jungian dream interpretation.

Here in Palestine (and Palestine is already the intellectual center) the Jews are living as a people, resident, earth-bound,[41] and self-reliant, not in the middle of another culture. I wish you could see some of these new types of Jews.

However, all of this (return to the soil, to the homeland) is only the presupposition for something much more important. Surely we are an ancient culture. Certainly, we cannot create entirely new cultural values like the Teutonic people. Our tensions are differently determined – and comprise equally rich creative possibilities. In Faulhaber's[42] words, since Christ, the Jews have been excluded from the revelation. We made a vital mistake by rejecting Christ. Christ is *the* repressed complex of the Jew. However, just as everything changes in the individual life of a person as soon as a repressed complex enters into consciousness and comes alive, in the same way things can change collectively – and also creatively – with our repressed Christ-complex. I have a great number of proofs (dreams and images) to support my view that this Christ-complex is central in the Jew. On this basis one must understand the peculiar psychology and the peculiar fate of the Jew – and also anti-Semitism.

I believe you'll be able to confirm my interpretation. We are dealing with a collective standstill, a repression with all its consequences. Also we are not nomads, but rather a restless people that has lost its living God, despite all the warnings of the prophets. We even pronounced the dreadful word about Christ: His blood be on our head and that of our children.[43]

You are not the first, and will not be the last, whose warnings we cast aside. But I believe that – especially at this moment – your way will lead us back to the Living One and may be of enormous significance for the rebirth of the Jews. For this reason, it appears to me an irreparable harm if your voice should be silenced here.

I cannot imagine that what you write in your essay "Zur gegenwärtigen Lage der Psychotherapie"[44] is everything you have to say about the Jews. Would it not be useful if you published a detailed essay about the Jews here, too? I could arrange for a good Hebrew translation to appear in an excellent publication.

Please excuse this somewhat confused letter, but it was written from my heart. Could you answer me in detail?

With most cordial greetings, Ever faithfully yours, JAMES KIRSCH

---

41 In Jung's 1918 essay, "Über das Unbewusste" [On the unconscious], he had written that Jews lack the "chthonic quality" of the psyche (cf. "The Role of the Unconscious," CW 10, ¶18). He also proposed that *Erdgebundenheit* [earth-boundness] is essential to the psyche in his contribution to *Mensch und Erde* (cf. Jung, 12 August 1931, p. 21 and note). Cf. also Kirsch, "The Jewish Image of the World," summer 1931, p. 16 and note.

42 Michael von Faulhaber (1869–1952): Cardinal and Archbishop of Munich.

43 Direct quotation from the New Testament, Matt. 27: 25.

44 Cf. note 38 above.

Dr. C. G. Jung
Küsnacht-Zürich
Seestrasse 228

26 May 1934[45]

Dr. James Kirsch
Hayarkon str. 101
Tel-Aviv
Palestine

My dear Kirsch,

It gives me great pleasure that you've written to me again. It appears that amusing rumors are being spread about me. The only unquestionable fact which lies behind all this stupid gossip is that as the honorary chairman[46] of the International Society for Psychotherapy,[47] I could not desert the society at the moment when Kretschmer resigned.[48] I was urgently requested by the German physicians to retain this position[49] and have consequently done what anyone else would have done in my situation, namely, my duty toward the International Society. Essentially this consisted in preserving the umbrella organization and incorporating the German Society into it. This plan succeeded at the last Nauheim Congress,[50] and we can also register the gratifying fact that, at my suggestion,

---

45 Typewritten in German, on letterhead. Letter prev. pub. in *PP*, trans. by Ernest Harms ("Letters to a Friend, Part I," pp. 12ff). Letter also prev. pub. in *Letters I*. Harms's translation orig. pub. in his article, "Carl Gustav Jung – Defender of Freud and the Jews," *Psychiatric Quarterly,* April 1946 (cf. Kirsch, 22 December 1946, pp. 108f and notes).

46 *Ehrenvorsitzender*. In fact, Jung held this title only at the 1928 Congress, when he presided over the opening session. From 1930 to 1933 his title in the organization was *2. Vorsitzender* (Vice-president).

47 *der Internationalen Gesellschaft für Psychotherapie*: i.e. the IAAGP. In 1933, at Jung's insistence, the name and structure of the AAGP underwent an important change. (Cf. Appendix D, pp. 306f).

48 Ernst Kretschmer, Dr. med. (1888–1964): German psychiatrist and neurologist, professor at Tübingen and later at Marburg. One of the founders of the AAGP, of which he was president beginning in 1930, Kretschmer resigned his post on 6 April 1933, after cancelling the Congress which had been planned for later that month in Vienna (cf. Appendix D, p. 306 and note). Kretschmer continued to work in Germany during the war and at its end returned to Tübingen, where he directed a neurological clinic until 1959.

49 As general secretary of the AAGP, Walter Cimbal had written at length to Jung, begging him to take over the presidency: *"Durch die Amtsniederlegung von Herrn Prof. Kretschmer sind Sie zum geistigen Führer der Gesellschaft geworden, und ich bitte Sie persönlich und im Interessse der wissenschaftlichen Bewegung von ganzem Herzen, dieses Amt anzunehmen."* ["Due to the resignation of Prof. Kretschmer you have become the spiritual leader of the Society, and I ask you with all my heart, personally and in the interest of the scientific movement, to accept this position."] (Cimbal to Jung, 21 April 1933, ETH Library archive).

50 In May 1934 the "Seventh Congress for Psychotherapy" convened under Jung's leadership at Bad Nauheim, Germany. At this congress the new statutes of the IAAGP were adopted. A printed

a special paragraph was adopted which makes it possible for German Jewish physicians to join the international organization as individual members.[51] Thus they have become full members with equal rights.

I need hardly mention the other rumors. It is a downright lie to maintain that I said Jews are dishonest in analysis. People must think me extraordinarily stupid if they think I could hold such an idiotic opinion. Neither have I addressed Hitler over the radio or in any other manner, nor have I expressed anything concerning politics.

With regard to my view that, as far as one can see, the Jews will not create their own form of culture, this view is based on (1) historical facts, and (2) the additional fact that the specific cultural contribution[52] of the Jew evolves most clearly within a host-culture, where the Jew frequently becomes the very carrier of this culture, or its promoter. This task is so unique[53] and demanding that it is hardly to be conceived how, in addition, any individual Jewish culture could arise alongside it. Now, since Palestine presents very unique conditions, I have cautiously inserted "voraussichtlich"[54] in my sentence. I would in no way deny the possibility that something unique is being created there, but I don't know that as yet. I positively cannot discover anything anti-Semitic in this opinion.

Regarding your suggestion that I write a special piece about this question, this too has already been anticipated, in that I suggested an exchange of letters with

circular, dated 1 December 1934 and signed by Jung, announced the change: *"Auf dem letztjäh-rigen Kongress der 'Überstaatlichen allgemeinen ärztlichen Gesellschaft für Psychotherapie' ist beschlossen worden, den Verein in Form von Landesgruppen zu konstituieren..."* ["At the past year's congress of the 'International General Medical Society for Psychotherapy' it was decided to constitute the association in the form of national sections..."] (documents of C. A. Meier, ETH Library archive). (Cf. CW 10, ¶1035–38.)

51   Under IAAGP statutes, membership could be applied for either through one's national section or directly through the international society. The result (intended by Jung) was that Jewish doctors, no longer legally permitted to belong to professional organizations in Germany, could still be full members in the IAAGP. Cf. Appendix D, pp. 308f.

52   *die eigentliche kulturelle Leistung:* alternatively, "special cultural achievement."

53   *eigenartig:* lit. "of its own kind." This word, which occurs three times in Jung's paragraph (translated here as "unique"), was in general use at this time. In Nazi writings its connotations are most often discriminatory. Kirsch uses it positively, however, in his article, "Die Judenfrage in der Psychotherapie: Einige Bemerkungen zu einem Aufsatz von C. G. Jung" (*Jüdische Rundschau*, 29 May 1934; cf. Jung, 11 June 1934, p. 57 and note).

54   lit. "as far as one can see." Cf. Kirsch, 7 May 1934, p. 42 and note.

Dr. Neumann,[55] who has worked with me and now also lives in Palestine, which would deal with all the contentious questions.[56] Up to now, though, I've heard nothing from him.

The Jewish Christ-complex is a very remarkable business. As you know, I completely agree with you in this respect. The existence of this complex predisposes to[57] a somewhat hystericized general mental attitude, which has become especially clear to me in the course of the present anti-Christian agitation against me. The mere fact that I speak of a difference between Jewish and Christian psychology suffices for anyone to voice the prejudice that I'm an anti-Semite. Or, in the opinion of the Schweiz Israelitische Wochenblatt,[58] for instance, my assertion that I'm just as little an anti-Semite as an anti-Chinese proves my intention to compare the Jews with a Mongolian horde. This sensitivity is simply pathological and makes every discussion almost impossible. As you know, Freud previously accused me of anti-Semitism because I could not tolerate his soulless materialism. With this readiness to sniff out anti-Semitism everywhere, the Jew directly evokes anti-Semitism. I cannot see why the Jew, like any so-called Christian, is incapable of accepting that he is being personally criticized when one has an opinion about him. Why must it always be assumed that one wants to condemn the Jewish people? Surely the individual is not the people? I regard this as an inadmissible means of silencing one's adversary. In the great majority of cases, I've been getting along very well with my Jewish patients and colleagues. It happens in the cases of other people, too, that I have to criticize the individual; but they don't ascribe it to the fact that they are English, American or French. However, there is one exception I'd like to mention here, and that is the Germans. It has happened to me more than once that when I criticized an individual German, he immediately concluded that I am a hater of Germans. It is really too cheap to try to hide one's own inferiority behind a politicial prejudice. So, if you perceived my reserved attitude in Ascona

---

55 Erich Neumann (1905–1960): German-Jewish psychologist, Jungian analyst and writer. One of Jung's most gifted students, Neumann earned his Dr. phil. in 1927 in Erlangen and then studied medicine in Berlin. He and his wife, Julie, active Zionists, emigrated in 1933 to Zurich and from there to Tel Aviv, where they settled (cf. Kirsch, 8 June 1934, p. 53 and note). Neumann lived and worked in Tel Aviv until his death at the age of 55. Although he was disappointed by Jung's relative lack of interest in the plight of the Jews in Eastern Europe, he defended him in print against allegations of anti-Semitism (cf. Jung, 11 June 1934, p. 57 and note). Starting in 1947 Neumann lectured yearly at Eranos. He wrote classics of Jungian scholarship, including *Ursprungsgeschichte des Bewusstseins* (Rascher, 1949) [*The Origins and History of Consciousness*, Foreword by Jung, trans. R. F. C. Hull, Routledge, 1954]; *Tiefenpsychologie und neue Ethik* (Rascher, 1949) [*Depth Psychology and a New Ethic*, trans. Eugene Rolfe, Putnam, 1969]; *Die grosse Mutter: Die weiblichen Gestaltungen des Unterbewussten* (Rhein, 1956) [*The Great Mother: An Analysis of the Archetype*, trans. Ralph Manheim, Routledge, 1955]. Cf. also Jaffé, 3 March 1961, p. 265, note 81.
56 Jung also sought Kirsch's help to involve Neumann in this exchange (cf. p. 47 below).
57 *bedingt*: "requires," "necessitates." For Jung, the complex pre-exists the mental attitude, for which it sets the conditions.
58 Swiss Israelite Weekly.

as anti-Semitism, you missed the mark completely. I've already told you what gave rise to my attitude then.

In your place, I'd advise you to work toward advancing clarity in this respect. You can refer to the objective results of the Nauheim congress, which make it clear beyond all doubt that I can't be an anti-Semite.[59] In general, you really ought to know me well enough not to attribute to me uncritically a non-individual stupidity like anti-Semitism. You know well enough to what extent I approach each person as a personality, whom I endeavor to lift out of the collective conditioning and make into an individual. This, as you also know, is only possible if one acknowledges one's particularity, with which one is endowed by fate. No one who is a Jew can become a human being without knowing he is a Jew, since this is the basis from which he must reach out toward a higher humanity. This holds true for all nations and races. Nationalism is therefore a conditio sine qua non[60] – no matter how objectionable it is – but the individual must not remain stuck in it. On the other hand, insofar as he is a particle of the mass of the people, he must not elevate himself above it either. As a human being I am a European, as an atom of the masses I am a Swiss bourgeois, domiciled at 228 Seestrasse, Küsnacht near Zürich.

I hope these explanations are sufficient for you, otherwise I'll have to offer you witnesses and references, who would testify under oath to the truth of my statement. In judicial language this is called "probative tenders."[61]

When you see Dr. Neumann, please greet him from me and remind him that I am waiting to hear from him.[62]

Finally I want to inform you that my new book, "Wirklichkeit der Seele,"[63] has appeared. I've included in it a Jewish author on Old Testament psychology[64] in order to annoy the National Socialists and all those Jews who have decried me as an anti-Semite. The next thing that will be invented now is that I suffer from a complete absence of convictions and am neither an anti-Semite nor a Nazi. We happen to live in a period which overflows with lunacy. "Quem Deus vult perdere prius dementat."[65]

With best greetings, Yours C. G. JUNG et semper idem.[66]

---

59 Cf. pp. 44f, note 50.

60 indispensible condition.

61 *"Beweisofferte"*: evidence offered for purposes of proof. I.e. if Kirsch still doubts Jung's explanation, Jung will present proof in the form of sworn witnesses.

62 Cf. note 56 above.

63 Cf. Jung, 20 February 1934, p. 39 and note.

64 Hugo Rosenthal, "Der Typengegensatz in der jüdischen Religionsgeschichte" ["Opposite types in Jewish religious history"], in *Wirklichkeit*, pp. 355–409.

65 "Whom God wishes to destroy, he first drives mad." In his quotation of this proverb, Jung capitalizes "Deus" ("God"). In Ernest Harms's trans., the word becomes "deus" ("the god").

66 and ever the same.

Dr. med. James Kirsch
Hayarkon str. 101
Tel-Aviv

8 June 1934[67]

Honored, dear Dr. Jung!

Please accept my most sincere thanks for your detailed letter and your kind willingness to discuss the Jewish problem. Particularly I would like to thank you for accepting my writing with such gracious understanding. I have to admit that, without believing some of the specific accusations, my image of you was somewhat darkened, especially after Fräulein Wolff[68] told me that, if you had been a German, you would have voted for the Nazis.[69] I realize now that I was mistaken in this respect, or rather that I misunderstood you. I fell into the trap of accepting a collective prejudice, where you were intending to give me a personal criticism.

I did not go so far as believing you capable of a non-individual stupidity like anti-Semitism, but thought it necessary to inform you of these rumors, and since they've produced such a reaction from you, in the form of your clear and unequivocal letter, a great burden has been lifted from my heart. I need not reassure you that no further proofs are necessary. With great joy I welcome your successful achievement at the Nauheim Congress in today's Germany.[70]

---

67 Typewritten (pp. 1–5), with final page handwritten (p. 6), in German, on plain paper with return address stamped.

68 Antonia (Toni) Wolff (1888–1953): Zurich-born analytical psychologist, teacher, and a member of Jung's closest circle for over four decades. Born to a distinguished Zurich family, the young Antonia sought treatment with Jung in 1910 after her father's death. By the time of Jung's break with Freud in 1913, she was already his trusted co-worker and confidante. Working in coordination with Jung, Wolff became Kirsch's analyst and clinical consultant in 1929 (cf. Jung, 16 November 1928, p. 3 and note; cf. also Jung, 15 August 1930, pp. 9f, note 28). She was president of the Club for a time after its founding in 1916, and again with short breaks from 1926 to 1952. She taught at the C. G. Jung-Institut, Zürich, on whose founding committee she had served with Jung and Meier. At the founding of the institute, Jung singled out Wolff's essay, "Einführung in die Grundlagen der komplexen Psychologie" ["Introduction to the Foundations of Complex Psychology"] as "a work distinguished for its philosophical clarity" (CW 18, ¶1134). This important, 200-page essay first appeared in the Festschrift for Jung's 60th birthday, *Die kulturelle Bedeutung der Komplexen Psychologie* [The Cultural Meaning of Complex Psychology] (1935). It was republished after Wolff's death in a collection of her writings, *Studien zu C. G. Jungs Psychologie* [Studies in the Psychology of C. G. Jung] (Zürich: Rhein-Verlag, 1957). Jung's foreword to the latter volume appears in CW 10, ¶887–902.

69 *daß Sie als Deutscher die Nazis gewählt hätten*: In context, *wählen* may mean either "vote" or "choose." Thus Kirsch's statement could arguably be translated, "you would have taken the side of the Nazis." No such statement is found in Wolff's surviving letters to Kirsch. The remark may have been made in June 1933, when Wolff and Jung were both in Berlin; or else in Ascona during the Eranos *Tagung*, August 1933.

70 Cf. Jung, 26 May 1934, pp. 44f and notes 50f.

The following small memory from youth may make my reaction to you understandable. From my ninth year on, I had a very good Christian friend; he was my chum. When I was twelve and a half, from one day to the next, this friend stopped talking to me and never said another word. For an entire week I couldn't find out from him the reason for his strange behavior. I searched for all sorts of personal reasons in myself, of course, but found none. Finally I learned from classmates the motivation for the sudden break-up: I was a Jew "squared."[71] A thing like that sticks and shows the whole ambiguity of being a Jew in the midst of other peoples.

I recalled your wonderful explanations during the Berlin Seminar, where you demonstrated how the idea of ritual murder was projected onto Christians and later onto Jews, and the underlying subjective process experienced by the person originating such projections. So I also wondered where the hook might be located in you, on which the Jews can hang the projection of anti-Semitism. Obviously, I am taking into account the Jew's readiness to cry "anti-Semitism" whenever anyone expresses a personal criticism. I think it's possible to project anti-Semitism onto you because you have opinions about the Jew which may be correct, but only insofar as they reflect the Galut existence, as it is called in the Kabbalah,[72] the banishment of the Shekhinah[73] (the Jewish anima). Essentially you list four points to substantiate your interpretation of Jewish psychology.

I. They have had no culture of their own.[74]

1) In my opinion, the Jews did have their own culture. They lived a thoroughly creative life in pre-Christian times. True, they did not leave behind temples, artworks, or great music, but instead a great book, the Bible, which is a great literary collection of most diverse and antithetical, individual and national experiences of this people. This literary monument is governed by one theme: the relationship to God and God's predilection of Israel, God's authority among the Jewish people. This leading idea was absolutely capable of creating its own culture, and it is imprinted on the Jewish soul. It is amazing to discover in analyses how vividly this Jewish antiquity still lives in the Jewish soul of today. Of course, there are plenty of broadly oriental ideas in the Bible, but just as the Bible-Babel dispute[75] has shown, a creative conception existed in ancient Israel, distinct from

---

71 *zum Quadrat:* squared, four times over.

72 Kabbalah: a discipline and school of thought concerned with the mystical aspects of Judaism.

73 Shekhinah: a grammatically feminine word in Hebrew, its original meaning is "indwelling," refer-
    ring to the dwelling place of God, as well as the indwelling of God within the world and within
    each soul. By extension, the feminine presence of God.

74 Kirsch sets out to respond to Jung's four points numerically, but he soon drops the numerals. His
    remaining three points, below, are verbally noted as such.

75 *"Bibel-Babel Streit":* Named for a lecture, "Babel und Bibel," delivered by Assyriologist
    Friedrich Delitzsch in 1902. Delitzsch argued that Babylon was the source of many central ideas
    and institutions of the Old Testament. In two subsequent lectures he attacked the idea that the
    Old Testament presented an ethical monotheism superior to Babylonian religion, and urged that
    German Christians drop the Old Testament altogether. Responses were immediate and vigorous.

other oriental cultures. It's certainly similar to the relationship between German culture and European. As shown by Dr. Häussermann,[76] the significance of the great prophetic personalities was based on their connection with the unconscious. In his work, unfortunately, he did not mention the biblical texts that reflect the interpretation of dreams and other manifestations of the unconscious. You would see then that they conform exactly to yours. Just last week I wrote an essay for the Palestinian public which won't tell you anything new, but may be of interest to you in the overall context of these things. I'll put it in the mail to you in the same post.[77]

Now it is interesting – and with this begins the problem of post-biblical Judaism – that a new concept of the relationship with the divine emerged at the time of Jeremiah. The Jerusalem priesthood believed that national misfortune could be avoided, and God could be appeased, if ritual rules – they created new ones and codified old ones – were adhered to as closely as possible. A fence was erected around the teachings. It was the general principle to build as many new fences as possible. As a consequence the Jews got stuck in the narrows. In an effort to escape this narrows, they now needed other cultures. This practice of staying behind fences is *de facto* a fear of the unconscious. At this point began a stabilizing of the level of consciousness attained up to that point, and a desperate self-seclusion, avoiding new expansions of consciousness through the experience of the unconscious. Jesus and his way of redemption were necessarily rejected, a process which you've described precisely in *Types*, in the chapter on Prometheus and Epimetheus.[78] This relative consciousness, which you cite as a second point, has an entirely different character from (for example) the Chinese. As far as I can judge the Chinese intellectual, the Chinese path led to a whole – "completion" not "perfection".[79] Jewish consciousness, on the other hand, has the characteristic that something essential is missing; something suppressed lives in the Jewish soul, which induces even in the educated Jew the most peculiar affects and hysterical reactions.

This rejection of Christ has, it seems to me (Jews will never admit this) determined the fate of the Jews. From a Jewish viewpoint, Christianity is its

By 1904 some 1,350 short and 300 long newspaper and journal articles and 28 pamphlets had been published, arguing against Delitzsch's equation of Hebrew religion with other religions of the ancient Near East. (With thanks to Dr. Richard Corney.)

76 Friedrich Häussermann: Twentieth-century German scholar of the Old Testament. Author of *Wortempfang und Symbol in der alttestamentlichen Prophetie: Eine Untersuchung zur Psychologie des prophetischen Erlebnisses* [Verbal revelation and symbol in Old Testament prophecy: Research into the psychology of the prophetic experience], Giessen: Töbelmann, 1932.

77 With this letter Kirsch enclosed his two-page "Conclusion," typed with the same typewriter and in the same style as the letter. He refers here, however, to *eine Arbeit,* which he will send to Jung by the same post. This may refer to his sixteen-page lecture, written at about this time, "Then he will open the ears of men" (cf. Appendix A, pp. 267ff).

78 Cf. *Types,* CW 6, Ch. V, "The Type Problem in Poetry," esp. ¶310–13.

79 words orig. in English: "*completion* nicht *perfection.*"

shadow (and also *vice versa*, by the way, but that's the Christians' concern). It's historically demonstrable that in every era when the Jewish people attempted to realize the idea of the Messiah, great disturbances also erupted in the Christian world. Sabbatai Zwi[80] and the religious wars, Zionism – National Socialism. There's a striking coincidence here.

Concerning the third point, nomadism, I would like to believe that this phenomenon does not represent a nomadic nature but rather a restless wandering on the basis of a repressed complex. For that reason, too, the Christian legend has portrayed the Jew as *Ahasuerus*.[81] You certainly know many people who have become restless through being cut off from the unconscious, who project the anima and seek salvation in every possible and impossible way, e.g. even in psychoanalysis, but never within themselves. The same is true for the Jews as a people.

After the destruction of the temple, too, the Jews led a life in exile which was distinctly their own and – one may even say – they developed their own culture. Essentially it consisted of preservation and annotation (Talmud!)[82] and had something otherworldly about it.[83] At stake was always the preservation of what was their own, as the struggle with Hellenism clearly shows. The Jews assimilated Hellenism, they weren't devoured by it. Thus I have to concede to you – and this is the fourth point – that Greek antiquity had a great influence on Jewish psychology, but compared to what gave Jewish antiquity its character, it had only secondary importance.

Jewish culture in the Christian era presents a difficult and many-sided problem, but one can surely say it existed. It was simply of no consequence in world history any more. What was remarkable about the Spanish-Arabic period[84] was that two different cultures lived there symbiotically. There is no question that Spanish-*Jewish* culture was inspired by the Spaniards, but Jewish culture made its very own contribution, as its great *Hebrew* poets, philosophers and physicians show.

---

80 = Sabbatai Sevi (1626–1676): Rabbi and Kabbalist of Spanish descent, born in Smyrna. His career as a would-be Messiah took him to Salonica, Cairo, Constantinople, and back to Smyrna. He succeeded in gathering followers, who founded the Sabbataian movement. Sevi converted to Islam in 1666, and persuaded both Muslim authorities and his Jewish followers that he was a double agent. Banished, he died alone in Albania. Sabbataians continued, however, as a heretical movement within Judaism. Cf. Gershom Scholem, *Sabbatai Sevi: The Mystical Messiah*, trans. by Zwi Werblowsky, Princeton University Press, 1973. Cf. Jung, 18 November 1952, p. 143 and note; Kirsch, 10 December 1952, p. 150.

81 A name sometimes given to the Wandering Jew, a figure in Christian-European legends since the Middle Ages. In his essay "Wotan" (1936), Jung associates the projection of the Wanderer archetype onto Jews with the rise of anti-Semitism (CW 10, ¶374).

82 Kirsch's handwritten note in the left margin: "(Talmud!)"

83 *hatte teilweise etwas Gespentisches an sich.* Alternate trans: "had something ghostlike about it."

84 Between 711 and 1492, parts of the Iberian Peninsula were governed by Arab and North African Muslims.

Also, at a later time, the powerful movement of Hasidism[85] proves the creative energy of the Jewish people. But this creative achievement of Hasidism was very short-lived, because it failed to find the historic thread from the prophets to Jesus and did not have the strength to deal with rabbinical formalism and the "ethical" conception of religion. The evidence of Jewish culture is that the Hebrew language has survived almost continually, and all great works by Jews have been written in Hebrew (or Aramaic). (Zohar,[86] Hasidism, Ibn Gabirol,[87] Jehuda Halevi![88])

With the French Revolution a new historic era begins also for the Jewish people. Here begins the purge of Jews, dissolving the Jewish ways of life which had existed heretofore, the disavowal of Jewishness, assimilation and cessation of the living Hebrew language, which from then on was used only literarily by the so-called "Maskilim" (representatives of the Enlightenment). Only in this period, when the Jew could no longer lead his own life in any way, and felt himself to be a member of other nations, can I accept what you, dear Doctor, write about the Jews, namely that they are the upholders and promoters of other cultures. The fact that the Jews repressed their Jewishness during the era of assimilation explains – besides the Christ-complex – also the psychological break of personalities like Heine,[89] as well as the soulless materialism of such inspiring but destructive individuals as Marx and Freud. I find your criticism of Freud essentially correct; it matches the image of the Jews during their period of assimilation in the previous century, and such Jews still exist today in droves. I also understand, and it appears historically necessary, that the Germanic soul has protested against Freud's life-threatening psychology of godless- and homelessness and – thanks to you – has

---

85 Hasidism: a movement within Judaism, founded by Rabbi Israel Baal Shem Tov (1698–1760), stressing service of God through the mystical, the power of joy, love of God and one's fellow, emotional involvement in prayer, finding the divine in every aspect of existence, and the elevation of the material universe.

86 Zohar: lit. "splendor" or "radiance." Foundational work in the literature of Kabbalah. A group of books including commentary on the mystical aspects of the Torah (the five books of Moses) and scriptural interpretations, as well as material on theosophic theology, mythical cosmogony, and mystical psychology.

87 Solomon ibn Gabirol (c.1021–1058): Andalusian Hebrew poet and Jewish philosopher, born in Malaga, Spain. One of the first teachers of Neoplatonism in Europe, he had a profound influence on medieval Christian theology (scholasticism). Author of "Fons Vitae" (Latin trans., 1150, from a lost Arabic text).

88 Yehudah ha-Levi (c.1080–1141): one of the greatest Spanish Jewish poets. He was born in Toledo, Spain while it was under Islamic rule. A prolific writer of both Arabic and Hebrew poetry; also a physician and philosopher. Author of the "Kusari," a major exposition of the unique value of Judaism in a world in which Jews were in the minority.

89 *den seelischen Bruch solcher Naturen wie Heine.* Heinrich Heine (1797–1856): German poet and satirist. Born to a well-to-do Jewish family in Düsseldorf, Heine earned a doctorate in law in 1825 and converted to Lutheranism for professional reasons. He wrote lyrical poems of great beauty, many of which were set to music by various Romantic composers. A characteristic of his poems is the grace with which Heine establishes a Romantic theme, which he then dismantles with pointed irony.

discovered the creative depths. As two thousand years of suffering shows – and especially the sorrowful events of the year 1933 – the Jew has injured himself gravely by his negative valuation of the unconscious.

Since Moses Hess[90] (self-emancipation), Jews have been involved in a severe and bitter psychological analysis of Galut Jewishness. Extensive literature exists on the subject which elucidates particularly the psychological, sociological, and "salvation-historical"[91] situation of the Jews. The Jews no longer wanted to wait for the Messiah sent by God; they wanted to put an end to the Galut. Again they take their fate into their own hands and dare to be unhistorical, by trying to start *ab ovo*. Thus they returned to the historic soil of Palestine. Conditions and circumstances are fundamentally different here than in any of the lands of the Galut, but what will come of it is, of course, an entirely open question.

In order to respond properly to your letter, I had to give you this detailed account of my interpretation of history. You once told me your way could be very meaningful for the Jews. Since I've become very familiar with the Bible and have been living in Palestine, I understand now more than ever how enormously important for us is your vivid conception of the unconscious and the approach to the experience of the unconscious. For me, at least, it was only through you that it became possible to understand the experiences of the prophets, the Messianic idea, and to rediscover what was lost in the consciousness of the Jewish people since the time of the prophets. It is the pure draught from the unconscious. It goes without saying that for now this is only happening in a few individuals, but I believe that in this way the magic spell, the *Ahasuerus* curse, will be broken.

In closing, I would like to inform you that Dr. Neumann, who for some time apparently has been living in Tel Aviv, just around the corner from my place, has not yet found an occasion to get in touch with me. To be ignored in this manner does not really surprise me since – as I mentioned to Fräulein Wolff in Berlin – he was already describing himself in June 1933[92] as the only Jungian analyst in Palestine.

90 Moses Hess (1812–1875): socialist Zionist, admired by Theodor Herzl. Born in Bonn to an ortho-dox Jewish family, Hess started as a utopian socialist but moved toward scientific determinism. He contributed to Marx's "Communist Manifesto" (1848) the term "religion as the opium of the masses." Following the unification of Italy, the rise of nationalism in that country and the emergence of German anti-Semitism, Hess returned to his Jewish roots. In his booklet *Rome and Jerusalem: The Last National Question* (1862) he proposed a socialist Jewish State.
91 *"heilsgeschichtlich"*: a theological term, from *Heilsgeschichte*, the history of salvation. As told in the Hebrew Bible, the Jewish people's relationship with God opens with Creation and continues through the whole biblical narrative, pointing finally toward the prophetic and apocalyptic visions of the Last Days.
92 Erich Neumann did not actually move to Palestine until early 1934. In 1933 Erich and Julie Neumann emigrated to Zurich. Julie moved to Tel Aviv later that year, but Erich remained in Zurich a few months longer, to continue working with Jung. In December 1933, Jung wrote a certificate explaining the delay in Neumann's move to Palestine. The certificate confirms that Neumann has been studying with Jung, and that their work will resume on 15 January 1934 (Jung to Neumann, "Certificate," 14 December 1933 (*Analytical Psych in Exile,* p. 8).

In any case,[93] Zionism is a great experiment, which finds its foundation and its meaning in the fact that the Jews believe in their creative strength. Whether such creativity exists and will give the Jewish people a new character will be revealed in time. I strongly believe in it and am unconditionally bound to this experiment. To be an upholder and promoter of a culture would not give the slightest meaning to my existence. I would prefer to discover even the smallest truth, as long as it grows on my pile of manure, rather than disseminate the largest truth to a foreign culture.

I am planning to come to Ascona in August and hope to be able to speak to you then, but I'd be very happy if you would send me a reply to this letter.

With my most cordial greetings, As always,[94] yours truly, JAMES KIRSCH

Enclosure in Kirsch's letter of 8 June 1934:

Conclusion[95]

For the Palestinian Public

When one presents to the Jewish public a topic fraught with as many sensitive aspects as the Jewish question in psychotherapy, one has to reckon with a multitude of complex reactions. So it is no wonder that Jung – and I, too – have had the experience that our writing is not read correctly. Thus I must attempt the following corrections.

I.

I have never said a single word against Jung's assertion that the Jew has a particular tendency and ability to perceive the negative, the shadow. On the contrary, in my essay I expressly cited and relied on Jung's words regarding the human shadow side: "In many cases it is exceedingly salutary to confront human beings with their own most unpleasant truths"! Indeed, in every case in a daily practice, it is urgently necessary to shine light on the shadow side, the negative side of the unconscious. Obviously, this insight does not only apply to individual Jewish patients but to the entire Jewish situation of our time. Recognizing and valuing the Jewish shadow in this way, I wrote that among the Jewish people a thorough and

---

93 The final page of Kirsch's six-page letter is handwritten.

94 *unverändert*: lit. "unchanged".

95 *Schlusswort*: lit. "final word". Enclosure typewritten in German, on plain paper. From a phrase in the first paragraph, *"die Judenfrage in der Psychotherapie,"* ["the Jewish question in psychotherapy"], and from the quoted passage with which the writing ends (p. 56 below), it is a follow-up to Kirsch's essay in *Jüdische Rundschau* (cf. Jung, 11 June 1934, p. 57 and note).

bitter analysis has recently broken out (e.g. Mauschel[96] by Theodor Herzl[97]). No matter how I try, I cannot detect any "sugar-coating" here.

The great contribution of Jung (and this is clearly expressed in the essay in question) is that he has declared that the unconscious is *also* the creative foundation of the soul, and that he thus sees both aspects, the negative and the positive.

II.

The terms genotype and phenotype are borrowed from biology. The genotype describes the hereditary possibility existing in the germ plasma, while the phenotype is the individual manifestation transformed by experience and thus taking visible form. This clearly defines the contrast between essence and appearance. Whoever ventures to follow the phenotype of the Jew into his darkest abyss, that person cannot be accused of escaping into a non-existing image of a Jew. More likely one could conclude that this person is intent on penetrating into the essence of the Jew by way of individual manifestations.

III.

When Jung expressed his views concerning the current situation of psychotherapy,[98] he had to clarify to what extent Freud's particular Jewish attitude to the unconscious influenced all of modern psychology and psychotherapy. He does not, however, need to raise the question whether we Jews can acknowledge Freud as the genotype of the Jews. May we then – as it has already been hinted among Jews – regard Freud as a Jewish prophet? The prophet is legitimized by God's calling, i.e. on the positive foundation of the unconscious. (See e.g. Isaiah chap. 6). Freud, however, unequivocally rejects the positive aspect of the unconscious (see *The Future of an Illusion*).[99] We are therefore bound to continue working with and appreciating not only the negative but also the positive aspect, if we are to come

96 A polemical essay by Theodor Herzl (under the name Benjamin Seff), "Mauschel," appearing in *Die Welt*, Vienna, 15 October 1897, the weekly Zionist newspaper which Herzl founded. In it Herzl made use of stinging rhetoric to turn an anti-Semitic term, *Mauschel,* into a condemnation of anti-Zionist Jews, whom Herzl characterized as cowardly, greedy, opportunistic, and false to their own people.

97 Theodor Herzl (Binyamin Ze'ev) (1860–1904): Austro-Hungarian journalist, playwright, and political activist. Born in Pest, Hungary, to a Jewish family, he lived in Vienna and worked in Paris as a correspondent for *Neue Freie Presse*. There he covered the Dreyfus Affair. Rising anti-Semitism in Vienna led him to conclude that a separate Jewish state was the only answer to the so-called "Jewish question." In 1896 he published a widely read pamphlet, *Der Judenstaat* [The State of the Jews], presenting Zionism as a political program. The following year he planned the First Zionist Congress in Basel. Herzl is known as the father of modern Zionism.

98 *Wenn Jung sich über die gegenwärtige Lage der Psychotherapie aussprach...*: Kirsch's phrasing would have been recognized as a direct allusion to Jung's controversial essay, "Zur gegenwärtigen Lage der Psychotherapie" (cf. Kirsch, 7 May 1934, p. 42 and note).

99 Sigmund Freud, *Die Zukunft einer Illusion,* 1927. (Trans. by James Strachey, New York: Norton, 1961.)

out of our current spiritual situation of godlessness and homelessness. In this we are also justified to consider Freud, without detracting from his courageous discoveries, as a figure determined by the Galut[100] (the Galut phenotype), rather than as a timeless manifestation of the Jewish essence.

IV.

It is surely correct that the Jew is better able than the Teuton to endure "living with his shadow side in a friendly spirit of tolerance." Without doubting Jung's *specific* statement, I am (in contrast to Jung) of the opinion that it is particularly damaging and dangerous for us to destroy the connection with the unconscious as our creative original foundation. I emphasize this connection with the original foundation because the timeless type of the Jew has always expressed even the negative on the basis of his connection with the Eternal. Freud tried to strike a fatal blow against the religious life of the soul in *The Future of an Illusion*. To overcome this attitude of godlessness and homelessness, we need Jung's revelations about Freud and about the corresponding distortion[101] of Jewish psychology, and Jung's way – in contrast to Freud's – in order to arrive at the positive aspect of the unconscious through accepting the shadow as fully as possible. For that reason the final sentence of my essay was as follows: "In Jung's personality as well as in his psychology and psychotherapy, something is contained which speaks to the depth of the ailing Jewish soul and which may lead to its liberation."[102]

---

100 Cf. Kirsch, 7 May 1934, p. 42 and note.

101 *Abart*: A term used in National Socialist jargon to mean "degeneration," characterizing Jewish customs and institutions. It may also mean simply "variation." Kirsch uses it here in a negative sense.

102 *"Gerade in Jungs Persönlichkeit, in seiner Psychologie und Psychotherapie ist etwas enthalten, das die kranke jüdische Seele in ihren Tiefen anspricht und zu ihrer Befreiung führen kann."* Final sentence of Kirsch's article, "Die Judenfrage in der Psychotherapie," *Jüdische Rundschau* Nr. 43, 29 May 1934 (cf. Jung, 11 June 1934, p. 57 and note).

Dr. C. G. Jung
Küsnacht-Zürich
Seestrasse 228

11 June 1934[103]

Dr. James Kirsch
Hayarkon str. 101
Tel-Aviv
Palestine

My dear Kirsch,

As an enclosure I'm sending you a letter[104] to your patient Frau Silber.[105] I leave it to you what kind of use you want to make of it. In any case, I would ask you to let Frau Silber know that I've answered. I would not want, however, to correspond with her without your foreknowledge.

On a later occasion I must say something to you about your article in the Jüdische Rundschau.[106]

With warm regards, Yours truly, C. G. JUNG

---

103 Typewritten in German, on letterhead.

104 Jung's letter to Hildegard Silber, dated 11 June 1934, appears below in Appendix B, pp. 278f.

105 Hildegard Silber (later Hilde Kirsch) (1902–78): German-born lay analyst. In 1932, depressed by the illness of her husband, a merchant who had multiple sclerosis, she began analysis with James Kirsch. In early August 1933, two months after her husband's suicide, Hilde and her sons accompanied the Kirsch family to Switzerland, and from there to Palestine (cf. Jung, 31 August 1933, p. 37 and note). She began analytic work with Jung in spring 1935, while staying in Zurich for two months (cf. Kirsch, 19 June 1935, p. 70 and note). In 1936, living in London and married to Kirsch, she received her first clinical referral when Jung sent Michael Fordham to her (cf. Appendix B, p. 280).

106 Kirsch had written at length to a bi-weekly Zionist newspaper in Berlin, *Jüdische Rundschau* [Jewish Review]. The organ of the Zionistische Vereinigung für Deutschland [Zionist Union for Germany], with wide circulation, the paper appeared from 1902 to 1938. Kirsch's letter was given the title, "Die Judenfrage in der Psychotherapie: Einige Bemerkungen zu einem Aufsatz von C. G. Jung" ["The Jewish Question in Psychotherapy: Some Remarks on an Essay by C. G. Jung"]. In it Kirsch takes issue with Jung's "Zur gegenwärtigen Lage der Psychotherapie" ["On the State of Psychotherapy Today"] (cf. Kirsch, 7 May 1934, p. 42 and note), especially his description of the Jews as "nomads": *"Wir sind auch nicht, wie Jung meint, 'relative Nomaden', sondern ein rastloses Volk, ein Volk mit einer kollektiven Neurose, das infolge dieses Verlustes des Zusammenhanges seitdem keine bleibende Stätte gefunden hat"* ["Neither are we, as Jung believes, 'relative nomads', but a restless people, a people with a collective neurosis, which since this loss of connection, and as a result of it, have found no abiding place"] (trans. ACL). He also defends Jung, however, on the grounds that Jung's psychology supports the desire of Jews to return to their own land (*"Rückkehr zum eigenen Boden"*). He says that Jung has been unfairly attacked and silenced by Jews, and that Jung's psychology can give substantial help to a new kind of Jew (*"ein neuer Typ Jude"*) who affirms his own way of being (*"seine Eigenart"*) (*Jüdische Rundschau*, Nr. 43, 29 May 1934, p. 11). In the following weeks, *Jüdische Rundschau* published three more articles on the same topic (cf. Jung, 2 July 1934, p. 58 and notes).

Dr. C. G. Jung
Küsnacht-Zürich
Seestrasse 228

2 July 1934[107]

Dr. James Kirsch
Hayarkon str. 101
Tel-Aviv
Palestine

My dear Kirsch,

I just received a letter written to Dr. Adler[108] by the editors of the "Jüdische Rundschau." Adler has written a contribution[109] to the discussion in the Rundschau,[110] which was sent to you, as the Rundschau tells me. It would please me very much if you could arrange for this article to be published. With so many false opinions being spread about me, surely I have a moral claim to being presented accurately.

Thank you so much for your friendly gift. I'll write to you about that very soon. I couldn't do it up to now, for lack of time.

With best greetings, Ever yours truly, C. G. JUNG

107 Typewritten in German, on letterhead.
108 Gerhard Adler, PhD (1904–1988): German-Jewish "lay" (non-medical) analyst, at this time still located in Berlin. He had begun analysis with Kirsch in 1929, after which they remained lifelong friends and colleagues. Adler studied with Jung from 1931 to 1934. He emigrated to England in 1936, where he remained until his death, living in London. He was one of the founders of the Society of Analytical Psychology (SAP), 1946, in which he was a non-medical member. He later served on the editorial committee for the CW and edited the *C. G. Jung Letters* (Cf. *Jung–White Letters*, pp. xxi, xxviii.) Among Adler's published works are *Studies in Analytical Psychology* (1948) and *The Living Symbol* (1961).
109 Adler's article, last in the series, appeared under the heading: "C. G. Jungs Stellung zum Judentum" [C. G. Jung's attitude toward Judaism]. His title asks, "Ist Jung Antisemitisch?" [Is Jung Anti-Semitic?]. He admits that some of Jung's phrases, taken out of context, can be read as anti-Semitic. But he defends Jung's critique of the collective Jewish shadow – rootlessness, homelessness – and compares Jung's statements on this topic with Buber's. He adds that many Jewish analysands have Jung to thank for helping them to reconnect with their tradition (*Jüdische Rundschau*, No. 62, 15 August 1934, pp. 2ff).
110 Articles by Otto Juliusburger and Erich Neumann also appeared in 1934 under the heading, "Die Judenfrage in der Psychotherapie." Neumann's article contradicted Kirsch's earlier column in certain respects. Jung later thanked Neumann for his contribution to the series and specifically for his criticism of Kirsch's statements about Jewish psychology(Jung to Neumann, 12 August 1934, *Analytical Psych in Exile*, p. 51). Neumann's article suggests that Jung's psychology is actually Zionist in spirit, because it teaches the psychological importance of being in contact with one's own ground (*Jüdische Rundschau*, No. 48, 15 June 1934, p. 5).

Dr. C. G. Jung
Küsnacht-Zürich
Seestrasse 228

16 August 1934[111]

My dear Kirsch!

I'm sorry I haven't got around to answering you. Even today I still cannot go into the details of your letters.[112] I merely wanted to assure you that the only cause of my silence is lack of time. I have to let my secretary read and answer a lot of letters. I want to deal with your letters personally, which will happen shortly – but first I must get through the meeting[113] in Ascona. I'll speak there about the archetypes, that is, about their particularly frequent forms.[114] With regard to your article, I want to thank you very much for your intervention. In the meantime some unimportant details, which I could have criticized, have been clarified by Neumann's article.

Might I ask you to send the enclosed manuscript back to Neumann? I wasn't sure if I was reading his address correctly – SIRKIUS Street?

How are you and your wife? Here in the madhouse of Europe nothing is beautiful any more but Nature.

Ever yours faithfully, C. G. JUNG

Dr. med. James Kirsch
Hayarkon str. 101
Tel-Aviv

26 August 1934[115]

Dear Dr. Jung!

Your letter brought me extraordinary joy. I am very aware of your chronic lack of time, and I understand it. I'm only sorry that on account of being so overextended, you can't get around to publishing a major work. For instance, we are all eagerly awaiting your book on dreams. That reminds me, in Berlin I asked

---

111 Hastily handwritten in German, on letterhead. Prev. pub. in *PP*.
112 Kirsch's letters in the interim are missing.
113 *Tagung*: gatherings at Eranos, being informal, were always referred to by this term, rather than the more organizational *Kongress*.
114 Jung's Eranos lecture in 1934 was "Ueber die Archetypen des kollektiven Unbewussten" [On the Archetypes of the Collective Unconscious]. Stanley Dell trans.: *The Integration of the Personality* (New York: Farrar & Rinehart, 1939; London: Kegan Paul, 1940). Revised version, R. F. C. Hull trans.: CW 9(i), *The Archetypes and the Collective Unconscious*, ¶1–86.
115 Handwritten in German, on plain paper with stamped return address.

for your permission to translate a number of your works into Hebrew.[116] To begin with I thought of translating shorter, freestanding pieces. The best one to start with seems to me *Die Bedeutung der Psychologie für die Gegenwart*.[117] Would you agree with this? From what I know about the book-publishing business, I probably would have to discuss the details regarding honorarium, etc. with Rascher. Of course, a Hebrew edition would only have a relatively small audience, but those readers are deeply interested in everything to do with psychology, and they are located not only in Palestine but mainly in the United States, in South Africa, Poland and Lithuania. I'm very curious myself to see how this essay of yours would be received by a Hebrew-reading public.

Personally I'm doing quite well. My practice already fills almost the full day. I regularly have the evenings to myself. There is little thought of scientific work, because it is extremely difficult to procure books. Every Tuesday evening I give a seminar where I rigorously and thoroughly discuss the dreams of a woman patient. I've been learning a lot this way, because a number of the participants are very knowledgeable about Jewish subject matter and bring a lot of material from old legends and sagas to the understanding of dreams and problems of common interest.

I've been tolerating the heat very well, my wife much less so. Since I spent my childhood in Guatemala, I am probably able to adapt more easily to this climate. Radiation is enormously high in Palestine. The worst of it isn't the heat, but the unbelievable abundance of ultraviolet light, which is much higher than for instance in Davos. Luckily we live by ourselves in a beautiful little house with a garden, right by the sea.

The political circumstances are not exactly splendid. As a matter of fact they are similar – remarkably similar – to the state of affairs during Roman times. We have our Nazis, i.e. a party which wants to elevate the "Führer" to be the King of Palestine and is organized like the military. They wear brown !! shirts, are responsible for acts of terror, and they murdered the most important labor leader. With this we prove that we have learned nothing in our 2000-year history of suffering, and have succumbed to the power principle just like many European nations.

Points of light are a whole series of settlements in the countryside which exhibit a wonderful pioneer spirit, and the reconstruction of farmland is really impressive. Most interesting for me are the religious problems. On one side, there are Rabbis who instruct their pupils strictly and in great detail about sacrificial offerings, in anticipation of the "Führer's" entrance into Jerusalem as king, which they expect in the

---

116 To date a modest list of Jung's works have been published in Hebrew. These include (in order of their Hebrew editions) *Psychology and Alchemy* (1951); *Psychology and Education* (1958); *Ego and the Unconscious* (1973); *Psychology of the Unconscious* (1973); "What did Jung say to *Mishmar*'s correspondent in Switzerland 29 years ago?" (1974); *Dreams* (1982); *Memories, Dreams, Reflections* (1993); *Psychology and Religion* (2005); *Answer to Job* (2005). (Cf. GW 19, Walter Verlag, 1983; also Juliette Vieljeux, *Jung: Catalogue chronologique des Écrits*, 2004.) With thanks to Ulrich Hoerni.

117 (Lit: The significance of psychology for the present time.) Jung had expanded his 1933 lecture, "Über Psychologie," and retitled it for publication in *Wirklichkeit* (1934). In Hull's translation, it appears as "Psychology for Modern Man," CW 10, ¶276–332.

foreseeable future, believing that he will raise the temple again; and in that event, enough people would be required who know the sacrificial ritual and can execute it. This in the year of grace 1934! On the other hand, there are a few individuals who consider the religious question from a psychological viewpoint, so that one is under the impression that they must already know you. This is a wide field. Maybe I'll have a chance to tell you about it in person. The majority of those involved in the reconstruction are strongly anti-religious. If the words "religion" or "religious" are merely uttered, they wrap themselves in icy silence. At the same time, the festivals celebrated here by the young people are entirely new, deriving their meaning from the reconstruction of the land, for example the festival of the presentation of the first fruits.

In conclusion, I would like to ask you about a personal matter. In your letter you wrote to me for a second time about the "madhouse in Europe where nothing is beautiful anymore but nature."[118] I share this view, but wonder what you are referring to *in particular*. You write about it with special affect, so I suspect you're speaking of specific experiences in this regard. I assume that the "Third Reich" plays a small role[119] in this.

Incidentally, do you know that our colleague Heimsoth[120] – whom I introduced to you at the Dresden Congress in 1931 and subsequently saw near you on several occasions – was shot to death in the course of the Action of June 30 (as it is called in such cheerful terms)? He knew too much, and it cost him his life. These are strange times indeed!

> With cordial greetings, thinking of you, yours faithfully, JAMES KIRSCH

> Dr. C. G. Jung
> Küsnacht-Zürich
> Seestrasse 228
>
> 29 September 1934[121]

My dear Kirsch,

Unfortunately I had so many urgent tasks to cope with that I never found a quiet moment to write to you. With regard to your article, I agree entirely with

---

118 Cf. Jung, 16 August 1934, p. 59, and 29 Sept. 1934, p. 61.

119 *dass das 'Dritte Reich' dabei kleine Rolle spielt [sic]*: Kirsch seems to have omitted the indefinite article in the phrase *eine kleine Rolle,* "a small role." It is also possible he intended to write, *keine Rolle,* "no role." By either reading, the phrase is ironic.

120 Karl-Günther Heimsoth, Dr. med. (1899–1934): Berlin neurologist and psychotherapist, a long-time member of the AAGP and a colleague of both Jung and Kirsch. Heimsoth was murdered by a faction of Hitler's stormtroopers on 30 June 1934, during what came to be known as the Röhm-Putsch, or the Night of the Long Knives (30 June–2 July 1934). He was the personal physician of the main target of the purge, Ernst Röhm. (Cf. also Jung, 29 September 1934, p. 63.)

121 Handwritten in German, on letterhead. Final paragraph prev. pub. in *PP*. Longer passage prev. pub. in *Letters I*.

its intention and conclusion, and only object to the inference that in some way I identify the Jew with Freud. First, I don't do that, and second, it is always emphasized, especially from the Jewish side (e.g. most recently by Kronfeld[122]), that psychotherapy (= Freud and Adler) is Jewish in spirit. If that is being said by the Jews themselves, I am virtually compelled to assume that at least a large number of authoritative Jews completely identify themselves with Freudian psychology. From this one must conclude that they experience the reductive standpoint as being in accord, to a large extent, with their own psychology, especially as no other standpoint has been espoused from the Jewish side. Silence in this matter may pass for consensus. I entirely share your opinion that, *especially* for the Jews, it would be extremely important and beneficial to see the positive side of the unconscious.

My greatest wish would be[123] if a way could be found to combat the touchiness and affectivity that poison everything. As it is, one can never reach an objective understanding. Formerly I was considered a hater of Germans because I criticized their barbarism; now the Jews are accusing me of trying to curry favor with the Germans (and meanwhile Palestine's foreign trade with Germany happily increased last year, despite the boycott!).

Your "Conclusion" is very good. I hope it will have some effect. *Adler*'s article was *not inspired* by me. He wrote quite independently. The Jüd. Rundschau did not send me an inquiry. I think it's unnecessary for me to say anything more at this time.

Many thanks for your birthday wishes, and those of your wife!

With regard to your patient,[124] it's quite correct to say that her dreams have been induced by *you*. The feminine mind is earth which awaits the seed. This is the meaning of transference. The less conscious one always receives spiritual fertilization from the more conscious. Hence the *guru* in India. This is a very ancient truth. As soon as certain patients start treatment with me, the type of their dreams changes. In the deepest sense, all of us do not dream *out of ourselves* but out of that which exists *between myself and the other*.

Cordial greetings from, Ever yours truly, C. G. JUNG

122 Arthur Kronfeld, Dr. med. et phil. (1886–1941): German-Jewish psychiatrist; researcher in sexology; expressionist poet, and independent psychotherapist. Kronfeld's critique of psychoanalysis, *Über die psychologischen Theorien Freuds und verwandte Anschauungen* [On Freud's psychological theories and related views] (Leipzig: Engelmann, 1912), was widely read across Europe. With Ernst Kretschmer he helped to found the AAGP, on whose board he served and whose *Zentralblatt* he edited. He also served on the Berlin board of the International Union for Individual Psychology until 1931. That year he was named Professor of Psychiatry and Neurology at the University of Berlin. In 1933, feeling that Nazi politics had infected the *Zentralblatt* under Jung's editorship (cf. Appendix D, pp. 307f and notes), Kronfeld left the IAAGP and started a rival journal, *Psychotherapeutische Praxis*. Stripped of his university professorship in 1935, he fled to Switzerland but was denied asylum. In 1936 he accepted a research professorship in Moscow. There, fearing the advance of Hitler's troops and also the threat of persecution by Stalin, Kronfeld and his wife committed suicide in 1941.

123 *am meisten läge es mir am Herzen.*

124 *die Pat.*: lit. "the (female) patient." Kirsch's previous letter is missing.

II.[125]

I am truly sorry I haven't answered your wife's inquiry before now.[126] Her letter arrived while I was traveling in Italy, and so it landed in a pile of correspondence that I'm only now starting to burrow through. I won't be giving a seminar in Zürich, though I will in Basel, Oct. 1–7[127] – but only about *elementary* things. Not worth the trouble. In the fall, unfortunately, I am unable to book any more patients; I am completely overrun.

Re: translation,[128] you have to come to an understanding with Rascher & Co., Limmatquai, Zürich. It's fine with me.

I'm glad to hear your practice is going well. What you say about political conditions is similar to Europe these days. A *madhouse*[129] for sure, especially Germany. But everyone else is more or less going along with it. The world seems to be going through an immense shift. Aquarius is announcing himself powerfully. The anti-religious attitude is a powerful reaction against the worn-out spirit[130] of the past. In psychology we have already reached the other side; the anti-religious are just starting to turn away from the past.

The fate of Heimsoth[131] is shattering – … The German leaders themselves are quite unsure [and doubtless] nervous.[132] Hitler persistently shirks the religious conflict, which signifies much the same as the end of Protestantism in Germany. What comes next is the conflict with the Catholic Church. In Austria they are now placing Protestant and Jewish children together in special schools. I wonder if it will lead again to religious warfare, as before?

Best greetings, J.

---

125 Jung's roman numeral "II" indicates both the letter's second page and its second section. This undated addendum, hastily handwritten in German on letterhead, discusses items which Jung had apparently overlooked on his desk. In the 2011 edition of *The Jung–Kirsch Letters,* this page was mistakenly assigned to Jung's letter of 16 August 1934, whose letterhead and handwriting it matches. Jung's references, to Heimsoth's death and Kirsch's offer to translate, however, suggest that this postscript belongs to the letter of 29 September. With gratitude to Robert Hinshaw and Thomas Fischer.

126 Referring evidently to a letter from Eva Kirsch (not preserved), asking about forthcoming opportunities to analyze and study with Jung in Zurich.

127 Jung's seminar in Basel, 1934, is described in an unpublished report, "Bericht über das Basler Seminar."

128 Cf. Kirsch, 26 August 1934, p. 60 and note.

129 Cf. Jung, 16 August 1934, p. 59, and Kirsch, 26 August 1934, p. 61.

130 *gegen den faulgewordenen Geist der Vergangenheit*: lit. "against the spirit of the past which has become rotten (or lazy)"; *faul* has both meanings.

131 Cf. Kirsch, 26 August 1934, p. 61 and notes.

132 Defective passage in original. The lower right corner of the first page is torn. At the top of the second page the last syllable of a word can be read: *"… los"* – perhaps for *zweifellos* [doubtless].

1935–1938

LONDON

Dr. C. G. Jung
Küsnacht-Zürich
Seestrasse 228

17 February 1935[1]

My dear Kirsch!

I hope my letter will reach you in time. It's atrocious how I neglect you, but the things I perceived via your wife[2] were so wide-ranging and made everything about your future seem so uncertain to me that I instinctively shrank from them. Somehow I wanted to be "not involved." That you're coming back to Europe and your other insights have lightened the pressure, so it seems that something wants to get back on the right track. I will see what I can do for you.[3] My work load is more than I can really bear, so I simply have to leave many things undone, as immoral as that may be. My winter holidays were also chopped up by all sorts of urgencies. I shared your letter with Fräulein Wolff. Of course, she is also very busy. Around the 22nd of March I will break off my work, since the Nauheim Congress[4] starts soon after.

To your earlier letter,[5] I have to note that schizophrenia is not an unequivocal matter. Certain cases are certainly organic in nature, i.e. *more* organic than

---

1   Handwritten in German, on letterhead. Second paragraph prev. pub. in *PP*.
2   The reference is presumably to Eva Kirsch (cf. Jung, 19 August 1929, p. 5 and note; cf also Figure 3.1 p. 69). She returned to Berlin soon after this, taking the children with her. James Kirsch visited Berlin in early 1935 to drop off Hilde Silber's sons temporarily with their paternal grandparents. He then moved to London, stopping first in Zurich for the summer. Hilde Silber went to Zurich in March to work with Jung. In September she and James Kirsch moved to London, taking her sons with them. On 11 September 1935 James and Hilde Kirsch were married. A few days later Kirsch's seven-year-old daughter, Gabi (now called Ruth), no longer safe in Berlin and having been expelled from her school, also came to live with her father and step-mother. (Thanks to Jim Silber and Ruth Kirsch for details of this account.)
3   Jung wrote an "Attest" (certificate), to help Kirsch find work in England. Cf. Jung, 7 June 1935, p. 69 and note.
4   The eighth Congress, Bad Nauheim, Germany, 27–30 March 1935, co-sponsored by the IAAGP (C. G. Jung, President) and the German *Landesgruppe* (M. H. Göring, President). Cf. Appendix D, pp. 304–12. Matthias Heinrich Göring, Dr. jur. & Dr. med. (1879–1945) was a German physician and psychiatrist, as well as a Nazi party member and distant cousin of Hitler's Reichsmarschall. M. H. Göring studied psychiatry with Kraepelin and received a training analysis from Leonhard Seif, an Adlerian; he opened his practice in Elberfeld in 1923. A member of the AAGP from its inception in 1926, Göring became president of the German chapter of the IAAGP in mid 1933 and thereafter corresponded with Jung and C. A. Meier concerning the content and policy of the *Zentralblatt*. Starting in 1937 he directed the *Deutsches Institut für Psychologische Forschung und Psychotherapie* [German Institute for Psychological Research and Psychotherapy] in Berlin (hereafter the Göring Institute). (Cf. Geoffrey Cocks, *Psychotherapy in the Third Reich*, *The Göring Institute*, 2nd ed., New Brunswick and London: Transaction Publishers, 1997.) M. H. Göring died in captivity in Poland in 1945. Cf. also Jung, 19 July 1938, p. 92, note 111.
5   Kirsch's previous letter is missing.

psychic, while others are more psychic. Antidotes or drugs affecting metabolism are also of no help here. The case is remarkable. It is extremely rare, but cannot be doubted, that deepest insights can emerge from a psychotic episode. *But such an acquisition is dangerous!* That is to say, a leaky spot may develop where other things can also seep through.

I'm sending this letter by airmail.

With best greetings, Ever faithfully yours, C. G. JUNG

Dufourstrasse 49
Zürich

28 May 1935[6]

Dear Dr. Jung!

Please accept my most heartfelt thanks for your kind willingness to help me build a new life. Listed below are the dates and times I worked with you or consulted with you on the occasion of seminars, etc. I don't know whether it's more appropriate to list dates in a certificate or to write something confirming that you were in touch with me and my work during recent years. I hope that such a document will achieve the same wonders as the one you wrote for me in the past, which I enclose,[7] and which assisted me at that time in being anointed with the title of "Medical Specialist."

With cordial greetings, Yours truly and gratefully, JAMES KIRSCH

1929	(1)	May and June – Analysis and Engl. Seminar
1930	(2)	at the time of your lecture in Berlin in January
	(3)	" of the Congress in B.-Baden, April
	(4)	" of the German Seminar, October
1931	(5)	" of your lecture in Berlin, January
	(6)	" of the Congress in Dresden, May
	(7)	" of the German Seminar, October
1932	(8)	" of the Hauer Seminar,[8] October
1933	(9)	" of the German Seminar in Berlin, June
1935	(10)	Analysis & Engl. Seminar in March and May

6   Handwritten in German, on plain paper.
7   Cf. Jung, "Certificate," 6 June 1932, p. 28. No enclosure found with the present letter.
8   Cf. Jung, 25 June, 1932, pp. 28f, note 117.

Prof. Dr. C. G. Jung
Küsnacht-Zürich
Seestrasse 228

7 June 1935[9]

Dr. James KIRSCH has worked with me in 1929 during 2 months. He already then enjoyed a good psychological preparation, before he began his work with me.[10] Between the years 1930 and 1935 he continued his education in psychotherapy by practical work with patients as well as through attending to 4 holiday-courses about analytical psychology. Repeatedly he distinguished himself by lecturing on psychological subjects.[11] During the last 6 years he practiced psychotherapy in Berlin as well as in Palestine.

I can recommend Dr. Kirsch as a sufficiently equipped specialist for psychotherapy.[12]

C. G. JUNG

Figure 3.1 **Eva Kirsch with Gabi and Michael, Berlin, mid 1935.** After moving to London in September 1935, Gabi Kirsch was known as Ruth. *Photographer unknown. Courtesy Ruth G. Kirsch.*

9 Typewritten in English, on letterhead, now including Jung's academic title, *Prof. Dr.*
10 Jung's certificate for Kirsch, originally in English, was written in haste and includes some non-standard wordings.
11 Cf. Jung's 1932 certificate for Kirsch, p. 28. There Jung refers to *Vorträge in Arbeitsgemeinschaft* ("lectures in a collaborative context"). Here the reference to collaborative work has been dropped, possibly because when he left Europe in 1933, Kirsch had allowed his membership in the AAGP to lapse.
12 Jung validates Kirsch's professional identity in the broadest terms, as a psychotherapist, rather than as an analytical psychologist or psychiatrist. The main intention of the certificate is to help Kirsch find work in England in any capacity. After his arrival in England, Kirsch quickly received permission to practice as a Jungian analyst (cf. Kirsch, 9 July 1935, p. 72).

Dr. James Kirsch
77, Cambridge Terrace,[13]
Hyde Park, W.2.
Tel. Paddington 4552

London, June 19, 1935[14]

Dear Dr. Jung,

First of all my most warmest thanks for your kind letter of recommendation, which I hope will be very effective. Strictly on the external level, everything seems to be working well so far, and I have to admit that I'm feeling very much at ease and sensing the land and the atmosphere in this country to be very congenial.

During one of her last sessions,[15] Hilde also talked to you at some length about me and my problem. To begin with, I have to tell you that the reason for my departure was not the land of Palestine, but the Jews. The Jews do not accept the land and the primitiveness there and instead attempt, consciously and unconsciously, to perpetuate their exile. When they say that they are sacrificing themselves there, this is not meant in a Christian sense; rather, they view themselves as a sort of compost for future generations. The consequence is that they are thinking only of the economic development of the land, and whenever significant problems arise, they say their children will have to solve them. They push everything away to the future and sacrifice *individuation*. If it were my destiny to live there, I think I would do it, or at least give it a try. But I don't think it is my fate.

May I bring up another point that Hilde touched on in her consulting hour? Probably you told her something to the effect that I cannot reach my own depth, because I don't realize my shadow sufficiently and am shirking the primitive within myself; my psychology seems as if I were floating, like a drop of oil, above my depth. I have to acknowledge this as absolutely correct and would like to ask for your help in this regard, even though I have certain misgivings about burdening you with this because I know that my shadow may ask things of you which I should actually ask of myself, and so it seems doubtful to me that it's even right to ask you for help. But I'd like to send you two dreams, and wonder if you can give me any indications as to how I can get out of this situation, which I myself recognize as burdensome and dangerous.

---

13 First London address of James Kirsch and Hilde Silber, until their marriage (cf. Jung, 16 September 1935, p. 75 and notes). It was also Kirsch's temporary business address.

14 Handwritten in German, on plain paper.

15 On 1 March 1935 Hilde Silber arrived in Zurich, hoping to begin analytic sessions with Jung. According to her son Jim Silber, while still in Tel Aviv she had read in the *I Ching* that she should see "the man over the great water." On arriving in Zurich she tried to make an appointment with Jung but was initially refused. When a woman in the same rooming house was taken ill and cancelled her session, Hilde requested the vacant hour and was accepted (cf. Jung to Hilde Kirsch, Appendix B, p. 279 and note).

1. I'm going down the street in a large city, which leads downhill. Go around a corner. There are wide green fields. Nazis have assembled there. Everybody knows that this is the time when they meet there, move out, and begin to shoot. But no one has attempted to stop them. They are just about to march off toward the city, to carry out their extermination work. The last group starts to point its machine guns toward the green field. I ask, "What are you doing here?" "Oh," they say, "Here the soldiers of the previous World War can witness how they shot each other." My brother is pulling me toward the middle. Here we're in the safest place, it seems to me. But the opposite is true. They are pointing their guns at me. I wake up with emotion.

2. Arnold Zweig[16] had written a book in which he described how on a historical day – like Armistice Day – people of diverse races celebrated the same event. He described the encounter somewhere in the mountains. I was in a gigantic house (like one of the physicians' houses in Harley St.) and wanted to imitate this event and appreciate it. I ascended the gigantic staircase; the steps were carved in marble. From the top an *Arab* descended the narrow steps in a light-footed way. I attempted to go upstairs but managed only a short distance. Then I could not go on and had to descend.

I arrived in a room. In it Arnold Zweig was just unpacking his suitcases. One bed was still free. I said to A. Z., "Let me stay here today." A large mattress was suspended as a hammock. I started to swing, also trying to imitate something from a story by A. Z. Many neckties were hanging around my neck. A. Z. said to me, "Not this way, you'll swing too high." The wind had caught the ties, and they were acting like sails, accelerating my swinging. He said, "Psst, swinging so hard, you're drawing attention to yourself. The Nazis are coming now."

I understand dream 1. to mean that the ucs. is against me, that primitive forces are at work, which will ruthlessly and definitively annihilate European culture. The shadow leads me into this. But I am fighting this process.

Of course, I asked myself what kind of attitude is preventing me from accepting this process, and I believe that dream 2. contains a detailed response. A. Z. is a

16 Arnold Zweig (1887–1968): German-Jewish novelist, playwright, literary essayist, and anti-war activist. From 1923 until he fled Germany in 1933, he was Editor-in-chief of the Zionist newspaper in Berlin, *Jüdische Rundschau* (cf. Jung, 11 June 1934, p. 57 and note). Zweig underwent a Freudian analysis in the 1920s. In 1927 he expressed fervent thanks to Sigmund Freud, and they corresponded for the next twelve years. (Their letters, edited by Ernst Freud, were published in 1968.) Zweig left Germany when Hitler came to power and lived in Haifa for 15 years. Eventually he turned away from Zionism. In 1948 he accepted the invitation of the East German government to move to the Russian Zone (later the GDR), where he spent the rest of his life, working in government and the arts, the World Peace Council, and the German Academy of the Arts. He died in East Berlin.

typically Jewish man of letters, with a tolerably good style, but everything in him is "adopted sentiments," inauthentic. He *constructs* fantasies and considers himself a representative of European culture, which he serves and believes – in a sentimental way – he has to save. The dream speaks abundantly of "adopting sentiments," imitation, and fear of the brutality and ruthlessness of the Nazis. I think it's this attitude toward Europe and its culture which prevents me from accepting the Arab – the Primitive. As a Jew I find it doubly foolish and damned sentimental to defend European works which are on the point of death anyhow. The word "hammock" leads to Guatemala, because it is a bowdlerized Indian word from the West Indies (originally *hamaka*). This Arab is not an urban Arab but a genuine Bedouin who belongs to a clan[17] and, as such, places extraordinary importance on his individual freedom. He would consider it an insult to be asked about the state of health of his wife or mother. On the other hand, the writer A. Z. never leaves any woman unshorn. He likes to write romans-à-clef, scandalous stories presented from a distorted slant.

When I look at this shadow side of mine, I become thoroughly frightened. I myself am aware how slanted my attitude is. I hope I'm not burdening you too much with this letter. It seems very important to me to finally let go of this "oil-on-water" psychology.

With most cordial greetings, also to your wife and Fräulein Wolff,

Gratefully yours, JAMES KIRSCH

Dr. James Kirsch
77, Cambridge Terrace,
Hyde Park, W.2.

London, 9 July 1935[18]

Dear Dr. Jung,

Today I can send you the happy news that the "Home Office" has given me permission to practice analytical psychology here in London.[19] Allow me to take this opportunity once again to express my most heartfelt thanks to you. I am fully aware how much I owe to you in all respects.

---

17   word orig. in English.
18   Handwritten in German, on small sheets of notepaper.
19   On 1 October 1935 Kirsch was invited to join the staff of the Tavistock Clinic, London. Seven months later, however, his status was changed to "collaborating doctor," after the Home Office stipulated that he might practice only in collaboration with a doctor registered in England. The Medical Director of the clinic informed him of this change, adding, "[A]ll of us on the staff regard you in precisely the same way that we should if you were [a] member of the Staff" (J. R. Rees to Kirsch, 1 May 1936, Kirsch archive).

I've heard that Dr. Bennet[20] has just left for Zurich in order to talk to you. I was quite astonished that you are able to see him now, when it's actually your vacation time. In Bennet's interest, though, I would hope very much that you can receive him and work with him intensively. I have a high opinion of him, in that he handles himself and the problems of psychotherapy with great self-reliance and without bias. He is regarded here, rightly in my opinion, as one of the most capable and responsible psychotherapists.[21]

With respectful greetings, Gratefully yours, JAMES KIRSCH

Prof. Dr. C. G. Jung
Küsnacht-Zürich
Seestrasse 228

31 July 1935[22]

Dr. James Kirsch
8 Park Square West[23]
Portland Place
London N.W.1

My dear Kirsch,

Please accept my best thanks for your kind[24] congratulations.

The situation in England seems to have taken shape for you in a favorable way. More favorable, anyway, than one could have hoped. I hope you'll succeed in gaining a firm footing there.

Concerning the translation of my more recent essays, this matter is already planned. For years now, Dr. Cary Baynes[25] has been looking after the translations. We just have to wait, as usual, until a sufficient number of suitable essays is collected.

With best greetings, Ever yours truly, C. G. JUNG

---

20 E. A. Bennet, English psychiatrist and Jungian analyst, practicing in London. Author of *C. G. Jung* (1961) and *What Jung Really Said* (1966). Cf. Kirsch, 11 September 1936, p. 91 and note.

21 *einer der fähigsten und saubersten* ("cleanest," in the sense of "having integrity") *Psychotherapeuten*.

22 Typewritten in German, on letterhead.

23 Kirsch's first private practice address in London.

24 *freundlich* (lit. "friendly"): A term often used in German business correspondence, corresponding to the formulaic English use of "warm" or "kind."

25 Cary F. Baynes, MD (1883–1977): American physician who analyzed with Jung in the early 1920s and served as his editorial assistant and translator. Born Cary Fink, she was married from 1910 to 1922 to Jaime de Angulo, whose study of American Indian culture later inspired Jung's visit to Taos, New Mexico. In 1923 Cary de Angulo moved to Zurich, where she was eventually married for a few years to H. G. Baynes (cf. Kirsch, 25 December 1935, p. 75 and note). She was authorized

8, Park Square West,
Portland Place,
London, N.W.1

[August 1935][26]

Dear Dr. Jung,

As you know, I am still constantly in great financial difficulties. I'm only now able to send you a portion of the amount I owe you. May I ask if you agree that I may send you the balance in about 2–3 months?

I would welcome the opportunity to speak with you briefly during your visit here. In spite of all these difficulties, would you be able to grant me a half-hour?

With cordial greetings, Gratefully yours, JAMES KIRSCH

Prof. Dr. C. G. Jung
Küsnacht-Zürich
Seestrasse 228

Küsnacht-Zürich, 30 August 1935[27]

Dr. James Kirsch
8 Park Square West
Portland Place
London N.W.1

Dear Kirsch

Many thanks for your check. Of course, it's all right with me if you send the balance in about three months.

I'll see you in London, naturally. A morning would be best, if your clinical activity permits.

With best greetings, C. G. JUNG

to take stenographic notes at Jung's Club seminars in summer 1925. She also translated several of his early works, working with H. G. Baynes, including *Two Essays on Analytical Psychology* (1928) and *Modern Man in Search of a Soul* (1933). In 1950 she published the work for which she is probably best known, her English retranslation of Richard Wilhelm's German version of the *I Ching or Book of Changes,* with Foreword by Jung.

26 Handwritten in German, on small letterhead. This undated letter predates Jung's reply of 30 August 1935.

27 Typewritten in German, on pre-stamped postcard. On front side of postcard are handwritten notes, probably by Hilde Kirsch: *"Kl. Sofa"* [small sofa]; *"1 Schreibtischstuhl"* [one desk chair]; in same handwriting, in English: "Touch the doors in the nursery.... all the smooth work... floor must be done in nursery... large bedroom."

Prof. Dr. C. G. Jung
Seestrasse 228
Küsnacht-Zürich

Küsnacht, 16 September 1935[28]

Dr. James Kirsch
25 Temple Fortune Hill[29]
London N.W.11

My dear Kirsch,
Accept my most heartfelt congratulations,[30] and please convey the same to your wife.[31]

With warm regards, Ever yours truly, C. G. JUNG

8, Park Square West,
Portland Place,
London, N.W.1

25 December 1935[32]

Dear Dr. Jung,
I was contacted by Dr. Kitchin[33] for analysis. She told me that many years ago – in 1920, I think – she worked with you for three months. I've only known her socially up to now, and seen her at my office only once for analysis. Baynes,[34]

---

28 Typewritten in German, on pre-stamped postcard.
29 Kirsch family's home address in London, following the marriage of James and Hilde.
30 James and Hilde Kirsch were married in London on 11 September 1935.
31 *Ihre Frau Gemahlin* (lit. "your lady spouse")
32 Handwritten in German, on small letterhead.
33 *Frau Dr. Kitchin*: Kathleen Kitchin, MSc, MB, BS: English physician and Jungian analyst. In 1939 she was one of the founders of the Guild of Pastoral Psychology (GPP), where she delivered a lecture titled "The Third Reich: a Plea for the Guardian Angel." In the 1940s, under her maiden name, K. Forsaith Lander, she gave two more GPP lectures, "A Map of the Psyche" (1943) and "The Anima" (1944). (Thanks to Diana Grace-Jones for information about Kathleen Kitchin and the GPP.) Cf. Jung, 3 January 1936, p. 76. An exception has been made in printing this patient's name. The editor has searched exhaustively for her heirs, without success. She is a historical figure. The possibility that she is living now, nearly 80 years after the letters in question, seems remote. So, after consultation with all concerned parties to the book, we have decided to let her name stand.
34 H. G. (Helton Godwin) Baynes, MB (1882–1943): English-born psychiatrist, Jungian analyst, and lifelong friend of Jung's; often called Peter, Jung's nickname for him. Baynes analyzed with Jung in 1920 and served as his confidential assistant in 1921–22 and 1929–31. In 1922 he co-founded the London Psychological Club (APC) and was its first chairman. He translated some of Jung's

with whom I consulted about her weeks ago, told me she's a psychosis.[35] He said it with affect, and since I've heard from her that strong tensions exist between her and Baynes, I'm interested also in knowing your opinion. My own is that indeed she has a deep-seated problem, but is by no means a psychosis. Of course, analyses of analysts are always peculiar! and I now work with five analysts in analysis. As you see, I'm doing quite well, and even though not all difficulties have been surmounted yet, everything looks promising now.

When will your new book be published? I heard you'll be going to the United States soon, is that true?

With warmest greetings to you and your family, and best wishes for the New Year.

Faithfully yours, JAMES KIRSCH

Prof. Dr. C. G. Jung
Küsnacht-Zürich
Seestrasse 228

3 January 1936[36]

Dr. James Kirsch
8 Park Square West
Portland Square
London N.W.1

Dear Kirsch,

When I analyzed Dr. Kitchin,[37] the issue was not a psychosis but only an extraversion which exceeded all bounds. Since then I haven't become aware of

---

early works, including *Psychological Types* (1923), and, with Cary F. Baynes (cf. Jung 31 July 1935, p. 73 and note), *On the Relation of Analytical Psychology to Poetry* (1923). In 1925–26 he accompanied Jung to East Africa. In 1931 he returned to England, where in later years he wrote *Mythology of the Soul* (1939), *Germany Possessed* (1941), and *Analytical Psychology and the English Mind* (1950).

35 The phrase, "she's a psychosis," is an indirect quotation from H. G. Baynes (*"Baynes, den ich vor Wochen nach ihr fragte, sagte mir, sie sei eine Psychose"*). This turn of phrase, reducing the patient to a diagnosis, occurs nowhere else in the Jung–Kirsch correspondence. It seems to be quoted here with irony. Baynes's diagnosis is questioned by Kirsch and emphatically contradicted by Jung (cf. Jung, 3 January 1936, pp. 76f).

36 Typewritten in German, on letterhead.

37 Cf. Kirsch, 25 December 1935, p. 75 and note.

anything different. Difficulties with Baynes[38] don't prove that the other person is crazy. You are quite right, the analysis of the analyst is a chapter unto itself. I could also tell you something about that.

My new book[39] is far from being finished.

Next summer I'm really going to America, where I'm invited to the Harvard University tercentenary.[40]

With best greetings and New Year's wishes also to your wife,

Ever faithfully yours, C. G. JUNG

8, Park Square West,
Portland Place,
London, N.W.1

14 January 1936[41]

Dear Dr. Jung,

Please accept my most heartfelt thanks for your friendly letter with the New Year's wishes. I am certain that you could tell many stories about the analysis of analysts – and with all my heart I wish for a quiet hour to discuss this and that with you. Since I myself am now one of those analysts about whom tales could be told, I'd like to report to you a dream I had recently. You know what difficulties I've had in finding the way to myself, and I am sending you the dream because it appears to me to announce a breakthrough. If your time allows, I would be delighted if you could send me a few words about it.

---

38 ibid.

39 Reference to "my new book" is unclear. Perhaps *Psychologie und Alchemie* [Psychology and Alchemy] on which Jung was already at work, and on which he would work for eight more years: *Psychologie und Alchemie* (Psychologische Abhandlungen 5. Zürich: Rascher, 1944). Somewhat revised, this work became GW 12, *Psychologie und Alchemie* (1952). The English translation appeared a year later: CW 12, *Psychology and Alchemy* (1953/1968) (Hereafter *Psych & Alch*). Two other works were also now in revision: *Das Geheimnis der goldenen Blüte: Ein chinesisches Lebensbuch* [The Secret of the Golden Flower: A Chinese Book of Life], Jung's first work on alchemy, written with Richard Wilhelm (orig. pub. 1929), was being prepared for its second edition (Zürich: Rascher, 1938) (cf. CW 13.1; CW 15.5). Meanwhile Jung's foundational work *Wandlungen* (cf. Jung, 12 August 1931, p. 21 and note) was being revised for its third edition (Leipzig & Wien: Franz Deuticke, 1938).

40 In August 1936 Jung sailed for New York. In September, during the tercentennial celebration at Harvard, he lectured on psychological and mystical quaternities and received the Doctor of Science, *honoris causa*. He then went to Bailey Island, Maine, where he lectured on dream analysis to about 100 members of the New York APC. He lectured again at the APC in New York and visited friends in Providence, RI, before returning to Europe in October.

41 Handwritten in German, on plain paper.

There was enormous fear that the war should break out. The onset of the war was expected at any moment. I was standing at the railway line with huge crowds of people. A gigantic locomotive, the "Russian" one, a sort of powerful tank, was moving on the rails, just about to cross over the nearest border into the other country, to bring war and destruction to the neighbor country. Other cars were moving in front of it. It moved forward as it could, step by step. "It's in a hurry," I thought, and I ran in the opposite direction to look for shelter.

I ran along a pond which had the shape of a half-moon, under trees by a river, but found no real shelter anywhere. Then in the distance I saw balloons throwing bombs and smoke rising. Soon one of them was above me, like the Homunculus in Faust.[42] It dropped a small pouch toward me, containing some kind of chemical. A voice said, "He is attracted by humidity and alkali, for – as is well known! – the soul is always alkaline in order to find 'personality'." Apparently the Homunculus in the balloon was blind and thus had to discover "personality" through chemical affinities. During this process a woman stepped out of me; she was seized by the chemicals and should really be dead. She was in a celluloid shell, so she looked like a doll from the outside. Her celluloid nose was then broken off by the Homunculus, and underneath was the real woman. But to everyone's horror, she was not dead. Everyone considered her to be a miracle of nature, since she had survived this process. A voice said, "Previously, the Jewish gold was like that: (Yet I saw it.) HAW + LAH[43] .... Now the gold of the HAWDAWAH has been added:[44] ...."

---

42 In Goethe's *Faust, Part II*, a miniature human figure is brought to life inside an alchemist's vial (vv. 6819ff). In his glass vessel he floats above the sleeping Faust (v. 6904ff), casting a bright light and speaking with supernatural authority. Other characters comment that the Homunculus (lit. "little man") wishes to be incarnate (vv. 8251f); is a virgin's son (v. 8253); is a hermaphrodite (v. 8256). (Cf. CW 12, *Psych & Alch*, ¶84, pp. 63–67, and Fig. 22, p. 66.)

43 Kirsch's hand-drawn symbol follows: a four-branched Hebrew "Shin," leaning left.

44 Another hand-drawn symbol follows: an eight-branched Shin, four branches leaning left and four right. Cf. Figure 3.2, p. 79.

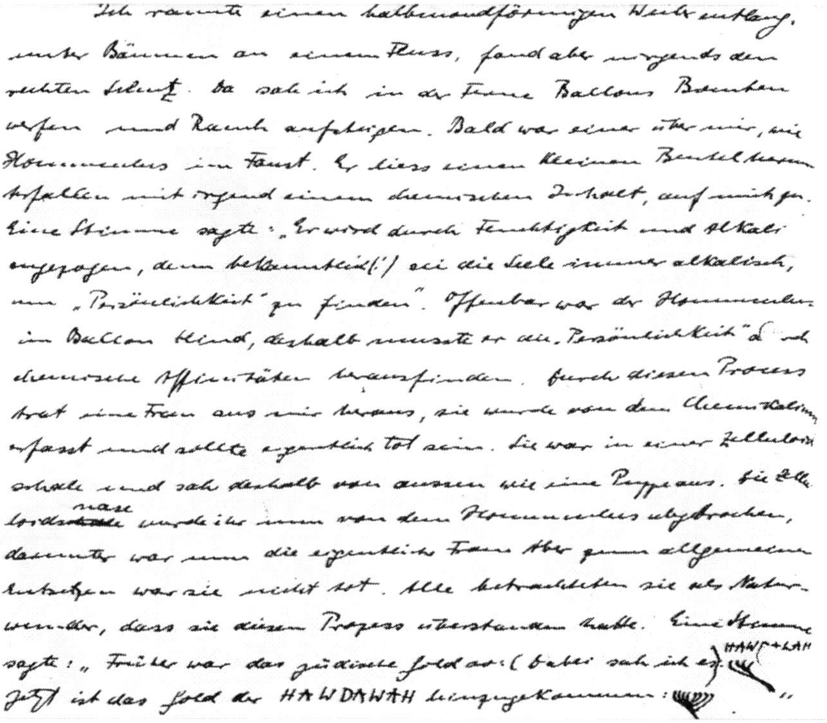
Ich rannte einen halbmondförmigen Weiher entlang,
unter Bäumen an einem Fluss, fand aber nirgends den
rechten Schlupf. Da sah ich in der Ferne Ballons Bomben
werfen und Rauch aufsteigen. Bald war einer über mir, wie
Homunculus im Faust. Er liess einen kleinen Beutel herun-
terfallen mit irgend einem dunkelsehen Inhalt, auf mich zu.
Eine Stimme sagte: „Er wird durch Feuchtigkeit und Alkali
angezogen, denn bekanntlich(!) sei die Seele immer alkalisch,
um „Persönlichkeit" zu finden". Offenbar war der Homunculus
im Ballon blind, deshalb musste er die „Persönlichkeit" d[urch] d[ie]
dunkelsehe Affinitäten herausfinden. Durch diesen Prozess
trat eine Frau aus mir heraus, sie wurde von dem Chemikalium
erfasst und sollte eigentlich tot sein. Sie war in einer Zelluloid
schale und sah deshalb von aussen wie eine Puppe aus. Die Zellu-
loidnase wurde ihr nun von dem Homunculus abgebrochen,
darunter war nun die eigentliche Frau. Aber gegen allgemeinen
Entsetzen war sie nicht tot. Alle betrachteten sie als Natur-
wunder, dass sie diesen Prozess überstanden hatte. Eine Stimme
sagte: „Früher war das jüdische Gold aus: (dabei sah ich ein) HAWDAH
Jetzt ist das Gold der HAWDAWAH hinzugekommen: "

Figure 3.2 **Excerpt from Kirsch's letter of 14 January 1936.** *Photo: ©2010, Ann Lammers. Courtesy ETH Library archive/Estate of James Isaac Kirsch.*

My wife only understands this dream negatively, while it appears to me that – after the initial fear and flight – the process of individuation prevails and this under alchemical symbols (which I do not understand). In this way the anima is, so to speak, exposed as a "personality," which evidently may also be a reference to the Jewish soul, which was changed into a chrysalis by the exile (rationalism? hair-splitting?). The symbol at the end corresponds to the four-limbed Hebrew letter "Shin" – the name of God.[45] Havdalah means "differentiation" and is a rite which is performed with a prayer at the end of Sabbath. During it one smells certain spices, and in the prayer God is thanked for teaching us to differentiate between weekdays and the Sabbath.

45 The letter Shin can refer to one of the names of God in Hebrew, Shaddai. In Kabbalistic tradition, the three-branched Shin originally had four branches. The lost branch is given various meanings in Kabbalah, including the "evil aspect," which will be integrated when the missing branch is restored at the coming of the Messiah. Thanks to Nomi Kluger-Nash, who cites the teaching of Gershom Scholem. Thanks also to Dr. Richard Corney, who cites David Leitner, *Understanding the Alev-Beis: Insights into the Hebrew Letters and the Methods of Interpreting Them*, Jerusalem/New York: Feldheim Publishers, 2007, pp. 313f.

"Hawdawah" does not exist in Hebrew. But there is a root form, "Badoh,"[46] from which one could form a noun "Habdawah," which then could mean "creative recall," thus creative "fantasy" or imagination. The new symbol is thus composed of a left-leaning and a right-leaning "Shin," and is ultimately a tree with eight branches.

Dear Dr. Jung, I have another important request for you. During my move here from Palestine, the "Sermones ad Mortuos"[47] were unfortunately lost. Might I ask you to send them to me again?

With cordial greetings, Your deeply indebted JAMES KIRSCH

Prof. Dr. C. G. Jung
Küsnacht-Zürich
Seestrasse 228

27 January 1936[48]

Dr. James Kirsch
8 Park Square West
Portland Place
London N.W.1

Dear Kirsch,

Dr. Kitchin has asked me for the Sermones. I'm far too little acquainted with her to agree right away to this request. If you're of the opinion that she'll make no idiotic[49] use of it, however, I'm prepared to go along with her request. Please send a card.

Your dream actually concerns the separation and differentiation of the anima. The Homunculus who takes care of this process is the Self.[50] The alchemical form of the procedure follows from the fact that alchemical philosophy is the

---

46 or *Badah* (handwriting unclear). The primary meaning of the Hebrew root is "make up, concoct, fabricate, invent." In certain forms the verb also means, "lie, falsify" and "be proved untrue." Here, as elsewhere, Dr. Corney has kindly advised about Hebrew lexical items, etymology and usage.

47 Cf. Jung, 13 February 1931, p. 14 and note.

48 Typewritten in German, on letterhead.

49 *blödsinnig* (lit. "feeble-minded"). Jung's concern about sending *VII Sermones ad Mortuos* to Dr. Kitchin is based on the peculiar nature of this early piece of writing (ibid).

50 Cf. Kirsch, 14 January 1936, p. 78 and note. Lecturing at the Club on 8 October 1949, Jung calls Homunculus *"ein Symbol der Ganzheit in der Alchemie"* ["a symbol of wholeness in alchemy"] ("Faust und die Alchemie," lecture transcript by Rivkah Schärf, unpublished typescript, ETH Library archive, p. 25). With thanks to Ulrich Hoerni.

nearest analogy. It is a kind of yoga, aiming for the creation of the Self through "Imagination." The Self appears under many names, such as gold, stone, divine water, the squaring of the circle, etc. Recently I gave three lectures on this question at the Club.[51]

With warm regards, Yours truly, C. G. JUNG

3, Devonshire Place,[52]

W.1.

Welbeck 7023

1 February 1936[53]

Dear Dr. Jung,

I believe that you can send the Sermones to Dr. Kitchin without special apprehension. She is evolving very well and will certainly make proper use of the Sermones.

At an English social event about three months ago, I met a gentleman – stutterer! – who had read the Sermones as the only one of your books! He told me the name of your patient who gave him the Sermones, but I've forgotten it. I believe it's right to take this opportunity to relate this to you.

In the meantime I received the Eranos book[54] and thank you for all the explanations you've given me therein. The consequences are far-reaching. Could you also send me the three lectures you presented at the Club?[55] Please excuse the brazen request but I really have a "burning" need of them.

In the dream I sent you, the gold is the 8-branched tree with eight branches on a "tree-interior" box.[56] It thus contains certain scents. In later dreams there are

---

51 Jung's three lectures at the Club, "Über die Philosophie des Steins der Weisen" [lit. "On the Philosophy of the Stone of the Wise"], are not published in their entirety. Their main concepts, images and literary references appear in Jung's 1935 and 1936 Eranos lectures, on which his later *Psych & Alch* is based (cf. CW 12, esp. Part 3, Section 4, "The Prima Materia," ¶425ff; cf. also Kirsch, 22 June, 1946, p. 103 and note).

52 Kirsch's new private practice address, located in a prestigious London neighborhood.

53 Handwritten in German, on half-sheets of letterhead.

54 Olga Fröbe-Kapteyn, ed., *Eranos-Jahrbuch 1935: Westöstliche Seelenführung* [Western and Eastern Guidance of Souls], Zürich: Rhein-Verlag, 1936. (Cf. note 57 below.) The lectures of each year's Eranos Tagung were edited by Fröbe-Kapteyn and published by Rhein-Verlag in annuals (*Eranos-Jahrbuch, -Jahrbücher*; hereafter *EJ*).

55 Cf. note 51 above.

56 *"Bauminnen büchse"*: invented word. *"Bauminnen"* [lit. "interior of a tree"] alludes to an alchemical image. Cf. Jung, "The Philosophical Tree," CW 13, *Alchemical Studies,* esp. Part I, ¶304–49 and Figures 13, 20–22. Cf. also Jung, 29 January 1953, p. 158 and note.

further offensive scents which, however, when I inhale them, make life possible for me within the fiery transformation process. You also mention a Latin text: *conjungite ergo . . . . . . suae odoriferae! uxori . . . .* (p. 82).[57] Are they perhaps the exhalations of my own inferiority, which I have to endure – a kind of test of courage?

Enclosed is a check in the amount of 139 francs. According to my records, I owe you 135 francs for my wife's sessions and my own, and 4 francs for the Sermones. Please let me know whether the amount is correct.

My practice is doing *very* well.

With cordial greetings, Faithfully yours, JAMES KIRSCH

7 February 1936[58]

Dr. James Kirsch,
8 Park Square West,[59]
Portland Place, N.W.1

Dear Kirsch,

Unfortunately I cannot send you the alchemy lectures because I didn't write them out.[60] Odors are referred to occasionally in the alchemical writings. Psychologically they may be related to psychological exhalations, as you suspect.

Many thanks for the check.

The Sermones for Dr. Kitchin are being sent to you today.

Ever faithfully yours, *[carbon copy unsigned]*

---

57 Kirsch underlines and adds an exclamation point to *odoriferae* [odorous]. The text comes from a footnote to Jung's 1935 Eranos lecture, under a paragraph on the importance of bringing the inferior function to consciousness: *"Diese Synthese betrachtete die Alchymie als eine ihrer hauptsächlichsten Aufgaben: conjungite ergo masculinum servi rubei filium suae odoriferae uxori et iuncti artem gignunt (Turba Philos. Ed. 1572,* p. 26)"* ["Alchemy regarded this synthesis as one of its most important tasks: therefore join the masculine son of the red slave to his scented bride, and the couple will give birth to the art"] ("Traumsymbole des Individuationsprozesses: Ein Beitrag zur Kenntnis der in den Träumen sich kundgebenden Vorgänge des Unbewussten." *(Eranos-Jahrbuch 1935,* p. 82, note). Parallel citations, with thanks to Dr. Ribi, are found in CW 14, *Mysterium Coniunctionis* (¶498) and in the *Aurora consurgens* of M.-L. von Franz (GW 14/ III, ¶534) (cf. Kirsch, 23 November 1952, pp. 146f and note).

58 Typewritten in German, on plain paper (unsigned). A photocopy of the secretary's carbon copy was kindly provided by the Stiftung der Werke von C. G. Jung. No original has been found.

59 Jung continued to address mail to Kirsch's former office address until Kirsch called his attention to the error (cf. Kirsch, 3 May 1936, p. 84, note 66).

60 Cf. Jung, 27 January 1936, p. 81 and note. The three handwritten lectures were never typed up or published in their original form. Holograph texts are available in microfiche at the ETH Library archive.

3, Devonshire Place,
London W.1

9 March 1936[61]

Dear Dr. Jung,

For the past few weeks, a young colleague from New Zealand has been working with me, Dr. U[…],[62] who has had two years of Freudian analysis in New Zealand because of severe bouts of depression. It did not damage him substantially. He has a deep inner concern with religious problems. Originally he wanted to become a pastor, then studied medicine which also left him deeply[63] dissatisfied. The depression disappeared when it turned out that the ucs. was evidently guiding him toward becoming an analyst, and that he has within himself an inescapable inner vocation to be an analyst. The Freudian analyst strongly recommended that he become an analyst, but he always rejected it. After he became acquainted with the other way, through me, the analytic profession forced itself on him *against* his will. He accepted this idea only with hesitation, and I was also not certain about it. For this reason I referred him to Baynes, who absolutely didn't understand the situation and talked common sense to me.[64]

Dr. U. is a modest, gentle man of great intelligence, very congenial, diligent, very honest, and also, based on his medical training, very suitable to become an analyst. I ask you most sincerely to do whatever[65] is possible to further him in his psychological development. Perhaps you could see him once here in October and later accept him for analysis in Zurich.

With cordial greetings, Yours very gratefully, JAMES KIRSCH

---

61 Handwritten in German, on half-sheet letterhead.
62 Apart from the first initial, the name is illegible in Kirsch's holograph.
63 *im Tiefsten* (?) (paper perforated): lit. "in the deepest (part)."
64 *und mir common sense talkte.* Borrowing the English phrase "talked common sense," Kirsch jokingly treats "talk" like a German verb.
65 *alles was* (?) (paper perforated).

3, Devonshire Place,
London, W.1
Welbeck 7023

3 May 1936[66]

Dear Dr. Jung!

May I ask for your help in coming to an understanding of a dream? For some time (after this dream), I've been reading alchemical texts and am intensely preoccupied with the manufacture of the "philosophers' stone."[67]

> Evchen (my first wife)[68] had apparently committed a crime (presumably murder) and was now busy removing the last traces of it. We were expecting a commission of inquiry. But as hard as Eva tried, some of the traces kept reappearing. We were standing next to the oven where something connected to the murder had been burnt. It was absolutely cold, that is, there was no fire, and consisted of two sections. I stirred whatever was in the upper part: (1) ash. From this came (2) an exactly cube-shaped stone and (3) a peculiar salt, shiny white crystals with a bluish shimmer. I took a rubber pouch (like an ice bag that's placed on a patient's heart), put the salt into it, and took it out to the garbage can. But some of the salt still remained in the oven, and the commission of inquiry will find it.

Dear Dr. Jung: What is the crime? That no fire was in the oven? Or that the stone was even produced? Or the murder of the "bodily" human being? Is the salt the "sophic salt?"[69] and what is it psychologically? Does the rubber pouch correspond to the "subtle body"?[70] or the "vas?"[71] Is consciousness represented by the "commission of inquiry"?

With most cordial greetings, Faithfully yours, JAMES KIRSCH

---

66 Handwritten in German, on half-sheets of letterhead. Kirsch's Park Square West address is crossed out, the new address added by hand.
67 Cf. Jung, 27 January 1936, p. 81 and note.
68 Cf. Jung, 19 August 1929, p. 5 and note.
69 phrase orig. in English.
70 phrase orig. in English.
71 (Latin) "vessel".

Prof. Dr. C. G. Jung
Küsnacht-Zürich
Seestrasse 228

19 May 1936[72]

Dr. James Kirsch
3 Devonshire Place
London W.1

Dear Kirsch,

For lack of time it's unfortunately not possible for me to go more deeply into your dream. I'd just like to note that the theme of crime has to do with the secret of alchemy, since the latter concerns itself with breaking through the generally valid state of consciousness. You must avoid carelessness and not lure a person who is meant for the collective into the path of danger. Nonnulli perierunt in opere nostro![73]

Please greet your wife from me, too, and tell her I'm afraid I'm not able to commit myself very reliably yet with regard to the winter semester. All kinds of assignments are waiting for me in the future, which I can't take account of. So I prefer not to make any definite promises yet.

With best greetings, C. G. JUNG

3, Devonshire Place,
W.1
Welbeck 7023

20 June 1936[74]

Dear Dr. Jung,

I would just like to let you know that although my wife had a somewhat complicated delivery, all in all it went well, and she's recovering beautifully.[75] The boy weighs 9 lbs 9 oz. and is correspondingly strong.[76]

---

72 Typewritten in German, on letterhead.
73 Not a few have perished in our work! (cf. *Psych & Alch*, CW 12, ¶188). The warning is common in alchemical literature. Dr. Ribi cites a text in *Rosarium Philosophorum, Artis Auriferae II*, p. 264: "Hoc est magnum signum, in cuius investigatione nonnulli perierunt…" Similarly, in Jung's *Alchemical Studies,* Part V, "The Philosophical Tree," the section titled, "The Dangers of the Art" opens: "*Aurora consurgens I* says in regard to the dangers which threaten the artifex: 'O how many understand not the sayings of the wise; these have perished because of their foolishness…'" (*Alchemical Studies,* CW 13, ¶429).
74 Handwritten in German, on half-sheet letterhead.
75 … *auch das Wochenbett tadellos ist* [lit. "… the days following the birth are also without complaint"].
76 Thomas B. Kirsch was born 14 June 1936.

Thank you from the bottom of my heart for your last letter. I'm trying very hard to heed your warning, hoping to succeed.

Cordial greetings, Faithfully yours, JAMES KIRSCH

Figure 3.3 **James Kirsch with Thomas, 1937.** *Photographer unknown. Courtesy Thomas B. Kirsch.*

25 June 1936.[77]

Dr. James Kirsch,
3 Devonshire Place,
London W.1

Dear Kirsch,

May I send you and your wife my heartiest congratulations on the birth of your child.

With best greetings, Ever yours truly *[carbon copy unsigned]*

---

77 Typewritten in German, on plain paper (unsigned). No original has been found. Copy of letter kindly provided by Stiftung der Werke von C. G. Jung.

10, Cavendish Place,[78]
London W.1

25 July 1936[79]

Dear Dr. Jung,

Please accept my most heartfelt congratulations for your birthday. I gladly take this opportunity, at least once a year, to express my deepest thanks to you for the inexpressible totality of what you've given me all these years.

I was told that you had nothing by Agrippa,[80] which I couldn't imagine. If you do not own this yet (I know you like it a lot, since you cited the motto in your Paracelsus essay[81]), please let me know. If you already have it, I could send you a very beautiful Latin-Greek edition of the Hermes Trismegistus Poimandros[82] by Flussas from the year 1574 (which Mead[83] considers to be very reliable) or "Arcana Arcanissima" by Michael Maier.[84]

With most cordial greetings and wishes, Faithfully yours, JAMES KIRSCH

---

78 Kirsch's new private practice address, in the same desirable neighborhood. (With thanks to Thomas Kirsch for information about his father's London offices.)

79 Handwritten in German, on plain paper. Letterhead added by hand.

80 Agrippa von Nettesheim, Heinrich Cornelius (1486–1535): German physician, theologian, philosopher. With this letter, Kirsch sent Jung a Latin edition of Agrippa's *De incertitudine et vanitate scientiarum* (1527). (Cf. Jung, 1 August 1936, p. 88 and note.)

81 Jung's lecture to the Zurich Literary Club, "Paracelsus: Ein Vortrag gehalten beim Geburtshaus an der Teufelsbrücke bei Einsiedeln am 22. Juni 1929." ["Paracelsus: A Lecture given at the house of his birth, on the Devil's Bridge at Einsiedeln on the 22nd of June 1929"] (*Lesezirkel*, XVI.10, September 1929, pp. 117–25), Part I of CW 15, *The Spirit in Man, Art, and Literature*. The motto is from Agrippa's *De incertitudine et vanitate scientiarum*: "Nullis his parcet Agrippa, / contemnit, scit, nescit, flet, ridet, / irascitur, insectatur, carpit omnia, / ipse philosophus, daemon, heros, deus et omnia" ["Agrippa spares no man; he contemns, knows, knows not, weeps, laughs, waxes wroth, reviles, carps at all things, being himself philosopher, demon, hero, god, and all things"] (ibid, ¶9 and note).

82 "Poimandros": sixteenth-century Hermetic text. In a long footnote to Jung's Terry Lectures, "Psychology and Religion" (1937), he quotes from *Hermetica, the ancient Greek and Latin writings ascribed to Hermes Trismegistus,* edited and translated by Walter Scott; *Libellus I: The Poimandres* (Vol. I, p.114). Cf. CW 11, *Psychology and Religion: West and East,* ¶47 n.21, pp. 29f (hereafter *Psych & Rel*).

83 George Robert Stow Mead (1863–1933): British theosophist, founder of the Quest Society, a scholar in Neoplatonism, Gnosticism and Hermeticism. Jung refers frequently to G. R. S. Mead's work, especially to *Pistis Sophia* (translator, 1896), *Fragments of a Faith Forgotten* (author, 1900); *Thrice Great Hermes: Studies in Hellenistic Theosophy and Gnosis,* (translator, 1906); and *A Mithraic Ritual* (author, 1907).

84 Count Michael Maier (1566–1622): Prussian-born physician, diplomat, philosopher, and alchemist. He studied medicine in Basel and lived several years in Prague, later also in London. His first published work, "Arcana Arcanissima" (London, 1614), discovers hidden meanings – philosophical, alchemical and Christian – in the ancient texts of Egyptian, Greek and Roman mythology.

Prof. Dr. C. G. Jung
Küsnacht-Zürich
Seestrasse 228

1 August 1936[85]

Dr. James Kirsch
10 Cavendish Place
London W.1

Dear Kirsch,

Many thanks for the friendly birthday wishes and for the beautiful edition of Agrippa. I actually have it only in a German edition and am very happy now to own also a Latin edition of this special work.[86]

What you write to me, though, about the 1574 edition of the Corpus Hermeticum[87] decidedly piques my appetite. If the thing isn't too expensive, I'd like to make a grab for it.

With best greetings, Ever yours truly, C. G. JUNG

10, Cavendish Place,
London W. 1
Landham 3289

4 August 1936[88]

Dear Dr. Jung!

I'm very happy I was able to give you pleasure with the Agrippa. Now I'm only interested in knowing which one of us two was tricked by the unconscious. As far as I remember, I wrote to you that I had a Latin-Greek edition of "Poimandros"

---

85 Typewritten in German, on letterhead.
86 Cf. Kirsch, 25 July 1936, p. 87 and note. Two of Agrippa's works are found in Jung's personal library: *De incertitudine et vanitate omnium scientiarum* (in two editions), and *De occulta philosophia libri tres.* (With thanks to Ulrich Hoerni and Andreas Jung.)
87 Jung has evidently mistaken the title (cf. Kirsch, 4 August 1936, p. 89 and note). The *Corpus Hermeticum* is unrelated to the *Museum Hermeticum.* Classic edition: *Hermes Trismégiste, tome I-IV,* edited by A. D. Nock and A.-J. Festigière (Paris: Les Belles Lettres, 1945). Cf. also *Corpus Hermeticum Deutsch,* C.Colpe u. Jens Holzhausen (2 vols. Stuttgart: Bad-Cannstadt, 1997); and *Hermetica,* English trans. by Brian Copenhaver (Cambridge University Press, 1992). With thanks to Dr. Ribi.
88 Handwritten in German, on printed letterhead. Kirsch mistakenly wrote the year as "1933," but context places this letter in 1936.

by Hermes Trismegistos from the year 1574 ready for you. On the other hand, I had also thought of another book called "Museum (not 'Corpus') Hermeticum Reformatum," 1677,[89] containing 21 treatises. For the most part they are translated from German into Latin, e.g. the Secret Symbols of the Rosicrucians,[90] Lambspring,[91] and others. I had carefully pondered whether I should send you that book, but surmised that you would know the important treatises *in German*.[92] Apparently, then, the unconscious wants you to receive it. Unfortunately it doesn't include the illustrations of the "Secret Symbols," but it has all the illustrations of Lambspring, the 12 Keys[93] of Basilius Valentinus[94] and Janitor Pansophus.[95]

Please let me know which one you prefer: the Poimandros[96] or the Museum Hermeticum.

89   *Museum Hermeticum Reformatum et Amplificatum*, Johann Daniel Mylius, ed. (Frankfurt a.M.: L. Jennis, 1625, 1678), a collection of alchemical treatises. A facsimile of the work has been published by the Akademischen Druck- und Verlagsanstalt (Graz, 1970). It also exists in English translation, "The Hermetic Museum restored and enlarged" (trans. by Arthur Edward Waite, 1893; later republished, two volumes: New York: S. Weiser, 1974). With thanks to Dr. Alfred Ribi.

90   "Secret Symbols of the Rosicrucians": An eigteenth-century compendium of earlier sources, important to Rosicrucian thought. The Rosicrucians arose in medieval Germany as a mystical-theological society, which became influential in Freemasonry and Protestantism. The "secret symbols" convey a vision of God and the cosmos in elaborate diagrams, combining themes famil-iar to alchemy and Kabbalah: light and darkness, matter and spirit, male and female, divine and human, life and death.

91   *De lapide philosophorum, Figurae et emblemata* ["On the Philosopher's Stone, Figures and Emblems"] is included in *Museum Hermeticum* (1625, 1678, op. cit.). Fifteen wood-cut images depict the alchemical process as a psychological progression. Lambspring (Lambspringk), the purported author, is identified in an introductory verse only as "a noble ancient philosopher." The treatise itself is described as "concerning the Philosophical Stone; rendered into Latin verse by Nicholas Barnaud Delphinas, Doctor of Medicine, a zealous student of this art" (trans. by A. E. Waite). Jung uses Lambspring's emblems in CW 12, *Psych & Alch* (Fig. 168, p. 331; Fig. 179, p. 342; Fig. 240, p. 436).

92   E.g. *Geheime Figuren der Rosenkreuzer, aus dem 16ten und 17ten Jahrhundert. Aus einem alten Mscpt. zum erstenmal ans Licht gestellt* [Secret Figures of the Rosicrucians from the 16th and 17th century. From an old manuscript, brought to light for the first time] (Altona: Gedruckt und verlegt von J. D. U. Eckehardt. Vol. 1, 1785; Vol. 2, 1788).

93   *Ein kurtzer summarischer Tractat, von dem grossen Stein der Uralten* [A brief summary tract, on the great stone of the ancients], attributed to Basilius Valentinus, Eisleben, 1599. Illustrations of the "twelve keys" first appeared in the Leipzig edition, 1602. A Latin edition was published in Frankfurt, 1618, under the editorship of Michael Maier. Latin, French, English and German edi-tions appeared in the seventeenth and eighteenth centuries. This text also appears in the *Museum Hermeticum* (op. cit.), from which Jung illustrates his work (cf. CW 12, *Psych & Alch,* Fig. 146, p. 292).

94   Basil Valentine (Basilius Valentinus): sixteenth-century German Benedictine monk and alche-mist. Works attributed to him include the "Twelve Keys" (op. cit.) and "Triumphal Chariot of Antimony" (Latin trans. by Theodore Kerckring, Amsterdam, 1685; English trans. by Arthur Edward Waite, London: James Elliott & Co., 1893).

95   "Janitor Pansophus": an anonymous component of the *Museum Hermeticum*. The 1678 edition includes illustrations.

96   Cf. Kirsch, 25 July 1936, p. 87 and note.

During the past week I have read your Wotan essay[97] and your commentary on the Tibetan Book of the Dead.[98] Especially in connection with alchemy, it gave me an amazing amount and opened new aspects for me, which are so broad and deep that at times I'm quite stupefied. I am looking forward *very much* to seeing you here in October.

With cordial greetings, Faithfully yours, JAMES KIRSCH

Prof. Dr. C. G. Jung
Küsnacht-Zürich
Seestrasse 228

Küsnacht-Zürich, 12 August 1936[99]

Dear Kirsch,

The "Museum Hermeticum" is already in my possession,[100] the Poimander[101] would really interest me more.

With many thanks for your news and best greetings,

Faithfully yours,[102] C. G. JUNG

10, Cavendish Place,
London W.1
Langham 3289

11 September 1936[103]

Dear Dr. Jung!

I'm told you won't see any patients this year during your stay in London, and that you will use your time mainly for the British Museum[104] and the Warburg

97 C. G. Jung, "Wotan," *Neue Schweizer Rundschau*, III.11, March 1936, pp. 657–69. Republished in *Aufsätze zur Zeitgeschichte* [Essays on Contemporary Events] (Zürich: Rascher, 1946). Cf. CW 10, ¶371–99.

98 C. G. Jung, "Einführung," *Das tibetanische Totenbuch* (W. Y. Evans-Wentz, ed., Zürich: Rascher, 1935): CW 11, *Psych & Rel*, "Psychological Commentary on 'The Tibetan Book of the Dead,'" ¶831–58.

99 Typewritten in German, on pre-stamped postcard.

100 Cf. Kirsch, 4 August 1936, p. 89 and note. According to a handwritten notation on the flyleaf, Jung's copy of the *Musaeum Hermeticum Reformatum et Amplificatum* (Francofurti, Apud Hermannum A. Sande., 1678), which is still in his library, came originally from Biblioteca Admontensis. Thanks to Andreas Jung.

101 Cf. Kirsch, 25 July 1936, p. 87 and note.

102 Handwritten closing.

103 Handwritten in German, on half-sheets of letterhead.

104 The British Museum, founded in 1759, includes a highly esteemed Reading Room, opened in 1857. Until the year 2000, this exclusive library was accessible only through a formal application.

Institute.[105] But if you can somehow arrange it, my wife and I would be very happy to see you and your wife[106] at our house. Our preference would be, of course, to have you with us for dinner, but I'm afraid this time may already be otherwise occupied. In which case, I'd suggest a late afternoon, when the libraries have closed.

In case you can make use of my consulting room, it goes without saying that it will be at your disposal anytime during your stay in London. It's located beside the Langham Hotel, and I imagine that there may be persons who wish to speak to you without Dr. Bennet's[107] knowledge.

I hope very much for a positive answer from you and your wife.

With cordial greetings, Faithfully yours, JAMES KIRSCH

10, Cavendish Place,
London W.1
Langham 3289

13 July 1938[108]

Dear Dr. Jung!

I would be much indebted to you if you could arrange to give me a consultation session during the Oxford Congress.[109]

---

105 The Warburg Institute (originally *die Kulturwissenschaftliche Bibliothek Warburg*), founded in Hamburg in 1919 based on the personal library of Aby Moritz Warburg (1866–1929), which emphasized the intellectual and social context of Renaissance art. The library was relocated to London in 1933 to escape Nazi persecution. It is now a part of the University of London.

106 Emma Jung-Rauschenbach (1882–1955): wife of C. G. Jung and herself a practicing analyst, was born to a wealthy industrialist family in Schaffhausen, Switzerland. She and Jung were married in 1903 and raised five children. Emma underwent analysis with Jung in the early years of their marriage, and became thoroughly committed to his psychology. She published two important papers on animus (1931/1934) and anima (1955), which later appeared in translation as a book, *Animus and Anima* (1957) (cf. Kirsch, 1 January 1954, p. 187 and note). Her greatest work, a study of the Arthurian epic, was left unfinished at her death. It was completed thereafter by Marie-Louise von Franz and published under both their names: *Die Graalslegende in psychologischer Sicht* [The Grail Legend in psychological perspective] (Zürich und Stuttgart: Rascher Verlag, 1960). English edition: *The Grail Legend* (trans. Andrea Dykes; New York: C. G. Jung Foundation, 1970; 2nd ed., Princeton University Press, 1998).

107 Cf. Kirsch, 9 July 1935, p. 73 and note. If tensions existed between Jung and Bennet, as Kirsch hints, they may have reflected current stresses within the IAAGP (cf. Jung, 19 July 1938, p. 92 and note).

108 Handwritten in German, on half-sheet of letterhead. Nearly a two-year gap exists between Kirsch's last letter and this one. Though there is no evidence of a rift in their relationship, it is possible that in this stressful period neither Jung nor Kirsch wrote to the other, or that a letter or letters became lost.

109 The tenth Congress of the IAAGP was held in Oxford, 29 July to 2 August 1938. Cf. Kirsch, 28 July 1931, p. 18, note 69; Jung, 19 July 1938, p. 92 and note.

I hope you're again in good health and have once again completely vanquished the amoebae.

With cordial greetings, Yours, JAMES KIRSCH

19 July 1938[110]

Dr. James Kirsch,
10 Cavendish Place
London W.1

Dear Colleague,

I hope it will be possible for me to speak to you privately, but I cannot promise unconditionally, because I don't know to what extent the business of the congress will make demands on me.[111] In Oxford I'm not my own master, after all, but the servant. In serviento patrimonio consumor![112]

With warm regards, Ever yours truly *[carbon copy unsigned]*

110 Typewritten copy of letter, in German. No original has been found. This copy was kindly provided by the ETH Library archive.

111 Jung's agenda at the Oxford congress was complicated. He had a public function to perform, but behind the scenes he wanted to plan his resignation as president of the IAAGP, with help from English colleagues. On 1 August 1938, in Oxford, Jung and Meier met with several of these – Baynes, Bennet, Crichton-Miller, Dicks, Hadfield, Hargreaves, Lowenfeld, Rees, Stephen, Strauss, and Wilson – to discuss how to conclude Jung's term as president while preserving the international neutrality of the IAAGP. It was agreed to have another meeting in August 1939, in Zurich, to decide the question of Jung's presidency and to arrange the next IAAGP Congress in a land other than Germany (cf. *"Protokoll der ausserordentlichen Sitzung mit den englischen Delegierten und Mitgliedern am 1.August 1938, 11 Uhr im Taylorian Institute, Oxford,"* typescript, ETH Library archive). Despite all efforts, when Jung submitted his resignation as president in July 1940, Matthias Göring promptly took over as president of the IAAGP and editor of the *Zentralblatt* (cf. Jung. 17 February 1935, p. 67 and note).

112 For *in serviendo...* : "In serving the patrimony I consume myself!" Paraphrased from Bismarck, 1881: *"Patriae inserviendo consumor"* [In serving my country I consume myself]. The phrase appears earlier in Hartmann von Aue, *Der arme Heinrich* (vv. 97ff). (*Geflügelte Worte: Der klassische Zitatenschatz*, gesammelt und erläutert von Georg Büchmann, neu bearbeitet und aktualisiert von Winfried Hofmann, München: Ullstein, 1864/2007, p. 449).

1940–1947

LOS ANGELES

Walnut 9229
936 South Windsor Blvd
Los Angeles, Cal.

19 November 1940[1]

Dear Professor Jung!

Quite a long time has gone by since you heard from me. Now I have an important announcement to make: My family and I have moved to Los Angeles.[2] The war brought this about. What we've lived through in recent times I need hardly describe to you. I'm happy that we escaped with our lives. Psychological work had become almost impossible. During the war any kind of activity became almost impossible for us foreigners. All my books are burnt, even my seminar notes are gone. Yet all these are small losses compared to the major upheavals which occurred in the spiritual lives of the English. I was very sorry to leave, because I loved England and the English people very much.

Now I am in California, in a climate which is quite similar to Guatemala's, and have peace again and the possibility of regaining strength. For my wife it's a blessing to be out of the war zone.

All along I had been hoping to be able to have an in-depth conversation with you. I'm afraid this will have to wait for some time yet. For several reasons I did not go to New York, even though my prospects were best there. Jung Clubs are a thorny problem, however, as you know better than anyone, and the effect of analysis on Jungian analysts (myself included!) gave rise to all sorts of questions in me, for which I have no answer.

Please give my warmest greetings to your dear wife and to Fräulein Wolff, and do pass on my new address to them.

1   Handwritten in German, on plain paper with handwritten letterhead.
2   In the fall of 1940, during the early days of the London Blitz, the Kirsch family – consisting of James and Hilde with their son Thomas, Hilde's two sons from her first marriage, and James's daughter from his first marriage, sailed out of Liverpool on board the *Samaria* – a Cunard Liner from New York. They arrived safely in New York, but once there, due to a problem with their immigration papers, they were kept on Ellis Island, which at this time was run as a prison. By a lucky turn of fate, their whereabouts were noted in a newspaper article and they were found by one of Kirsch's oldest friends from Berlin. With help from Werner Engel (cf. Kirsch, 7 June 1954, p. 203 and note), they were freed and lived for two months on West 110th Street. They then moved to California by train, to settle in Los Angeles. (Thanks to Jim Silber and Ruth Kirsch for details of the family's move.) Cf. Jung, 6 January 1941, p. 96; cf. also Jung to Hilde Kirsch, 5 May 1941, Appendix B, p. 282.

I've had no direct news recently from Fräulein Rosenbaum[3] and Westmann[4] because the telephone connection was interrupted. But I've learned indirectly that they're both living in the country.[5]

With cordial greetings, Yours, JAMES KIRSCH

Prof. Dr. C. G. Jung
Küsnacht-Zürich
Seestrasse 228

6 January 1941[6]

Dr. James Kirsch
936 So. Windsor
Los Angeles, Calif.

Dear Colleague,

You're to be congratulated for getting out of the hell of London.[7] In Los Angeles you will surely have every opportunity to make your own way.[8] I hope you will succeed.

That one gets into the most difficult problematic through analysis has also become clear to me with the passing years. I have even found this to be quite logical. Thus a saying of Nietzsche's has been on my mind for many years: "You sought the heaviest burden and found yourself!" That says everything that's needed.

Please give your wife my best greetings, too.

With warm regards and wishes, Yours truly, C. G. JUNG

3 Probably Erna Rosenbaum, a Jungian analyst from Berlin. She had trained with Jung, who in 1931 sent Wolfgang Pauli to her for analysis (Deirdre Bair, *Jung: A Biography*, Boston, New York, London: Little, Brown & Co., 2003, p. 366). Later she fled Germany, settling in London (ibid., p. 504).

4 Probably Heinz Westmann (1902–1986), another Jungian analyst from Berlin. He and Kirsch were close friends, who helped each other to escape from Germany. Westmann, who had analyzed with Jung and attended meetings at Eranos, emigrated to Switzerland in 1935, then to London in 1937, where he co-founded the Society of Analytical Psychology. In 1955 he moved to New York, where he continued to practice and anglicized his name (Westman). He finally settled in Maine. His major publications include *The Springs of Creativity* (Routledge, Kegan and Paul, 1961) and The *Structure of Biblical Myths: The Ontogenesis of the Psyche* (Spring, 1984). (Cf. also Jung to Westmann, 12 July 1947, *Letters I*, p. 472.)

5 Kirsch guesses that, like many Londoners, these colleagues fled the city during the Blitz.

6 Typewritten in German, on letterhead.

7 Cf. Kirsch, 19 November 1940, p. 95 and note.

8 *"Ihren eigenen Weg mach[en] zu müssen"*: lit "to have to make your own way."

James Kirsch, M.D.
6120 Barrows Drive
Los Angeles 36, Calif.
Walnut 9229

25 November 1944[9]

Prf. C. G. Jung
Küssnacht-Zürich *[sic]*
Switzerland

Dear Prf. Jung:

I saw with great joy that it is again possible to write letters to Switzerland, and so I take the first opportunity to write to you and to let you know that Mrs. Kirsch and I are well.

In 1943 I went to New York and took there my Medical State Board examination.[10] My practice has been going well, Mrs. Kirsch sees some clients regularly, and we have been able to interest a number of people in Analytical Psychology. So we were able at last to found a Club[11] which has shown a small, but steady growth.

Last year and this year, we have had a "Seminar", in which I discussed a series of dreams.[12] It takes place every Wednesday evening and has contributed to interest the public in Analytical Psychology. Besides, I have given a Seminar on

---

9 Typewritten in English (front); handwritten in English and German (back), on one sheet of onion-skin paper. The letter is slightly water-damaged. Both sides are marked by the wartime censor with heavy diagonal marks, which occur in the same order on both sides: beige, pink, blue, gold, brown, gold. Despite these marks, the letter is legible, although portions of Hilde Kirsch's handwriting are faded. Kirsh's English is unedited in these letters.

10 For extended periods in 1942 and 1943 Kirsch lived in New York, leaving his family in Los Angeles. He had originally thought of settling in New York, but found he could not work with the leading analysts of the New York APC (cf. Kirsch, 19 November 1940, p. 95 and note). While in New York in 1942 he studied the Rorschach technique with Bruno Klopfer (cf. Kirsch, 18 November 1945, p. 102 and note) and explored medical licensure. He earned his New York State medical license in 1943. Since licensure proved difficult in California (cf. Kirsch, 10 December 1952, p. 152 and note; 17 March 1953, p. 162 and note), Kirsch periodically reconsidered moving to New York over the ensuing decades (cf. Jung, 12 February 1960, p. 260).

11 The Los Angeles APC was founded in 1944, with James Kirsch as its president. In 1953 the C. G. Jung Clinic was founded, and also the Society of Jungian Analysts of Southern California (cf. Kirsch, 17 March 1953, p. 162 and note; 9 May 1953, p. 169 and note). In 1967 the C. G. Jung Institute of Los Angeles was founded. Kirsch played a central role in organizing all three, and both he and Hilde Kirsch contributed actively to their programs.

12 In 1941 Kirsch held two series of evening seminars at his residence in Los Angeles (6621 Drexel Ave.), which he publicized as "Informal Lectures on Analytical Psychology." One series was titled, "The Importance of Dreams in our Personal Life" (printed announcement, 1941, Kirsch archive).

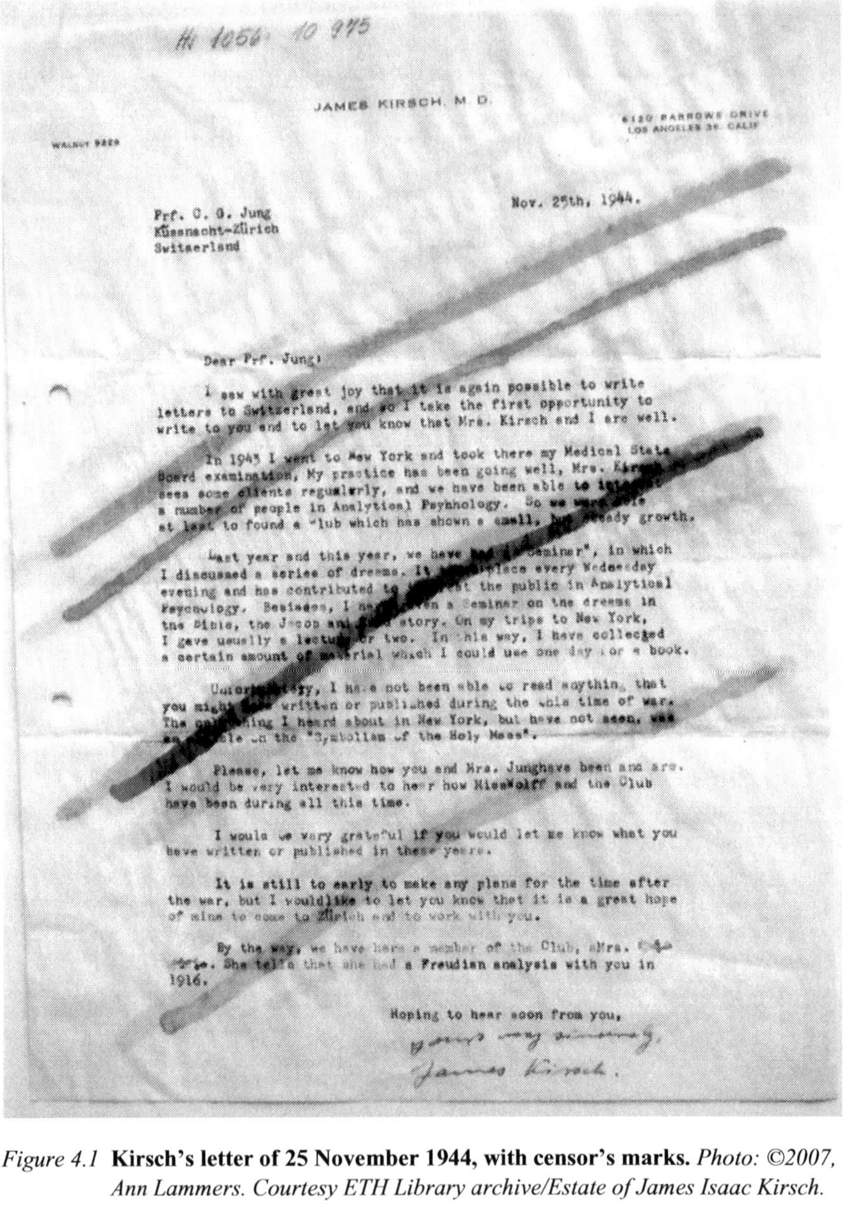

Figure 4.1 **Kirsch's letter of 25 November 1944, with censor's marks.** *Photo: ©2007, Ann Lammers. Courtesy ETH Library archive/Estate of James Isaac Kirsch.*

the dreams in the Bible, the Jacob and Esau story.[13] On my trips to New York, I gave usually a lecture or two.[14] In this way, I have collected a certain amount of material which I could use one day for a book.

Unfortunately, I have not been able to read anything that you might have written or published during this time of war. The only thing I heard about in New York, but have not seen, was an article on the "Symbolism of the Holy Mass".[15]

Please, let me know how you and Mrs. Jung have been and are. I would be very interested to hear how Miss Wolff and the Club have been during all this time.

I would be very grateful if you would let me know what you have written or published in these years.

It is still too early to make any plans for the time after the war, but I would like to let you know that it is a great hope of mine to come to Zürich and to work with you.

By the way, we have here a member of the Club, a Mrs. W[…].[16] She tells that she had a Freudian analysis with you in 1916.[17]

Hoping to hear soon from you, Yours very sincerely, JAMES KIRSCH

Hilde Kirsch's handwritten note, in German, on reverse side of Kirsch's letter:

Dear Prof. Jung

Having thought and wondered about you so much, I was so glad to hear, we can write again to Switzerland. Please, let us know how you all are, physically and psychologically. My best wishes for you all for Christmas and[18]

A happy beginning of 1945.[19]

Yours, HILDE KIRSCH

---

13 The other series of lectures was titled, "Dreams in the Old Testament: A study in religious psychology" (ibid.). From it Kirsch developed a two-week seminar which he taught at the New York APC in August 1943, "Seminar on the Pentateuch" (117-page typescript, compiled from listeners' notes; Kristine Mann Library archive, C. G. Jung Foundation of New York; hereafter KML archive).

14 Kirsch's lectures at the New York APC in this period included "The Nazi and his Significance in the Unconscious" (typescript, 20 November 1942, Kirsch archive) and "Balaam, A Myth" (APC Bulletin, Nos. XXII-XXIV, supplement; March 1943, KML archive).

15 C. G. Jung, "Das Wandlungssymbol in der Messe" [Transformation Symbolism in the Mass], *EJ 1940/41* (Zürich: Rhein Verlag, 1942). This lecture was also given to the Club, Zurich, 17 May 1941. English trans. by R. F. C. Hull in *The Mysteries: Papers from the Eranos Yearbooks, 2* (New York: Pantheon, 1955; London: Routledge & Kegan Paul, 1956); variant trans., CW 11, *Psych & Rel*, ¶296–448.

16 American Jungian psychotherapist, living in Los Angeles, who was only briefly a member of the Los Angeles APC. Name concealed in consideration of clinical confidentiality.

17 Cf. Jung, 3 August 1945, p. 100 and note.

18 Although Hilde wrote this note mainly in English, her closing follows the conventions of German letter-writing.

19 *Ein … froher [?] Anfang 1945.* The phrase is obscured by water damage. A space occurs after *"Ein,"* perhaps indicating a missing word. The next word is difficult to read; *"froher"* is a likely guess.

Prof. Dr. C. G. Jung
Küsnacht-Zürich
Seestrasse 228

3 August 1945[20]

Dr. James Kirsch
6120 Barrows Drive
Los Angeles 36
California

My dear Kirsch,

I received your letter of November 1944 with great delay but it really arrived. We didn't know then whether the mail from Switzerland to the U.S. worked equally well, so I waited until we had more definite proof that letters arrived.

In the meantime I reached my 70th birthday, for which I received in due time the congratulations of the Analytical Psychology Club of Los Angeles.[21] Beside my gratitude for your kind remembrance I was very interested in the fact that such a new club has sprung up in Los Angeles. Please convey my thanks to the members of the club whose president you are.

I thank you for the news of your letter which have interested me very much. Concerning your wish to know something about my publications since the war I enclose a list of them[22] and if something new should turn up I would send you a copy if possible.

There has been a Mrs. W[…][23] under my care in 1916, and if she says that she has had a Freudian analysis, then it is probably true.[24] I remember something of the kind. Our group in Zürich has flourished and never ceased its activities during the whole war. We passed through anxious times because we were twice immediately threatened by invasion and once it seemed to be inevitable,[25] but miraculously

---

20 Typewritten in English, on letterhead.
21 Cf. Kirsch, 25 November 1944, p. 97 and note.
22 Enclosure not found.
23 Cf. Kirsch, 25 November 1944, p. 99 and note.
24 For years after his bitter estrangement from Freud in 1913, Jung continued to do psychoanalysis with some of his patients, and to give credit to Freud when he did so.
25 In May 1940, when a German invasion was feared imminent, many citizens in unfortified parts of Switzerland – including the towns on the northern shore of Lake Zurich – took the advice of the federal government to evacuate to interior regions that were less threatened and more defensible. (cf. Edgar Bonjour, *Geschichte der Schweizer Neutralität: Vier Jahrhunderte Eidgenössischer Aussenpolitik*, Band IV: 1939–1945, Basel & Stuttgart: Helbig & Lichtenhahn, 1970, pp. 78–82). Jung and three generations of his family fled to Saanen, a small town in the Bernese Alps, where they lived for several months and where one of Jung's grandchildren was born. With thanks to Peter Jung and Ulrich Hoerni for reference and historical details.

enough we were spared. You can hardly imagine the devilish atmosphere in which we lived in Europe. It was psychically the hardest time I ever went through.

My birthday has brought me such a flood of letters that I cannot tell you more for the time being.

Please give my best regards to Mrs. Kirsch.

Sincerely yours, C. G. JUNG

James Kirsch, M.D.
6120 Barrows Drive
Los Angeles 36, Calif.
Walnut 9229

18 November, 1945[26]

Dear Dr. Jung:

I believe you can not imagine with what joy I received your letter of August 3rd, 1945. Since I wrote you my first letter after the war I had made a trip to New York, and there I heard that you had been ill.[27] Such news is always difficult to take, especially as nobody seemed to know exactly what you were suffering from, and frankly, it was a reason why I did not write to you before. In my mind I had written many letters to you, in which I told you many of the things which had happened since I saw you last, and discussed many questions which were uppermost in my mind. I like it very much here in Los Angeles, but one of the things I do not like about Los Angeles is that we are here rather isolated from any news about you and the life in Zürich. Lately, I had a letter from England mentioning your illness. It did not say whether it referred to an illness in 1944 or to something new. I do hope that you are well and continue working and writing.

A few weeks ago, I received your book "Psychology and Alchemy",[28] and I feel that I have been again in constant contact with you. For the last 3 years, I have been teaching here. The groups I have been teaching have grown all the time. Nevertheless, I have not been inclined to write a book, but feel that the time is approaching when I can do this.

---

26 Typewritten in English, on plain paper with stamped letterhead.
27 In February 1944 Jung's leg was broken, after which he suffered several embolisms and a heart attack. Cf. Jung, 25 July 1946, p. 107 and note.
28 Cf. Jung, 3 January 1936, p. 77 and note. Although Kirsch gives the title in English, at this date only the German-language Swiss edition had been published.

Besides my analytical work, Dr. Bruno Klopfer[29] has introduced me to the Rorschach Technique, and so about 1/3 of my work is now Rorschach work. It helped me to stay more in touch with general Psychiatry.

There is one more point I would like to mention in my letter to-day. I hear it again and again that you are a Nazi. It is such a ridiculous thing. In each case, I have been able to trace it to some Freudian, and it fits very well into the Freudian attempt to be considered the one and only form of depth-psychology. In each case I have been able to refute this insidious propaganda. But as you know it is very difficult to fight such a whispering campaign. Recently, a vile article has been published in the official organ of the American Psychiatric Association,[30] and maybe, this time we can kill this snake thoroughly. I do not know how you feel about it, but I feel that a public statement might do some good. I have not the original of your article of 1934,[31] on which all this propaganda is based. It would be wonderful if you could write something against this article in the "Journal", or if you would authorise me to make a statement.[32]

29 Bruno Klopfer, MD (1900–1971): German-born psychologist and psychotherapist, specializing in the Rorschach technique. A baptized Jew, he practiced in Berlin and analyzed with Gerhard Adler, until 1933 when he fled to Zurich. There he analyzed briefly with Neumann and Jung, before emigrating to New York in 1934. Klopfer taught at Columbia University for 12 years. In 1946 he moved to Los Angeles to teach clinical psychology at UCLA and at Claremont College. Kirsch saw Klopfer as a brilliant diagnostician, but primarily as a Freudian (J. Kirsch to E. Neumann, 6 December 1948, Kirsch archive), and for this reason vehemently opposed his application to the San Francisco MSAP (Medical Society of Analytical Psychology) and the Los Angeles APC (cf. Kirsch, 26 December 1948, pp. 121f, 27 June 1949, p. 125 and note; 2 July 1949, p. 126 and note; 5 August 1949, pp. 128f and note). In early 1950 Klopfer was accepted by the MSAP as a "psychotherapist with a Jungian orientation" (Kirsch to Wolff, 26 January 1950, Kirsch archive). After this Kirsch and Klopfer were reconciled (cf. Kirsch, 7 June 1954, p. 201), and Klopfer became an influential member of the Society of Jungian Analysts of Southern California (cf. Thomas B. Kirsch, *The Jungians: A Comparative and Historical Perspective*, London & Philadelphia: Routledge, 2000, pp. 98f; hereafter *Jungians*).

30 An article by S. S. Feldman, MD, in the *American Journal of Psychiatry* ("Dr. C. G. Jung and National Socialism, *Am. J. Psychiatry*, Vol. 102.2, September 1945, p. 263) had painted Jung as an anti-Semite and a defender of Hitler. Feldman opens with a quotation from Freud, in 1914, attributing to Jung "certain racial prejudices." Then he quotes from Jung's "Zur gegenwärtigen Lage der Psychotherapie" (cf. Kirsch, 7 May 1934, p. 42 and note) in his own translation, to suggest that in 1934 Jung felt "admiration" for the Nazi movement. Finally he quotes a statement by Jung, from a newspaper interview published on V E Day (C. G. Jung, "Nach der Katastrophe," *Neue Schweizer Rundschau* XIII, Zürich, 1945; cf. CW 10, ¶400–43), to the effect that the Nazis and their opponents should all repent equally for the war's atrocities.

31 "Zur gegenwärtigen Lage der Psychotherapie" (cf. Kirsch, 7 May 1934, p. 42 and note).

32 Jung's response to this query is missing. Apparently he declined to publish any refutation in the *Am. J. Psychiatry*, and asked his followers to refrain from defending him in print. Two defenders, however, Gerhard Adler and Ernest Harms, wrote letters to the journal (cf. Kirsch, 22 June 1946, p. 105 and note). Kirsch later wrote to a friend: "After Adler's article was published, Jung did not allow any of his followers to publish anything in his defense. He was of the opinion that whoever touches pitch will be defiled" (Kirsch to Ernst Simon, 19 June 1962, Kirsch archive).

I am planning to come to Zürich next year, that is as far as one can make such plans these days. I should like to know whether you believe that you will want to see patients next year, or whether you prefer to write. How anxious I am to see you is difficult to put on paper.

With my very best wishes, yours very sincerely, JAMES KIRSCH

James Kirsch, M.D.
6120 Barrows Drive
Los Angeles 36, Calif.
Walnut 9229

22 June 1946[33]

My dear Dr. Jung:

I have written you so many letters which were never mailed that, when it comes to sitting down at my desk and really writing down what I want to say other things come to the foreground. These letters which never reached [you] were gossipy or full of questions. I have been feeling very close to you during these last two years in the U.S. Lately, I have been dreaming a great deal about you. Usually, it was a scene in which you came to Los Angeles and gave a series of lectures. Sometimes I could catch a great deal of what this dream figure had to say, like in a lecture on the relationship between the Atom-bomb and the Osiris myth. In another dream, you had quite a lot of luggage. I offered to carry it, but when I did the figure changed into that of Elias[34] and the Eternal Jew. I am very much aware of these continuing changes of the "Old Wise Man", but I don't know somehow how to carry the heavy burden that is meant by it. At last, I received your latest books (Psych. and Alchemy,[35] Paracelsica[36]) and am deeply moved by it. To read your books is a wonderful "Zwiegespräch"[37] beyond time and space. I would like very much to come to Zürich and discuss as many things as possible with you. I understand you see few patients these days and give most of your time to writing for which I am deeply grateful. Please, let me know if you make plans to see patients next Spring (1947), and if so, could you make time for me?

33 Handwritten in English, on letterhead.
34 (German): Elijah.
35 Cf. Kirsch, 18 November 1945, p. 101.
36 C. G. Jung, *Paracelsica: Zwei Vorlesungen über den Arzt und Philosophen Theophrastus.* [Two lectures about the physician and philosopher Theophrastus], Zürich und Leipzig: Rascher, 1942. The two lectures are separately published in English: "Paracelsus the Physician," CW 15, *The Spirit in Man, Art and Literature,* ¶18–43; "Paraceslus as a Spiritual Phenomenon, CW 13, *Alchemical Studies,* ¶145–238.
37 "dialogue".

In our Club, we devote the last meeting of the year to read something out of your books which have not yet been published in English. This year, I read about $^3/_4$ of the preface to "Psych. and Alchemy". I had done the translation. The Club found my translation excellent, and I felt that I had given faithful account of what you had tried to say. So I was asked to do some more translating of your books. I understand "Psych. & Alchemy" has already been translated and will shortly be published in England. I was asked by several book sellers to tell you what the situation is here in the U.S. in respect of your books. They are constantly read in all libraries, and it's difficult to lend[38] them, because they are circulating so much. It is impossible to buy them if they were not printed here in the U.S. The reason for this is the fact that there is a great paper shortage in England, and only few copies are sent over here. I wonder whether you have any agreement with Rascher to have them printed in the U.S.? What could be done to have more copies of your books here?

I intended to send you a copy of what I have translated, but as the whole book has been translated I don't see much sense in sending it to you. If you would like me to do so I shall gladly send it to you. There are only 2 copies of it in existence, one my personal copy, and the other one in the Club library. So I hope I have not violated any copyrights.

What I should like to ask you is: Is there any of your later books which has not yet been translated into English, and for which no arrangements in respect of an English translation have been made? In case there are no such arrangements f.i. for Paracelsica and it is agreeable to you, I would like to do such a translation and arrange with an American publisher all the necessary details. The important thing would be to have it published by an American publishing house.

I enclose the letter and 3 articles[39] of a very interesting man. He is a Frenchman who has lived here for 25 years and is considered a leading Astrologer.[40] Besides he is a composer, poet and author of a number of philosophical books. He lacks a great deal of Earth, many things he says are "sublimations." He never had an analysis. Nevertheless, I find him very worthwhile. He publishes about 10,000 words a month, as he says, and quotes constantly from your books. For comparison, I would like to mention that Columbia University still teaches nothing but Behaviorism.

---

38   Kirsch seems to have substituted "lend" for "borrow." German uses one verb, *leihen*, for both.
39   Enclosures not found.
40   Dane Rudhyar (1895–1985): transpersonal astrologer, modernist composer and philosopher. Rudhyar was born in Paris as Daniel Chennevière. He moved to New York in 1916 and later settled in San Francisco, where he became influential in the New Age movement of the 1970s. As a student of Jung's psychology, Rudhyar interpreted astrology synchronistically rather than causally. Among his many published works, his first major publication on this topic is titled, *The Astrology of Personality* (1936).

It seems that Adler's and Harms' article[41] have done some good. I would like you to know that I completely agree – now – with the position you have taken[42] after the poisonous article appeared in the Am. Psy. Journal.

Hoping very much for *ein Wiedersehen*.[43]

Yours, JAMES KIRSCH.

To-morrow, I'll fly to Guatemala.[44]

5 July 1946[45]

Dear Prf. Jung:

At last, I have succeeded to come back to Guatemala. It is a strange experience to touch the old soil again. I have gone along old Maya trails as much as possible. The Indios hold on to their primitive religion, but do not give their secrets away to the white man.

You certainly know this old "calendar" stone.[46] It is amazing how simple their system is to use this mandala for calendar purposes. This calendar stone is valid for 52 years and includes Venus. It weighs many, many tons and has lain buried for several hundred years. Now it is in the Museum in Mexico. The face in the center speaks a strange and fascinating language.

With best wishes, Yours, JAMES KIRSCH

---

41 Two responses to Feldman's article (cf. Kirsch, 18 November 1945, p. 102 and note) appeared in the *American Journal of Psychiatry.* The editor of the journal, Gotthard Booth, criticized Feldman's translations (*Am. J. Psychiatry*, January 1946, Vol. 102.4, p. 555). Then, under "Correspondences," letters by Gerhard Adler and Ernest Harms were excerpted and summarized. Adler and Harms testify to Jung's character and criticize Feldman's mistranslations, pointing out his historical ignorance of the AAGP, the IAAGP, the *Zentralblatt,* and Jung's roles in each during the 1930s (*Am. J. Psychiatry,* March 1946, Vol. 102.5, pp. 702f). Kirsch later complained that "50% of [Adler's] article was cut out by the editors, and this 50% of course contained all the facts" (Kirsch to Ernst Simon, 19 June 1962, Kirsch archive).

42 Jung had asked his followers not to respond any more to published attacks (cf. Kirsch, 18 November 1945, p. 102, note 32).

43 a reunion.

44 Final line written sideways in left margin. Kirsch, who had become a US citizen in April 1946, made this trip with his son Thomas.

45 Handwritten in English, on plain onionskin.

46 Evidently a photograph or drawing was enclosed in the letter. This enclosure is unfortunately lost.

Prof. Dr. C. G. Jung
Küsnacht-Zürich
Seestrasse 228

25 July 1946[47]

Dr. James Kirsch
6120 Barrows Drive
Los Angeles 36
California

Dear Dr. Kirsch,

Thank you for your letters and for the reprints you have sent me, also for the calendar-stone which I knew already; it is a nice mandala.

My book about "Psychology and Alchemy"[48] will appear in England, but there is an arrangement with an American Editor who is going to publish it in America almost simultaneously. I want to call your attention to the Bollingen Series,[49] in which this book will appear together with other books of psychological interest.

I see from your letters that you have heard that foolish rumour that I'm a Nazi. If the Germans had invaded Switzerland they certainly would have put me into a concentration camp or against a wall. My books were suppressed in Germany and destroyed in France. If I had been a Nazi they surely wouldn't have behaved like that. Moreover whoever knows my psychology knows that I warned the world of the things that were preparing in Germany. This rumour has been started chiefly for the reason that my little book published by the Yale University Press, "Psychology and Religion",[50] had 5 editions during the war. Thus I came a little bit too much before the public mind for certain people who are not too happy about it.

---

47 Typewritten in English, on letterhead. When working with an English-speaking secretary, Jung often dictated in English (cf. Jung, 18 November 1952, p. 141 and note). Parts of this letter prev. pub. in *PP*.

48 Cf. Jung, 3 January 1936, p. 77 and note.

49 The Bollingen Series sponsored the publication of Jung's Collected Works, the *C. G. Jung Letters*, etc. Its work was underwritten by the Bollingen Foundation, founded in 1945. The official English translator for the series was R. F. C. Hull (cf. Jung, 28 November 1952, pp. 149f and notes). The concept for the foundation and series had been formed as early as 1941 by Mary Mellon (1904–1946), who was Editor-in-Chief until her early death. Initially the series was intended only to publish an English edition of Jung's collected writings, together with selected Eranos lectures. Later it included works by writers in related areas of humanistic scholarship (cf. *Letters I*, p. 283n). The Bollingen Foundation ceased activity in 1969, after making a grant to Princeton University Press, which continued the Bollingen Series for almost 30 years longer before declaring Jung's part of the series closed. For an insider's personal view, cf. William McGuire, *Bollingen, an Adventure in Collecting the Past*, Princeton University Press, 1982.

50 C. G. Jung, *Psychology and Religion*, New Haven: Yale University Press, 1938. Jung's Terry Lectures, written in English and delivered at Yale in 1937, were later somewhat revised and translated into German. A revised English version appears as the first part of CW 11, *Psych & Rel*, ¶1–168.

As there will be an arrangement made with the firm of Kegan Paul in London for a complete edition of my works the question of translations has already been more or less settled. There is an editorial committee that handles now this question. Thank you for your readiness to be of help. The next thing that will appear is "Psychology and Alchemy" and the "Essays on Contemporary Events".[51] After that my book on transference[52] will follow. This latter book is just about to appear in German. It is a book for Doctors and practical Psychologists.

My illness[53] has been a serious thing. I had a fracture of my right fibula with a big haematoma; on account of it a thrombosis developed in the right leg first and then it went over to the left leg, reaching as far as the vena cava. And then the worst came: two embolisms in the lungs and an embolism in the posterior part of the heart. That was the thing that almost knocked me out, but I recovered slowly. This was in February 1944. In the following two years I got slowly better and now I must say that this summer I feel ever so much stronger than last year. Mountain climbing is out of the question of course, but I can do some sailing instead which I enjoy very much. I'm now 71 years of age and I feel disinclined to do work with patients. I take on no new patients but of the old ones there are left enough to keep me busy. Moreover there are always thousands of other things which have to be done, but I try my best to cultivate leisure in the true Chinese style inasmuch as the world permits me to do so.

I shall write to Mr. Rudyar[54] personally. His reprints are quite interesting. I really had no idea that astrology would make so much of my psychology.

Hoping you are always in good health

I remain yours sincerely C. G. JUNG

---

51 C. G. Jung, *Aufsätze zur Zeitgeschichte*, Zürich: Rascher, 1946 (*Essays on Contemporary Events*, London: Kegan Paul, Trench, Trubner, 1947). The collection includes "Wotan" (1936) and several pieces from the 1940s: "Individual and Mass Psychology," "Psychotherapy Today," "Psychotherapy and a Philosophy of Life," and "After the Catastrophe." These essays, as well as Jung's Foreword and Epilogue, appear, in English translation, as sections of CW 10 and CW 16.

52 C. G. Jung, *Die Psychologie der Übertragung. Erläutert anhand einer alchemistischen Bilderserie. Für Ärzte und praktische Psychologen* [The Psychology of the Transference. Interpreted on the basis of a series of alchemical images. For physicians and practical psychologists] Zürich: Rascher, 1946 (hereafter *Transference*). Cf. CW 16, *The Practice of Psychotherapy*, Part 13: "The Psychology of the Transference," ¶353–539.

53 Cf. Kirsch, 18 November 1945, p. 101 and note. Jung recounts this close encounter with death, and the para-psychological visions which accompanied it, in "Visions," Chapter 10 of *Memories*. Another near fatal illness occurred in late 1946, when Jung suffered a heart attack (cf. *Jung–White Letters*, pp. 55–61).

54 Cf. Kirsch, 22 June 1946, p. 104 and note. No letter to Rudhyar is published in the *C. G. Jung Letters*.

James Kirsch, M.D.
6120 Barrows Drive
Los Angeles 36, Calif.
Walnut 9229

22 December 1946[55]

Dear Dr. Jung:

As usual, I have wanted to write to you and to thank you from the depth of my heart for your letter very often. You know that many letters remained unwritten, because my mind and my mind[56] are so occupied with you and your work. Your 2 latest books which I got hold of here, Psychology and Alchemy and Übertragung,[57] opened great vistas, are extremely helpful in my daily work with patients – and very much with myself. It is quite evident to me that you would understand me, the extraordinary events the analyst meets; I am so grateful for teaching me again and again patience and love with myself, my patients and friends. Certainly, I have seen changes and "cures" in patients which one can only call miracles.

I enclose a dream[58] of a woman of 33 y., Jewish, who suffered from extraordinary obsessive thoughts that her husband and child might be killed. She has seen a picture of you in my office, but has not read anything of your books yet. After 3 months of analysis, she has very few of those thoughts and is altogether much better adjusted to her particular conditions.

I believe you saw Dr. Harms'[59] article: "Carl Gustav Jung – Defender of Freud and the Jews."[60] I hope you did not mind that your letter to me from 1934[61] was partly reproduced in this article. I did not directly authorize Dr. Harms to publish this letter. I sent it to a committee which collected material in New York to refute the stupid accusation that you are a Nazi. I heard later that you stopped this

55 Handwritten in English, on letterhead.
56 Error in original, possibly for "heart."
57 Transference (i.e. *Psychology of the Transference*). Cf. Jung, 25 July 1946, p. 107 and note.
58 A dream text, written like a poem. The dreamer sees Jung as a rejected prophet and tells of a god-like figure, a "man-made man," embodying "the torture of the many long dead."
59 Ernest Harms, Dr. phil. (1895–1974): German-Jewish psychologist, educator and philosopher, then living in New York. After earning his doctorate in Würzburg in 1919, Harms studied further in Paris and London and at Harvard and Duke Universities in the United States. In 1936 he emigrated to New York, where he worked as a clinician and lecturer and directed child guidance clinics at Beth David and Grand Central Hospitals. He published *Hegel und das zwanzigste Jahrhundert* (1933); *Handbook of Child Guidance* (1947); *Awakening in Consciousness of Subconscious Collective Symbolism* (1947); *Origins of Modern Psychiatry* (1967), and many volumes on the treatment of children and adolescents.
60 Ernest Harms, "Carl Gustav Jung – Defender of Freud and the Jews: A chapter of European psychiatric history under the Nazi yoke," *Psychiatric Quarterly* Vol. XX, 1946, pp. 199–230. Although Harms and Kirsch had a friendly relationship, Harms was not a Jungian, a fact which gave his essay added weight.
61 Cf. Jung, 26 May 1934, pp. 44ff. Harms had translated Jung's letter to Kirsch and included it in his 1946 article without seeking copyright permission.

committee of the A.P.C. in N.Y. from answering those accusations.[62] But Dr. H. published it. I could not help being very glad that this wonderful letter of yours was published – and I hope it finds your belated consent.

To-day, I saw a letter by Heyer[63] to one of his former Jewish patients who lives here in Los Angeles. He was evidently hit in his guilt-complex by your article in the "Schweizer[64] Weltwoche." It is very sad to see that a psychologist is unable to face his shadow, his national shadow. It makes me very anxious about the German future. Is it easier for us because we are Jews? Or because we are farther away from Germany with its terrible mass psychology? It is certainly not easy to bear the Jewish shadow, and I certainly carried – and still do – a great deal of the German shadow. The influence of mass psychology is certainly tremendous here in the U.S. I have not seen a single German here who has accepted his collective guilt. I hope you have.

2 days ago, I became a grandfather.[65] So I am growing older too.

The situation has not yet changed here as far as your books are concerned. It is quite easy to find copies of "Psychology and Religion", "Modern Man",[66] but the "2 Essays"[67] are unobtainable, and we are certainly very anxious for your latest books.

I can understand so well that you do not see any new patients. There are certainly enough of the old ones, but it seems most important to me that you continue your writing. Your latest book on "Übertragung" is so alive and so personal that I feel very much like sitting in your study and talking to you and listening to you.

---

62   Cf. Kirsch, 22 June 1946, p. 105 and note.
63   Gustav Richard Heyer, Dr. med. (1890–1967): German psychiatrist and Jungian analyst, located in Munich. A trusted follower and close friend of Jung in the 1920s and 1930s, Heyer lectured at Eranos and taught at the Club. He headed a group of Jungian analysts, the Münchener Psychologischer Arbeitskreis (cf. Jung, 20 July 1931, p. 17, note 63) and practiced with his wife, Lucy Heyer, a body therapist specializing in relaxation therapy. Leaning toward National Socialism, Heyer joined Matthias Göring on the executive committee of the German section of the IAAGP (*Zentralblatt* VI.3, December 1933, p.141) and taught at the Göring Institute starting in October 1939 (G. R. Heyer to C. A. Meier, 14 July 1939, ETH Library archive). Once Heyer officially joined the Nazi Party, Jung gave up contact with him (his last known letter to Heyer is dated in 1941). Athough Heyer quit the Party again in 1944, Jung did not resume contact. Heyer's published work includes *Der Organismus der Seele* (1933) and *Reich der Seele* (1937).
64   No publication by this name exists. From context, Kirsch may have confused *Die Weltwoche* (a Zurich periodical) and *Neue Schweizer Rundschau*. Jung's "Nach der Katastrophe" [After the Catastrophe] was published in the latter (*Neue Schweizer Rundschau*, XIII.2, June 1945). (Cf. CW 10, ¶400–43.)
65   Kirsch's first grandchild, Kathleen Ruth Andersen (later Sprekelmeyer) was born 20 December 1946 to his daughter, Ruth Gabriele Kirsch, and Douglas Eugene Andersen.
66   C. G. Jung, *Modern Man in Search of a Soul* (trans. by W. S. Dell and Cary F. Baynes, orig. pub. New York: Harcourt Brace; London: Kegan Paul, 1933) comprises eleven papers by Jung, orig. in German, dating from 1928 through 1932. They are available in various volumes of the CW.
67   C. G. Jung, *Two Essays on Analytical Psychology* (trans. by H. G. and Cary F. Baynes, orig. pub. New York: Dodd, Mead; London: Baillière, Tindall & Cox, 1928): two long papers by Jung, orig. in German, from 1926 and 1928. Cf. CW 7, *Two Essays on Analytical Psychology*.

Much remains unsaid, dear Dr. Jung. The other day, a handreader looked into my hands and exclaimed: "Dr. Kirsch, this is strange, there have only been 2 influences in your life, your mother and a decisive one when you were 28 y."[68] Well, Dr. Jung, I want you to know how deeply obliged I am to you, and very grateful to have met you in every sense of the word.

I sincerely hope that you have completely recovered from your latest heart attack and can enjoy sailing and leisure in the true Chinese style.

Thank you so much, Yours very sincerely, JAMES KIRSCH

Probably from Marie-Jeanne Schmid:[69]

21 October 1947[70]

Dr. James Kirsch,
6120 Barrows Drive,
Los Angeles 36. Calif.

Dear Doctor,

Sincere thanks, also in Prof. Jung's name, for sending the photos. He found though that he looks a little strange in them.

Your greetings are most kindly reciprocated by Prof. and Mrs. Jung.

I am also sending you best regards and wishes!

[carbon copy unsigned]

---

68 Kirsch began working with Jung in 1929, when he was 28 years old.

69 Marie-Jeanne Schmid (later Boller-Schmid), daughter of Hans Schmid-Guisan, MD, a pupil and friend of Jung's (cf. Jung, 23 May 1932, p. 27 and note). She became Jung's private secretary in 1932 and served in that capacity until her marriage in 1952. Working in close cooperation with Jung for 20 years, she was entrusted with confidential matters of all sorts and came to know many of Jung's friends and colleagues on a personal basis. Other secretaries also worked briefly for Jung during this period, so an unsigned letter is hard to assign with certainty. Based on style this letter appears to be hers. It is published with the kind permission of her estate.

70 Typewritten in German, on plain paper. No signature on carbon copy.

1948–1949

THE INSTITUTE

Prof. Dr. C. G. Jung
Küsnacht-Zürich
Seestrasse 228

7 July 1948[1]

Dr. James Kirsch
6120 Barrows Drive
Los Angeles 36
Calif.

Dear Dr. Kirsch,

This is to introduce to you Mr. Henry L. Drake[2] who has done some very intensive studies here in Zürich both privately and at the Institute.[3] He wants to continue his studies in California and I would like to recommend him to your benevolence. I shall be grateful for any help you can give him.

Yours sincerely, C. G. JUNG

James Kirsch, M.D.
6120 Barrows Drive
Los Angeles 36, Calif.
Walnut 9229

16 September 1948[4]

Dear Prf. Jung:

Mrs. Mary Crile[5] is a member of our Los Angeles Psychological Club and a very close friend of my family. She has been doing Rorschach work at the Los

---

1 Typewritten in English, on letterhead.
2 Henry L. Drake, PhD (1906–1978): American philosopher and analytical psychologist, who went to Zurich and studied at the newly founded C. G. Jung Institute (cf. Kirsch, 21 September 1948, p. 116). Drake later co-authored a two-year correspondence course, "The Basic Ideas of Man" (1953–54). He wrote *The People's Plato* (1958), and edited *Plato's Complete Works* (1959).
3 The C. G. Jung Institute, Zurich, was founded in spring 1948. Kirsch gave a five-week seminar there the following May and June. Cf. Kirsch, 21 September 1948, p. 116, notes 21, 22.
4 Handwritten in English, on half-sheet letterhead.
5 Mary Webb Crile (1890–1968): English-born psychologist, who emigrated to the United States in 1923. She analyzed with James Kirsch in New York in the early 1940s, then moved to Los Angeles and studied the Rorschach technique with Dr. Bruno Klopfer. She first met with Jung in the summer of 1948 and attended lectures at the Jung Institute, Zurich. She was also present at the Constitutional Meeting of the IAAP in Zurich, July 1955. Upon retirement she moved to Big Sur, and she died in Carmel, California.

Angeles Board of Education, having received her training from Dr. Bruno Klopfer in this field.

I should be very happy if time and circumstances would permit you to receive her.

Yours very sincerely, JAMES KIRSCH

James Kirsch, M.D.
6120 Barrows Drive
Los Angeles 36, Calif.
Walnut 9229

21 September 1948[6]

Dear Dr. Jung,

More than a year has already gone by since I saw you. Very often during the past year I wanted to write you but was always waiting for a quiet afternoon to write you a long epistle. But it seems there is "no peace for the wicked."[7]

Now I've received your letter recommending Mr. Drake to my "benevolence,"[8] and I would like to write to you. I can really say without exaggeration that I'm thinking of you very often, and the unconscious continues to present encounters between you and me in dreams. Generally speaking, these dreams are much less exciting than they used to be because, fortunately, no difficulty between you and me ever comes up in these dreams; and the last dream even confirmed explicitly that the images of the starry sky can now detach themselves from you. All in all I've been doing very well this year, and friends and patients have been saying that I look different and work differently now.

I thoroughly read Steward Edward White's[9] book twice, and am just as "puzzled"[10] as before. I did not let myself be disturbed by his quasi-journalistic style and a peculiar breeziness – or should one say: frivolity?[11] – with which

---

6 Typewritten in German, on letterhead.
7 Phrase orig. in English.
8 Word orig. in English.
9 = Stewart Edward White (1873–1946): American journalist, novelist and author, living in California. He wrote many novels and non-fiction works, one of the most famous being *The Betty Book: Excursions into the World of Other-Consciousness* (1937/1943/1977), a record of his wife's statements during spiritist trances. White and his wife became full trance mediums in the 1920s. His book *The Unobstructed Universe* (New York: E. P. Dutton, 1940) was later published in German as *Uneingeschränktes Weltall* (Zürich: Origo, 1948), with a foreword by C. G. Jung (cf. CW 18.6). It is to this work that Kirsch probably refers.
10 Word orig. in English.
11 A play on words: *Leichtigkeit* ("breeziness") and *Leichtfertigkeit* ("frivolity").

he says these things. I found many things therein, which I also rediscovered in dreams. The more deeply and intensively I study the unconscious, the more enigmatic it becomes.

In your speech at the opening of the Institute[12] I noticed a comment, that the investigation of pre- and post-mortal phenomena should be continued.[13] In regard to post-mortal, I can only imagine that you are thinking of phenomena which emerge from the unconscious of the living, and concern phenomena and persons that have already died. For many years I've observed such things, and have occasionally also spoken about the psychology of "ghosts."[14]

I'm enclosing a dream of a 22-year-old young person who worked with me two years ago.[15] I discussed this dream in detail in a seminar, but was in no way specific about its connection. I thought it was possible to give a psychological explanation referring almost entirely to this side, as it were; but I also indicated that some very different things could play a role here, a para-psychological phenomenon. The grandfather, who represented the father for this young man, died when the boy was six years old. It was a severe trauma for this boy and caused a hole, or a particularly thin spot. As a result of this trauma the young man is subject to very severe depressions – he calls them "yellow feeling"[16] – which render him unfit to work and prevent him from finding a lifetime career goal. When this dream occurred, he was somewhat conscious of the problem which the personal grandfather represented for him, but he hardly grasped the more general matter of death and of intrusions from a completely different world. Shortly before this dream, there was a dream in which a girl follows him, then he follows her; but when he actually faces her, he is filled with disgust and places a wire grate between himself and her.

---

12 C. G. Jung-Institut Zürich (also named, from the beginning, Institute for Analytical Psychology, Institut de Psychologie Analytique, and Institut für Komplexe Psychologie) was founded on 24 April 1948. For the first several years, classes were held at Gemeindestrasse 27, the large townhouse which still houses the Club. Jung's address at the founding of the institute appears in CW 18, *The Symbolic Life*, ¶1129–1141.

13 Mentioning future developments which might occur in the field of analytical psychology, Jung remarks in his address on "a dearth of fully elaborated case histories." In the same paragraph he points to the value of exploring "pre- and post-mortal psychic phenomena" (CW 18, ¶1138). Kirsch thus offers to teach a seminar at the Institute (cf. note 21 below) that may contribute toward both these ends.

14 Word orig. in English.

15 The text of the enclosed dream (typewritten, in English) opens with the dreamer's visit to a submarine, "manned by boys," which narrowly escapes being torpedoed thanks to the dreamer's prompt responses. Next come a school of jumping fish, which turn out to be the spirits (ghosts) of those buried at sea. One of these tells the dreamer how difficult it is for the ghost of a man to join with that of a woman. Finally a boy, fishing from the deck, catches a fish which turns out to be the ghost of an injured dog. Jung gives a full response to this dream (30 September 1948, pp. 119f).

16 Phrase orig. in English.

As you see, all these things are very unclear to me. I often reflect on our conversation about these topics in Bollingen. Dr. Kuenkel[17] told me that he has corresponded with you about Stewart Edward White.[18] I hope very much that someday you may write an article or a book about it. I could ask you many questions about this. My thinking on these matters isn't crystallizing yet.

With great joy we heard that the Institute has been founded. I hear from Mr. Drake that it's developing well and surprisingly quickly. The strict conditions stipulated by the Institute for the granting of diplomas have had an excellent effect here. Very soon I hope to hear from the institutes[19] in New York and San Francisco as to how we can collaborate.[20]

My wife and I are planning to come to Zurich next spring and to participate as auditors in the work of the Institute. If it is possible within the framework of the Institute, I would very much like to give a seminar about a series of dreams by the young man mentioned above.[21] I'll write about this to Dr. Meier,[22] too, who I believe is the appropriate channel.

17 Fritz Künkel, Dr. med. (1889–1956): German psychiatrist and psychotherapist, living in Los Angeles. Having trained with Alfred Adler in Vienna, Künkel (anglicized spellings: Kuenkel, Kunkel) practiced in Berlin from 1924 on, where he began to develop his own school of psychology, combining Adler, Freud, and Jung. From 1928 to 1935 Künkel published a six-volume work on character development, of which the major title was *Vitale Dialektik: Theoretische Grundlagen der individualpsychologischen Charakterkunde* [Vital Dialectic: Theoretical Foundations of the Study of Character in Individual Psychology] (1929). After the Nazi regime came to power, Künkel served on the faculty of the Göring Institute. His most famous work, *Wir-Psychologie* [We-Psychology], appeared in 1939. Finding himself in Los Angeles on a lecture tour at the outbreak of war in Europe, he stayed and founded The Fritz Kunkel School of We-Psychology, offering psychological training for ministers and theological students. In 1941 Kirsch attended a seminar of Kunkel's in Ojai, California (typed student list, 17 August 1941, Kirsch archive).

18 Referenced above, p. 114 and note.

19 The word may be an error. At the time of this letter, neither the New York nor the San Francisco Jungians had officially founded an institute. The C. G. Jung Institute of New York was founded in 1962, and that of San Francisco in 1964. The C. G. Jung Institute of Los Angeles followed in 1967. Earlier starting dates are sometimes cited for each, in view of the fact that each community had begun training analysts and established standards for such training decades before an institute formally existed.

20 From the beginning, collaboration between the Los Angeles community and those in New York and San Francisco required negotiation, as they differed in their prevailing understandings of Jungian theory and practice (cf. Kirsch, 7 June 1954, pp. 199f, note 77).

21 In summer 1949 Kirsch taught a five-week German-language seminar at the Institute, starting 30 May and meeting weekly for five weeks in two-hour sessions. Open also to members and guests of the Club, it was advertised as a course in *"Kasuistik"* [case study], being an examination of two clinical cases, one featuring rich imagery, with an opportunity to discuss para-psychological problems (announcement letter, signed "Das Curatorium," 23 May 1949, Kirsch archive).

22 C. A. (Carl Alfred) Meier, Dr. med. (1905–1995): Swiss psychiatrist and Jungian analyst, professor of psychology at the ETH, whose published works include *Jung's Analytical Psychology and Religion* (1959, 1977); *The Meaning and Significance of Dreams* (1987, 1990); *A Testament to the Wilderness* (1985); and *Atom and Archetype: The Pauli/Jung Letters 1932–1958* (PUP, 2001), which he edited at the end of his life (orig. title: *Wolfgang Pauli und C. G. Jung: Ein Briefwechsel*

Unfortunately I haven't made much progress with my own writing. At the College of Medical Evangelists I gave a lecture to several hundred physicians on the subject of "The Role of Instinct in Psychosomatic Medicine"[23] and was pleased that two journals wanted to print it. It will actually be published in November.[24] An article titled "From Hollywood to the Shores of the Spirit,"[25] dealing with the development of intellectual creativity, will be published in November.[26] I feel greatly inspired to write but, again and again, find it difficult to resist the demands of my practice and to find time for writing. The seminar which I gave last winter was written down for the most part word for word. It would be the material for a book. I'm very curious to find out what else has to happen, for me to sit down and write. The indications coming from all sides are pointing to a greater participation in collective life than with individual patients.

Mr. Drake reported to us that you were ill in June. I hope very much that you're fully recovered and back at work.

We sorely miss your books in English translations. I hope that the publication of the Collected Works will commence soon. "Die Symbolik des Geistes"[27] was announced for January, but so far I haven't been able to obtain it.

With many cordial greetings to you, your wife, and Fräulein Schmidt,[28]

Faithfully yours, JAMES KIRSCH

1932–1958, Berlin/Heidelberg: Springer-Verlag, 1992). For decades a close friend and confidant to Jung, with whom he had analyzed in the late 1920s, Meier served as General Secretary of the IAAGP in 1933–40. He was also the first vice-president of the Zurich Institute and worked closely with Jung in many other undertakings. In the 1950s Kirsch analyzed with Meier, and they also carried on an active correspondence (Meier usually signing with his nickname, Fredy). Meier visited Los Angeles in late 1954 to travel and to teach (cf. Kirsch, 1 January 1954, p. 187 and note; 27 November 1954, p. 209 and notes).

23 Title orig. in English.

24 James Kirsch, "The Role of Instinct in Psychosomatic Medicine," *American Journal of Psychotherapy,* Vol. III, No. 2, 1 April 1949. The paper is a revision of Kirsch's lecture at the sixth Congress of the AAGP, Dresden, 1931 (cf. Jung, 2 June 1930, p. 9, note 23).

25 Title orig. in English.

26 Kirsch read this paper to the APC of Los Angeles on 12 November 1948. Slightly revised, it appeared as "Dreams of a Movie-Maker" in *Spring 1950,* APC of New York, Inc.

27 C. G. Jung, Die Symbolik des Geistes: Studien über Psychische Phänomenologie [Symbolism of the Spirit: Studies on psychic phenomenology] (Psychologische Abhandlungen 6, Zürich: Rascher, 1948), with contribution by Rivkah Schärf (cf. Jaffé, 22 November 1952, p. 145 and note) (hereafter Symbolik).

  Symbolik never appeared as a whole in English. Jung's essays appear in various volumes of the CW: "On the Phenomenology of the Spirit in Fairy Tales" (CW 9(i)); "The Spirit Mercurius" (CW 13); "A Psychological Approach to the Dogma of the Trinity" and "On the Psychology of Eastern Meditation" (CW 11). "On the Phenomenology of the Spirit in Fairy Tales" is also Part I of *Spirit and Nature: Papers from the Eranos Yearbooks* (New York: Pantheon, 1954; London: Routledge & Kegan Paul, 1955).

28 = Marie-Jeanne Schmid (cf. unsigned letter of 21 October 1947, p. 110 and note).

6120 Barrows Drive
Los Angeles 36, Calif.
Walnut 9229

29 September 1948[29]

Dear Dr. Jung,

Please allow me to add a few points which I forgot to mention in my earlier letter.

Dr. I. J. Dunn,[30] a young Jewish psychiatrist and a student of mine, will be coming to Zurich to work with Frl. Wolff and Dr. Meier and to audit lectures at the "Institute." He has his inferiority-complexes, as a Jew and an osteopath, but he is a very promising young man.[31] I would be very pleased if you could receive him at some time.[32]

Mrs. Mary Crile,[33] an English lady with all the attributes of the English national character, but who has been living in the United States for the past 26 years and is a charter member of our Club, will be coming to Zurich and would like to deliver our greetings to you. I hope you'll be able to see her for a brief time.

Then I would like to draw your attention to a dreadful mistake in translation. On page 115 of "Aufsätze zur Zeitgeschichte,"[34] "nigger"[35] is used as a translation of "Neger."[36] Here you are not speaking at all of the American Negro. But "nigger" identifies you with the attitude of the "Deep South."[37]

With cordial greetings,[38] Faithfully yours, JAMES KIRSCH

---

29 Handwritten in German, on half-sheets of letterhead.
30 I. Jay Dunn, D. O. (d. 1970): American-born osteopath and one of the early Jungian analysts in Los Angeles. Having been Kirsch's patient, he became his friend and colleague. In 1949 Dunn shared office space with James Kirsch and Max Zeller (Kirsch to Wolff, 27 February 1949, Kirsch archive). With his wife, Dunn was an active member of the Los Angeles APC, where in October 1960, as a training analyst, he presented a four-hour seminar, "The Psychology of Primitives" (printed announcement, Kirsch archive). The C. G. Jung Institute of Los Angeles lists him as its president, 1958–60.
31 Final clause orig. in English.
32 A hole in the paper obscures the word *ihn* ("him").
33 Cf. Kirsch, 16 September 1948, p. 113 and note.
34 C. G. Jung, *Essays on Contemporary Events,* trans. Elizabeth Welsh (London, 1947).
35 Word orig. in English.
36 Negro. At the time, *Neger* was still a neutral term in German, used generally for dark-skinned peoples (of whom few were seen in Central Europe until after the second World War). Usage has since changed; the word is now avoided. In his translation of the referenced passage, Hull uses the phrase, "the colored races" (cf. "After the Catastrophe," CW 10, ¶431, p. 211).
37 Phrase orig. in English.
38 Closing written in left margin, sideways to text.

30 September 1948[39]

Dr. James Kirsch,
6120 Barrows Drive,
Los Angeles 36,
California

Dear Colleague,

Many thanks for your detailed news. It would certainly be of great interest for the Institute to hear one of your seminars. Recently Dr. Adler gave one which was highly valued.

The case of the young man you mention is interesting. The dream of the torpedo shows that an attack is being planned by the unconscious, or even that it is taking place. He has a negative attitude toward this activated content of the unconscious. Therefore it assumes a dangerous form (torpedo). What is intended however is a unification of the unconscious content with consciousness. In the next part of the dream there are now fish, which are well-known symbols of the contents of the unconscious. These fish are, as now becomes evident, ghosts.[40] The dream is very explicit in this respect, and so this hypothesis should be accepted, for "ghost" signifies a special characterization of a content which, due to the possibility that ghosts exist, should initially and cautiously be interpreted in no other way. At best we could speak of "contents of the unconscious," but these could be expressed just as well by either fish or torpedo. Therefore I would assume here that, indeed, something like "ghost" is meant. The last part of the dream is even more positive, in that the young man is no longer attacked by the fish, but catches it. The fish turns out to be a disguised dog, which is wounded. The dog represents the instinct accompanying Man who, in the case of the dreamer, is wounded. This wounding needs to be brought into connection with the torpedo attack. Thus he is injured in his instinctual sphere by, as one might say, a ghostly[41] attack. If the disturbance to his instinct can be healed through analysis, the ghostly attack will cease, from which it will then be concluded (wrongly) that the cause had been a common neurotic disturbance. If we look at the dream in a literal sense, however, the

---

39 Typewritten in German, on plain paper (unsigned carbon copy). Handwritten notation to the right of Kirsch's typed address: *Traumdeutung* [dream interpretation].

40 *Geister:* alternate translation, "spirits." The dream text to which Jung refers, enclosed in Kirsch's letter of 21 September, concerns the ghosts of "men who have been buried at sea and are all dead" (cf. Kirsch, 21 September 1948, p. 115). In his letter (written in German) discussing this dream text, Kirsch deliberately inserts the English word "ghosts" rather than the more ambiguous *Geister* (cf. Jung, 20 February 1932, p. 24 and note). An unpublished English version of this portion of Jung's letter (apparently made by Kirsch for his 1949 seminar at the Zurich Institute) straddles the alternatives, routinely rendering *Geister* as "spirits (ghosts)" and *geisterhaft* as "spiritual (ghostly)." (Cf. typescript, "Translation of Excerpt of Letter by Prof. Dr. C. G. Jung to Dr. James Kirsch dated September 30, 1948," Jung–Kirsch correspondence, ETH Library archive.)

41 *geisterhaft:* ghostly. Alternate translation: spiritual.

original cause was a ghostly activity which injured the dreamer's unconscious. But by this means the reality of the ghostly *agens*[42] is not got rid of. Thus analysis only integrates the effect of this attack, and with that fulfils the latter's purpose. One could say, for example, the grandfather wanted his grandson to make the spiritual progress which he was not able to achieve. I have seen quite a number of such cases and learned from them that we are the continuation of the lives of our ancestors, and we have to complete the tasks which the ancestors left unfinished.

With best greetings, *[carbon copy unsigned]*

James Kirsch, M.D.
6120 Barrows Drive
Los Angeles 36, Calif.
Walnut 9229

15 November 1948[43]

Dear Professor!

My most heartfelt thanks for your prompt response to my letter and for the wonderful analysis of the dream which the young man had about the dead. It explained a lot which I had not understood before. However, I prefer not to write in detail about it now since I'll be in Zurich for two months next year (Deo concedente), and I hope to have an opportunity then to speak with you about this and other things at greater length.

With cordial greetings I remain, Faithfully yours,[44] JAMES KIRSCH

James Kirsch, M.D.
6120 Barrows Drive
Los Angeles 36, Calif.
Walnut 9229

27 November 1948[45]

Dear Dr. Jung,

In the enclosure I am taking the liberty of sending you a copy of a lecture I recently gave at the Los Angeles Analytical Psychology Club.[46]

---

42   agent.
43   Typewritten in German, on half-sheets of letterhead.
44   Closing handwritten.
45   Handwritten in German, on half-sheets of letterhead.
46   Enclosure missing. Kirsch's lecture was titled "From Hollywood to the Shores of the Spirit" (cf. Kirsch, 21 September 1948, p. 117 and note).

At this time many topics are swirling around in my head. I hope that one day something suitable for publication will emerge from my work.

With cordial greetings, and hoping that you are in good health,

Faithfully yours, JAMES KIRSCH

James Kirsch, M.D.
6120 Barrows Drive
Los Angeles 36, Calif.
Walnut 9229

26 December 1948[47]

Dear Dr. Jung:

Today I would like to write to you about a matter which has been troubling me for some time, and that I actually wanted to discuss with you when I'm in Zurich next May. But it cannot wait that long.

It's about Dr. Bruno Klopfer.[48] He has helped me a lot in many ways. For instance, I am indebted to him for my whole training in the Rorschach test. He motivated me to earn my American M.D. degree in New York. Now, about a year ago, he's come to Los Angeles, and he has become a problem for us, i.e. the Club. It began when, even though he had been a member of the New York Club for many years, he refused to join our Club as a member. Nevertheless he regularly came to each of our meetings. The reasons he gave to the then president of our Club were that he cannot endanger his academic career by membership in a Psychological Club composed mostly of non-professional members.

Simultaneous with this somewhat ambiguous attitude toward the Club, he supports you very courageously at the university and in all his courses. On the other hand, one notices that in fact he has only a slight and superficial knowledge of your teaching and your books. His Rorschach analyses move almost exclusively along Freudian lines.

In discussions with him it is almost impossible to get to any factual material. Such conversations rarely go beyond the level of personal, psychological "gossip."[49] He is very active in academic life, always participates in organizing something, "has his finger in every pie".[50] At the same time, one has the impression that he's not at all interested in the project, except as it's useful to him. In this way he is casting a wide shadow and has provoked great resistance.

---

47 Handwritten in German, on letterhead.
48 Cf. Kirsch, 18 November 1945, p. 102 and note; 16 September 1948, p. 113.
49 Word orig. in English.
50 Saying orig. in English.

My affect about him was considerable, so I knew I had projected something onto him. Some time ago I also had a dream that he authored an illustrated book. The pictures were not exactly "projective material"[51] but showed the entrance of the Children of Israel into Palestine (antiquity) in almost photographic clarity.

So for a time I withdrew from him, to work through my affect *about* him internally. Now I feel completely free of affect toward him. As things sometimes happen, two individuals, one from New York and one from here, told me similar stories about him, i.e. that he is pressuring and influencing people for reasons which may be plausible but which always evoke suspicion.

We, i.e. various members of the Club, thus have the impression that he has hardly had any analysis and falls short of what we expect an analyst to be.

In addition, he has recently been training a lady as an analyst (supposedly as a Jungian analyst) whom none of us who know her consider qualified to become an analyst.

You see how difficult my position is. On one hand, I am personally indebted to him. I recognize his great psychological ability, which certainly has a touch of genius as far as diagnosis is concerned. His achievement in connection with Rorschach and other "projective techniques"[52] is really impressive. Where there is much light, there is also much shadow.

The difficulty begins at the point where he presents himself as an analyst and claims to be a representative of the Zurich orientation.[53]

Fortunately the Zurich Institute has now established clear guidelines as to when someone is qualified to be called an analyst. But how are things to be handled with respect to those who qualified before the foundation of the Institute?

I have tried to present to you the case of Dr. Klopfer as clearly as possible in a letter, and have also described my involvement with him. May I ask you how long he worked with you? Did you recognize him as an analyst? Did you recognize him as a "training analyst"?[54]

By the way, I forgot to mention in my earlier letters that I sent you Graves's book The White Goddess[55] which may be of interest to you on account of the enormous amount of mythological material it contains.

Recently I also sent you a few copies of the *Psychiatric Quarterly* because it contains a number of essays by Freudian analysts who reported on telepathic

---

51 Phrase orig. in English.
52 Phrase orig. in English.
53 *ein Vertreter der Züricher Richtung.* In addition to tensions of long standing between Jungian and Freudian schools of depth psychology, additional lines of tension had emerged within the worldwide Jungian community between what came to be called a "Zurich" (or archetypal) and a "London" (or developmental) orientation (cf. Jung, 12 November 1959, p. 250, note 22).
54 Phrase orig. in English.
55 Robert Graves (1895–1985): English poet, translator, novelist. One of his most famous publications, *The White Goddess* (London: Faber & Faber, 1948) is a historical study of poetic inspiration. Kirsch quotes extensively from this work in his essay, "Dreams of a Movie-Maker" (orig. "From Hollywood to the Shores of the Spirit"), *Spring 1950* (op. cit.), pp. 67f.

dreams and discussed them. If they observe such phenomena, one day they may also realize that the unconscious is something other than a receptacle for repressions.

With cordial greetings, Faithfully yours, JAMES KIRSCH

Pension Tiefenau
Steinwiesstr. 8
Zch 32

28 May 1949[56]

Dear Professor Jung,

It was a surprise and a little bit of a "shock"[57] when you told me that you wanted to come to my seminar.

During my afternoon with you, I was able to rid myself of my projection of the "mana" personality on you to such an extent that my inferiority-complexes are no longer obstructing my path, and I can tell you that I would be *very* pleased if you would come.

My secret, but nonetheless avowed, desire in giving such a seminar in Zurich, is to learn as much as possible from the case.[58]

With cordial greetings, Faithfully yours, JAMES KIRSCH

56 Handwritten in German, on plain paper, with sender's address handwritten at lower left.
57 Word orig. in English.
58 Cf. Kirsch, 21 September 1948, p. 115 and note. The case concerned a young man who had dreamed of spirits (ghosts) in the form of fish, representing those buried at sea. Cf. also Kirsch, 21 June 1949, p. 124.

Pension Tiefenau
Steinwiesstr. 8
Zch. 32

21 June 1949[59]

Dear Professor!

In my seminar yesterday I spoke of post-mortal phenomena and also briefly mentioned "Hamlet."[60] Next time it will be the big, long dream which I sent you a few months ago, and about which you were kind enough to send me a commentary.[61] It would be my great pleasure if you would do me the honor of coming to the seminar next Monday. Frau Jokl[62] will discuss the dream, and I asked her to limit herself to 15 minutes.

Here in Zurich I feel I'm receiving many rich gifts, especially from you personally. Thus it seems presumptuous to ask you to see me one more time. I know how enormously your time is in demand, but hope that you may be able to spare another $^1/_2$ hour to see me, possibly toward the end of the semester.

Might I perhaps come by this Thursday and read the Morienus[63] in a corner of your house? If the weather is good, in the garden?

With cordial greetings, Faithfully yours, JAMES KIRSCH

---

59 Handwritten in German, on plain paper, with sender's address handwritten at top left.

60 Kirsch's notes for the seminar session of 20 June 1949, four pages handwritten on onionskin, show that he used material from several sources in addition to Shakespeare's *Hamlet*, including alchemical works, dream material, and writings by Jung and C. A. Meier. He assigned a student to lecture briefly at each session. A line in his notes reads: *"Baynes*: the ghost as psychol. phenomenon" (undated holograph, Kirsch archive). Deborah Wesley, archivist at the C. G. Jung Institute of Los Angeles, kindly supplied this document.

61 Cf. Jung, 30 September 1948, pp. 119f and note.

62 Anna Maria Jokl, a student at the Jung Institute. Writing from 33 Plattenstrasse, she sends the notes for her brief presentation, asks for Kirsch's comments, and promises to stay within the time limit. Her letter ends, "Will anyone at all come on Monday, since Prof. Kerényi's lecture is awkwardly scheduled for the same evening?" (Jokl to Kirsch, 24 June 1949, Kirsch archive; trans. ACL).

63 Two-part volume on alchemy by Morienus Romanus, *Artis Aurifer, Volumina II*, Basel: Conrad Waldkirch, 1593. The fat, leather-bound book is still found in Jung's library. Pasted into its flyleaf is an illustrated bookplate with a hand-lettered epigram: *"Mors mortis morti mortem mors morte redemit"* [The death of death by death; death has redeemed death through death] (trans. suggested by Richard Corney). Cf. Lee Stavenhagen, "The Original Text of the Latin Morienus," *Ambix*, vol. 17, 1970, pp. 1–12; cf. also *A Testament of Alchemy*, ed. and trans. by Lee Stevenhagen, Hanover, NH: University Press of New England, 1974. (English-language references kindly provided by Dr. Alfred Ribi.)

Pension Tiefenau
Steinwiesstr. 8
Zürich 32
27 June 1949[64]

Dear Professor Jung:

Thank you very much for your kind invitation to tea on Thursday which I accept with the greatest pleasure.

I understand that you are awfully busy these days. It seems only natural that I shall not see you alone even for a few minutes. But may I submit the enclosed letter[65] to you and ask your help in my struggle to prevent Dr. Klopfer from being recognised as a training analyst by the San Francisco group of the M.S.A.P. (Medical Society of Analytical Psychologists)?[66] Address same as Joseph Wheelwright, M.D.[67] I should be very grateful if you would back me up by writing a letter to the M.S.A.P.

In my seminar last night, I did not discuss the question of what the dead mean in the patient's dream. I postponed it in the faint hope that you might find it possible to come next Monday. Your vacation is more important however.

Yours, JAMES KIRSCH

---

64   Handwritten in English, on plain paper, with sender's address handwritten at upper left.

65   Enclosed letter not found.

66   The first Medical Society of Analytical Psychologists (MSAP) was founded in the UK in 1936, for the purpose of setting standards for the training of Jungian physician-analysts. Kirsch, then in London, was one of its founding members. In 1943 a parallel organization was founded in San Francisco. In 1946 the New York Jungians followed, and after 1947, with Jung's blessing, "MSAP (US)," which consisted of a Western division, headquartered in San Francisco, and an Eastern division, headquartered in New York. Kirsch was accepted to the San Francisco MSAP in January 1949 (Kirsch to J. Henderson, 25 January 1949, Kirsch archive) as an Associate Member, i.e. a non-licensed MD. By the early 1950s, the member list of the San Francisco MSAP included eight Licensed MDs (all from San Francisco); two Associate Members; and three Accredited Lay Analysts: Hilde Kirsch and Max Zeller of Los Angeles, and Jane Wheelwright of San Francisco.

67   Joseph B. Wheelwright, MD (1906–1999): American psychiatrist and Jungian analyst, who had studied medicine at St. Bartholemew's Medical College, London, where he became friends with Joseph Henderson (cf. Kirsch, 18 April 1953, p. 167 and note). Wheelwright and his wife, Jane, both analyzed with Jung in the 1930s and became analysts. After returning to the US and taking up professional life in San Francisco, Wheelwright and Henderson together organized an analytic training program there, starting in 1945. Thus, almost 20 years before the San Francisco Institute came into existence (1964), formal training of analysts began, with oversight first from MSAP and then from the Society of Jungian Analysts of Northern California (formed in 1950). Wheelwright taught for 30 years at the Langley-Porter Psychiatric Institute, UCSF Medical Center. He was active in the San Francisco MSAP and the Society of Jungian Analysts, and served two terms as vice-president and two more as president of the IAAP (International Association for Analytical Psychology). He taught and administered in the Jung Institute of San Francisco from its founding until his retirement. (With many thanks to Marianne Morgan, acting archivist at the Virginia Allen Detloff Library, C. G. Jung Institute of San Francisco; hereafter VADL archive.)

Pension Tiefenau
Zch 32.

2 July 1949[68]

Dear Prof. Jung!

My wife sent me the "minutes"[69] of the M.S.A.P. (Med. Soc. of Analyt. Psychologists). The following is stated:[70]

> A letter was read which expressed doubt as to the analytical qualifications of Dr. Klopfer. As a result it was decided to invite all founding members to submit a fairly complete file of qualifications before approval of the list.

For this purpose, therefore, my wife (through me as her intermediary) asks you to write a rather detailed certificate for her, confirming her work with you and her qualifications as an analyst. Despite my bias in her regard, I can truly state that she has done excellent work with her patients during the past years. She discusses almost all her cases with me.

With best wishes for a wonderful and restful vacation.

Faithfully yours, JAMES KIRSCH

Mrs. Hilde Kirsch[71]
6120 Barrows Drive
Los Angeles 36, Calif.

---

68 Handwritten in German on plain paper, with sender's address handwritten at upper left.
69 Word orig. in English.
70 Following paragraph orig. in English.
71 Kirsch provides his wife's address to assist Jung in sending her the requested certificate.

Prof. Dr. C. G. Jung
Küsnacht-Zürich
Seestrasse 228

12 July 1949[72]

Dear Colleague!

Since I have an important conference on Thursday, I cannot free up any time for you. Besides, the ars geomantica[73] is a complicated matter about which I myself still understand far too little. It cannot be learned in a flash. A single experiment requires much time and effort. You simply must put this off to a later time.

I wish you a good trip and success in your work.

With best greetings, Yours truly, C. G. JUNG

James Kirsch, M.D.
6120 Barrows Drive
Los Angeles 36, Calif.
Walnut 9229

5 August 1949[74]

Dear Dr. Jung!

Please accept my most heartfelt thanks for your last letter from Zurich. I was very sorry not to see you again, but "by chance" on Tuesday of my last week in Zurich, Dr. Meier happened to speak of the Ars Geomantica and showed me two old Latin books on the subject, and I now understand how difficult this art

---

72 Handwritten in German, on letterhead.
73 geomantic art. (Kirsch's previous letter is missing. Cf. Kirsch, 5 August 1949, pp. 127f, note 75.) Gerhard Adler describes geomancy as "an ancient method of divination still widely practiced in the Orient, especially the Far East, [in which] earth or pebbles are thrown on the ground and the resultant pattern is interpreted.... A later development was to make dots at random on a piece of paper." (*Letters II*, p. 169n). Cf. CW 8, "Synchronicity," ¶866. Cf. also M.-L. von Franz, *Number and Time: Reflections Leading Towards a Unification of Psychology and Physics*, trans. by Andrea Dykes, London: Rider & Co, pp. 117ff; and *Rhythm and Repose*, London: Thames & Hudson, 1978, pp. 92ff.
74 Typewritten in German, on letterhead.

is, and how much time is required for even a single inquiry. Of course, this only heightened my interest, but I don't know how far I'll get with it here in Los Angeles.[75]

Never before was the departure from Zurich so difficult for me, and I decided – if at all possible – to come back to Zurich next year. By human estimation, it's certain that my wife will come to Zurich next summer and, if possible, will accept the invitation of your daughter (Frau Baumann) to my youngest son Thomas.

I don't need to tell you how grateful I am for everything that Zurich, the Swiss culture, the Institute with its many distinctive personalities, and especially you have given me. This time I owe a special debt for my work with Fräulein Wolff. It was very difficult to leave, because so many new and strong bonds have been established.

As was my intention, I recently spoke with Dr. Klopfer. After some face-to-face conversation in private, he felt it necessary to invite the ladies to be present also. Thus, the discussion was continued in the presence of his wife, my wife, and a mutual woman friend. I told him that you consider him neither analyzed nor entitled to call himself a Jungian analyst. His response was that you must have forgotten a great deal; that his more than 200 hours of Freudian analysis had been accepted as a basis for his Jungian analysis; that you had encouraged him to advance from the analysis of children to that of adults; that you had supervised two of his cases, and besides that you'd given him a letter of recommendation to the New York Club. A copy of that letter should be in your files. Dr. Klopfer surmised that my inquiry in his regard must have prompted your negative reaction. His reaction to my statements was entirely personal. He could not comprehend that Freudian and Jungian analyses are two entirely different things, and that one cannot simply assume that a Freudian analysis can take the place of a Jungian analysis when applying for membership at the New York Club or an organization which is being founded for the benefit of lay analysts. I am fully convinced that Dr. Klopfer did not want to deceive us, but that he was absolutely unconscious when he judged a Freudian analysis to be equivalent to a Jungian analysis.

I do not know what the outcome of all this will be. If Dr. Klopfer had been my patient, I certainly would not have stepped into his shadow in this manner. I felt that I had to do so, however, because it is simply unacceptable that such an unanalyzed individual should set the conditions as to who should be a Jungian analyst. Afterwards I sent him a friendly letter, drawing his attention to the fact that we consider it necessary for every analyst to undergo a follow-up analysis at five-year intervals, and that both Zeller and I had fulfilled this requirement recently in Zurich. I recommended that he do this as well. I don't have much hope that he will decide to have additional analysis, since his initial reactions

---

75 On 17 February 1952 Kirsch sent his geomantic chart to Liliane Frey-Rohn. She found most of his "geoscope" to be favorable, but warned him that "the critical problem seems to be related to the Puella (the inferior Anima)" (Frey-Rohn to Kirsch, 22 March 1952, Kirsch archive, trans. ACL).

have been directed at me quite personally and not at all to the point. For instance, he assumes that I challenged him out of "vindictiveness"[76] and/or "cherchez la femme" motives.[77]

By the way, the mother of the young man whose case I discussed in Zurich[78] came to see me recently. You may recall that at the time you were interested in finding out why the young man said, "that the Queen Elisabeth was coming 'down' the St. Lawrence River," while actually it was going 'up'.[79] She told me that she had been fascinated by the St. Lawrence River since her childhood and always wanted to go there and see it for herself. This summer she went to Canada by herself and stayed for several weeks in the different cities on the St. Lawrence River. There several people pointed out to her that from Quebec to Montreal, for example, one travels 'up' the St. Lawrence River and not 'down' as she had always said. So it's quite certain that the son adopted this from his mother. It's also an interesting coincidence that the mother was on the St. Lawrence River at the same time as we were discussing the dream in Zurich. Again, one of those coincidences.

With cordial greetings and best wishes to you, your family and Fräulein Schmid.

Faithfully yours, [80] JAMES KIRSCH

521 N. La Cienega Blvd.
Los Angeles 48, Calif.
Walnut 9229

9 September 1949[81]

Dear Dr. Jung:

Today I should like to write you about a case which has been keeping my mind occupied for quite some time. This lady, Mrs. H[82] (at the time of the dream about forty) has been my patient for about two years during the war years. After that, she came quite regularly to my dream seminar. She asked me for one appointment in

---

76 Word orig. in English.
77 *Motiven:* added in handwriting. (Klopfer implied that Kirsch was motivated by professional or romantic rivalry.)
78 Cf. Kirsch, 28 May 1949, p. 123 and note.
79 Statement orig. in English.
80 Closing handwritten.
81 Typewritten in English on letterhead, and signed. With typewritten attachments, also in English. This original document was found only in the Kirsch archive. It may be Kirsch's rough draft for a letter which was later mailed. If so, the final copy is missing from Jung's papers. There is no record of Jung's reply.
82 Patient's name concealed in Kirsch's original.

April '48, because she had a series of frightening dreams. At this single interview, which took place sometime in May '48, she read the enclosed series of dreams and then asked me whether they were death dreams. She thought of that because of the mentioning of St. Peter's gate, and because of the extraordinary emotion which accompanied the first dream.[83] Her main association to the Green Dolphin Street was rather long, telling of the story of the book, *The Green Dolphin Street*, in which a young woman is in terrible danger of life and in utter emergency finds a shaft within a rock which is far out to sea, and climbs this dangerous shaft which is like an elevator shaft and arrives then on top at a nunnery. The gate between this shaft and a little garden is called St. Peter's Gate in the book. When she asked me whether this dream did not indicate death, I must admit that I had that thought too, but there was a healthy woman sitting in front of me, and I just did not have the heart to agree with her question. I do not know whether I acted right, and I believe that is my first lie in a very, very long time that I told a patient.

Sometime in October of '48 she came to the seminar and looked very bad, and I asked her why she looked so sick, and she said she did not know, but suddenly at four o'clock sharp she felt something like an explosion in her, and very sick after that and has not yet recovered. When she came to the next seminar meeting a week later she told me that her brother-in-law had committed suicide by shooting himself at four o'clock sharp that day. This brother-in-law played a certain role in her analysis as he was a doctor and gave a certain amount of medical advice to her and her children, but there was no close personal relationship between my patient and her brother-in-law at any time, and at the time of the suicide they had not met or seen each other for a number of years.

In May '49, when I was in Zürich, I received a letter from one of her friends that she had been operated of cancer of the breast. She afterwards sent me a number of dreams[84] which at the time I discussed also with Fräulein Wolff. Since my

83 In the patient's first dream, dated 1 April 1948, she faints and then, conscious that she has fainted, has another dream within her dream. She is now in a rocky shaft, being forced upward by "a wind of tremendous force." This reminds her of a movie, "Green Dolphin Street." As in the movie, the rocky shaft opens at "St. Peter's Gate." The dreamer is finally expelled into a pool of water in a peaceful setting, far below. Sinking below the surface, she has great difficulty coming up for air. After waking, she feels physically as if she had spent a long time under water.

84 In the patient's second dream, dated 26 April 1948, she sees a room in which a fire is burning in the shape of a quarter-circle. Beyond it are rich foods, jewels and treasures, guarded by a dragon. The dreamer wakes and sleeps again. In her next dream she is speeding through space with a group of people, one of whom says, "Mercury is really doing a good job this trip." Then she stands with a child in an ancient plaza, through which a small train passes. Nearby in a "religious building" they see an ancient beehive oven, with flames rising from it. Figures walk by in procession, "the dying carrying the dead," and enter the religious building. Inside it "a woman of commanding appearance" is asked to say a blessing. The woman leans over and wraps her feet in strips of cloth.

return to Los Angeles I have seen her regularly once a week. All her dreams point undoubtedly to a fatal outcome: dreams like, "My mother (but not my personal mother) has irrevocably decreed that I must be executed," or "An uncle who died eight years ago of cancer is digging a grave." Then there are other dreams which tell her to give up all thoughts of love, life, marriage, interest in people, and dedicate herself to something religious. Shortly before and after her operation in May she had some experiences in which she had completely resigned from life and felt something of what is beyond life. These experiences had given her, who is otherwise a very simple, practical, extraverted American woman, a wonderful detachment, an indescribable relaxed kind of wisdom.

A few weeks after the operation she recovered physically to a large degree and felt much stronger, and this experience of death receded and she made attempts to go back into life, although half of all the dreams were nothing but announcements of quickly approaching death. Now her strength is waning, she has pleuritis, bronchitis and other symptoms indicating a rapid growth of the cancer through the chest.

I am so very puzzled because I do not understand this dream, the psychology (or what-have-you) meaning of this dream, and secondly because I do not know what to tell her. When I discussed it with Miss Wolff she said: "Don't rub it in." It would be my inclination to tell her quite frankly that her time of life is limited, and that she should realize it so that she could take care of her three children in the best possible way and prepare properly for death. On the other hand, I just haven't got the courage to tell her that. She herself does not interpret her present symptoms, pleuritis and bronchitis, as what it really is. If she herself would have a realization of what is happening to her, the work on her dreams would be more fruitful. Another complication is that her thinking does not seem to me as clear as it used to be. I am not sure whether this is due to drugs that she receives to a large degree, or whether possibly the cancer has gone into the brain.

Pardon me for writing so extensively about this case, but I would appreciate your help in it.

With cordial greetings,[85] Faithfully yours, JAMES KIRSCH

---

85   Closing handwritten in German.

1950–1952

AION AND *JOB*

James Kirsch, M.D.
6120 Barrows Drive
Los Angeles 48, Calif.
Walnut 9229

1 October 1950[1]

Dear Professor Jung,

I'm sorry to say I've had no answer to the last letter I wrote you.[2] Maybe it was for the best. But I have been anxiously awaiting a word from you. For four months, the secret[3] (which really was no secret) exerted its destructive influence on me. Too late, unfortunately, I realized where it truly struck me. On Sept. 24 it finally came out, and since then my relationship to Hilde is in order. I take responsibility[4] for this process and am very accepting of it. I've suffered terribly, but finally now this wound is only internal. How it may heal, and whether it will ever heal, I do not yet know. Astrology[5] was very helpful, since Bernhard[6] had sent me the constellations with exact dates; so I knew the secret would finally come out on Sept. 24.

---

1   Typewritten in German, on letterhead.
2   A letter from Kirsch has evidently been lost.
3   According to Thomas Kirsch, the "secret" here is related to an extramarital relationship in which his father was involved. In late May 1950 a crisis had occurred, and for several weeks James and Hilde Kirsch had planned to separate. In late September another aspect of the situation was revealed, and the marital crisis to some extent resolved.
4   *ich stehe Gevatter:* lit. "I stand as Godfather."
5   Both James and Hilde Kirsch were strongly influenced by astrology. At various points they sought consultation with astrologers, relating to events in their lives or to important relationships.
6   Ernst Bernhard, Dr. med. (1896–1965): German-Jewish pediatrician, Jungian analyst and astrologer. A cousin of Max Zeller and close colleague of James Kirsch, Bernhard analyzed with two Freudians, also with Toni Sussmann and Käthe Bügler in Berlin, and for five months with Jung (Bernhard to Kirsch, 29 June 1936, Kirsch archive) and Toni Wolff. After attempting to emigrate to London (Bernhard to Kirsch, 31 July 1936, ibid.), but being denied asylum due to his interest in astrology (cf. A. Carotenuto, *Jung e la cultura italiana*, Roma: Astrolabio, 1977, p. 45), Bernhard and his wife settled in Rome. In 1940–41 he was sent to an Italian internment camp, but was released and confined to his apartment for the duration. Carotenuto credits Bernhard with freeing post-war Italy from provincialism, by editing the works of Jung, Jungians, and anthropologists for the Astrolabio series "Psiche e Coscienza." In 1949 Jung used Bernhard's horoscopes of married couples to support his work on synchronicity (CW 8, ¶873ff). (Giovanni Sorge, ed., *1934–1959 Lettere Ernst Bernhard–Carl Gustav Jung*; enc., *Rivista di Psicologia analitica*, 12, 64; Roma: Vivarium, 2001, p. 41). With thanks to Dr. Sorge for references and information.

Figure 6.1 **Ernst Bernhard.** *Photo: ©1957, James Kirsch. Courtesy Thomas B. Kirsch.*

I would like to relate (slightly post festum) a dream that I had on Sept. 8, since in it I asked you about the effect of the secret, and my inner situation is described:

> I was on a ship. Then saw that a young girl was making a phone call in a telephone booth that was like the installation they put around an electroencephalograph. Suddenly lightning struck this installation and killed the young girl. I thought, the newspapers will write what a frightful accident, but I knew there was a meaningful connection. Dangers were threatening us all around, I had warned Hilde about them. All at once came a huge quantity of water (I thought: "heavy water") and it rushed in through the open hatch. I assumed, of course, that the water would also gush through the corresponding hatch on the other side, but after some time I noticed this was not the case, opened the hatch, went out, and led the others to the outside. I went along a moulding which, on account of the impaired balance of the ship, allowed us to walk on it and reach safety. In the process I realized that I did not react well to dangers, because I was so frightened.
>
> Then I spoke with you. You said many important things. Now Mrs. Baumann (née Fish) arrived and interrupted us. I was annoyed

at this. After she left, I asked you about the effect of the secret. You answered: "If it is a new marriage, then the secret will destroy the marriage. But if it's an old one, perhaps it may work out." I said, "It's a new one, because the old one has absolutely ended." You then added, "You are never alone, I am with you on the human side, and God is with you on the spiritual side." I do not wish to burden you further, I said, and took my leave.

With most cordial greetings and best wishes,[7]
Very truly yours, JAMES KIRSCH

Küsnacht-Zürich

16 October 1950[8]

Dr. James Kirsch,
521 North La Cienega Boulevard,
Los Angeles 48,
California

Dear Kirsch,

Unfortunately it's impossible for me to answer all letters *in concreto.*[9] There are just too many of them. I read yours and thought that you should proceed without my assistance.

By the way, your dream of September 8[10] gave you the correct answer. Maturation costs not only time but also suffering.

With warm regards, Yours truly *[carbon copy unsigned]*

---

7 Remainder of closing handwritten.

8 Typewritten in German, on plain paper (unsigned). No original has been found.

9 Kirsch had been distressed by Jung's failure to answer (cf. Kirsch, 1 October 1950, opening, p. 135 and note).

10 ibid., pp. 136f.

Prof. Dr. C. G. Jung
Küsnacht-Zürich
Seestrasse 228

16 May 1951[11]

Dr. James Kirsch
Hotel Sonnenberg
Zürich

Dear Colleague,

I have arranged for either the MS or page-proofs of my work on the symbolism of the Self[12] to be sent to you.

At the moment I don't yet feel up to giving consultations. First I need a little more rest. Please let me know how long you're planning to stay in Zurich.

Meanwhile with best greetings, Yours truly C. G. JUNG

Hotel Sonnenberg Zürich
Aurorastrasse 98
Telephon 24 47 47

20 May 1951[13]

Dear Professor Jung,

Please accept my most sincere thanks for your kind letter and especially for the information you sent me via Dr. Frey.[14]

---

11 Typewritten in German, on letterhead.
12 C. G. Jung, *Aion: Untersuchungen zur Symbolgeschichte* [Aion: Researches in the history of a symbol]. Unter Mitarbeit von M.-L. von Franz. Psychologische Abhandlungen 8, Zürich: Rascher, 1951. This work had originated with Jung's Eranos lecture of 1948, "Über das Selbst" ["On the Self"], which became the core of its two central chapters. Cf. CW 9(ii), *Aion: Researches into the Phenomenology of the Self*, 1958/1968 (hereafter *Aion*).
13 Handwritten in German, on two sides of a small sheet of hotel letterhead.
14 Liliane Frey-Rohn, Dr. phil. (1901–1991): Swiss-born Jungian analyst, one of Jung's closest collaborators. She earned her doctorate from the University of Zurich and practiced in that city for more than 50 years. In 1947–48 she served on the five-person committee (with Meier, Binswanger, Jacobi and Jung) preparing to found the C. G. Jung-Institut Zürich. In 1951–52 Frey-Rohn was Kirsch's analyst, for a total of 70 hours (handwritten record, late 1952, Kirsch archive). Thereafter they maintained a voluminous and affectionate correspondence until Kirsch's death. Frey-Rohn published several works, two of her best-known being *From Freud to Jung: A Comparative Study of the Psychology of the Unconscious* (1974; pub. in German 1969) and *Friedrich Nietzsche: A Psychological Approach to His Life and Work* (1988; pub. in German 1984).

In addition, almost like magic, your new book[15] came to me on the same day, and I'm now in the middle of it. I'll definitely stay here until the middle of July and perhaps longer.

With cordial greetings, Faithfully yours, JAMES KIRSCH

Prof. Dr. C. G. Jung
Küsnacht-Zürich
Seestrasse 228

pro tem. Bollingen, 12 July 1951[16]

Dear Colleague!

Until now I haven't even started my actual vacation,[17] because I had to take care of a number of business matters from here, which had remained undone since the time of my illness. As a result of the inordinate amount of work I accomplished during the past two weeks, I collapsed and now urgently need rest. So I won't be able to see you until later, around the end of this month.

Your dream hits the nail on the head.[18] Freud is indeed significantly cheaper. But in return one does not make any progress. Moreover, it was not I who invented the entire complication of the soul, nor did Freud succeed in removing it from the world.

Meanwhile with best greetings, Yours truly C. G. JUNG

---

15 Aion. Cf. Jung, 16 May 1951, p. 138 and note.

16 Handwritten in German, on letterhead. Second paragraph prev. pub. in *PP*.

17 Jung had been staying at the Tower in Bollingen, where normally he would have rested. But he had brought a quantity of work with him, and only now, after two weeks, was he was able to relax.

18 Kirsch's previous letter is missing.

From Una Thomas:[19]

20 October 1952[20]

Dr. James Kirsch,
6120 Barrows Drive,
Los Angeles 48
Calif.

Dear Dr. Kirsch,

Professor Jung has asked me to write to you on his behalf to tell you that he has read your letter[21] but regrets very much to have to tell you that it is not possible for him to answer it at the present time. He is in bed and under strict doctor's orders not to do any work.[22] However, Professor Jung thinks it might interest you to know that Dr. Hurwitz[23] (Dr. S. Hurwitz, Rigistr. 54, Zürich 6) who is interested in similar questions might be able to be of some assistance to you.

Sincerely yours, UNA THOMAS, Secretary

---

19 Una G. Thomas (1898–1996): An Englishwoman who lived in Zurich, Thomas had been in analysis with Jung in the 1920s and was a member of the Club (cf. Christmas greetings, p. 246). She had assisted Barbara Hannah and Elizabeth Welsh in recording an English version of Jung's ETH lectures (*Modern Psychology*, Vol. 1 and 2: Notes on Lectures given at the Eidgenössische Technische Hochschule, Zürich by Prof. Dr. C. G. Jung, October 1933–July 1935) (1959). Thomas took over temporarily as Jung's secretary in September 1952, when Marie-Jeanne Schmid left to get married (cf. Jung, 18 November 1952, p. 141 and note).

20 Typewritten in English, on Jung's letterhead.

21 Kirsch's previous letter is missing.

22 Jung had recently suffered an attack of tachycardia and arrhythmia. Cf. Jung, 18 November 1952, p. 141 and note.

23 Siegmund Hurwitz, Dr. med. dent. (1904–1994): Swiss-Jewish scholar, writer, and later in life a Jungian analyst. Dentistry was his original profession, and Jung was one of his patients. Hurwitz analyzed with Jung, Wolff, and von Franz and was a friend of many Zurich Jungians. His friendship with Kirsch began in the early 1950s, and the two families often went on vacation together. In December 1951 and January 1952, Hurwitz visited the United States and lectured on the Kabbalah in New York, Los Angeles, and San Francisco. After retirement, Hurwitz became an analyst. His published works include "Archetypal Motifs in Hassidic Mysticism" (3. Studien vom C. G. Jung-Institut, 1952); *Die Gestalt des sterbenden Messias: Religionspsychologische Aspekte der jüdischen Apokalyptik* [The Figure of the dying Messiah: Religious and psychological aspects of Jewish apocalyptic] (8. Studien vom C. G. Jung-Institut, 1957); *Psyche und Erlösung* [Psyche and Redemption]; and *Lilith – die erste Eva* [Lilith – the first Eve] with foreword by von Franz (1979). Cf. Jung, 18 November 1952, p. 143, note 43.

Prof. Dr. C. G. Jung
Küsnacht-Zürich
Seestrasse 228

18 November 1952[24]

Dr. James Kirsch
6120 Barrows Drive
Los Angeles 48
Calif.

Dear Kirsch,

I am sending you an English letter this time as I am still unable to write longhand letters myself.[25] I had another attack of arrhythmia and tachycardia due to overwork.[26] I am now slowly recovering and my pulse is normal again since almost a week, but I am still tired and have to go slowly.

Your question[27] is a very important one and I think I can understand its full import. I would not be able to give you a satisfactory answer, yet having studied the question as far as possible, I can call your attention to the extraordinary development in the Cabbala. I am rather certain that the sefirot tree[28] contains the whole symbolism of a Jewish development parallel to the Christian idea. The characteristic difference is that God's incarnation is understood to be a historical fact in the Christian belief, while in the Jewish Gnosis it is an entirely pleromatic process symbolized by the concentration of the supreme Trias[29] of Kether, Chochma and Bina[30] in the figure of Tiferet.[31] Being the equivalent of the Son and the Holy Ghost, he is the sponsus[32] bringing about the great solution through his

---

24 Typewritten in English, on letterhead. Prev. pub. in *PP*; also in *Letters II*.
25 Jung dictated the letter in English, since his secretary at the time, Una Thomas, was English-speaking.
26 This cardiac condition occurred in October 1952. Jung recovered slowly, but was concerned that his symptoms might recur. In late October 1952 he wrote to another correspondent: "The news is that I have to reduce my work still more and make of myself a confirmed recluse in order to avoid all temptation to overwork. It got me this time good and proper and I do not want to repeat this experience" (Jung to Victor White, 31 October 1952, *Jung–White Letters*, pp. 207f). He suffered a relapse in April 1953 (cf. Jung, 28 May 1953, p. 170 and note).
27 Kirsch's previous letter is missing.
28 In the Kabbalah, the ten *sefirot* represent "stages in the revelation of God's power" (Scholem, *Major Trends in Jewish Mysticism*, 1941, p. 13), and are often drawn as ten circles arranged in the shape of a tree (*Letters I*, p. 356, n. 5; *Letters II*, p. 92, n. 3). They also represent stages in the ascent of the soul toward divinity. (Thanks to Dr. Steven Joseph, here and elsewhere, for his assistance relating to the Kabbalah.)
29 triad.
30 *Keter, Hokhmah, Binah*: Crown, Wisdom, Intelligence, the first, second and third *sefirot*.
31 *Tiferet*: Beauty, the sixth *sefirah*; also called *Rahamim*, Compassion.
32 spouse.

union with Malchut.[33] This union is equivalent to the assumptio beatae virginis,[34] but definitely more comprehensive than the latter as it seems to include even the extraneous world of the Klippot.[35] Professor Scholem[36] is certainly all wet when he thinks that the Jewish Gnosis contains nothing of the Christian mystery.[37] It contains practically the whole of it, but in its unrevealed pleromatic state.

There is a very interesting little Latin mediaeval book written either by Knorr von Rosenroth,[38] or at least under his direct influence. It is called "Adumbratio Kabbalæ Christianæ. Id est Syncatabasis Hebraizans, Sive Brevis Applicatio Doctrinae Hebræorum Cabbalisticæ Ad Dogmata Novi Foederis. Francofurti. 1684.[39] This little book is highly worthwhile; it contains a very useful parallel of the Christian and the Cabbalistic mystery and might give you much help as it has helped me in understanding this all important problem of the Jewish religious

33 *Malkhut,* Kingdom of God, also called *Shekhinah,* God's Dwelling Place: the tenth *sefirah,* representing the community of Israel and the material creation.

34 Assumption of the Blessed Virgin: dogma of the Roman Catholic Church, promulgated in 1950, stating that at her death the Virgin Mary was assumed bodily into heaven.

35 *Kelipot,* shards, shells: forces of evil. "According to the Kabbalist Isaac Luria (1534–1572), they originated in the "breaking of the vessels" of the *sefirot* which could not contain the power of God. The world of the *kelipot* is the counter pole to the world of the *sefirot.* Cf. "Answer to Job", CW 11, ¶595, n. 8, and Jaffé, *The Myth of Meaning,* pp. 122ff (*Letters II,* p. 92, n. 4). Cf. also Jung, 16 February 1954, p. 193 and notes).

36 Gershom Gerhard Scholem (1897–1982): Pre-eminent modern scholar of Jewish mysticism. Born to an assimilated Jewish family in Berlin, Scholem became a Zionist at fourteen and emigrated to Palestine in 1923. There he became a leader within the German-Jewish intellectual community. Living in Jerusalem for the rest of his life, he wrote 40 volumes and almost 700 articles, mainly in German or Hebrew. His first book in English, *Major Trends in Jewish Mysticism* (1941), transformed the study of Kabbalah. Jung valued and often consulted this work in English and later in its German edition, *Die jüdische Mystik in ihren Hauptströmungen* (1957) (cf. Jung, 16 February 1954, p. 195 and note). Scholem proposed that philosophical movements are historically shaped, and argued that the Sabbataian heresy (cf. Kirsch, 8 June 1934, p. 51 and note) belongs to the necessary dialectic of Jewish mysticism. Another of his major works, available in English, is titled *On the Kabbalah and its Symbolism* (trans. by Ralph Manheim, 1965).

37 Possibly a reference to Scholem's lecture at Eranos, August 1952. Cf. Kirsch, 10 December 1952, p. 151 and note.

38 Christian Knorr von Rosenroth (1631–1689): German-Christian Hebraist and Kabbalist, born in Silesia, educated at Wittenberg and Leipzig. In his interpretation of Kabbalah, the mystical Jewish figure of Adam Kadmon is seen as equivalent to the Christian figure of Jesus. Jung highly values the thought of Knorr von Rosenroth, whose work he mentions often in letters and footnotes, and occasionally in primary texts (cf. especially CW 14, *Mysterium Coniunctionis,* pp. 411f, ¶592–93).

39 Jung's edition of this slender volume, still found in his library, bears no author's name. Often attributed to Knorr von Rosenroth, it is an anonymous addendum to *Kabbala denudata* (1684) (cf. note 41 below), possibly written by a contemporary Flemish Kabbalist, Francis von Helmont (1614–1698). The final clause in the title, which Jung omits, reads: "Pro formanda hypothesi, ad Conversionem Judaeorum proficua." The full title may thus be translated: "An Outline of the Christian Kabbalah, that is a Hebraizing Accommodation to the doctrine of the New Covenant, useful for the Forming of a Hypothesis for the Conversion of the Jews." With thanks to Richard Corney for research and translation.

development. It would be highly commendable to translate the book. I am pretty certain that the extraordinary and venomous response of the orthodox rabbis against the Cabbala[40] is based upon the undeniable fact of this most remarkable Judeo-Christian parallelism. This is hot stuff, and since the 17th century, as far as my knowledge goes, nobody has dared to touch it, but we are interested in the soul of man and therefore we are not blindfolded by foolish confessional prejudices.*

This is about all I can do for you now. Hurwitz would probably know something more because he is in the fortunate position of being able to read the original texts. I must say I got enough from the study of Knorr von Rosenroth's "Cabbala Denudata".[41]

Sincerely yours, C. G. JUNG

P.S.   I believe in the anonymous authors' device "Quaeritur una salus".[42]

*S. Hurwitz has been preached against in the Synagogue.[43]

---

40   Jung's statement may reflect the personal experience of his friend, Siegmund Hurwitz (cf. post-script below and note 43). According to Steven Joseph, however, this view of Jung's is open to question. Although some orthodox rabbis have opposed Kabbalah, others maintain that it was and has remained at the very center of orthodox Judaism.

41   Knorr von Rosenroth published two major works titled *Kabbala denudata* [Kabbalah laid bare], both of which Jung owned. The first is subtitled, *Sive Doctrina Hebraeorum Transcendentalis et Metaphysica atque Theologica* (Sulzbach: Abraham Lichtenthaler, 1677–78). The second, sub-titled *Id est liber Sohar restitutus* (Frankfurt-am-Main: Johann David Zunner, 1684), appeared with an anonymous companion volume (cf. p. 144 and notes, above).

42   "A single salvation is sought." Quoting from the Latin motto on the page facing the title page in the 1684 edition of *"Adumbratio Kabbalae Christianae"*: *"Quaero, non pono: nihil hic determino dictans: / conjicio: conor: confero: tento: rogo: / Judaeos capto: melior tramite doctor / Si fueris, cedo: quaeritur una salus."* With thanks to Dr. Corney, a rough translation reads: "I seek [knowledge], I do not assert: speaking, I determine nothing here: / I conjecture: I strive: I apply myself: I ask: / I try to win over Jews: if you are a better leader / on the pathway, I yield: a single salvation is sought."

43   Jung's handwritten postscript. (Cf. Thomas, 20 October 1952, p. 140 and note.) In 1951 Hurwitz had lectured at the Club on Sabbatai Sevi (cf. Kirsch, 8 June 1934, p. 51 and note).

James Kirsch
Analytical Psychologist
6120 Barrows Drive
Los Angeles 48, Calif.
Walnut 9229

19 November 1952[44]

Dear Mrs. Thomas!

Please accept my most heartfelt thanks for your friendly letter of Oct. 20. I am deeply grateful to the Professor for his message.

Please convey to him and to Mrs. Jung my warmest greetings. Our thoughts and wishes are with him every day, and we are very glad that he is now feeling better and is again permitted to get up. Thanks be to God!

With cordial greetings and all good wishes also to Mrs. Jung,

Very truly yours, JAMES KIRSCH

---

44   Handwritten in German, on half-sheets of letterhead.

From Aniela Jaffé[45]

Gemeindestr. 27
Zürich 32

22 November 1952[46]

Dear Dr. Kirsch,

A Rabbi Dr. H[…][47] has approached Jung and sent him a letter with all kinds of questions about "Judaica." He appeared to be most wretchedly informed about all the Jewish material Jung has already published (in *Psych. & Alch.*, in *Aion*,[48] etc.). In my letter I referred him to these writings and also mentioned works by Hurwitz[49] and Riwkah.[50] Riwkah gave me permission to write that she would agree to have you lend Dr. H[…] the abbreviated English version of her "Satan" work,[51] if he should ask for it. Maybe he won't even ask, but we felt that one

---

45 Aniela Jaffé (1903–1991): Jungian analyst, editor, writer. Born in Berlin to Jewish parents, Jaffé fled Germany in 1933, just before finishing her medical degree at the University of Hamburg. She settled first in Geneva, where she was briefly married. After working as a secretary in Geneva in the late 1930s, she moved to Zurich to begin analytic work with Liliane Frey. Jung later accepted her for a long analysis. Later becoming an analyst herself, Jaffé became the first secretary of the C. G. Jung-Institut, 1948–55. In 1955 she came to work as Jung's full-time secretary and served in that role until his death in 1961. In the last four years of his life she worked closely with him as editor of his memoir, *Memories, Dreams, Reflections* (cf. Jaffé, "Jung's Last Years," in *From the Life and Work of C. G. Jung*, trans. R. F. C. Hull and Murray Stein, Einsiedeln: Daimon Verlag, 1989; hereafter *Life & Work*). Her published works also include *Apparitions: An Archetypal Approach to Death, Dreams and Ghosts* (1957); *The Myth of Meaning* (1970/1984); *C. G. Jung: Word and Image* (1979), and *Was C. G. Jung a Mystic?* (1989). Jaffé wrote an essay for Jung's last book, *Man and His Symbols* (cf. Jaffé, 3 March 1961, p. 265 and note). She also edited the three-volume German edition of Jung's letters, *Briefe C. G. Jung* (1972, 1973), and assisted Gerhard Adler in editing the two-volume English edition, *C. G. Jung Letters* (1973, 1975).

46 Typewritten in German, on stationery of the C. G. Jung-Institut, Zürich. At this time Jaffé was secretary of the Institute, but she also worked occasionally as one of Jung's part-time secretaries, replacing the recently retired Marie-Jeanne Schmid. Her use of Institute stationery seems to have been an oversight, since the letter belongs to Jung's personal correspondence.

47 Dr. H[…] (name concealed due to clinical context) was at this time the literary editor for a weekly Jewish newspaper (cf. Kirsch, 23 November 1952, p. 148 and note).

48 Cf. Jung, 16 May 1951, p. 138 and note.

49 Cf. Thomas, 20 October 1952, p. 140 and note.

50 Rivkah Schärf [later Schärf-Kluger], Dr. phil. (1907–1987): Swiss-Jewish Jungian analyst and teacher. She recorded in shorthand many of Jung's lectures at the ETH. Her doctoral work in religious studies won unusual recognition from Jung (cf. note 51 below). In 1950 she was invited to become one of the first lecturers at the Los Angeles Jung Institute. In 1954 she married Yechezkel Kluger (cf. Kirsch, 14 March 1954, p. 197 and note), and both taught at the Los Angeles Institute (cf. Kirsch, 10 February 1960, p. 259 and note). In 1969 they moved to Haifa. Schärf-Kluger's works include *Psyche and Bible* (Spring 1974), later republished as *Psyche in Scripture* (ed., Y. H. Kluger, Inner City Books, 1995), and *Gilgamesh: A Modern Ancient Hero* (ed., Y. H. Kluger, Daimon, 1991).

51 Rivkah Schärf's doctoral dissertation, "Die Gestalt des Satans im Alten Testament" ["The Figure of Satan in the Old Testament"], was printed in its entirety in Jung's *Symbolik* (1948). Cf. Kirsch, 21 September 1948, p. 117 and note.

should give him an opportunity. Apparently he likes writing about Jung, and does it a lot, in a "Jüd. Rundschau."[52]

Excuse my bothering you. I trust that you and your family are doing well and hope you aren't having the kind of early winter snow we're having.

Soon we'll write to Dr. Drake.[53] Dr. Meier is now "loaded"[54] which seems to me the necessary prerequisite for the appropriate tone.

Many cordial greetings and thanks for your H[…] help.

Yours ANIELA JAFFÉ

James Kirsch
Analytical Psychologist
6120 Barrows Drive
Los Angeles 48, Calif.
Walnut 9229

November 23rd, 1952[55]

Dear Professor Jung:

Thank you so much for your kind and very helpful letter. I am so glad to hear that you feel better now. My friends in Zurich wrote to me regularly about your illness.[56] I expect that your overwork means a new book. Your creative demon really plagues you. Mrs. Jung told me last summer that you had finished the

---

52 *Jüdische Rundschau* [Jewish Review]. The widely read Zionist weekly (cf. Jung, 11 June 1934, p. 57 and note), published in Berlin until 1938, had not reappeared after the war. Various later publications borrowed the name.

53 Henry L. Drake, PhD (cf. Jung, 7 July 1948, p. 113 and note) had sent out a mass-mailing of brochures and newspaper notices advertising his lecture series on Jungian psychology with the Philosophical Research Society.

54 *"geladen"*: i.e. "ready to fire" (implying an angry intention). Alarmed that Drake was using the name of Jung and of the Jung Institute in an irresponsible way, Kirsch wrote to C. A. Meier, asking him to write Dr. Drake a warning letter. As Director of the C. G. Jung-Institut, Zürich, Meier promptly sent a strongly worded letter, reminding Dr. Drake that he had visited Zurich for only a short time and that his analysis there had been merely fragmentary. If Drake wanted to advertise himself as representing Jung's psychology, Meier advised him, he should affiliate with the Los Angeles APC, "which body represents Jungian Psychology officially" (C. A. Meier to H. Drake, 6 December 1952, Kirsch archive).

55 Typewritten in English, on half-sheet letterhead. A long excerpt from this letter, also typewritten in English, is found in the Kirsch archive.

56 Cf. Jung, 18 November 1952, p. 141 and note.

Mysterium Coniunctionis.[57] I would love to read it soon. Your books have such a wonderful quality that one can read them again and again and feel that they are always new. I am giving 2 courses on the *Antwort auf Hiob*,[58] one to a larger group (about 30) and one to the analysts here, and yet these courses bring something very different out in the 2 groups. By the way, there is a very minor detail with which I cannot agree: On page 25 you write of Yahve and his relationship to the Chosen People, "dessen Urvater Adam er in einem offenbar speziellen Schöpferakt als den Anthropos, den Urmenschen schlechthin nach seinem Bilde geschaffen hatte. Die anderen Menschen, die es dazumal auch schon gab, waren …"[59] I always understood that the Protoplast carried the image of God for the whole of Mankind. The history of the Chosen People begins, as I understand it, with Abraham. It would seem awful to me if the Jews would have claimed that they were the only ones who could be impregnated with the image of God. I could accept it insofar as this was definitely Jewish mythology. But according to your reading of this story: "waren die anderen Menschen, die es dazumal auch schon gab, mit den anderen Arten des Wildes und des Vieh's auf der göttlichen Töpferscheibe geformt worden …"[60] Auch sind ja verschiedene Gottesnamen genannt: Elohim, spaeter Yahve Elohim und erst spaeter Yahveh allein.[61] I always

---

57 C. G. Jung, *Mysterium Coniunctionis: Untersuchung über die Trennung und Zusammensetzung der seelischen Gegensätze in der Alchemie* (GW 14; hereafter *Mysterium*). German edition published in 1955; English edition, in 1963: *Mysterium Coniunctionis: An Inquiry into the Separation and Synthesis of Psychic Opposites in Alchemy* (CW 14). The English edition is one volume, limited to Jung's work. The German edition is three volumes, including an *Ergänzungsband* [supplemental volume], which contains a major work by M.-L. von Franz: *Aurora consurgens. Ein dem Thomas von Aquin zugeschriebenes Dokument der alchemistischen Gegensatzproblematik* [*Aurora Consurgens*. A Document Attributed to Thomas Aquinas on the Problematic of Alchemical Opposites].

58 C. G. Jung, *Antwort auf Hiob* [Answer to Job], Zürich: Rascher, 1952 (hereafter *Job*). For several years this book, Jung's most controversial work on religion and theology, was available only in the original Swiss edition. Kirsch read the book in typescript in the summer of 1951 (cf. Jung, 29 January 1953, p. 157 and note). In 1952–53 Kirsch taught seminars in Los Angeles based on his own translation of *Job* (cf. note 64 below; also Kirsch, 17 March 1953, pp. 160f; and 18 April 1953, p. 167; cf. also Jung, 29 January 1953, p. 157 and note). With Jung's encouragement, he collaborated with Hull on the official translation (cf. Kirsch, 14 February 1954 and enclosure, pp. 190ff and notes). In 1954 *Job* was published in Hull's translation by Routledge & Kegan Paul, London. In 1956 it was republished by the Pastoral Psychology Book Club, Great Neck, New York. In 1958 it became part of *Psych. & Rel.*, CW 11, ¶553–758. Cf. also Jung's letters to Priestley and Murray, *Letters II*, pp. 192f and 322ff.

59 "whose forefather Adam he had created – apparently in a special act of creation – as the Anthropos, the first man, entirely in His own image. The other human beings, who must also have existed at that time, had been…" (alternate trans). Cf. CW 11, "Answer to Job," ¶570.

60 "the other human beings, who already existed at that time, had been formed together with other species of wild animals and livestock on the divine potter's wheel…" (alternate trans).

61 Different names of God are also used: Elohim, later Yahweh Elohim, and only much later Yahweh alone.

saw in these different names of God a definite development of Consciousness. It is only in Gen. 4, 26, with the birth of Enosch[62] (der Sterbliche)[63] that one began to call God by the name "Yahveh".

By the way, I have now a large part of your book in long hand in English.[64] I wonder whether it could be used for the eventual publication, but I suppose that, due to the special arrangements you have with the Bollingen Foundation, this is out of the question.

Dr. H[…],[65] who had recently written to you and just received an answer from you, has in the meantime started to do analysis with me. I'll try to answer his question about your so-called anti-Semitism.[66] I have written a letter to the "Jewish California Voice" of which I enclose a copy.[67] I try to write my letters to you in such a way that they do not require an answer. Please, do not overwork again, and my best wishes for your complete recovery,

Yours as ever, JAMES KIRSCH

62 Enosh [אנוש]: son of Seth, third son of Adam. The verse in which he is introduced concludes: "At that time men began to call upon the name of the LORD [Yahweh: יהוה]" (Gen. 4:26).

63 (the mortal one). In Hebrew and Aramaic, *enosh* is also an ordinary noun meaning "human being." In Aramaic texts, the phrase translated "Son of Man" (*Ben-Adam* in Hebrew) is *Bar-Enosh* (e.g. Dan. 7:13). As a biblical figure, Enosh "the mortal one" is distinct from Enoch [חנוך], a later descendant, who is taken up by God without undergoing physical death (Gen. 5:18–24). Jung seems to conflate the two when he describes Enoch's bodily ascent into heaven as an image of the Son of Man, while also referring to Enoch as "an ordinary human being and therefore mortal" (CW 11, "Answer to Job," ¶684ff, cf. esp. ¶686).

64 As the preceding passage shows, Kirsch has been working on his English translation of Jung's *Job* (cf. Kirsch, 20 May 1951, p. 139 and note). Using this translation, Kirsch taught seminars for analysts at the Los Angeles APC in 1952 and after. He also offered his translation to R. F. C. Hull, to assist the latter in translating *Job* for CW 11, and received a limited acknowledgment (cf. "Translator's Note," *Psych & Rel*, CW 11, p. vii; cf. also Kirsch, 14 February 1954 and attachment, pp. 190ff and notes).

65 Cf. Jaffé, 22 November 1952, p. 145 and note.

66 No record exists of Kirsch's response to this analysand. Later, however, in a Festschrift for Werner Engel, he published a discussion of the topic, "Reconsidering Jung's So-Called Anti-Semitism" (*The Arms of the Windmill: Essays in Analytical Psychology in Honor of Werner H. Engel,* New York: The Jung Foundation, 1984, pp. 5–27).

67 Enclosure not found.

Prof. Dr. C. G. Jung
Küsnacht-Zürich
Seestrasse 228

28 November 1952[68]

Dr. James Kirsch
6120 Barrows Drive
Los Angeles 48
California.

Dear Kirsch,

Concerning Adam, you are quite accurate yet too rational. When you read the Bible in the ordinary way, apparently all human beings derived from Adam, so quite certainly Jews who go right back to the primordial parents, but then you suddenly find that beside Adam and his children there must have been other human beings. Now where did those come from? That is my preoccupation. I have no intention to suggest that the Jews are the only ones that have received the divine imprint, since besides the Jews many other peoples and nations descend from Adam's children, but we have not heard that those human beings from whom Adam's sons took wives have received the divine image.

Thank you for your good wishes. I am slowly, very slowly, picking up.[69]

I could not say there was a new book, but a revision of old papers which will appear under the title *Von den Wurzeln des Bewusstseins*.[70]

You might write to Mr. Barrett,[71] Bollingen Foundation Inc., 140 East 62nd Street, New York 21. Perhaps they could use your translation. Of course they have

---

68 Typewritten in English, on letterhead. First paragraph prev. pub. in *PP*.

69 Cf. Jung, 18 November 1952, p. 141 and note.

70 C. G. Jung, *Von den Wurzeln des Bewusstseins: Studien über den Archetypus* [On the Roots of Consciousness: Studies of the Archetype] (Psychologische Abhandlungen 9, Zürich: Rascher, 1954 (hereafter *Wurzeln*). This work, which contains essays dating from 1935 to 1947, is not published in English as a whole. The essays appear separately in various volumes of the CW: CW 8, Part 8; CW 9(i), Parts 1, 3, 4; CW 11, Part 3; CW 13, Parts 2, 5; CW 18, Part 58.

71 John D. Barrett: President until 1969 of the Bollingen Foundation. Kirsch approached Barrett with two questions concerning his translation of *Answer to Job*. On 8 December 1952 he inquired about its possible use for the CW and asked whether copyright issues would arise if he handed out copies of his translation. Barrett replied on 16 December 1952, declining the offer of Kirsch's translation for the CW (cf. Kirsch, 28 December 1952, p. 153 and note), but assured him that no copyright violation would occur if he handed out his translation.

an official translator,[72] but he might be quite grateful for such a second translation, particularly in this case which is not altogether an easy one.[73]

Thank you also for your manful and courageous letter to the Editor.

With best wishes, Yours sincerely, C. G. JUNG

6120 Barrows Drive
Los Angeles 48
Calif.

10 December 1952[74]

Dear Professor,

When I saw you last in Ascona, I wanted to ask you a question which has been on my mind for many years, but which has become much more urgent since I read your book *Aion*.

I cannot even formulate it precisely. It is the question about the diversity, the relationship, or rather the compensatory relationship, of the individuation process in the Jewish and the Christian story.

In *Aion* you expand on the effects of the Christ-event in the human unconscious, and describe the historic manifestations of its reception. In several passages you also speak of Jewish developments, e.g. in connection with the problem of evil, or the fish symbol. The essential part of Christian development is the incarnation of God in the human being. Precisely this development of the realization of the Self is completely rejected within the Jew – or should I say repressed. On the other hand, the image of the Self became tremendously differentiated in the kabbalistic tree of life. The image of the Messiah remained projected for a long time until – in the 17ᵗʰ century – it fascinated and deeply gripped the Jews in the figure of Sabbatai Zwi.[75] This had tragic consequences. However, the image of the Self could again incarnate in real human beings, an event which manifested itself in the fact that

---

72 R. F. C. (Richard Francis Carrington) Hull (1913–1974): official translator of Jung's works from German to English for the Bollingen Series (CW). Hull also translated Jung's German-language letters for *C. G. Jung Letters* and Jung's letters to Freud, in *The Freud–Jung Letters* (cf. Jung to Hull, 24 January 1955, *Letters II*, p. 217).

73 Jung's encouragement led Kirsch to send his translation of *Job* to John Barrett, the Bollingen Foundation (Kirsch to Barrett, 8 December 1952, Kirsch archive). On 9 December 1953, at Hull's invitation (Hull to Kirsch, 2 December 1953, Kirsch archive), Kirsch and Hull met in Ascona for several days to compare their translations in detail (cf. Kirsch, 14 February 1954, and Kirsch to Hull, 11 February 1954, pp. 190ff and notes).

74 Handwritten in German, on plain paper with handwritten letterhead.

75 Cf. Kirsch, 8 June 1934, p. 51 and note.

the Zaddikim appeared as "saints" in the 18th and 19th centuries. Of course, this was connected with dreadful inflations, e.g. Rabbi Nachmann of Bratzlav,[76] about whose fairy tale "The Seven Beggars"[77] I once spoke here at the Club.

In the Cathedral of Strasbourg I saw a depiction of the conquered synagogue and the ecclesia triumphans,[78] and above it – in the middle and upper spaces – the coronation of Mary by Christ – a depiction which touched me deeply. In Ascona, I asked Professor Scholem[79] whether he was aware of corresponding themes in Judaism. "Absolutely not," he said; "that does not exist in Judaism." But subterranean connections must have existed all the same.[80] Your remark in *Aion* about the feebleness of the messianic element in Judaism impressed me profoundly.

I believe this problem of God's becoming human has a special meaning for the Jew and his tragic history. I also discovered that it concerns me quite personally. Recently I dreamt that a preceding dream had dealt with the question of freedom and possession. Then two ladies, one Jewish and one Christian, collided. The Christian lady insisted that the Jewish lady hand over her ring as compensation for the damage. The Jewish lady did so, much too quickly and out of a guilty conscience. The ring was your ring with the Gnostic black cameo!

---

76 Rabbi Nachmann (1772–1810): Ukrainian Tzaddik, teacher of Torah, Hasidic master and story-teller, specializing in spiritual fairy tales; spent the last eight years of his life in Breslov (Bratzlav). Great-grandson of Rabbi Baal Shem Tov, the founder of Hasidism, the rabbi was acclaimed even as a boy for his knowledge and dedication.

77 James Kirsch, "The Story of the Seven Beggars: A Contribution to the Understanding of Jewish Psychology" (lecture read to the APC of Los Angeles, 21 October1949; typescript, KML archive). Kirsch discusses one of the rabbi's most famous spiritual tales as an active imagination, connect-ing its themes to the Kabbalah, particularly the ten *sefirot* and the development of the feminine (the *Shekhinah*).

78 Church Triumphant.

79 Cf. Jung, 18 November 1952, p. 142 and note. In the early years of Eranos Scholem had been a frequent attender and speaker. After 1945 he declined to return, until he learned from Rabbi Leo Baeck that Jung had admitted to "slipping up" in some of his statements during the Hitler years. Cf. Jaffé, *Life & Work*, p. 100; also Kirsch, "Reconsidering," pp. 14f. Hearing of Jung's apology, Scholem resumed his attendance at Eranos, starting in 1947. He never softened his opinion, how-ever, that Jung had had "links" to Nazism in the 1930s, and that some of Jung's statements at the time had been harmful and unjustifiable from the perspective of Jung's own psychology (Scholem to Kirsch, 8. November 1973, Kirsch archive).

80 Kirsch later recalled this conversation with Scholem in greater detail: "I had visited the Münster in Strassbourg and had seen the representations of the Ecclesia and of the Synagogue, and then had had a conversation with Scholem at the Eranos meeting, in which I told him of my experience. I told him that this proved the constant occupation of the Christian with the Jew – and then asked him whether in his opinion there existed a parallel process with the Jews, in which they would be deeply occupied with Christ and the Christian mystery. His answer was that in the whole of Jewish literature there was nothing concerning X [Christ] or the Church. (Since he later wrote about Christian influences in Sabbatai Zwi, and even in Jacob Frank, he must have limited his remark to the Middle Ages.)" (Kirsch to Adler, 11 October 1966, Kirsch archive).

Although with the help of your book *Aion* the Christian side has become clear (or relatively clear) to me, I understand very little of the Jewish side in its psychological meaning, even though I know the Jewish history of ideas relatively well.

By the way, do you by any chance know the history of the Rabbi Acher?[81] He lived in the 2nd century. He maintained that the Jews had to take cognizance of the fact that according to Christian view, God had a son and thus was no longer one but two. He did not want the Jews to recognize him as the second, but only that this fact should be acknowledged. For this he was banned, excluded from Judaism, and given the name "Acher," the "Second."

All sorts of strange things have been happening lately. On the day I dreamt that I was registering as a licensed physician with the Board of Med. Examiners, I received the news that there was a possibility I would be admitted as a licensed physician in California.

Hoping you and your family are doing well, Faithfully yours, JAMES KIRSCH

6120 Barrows Drive
Los Angeles 48, Calif.

28 December 1952[82]

Dear Professor,

I greatly enjoyed receiving your letter of November 28th. I hope you're feeling better now and have once again been able to spend the holidays with your family. From friends in Zürich I've heard that you are not yet allowed to see them, because your nervous system is too easily excited. This is also why I waited so long before answering your letter. I have the advantage of being able to converse here with you every day. I keep reading your book *Antwort auf Hiob*[83] over and over, which has powerfully opened up new vistas for me and for so many other people I know. Your gospel: "One can love God, and one must fear God"[84] is very much alive in me and has brought me deeply moving and liberating experiences.

I wanted to ask you about several things, but then realized that I was being too rational. In seminars I get questions from Christian audiences which are new to

81 Elisha ben Abuyah, rabbi, born in Jerusalem before 70 CE. After adopting views considered heretical, he was no longer named by his fellow rabbis but called אחר (Acher), "the Other One."

82 Typewritten in German, on letterhead. This letter exists only as an unsigned carbon copy in the Kirsch archive. Presumably typewritten by Kirsch himself, it contains numerous small errors (e.g. accidental spaces and hyphens), which are silently corrected here.

83 *Answer to Job*. Cf. Kirsch, 23 November 1952, p. 147 and note.

84 Cf. *Job*, CW 11, ¶717; ¶732f.

me. For instance, one of these listeners said that, according to a widespread belief, we are only the adopted children of God, and that Christ alone is the begotten son (Christ the only-begotten son). For me as a Jew this thought is far removed, since – as Luther said long ago – the Jews are God's children, but Christians are only his nephews and nieces. Apart from this insight, I can fully accept the postulate that Christ is "the only Begotten one,"[85] if Christ is also an eternal mystery and one which was a unique historical event, and especially if the ego clearly distinguishes itself from the one who dwells within it.[86] Adoption[87] does not express for me the direct relationship that I experience. But it touches on the problem that you mentioned in your letter to me and also in your book: What is the origin of the human beings by whom Adam's sons had their children? Would there be a part in the human psyche which did not bear God's image? This is also unthinkable.

Another problem, which particularly occupies my wife, is the declaration (p. 61) that she (Mary) will not conceive her child in sin like all other mothers. To be sure, this is an assertion of the Catholic Church, but it certainly sounds as if you concur with it. The matter of original sin was indeed raised by us Jews, but it was rejected as a dogma. Hilde resists original sin out of her feminine feeling, but it appears to me a prerequisite and a given in the process of individuation. Psychologically it seems to establish the fact of creatureliness.[88]

On the question of translations, of course, I received a rejection from Mr. Barrett. In his letter he writes that four volumes have already been translated, and Mr. Hull is working on the fifth. But we see nothing! *Psychology and Alchemy* was promised to us for November 15th. Now it's supposed to be published on January 15th. Please God.

I couldn't get the book by Knorr von Rosenroth here. I'll search for it further.

A Mr. Bedford came to see me here at your instigation. I was able to give him information about Buber,[89] as I've known him since 1922. He hasn't become more

---

85 The phrases, "Christ the only-begotten son" and "the 'only Begotten one'," are originally in English.

86 Jung frequently writes about the interior image of God (*imago Dei*), i.e. the individual's personal experience of the Self within the psyche, but distinct from the ego. Among many instances in Jung's published work: "[E]ven the enlightened person remains what he is, and is never more than his own limited ego before the One who dwells within him…" (*Job*, CW 11, ¶758).

87 Word orig. in English.

88 *Creatürlichkeit.* In theological anthropology, a term pointing toward the difference between God and humanity. In Jung's psychology, this would be equivalent to knowing the difference between Self and ego. Kirsch sees the doctrine of original sin (i.e. the universal human tendency to choose wrongly and estrange ourselves from God) as a helpful confirmation of the individual's non-divine, creaturely existence, i.e. the ego's relativization by the Self.

89 Martin Buber (1878–1965): Austrian political and religious philosopher, born into a family of Jewish scholars. Buber played an important role in almost every aspect of Jewish life in Western Europe and Israel. His mature thought was influenced by Hasidism. His published works include *I and Thou* (1923), *Paths in Utopia* (1950), *Eclipse of God: Studies in the Relation Between Religion and Philosophy* (1952), *Hasidism and Modern Man* (1958), and *The Knowledge of Man* (1965). In 1923 Buber lectured at the Club in Zurich. In 1934 he and Jung both spoke at Eranos.

likable in the meantime. I also translated your response to Buber for Mr. Bedford. Of course, Buber's new book, containing his *Merkur* article,[90] came out in English without your response.

Now I'd like to close and am sending you and your wife my most cordial greetings and wishing you all the best for the New Year.

[JAMES KIRSCH] *[carbon copy unsigned]*

90 In "Religion und modernes Denken" (*Merkur*, VI.2, February 1952, Stuttgart) Buber accused Jung of Gnosticism. Jung responded with a long letter to the editor, published as "Religion und Psychologie" (*Merkur*, VI.5, May 1952), in which he discussed the difficulty of carrying on a dialogue between philosophically grounded theology and scientifically based psychology. (Cf. "Religion and Psychology: A Reply to Martin Buber," CW 18 ¶1499–1513.) Buber's response was printed in the same issue of *Merkur*. Both it and Buber's initial article were incorporated into Buber's *Eclipse of God* (1952). (Cf. *Letters II*, p. 43n.)

1953

JUNGIANS IN L.A.

29 January 1953[1]

My dear Kirsch!

I would like to thank you very personally for the great honor you've bestowed upon me[2] and for the great joy you've given me with it. I hope and wish for all good for the future of your Society.[3] If I had an honorary doctorate to bestow, I would set the well-deserved mortarboard on your head in recognition of your truly remarkable and meritorious activity on behalf of "my" psychology, in regard to which I don't claim any right of possession. This represents a movement of the spirit which took possession of me and which I had to and was allowed to serve all my life. It brightens the evening of my life and fills me with glad *serenitas,* that the grace was allotted to me to place my best in the service of a great cause.

What you write in regard to the effect of *Job* upon analysts[4] agrees with my own experiences: the number of individuals who are capable of reacting to it is relatively very small, and analysts are not exceptional people. Incidentally, a second edition of *Job* is just now being published, in which I've inserted the corrections you suggested.[5] I'll send you a copy when it comes out.

---

1   The original of this letter is missing. Handwritten (cf. "Letters to a Friend: Part II, *PP*, p. 168; *Letters II*, p.104), in German (cf. *Briefe II*, p. 320). English translations prev. pub. in *PP* and *Letters II*.

2   Jung had been invited to become an honorary member of the Society of Analytical Psychology of Southern California. Adler's note on this passage erroneously refers to the newly founded Analytical Psychology Club of Los Angeles (*Letters II*, p. 104n), an error repeated by Jaffé (*Briefe II*, p. 320n). In fact, the APC of LA was founded in 1944, whereas the Society of Analytical Psychology of Southern California was founded on 9 November 1953. A mistake on this point was natural, however. When editing *C. G. Jung Letters* for publication, Adler sought information from the letters' recipients. In this case, he received a misleading answer (Kirsch to Adler, 28 September 1967, Kirsch archive).

3   *Gründung* (foundation; organization). The Society of Analytical Psychology of Southern California was founded by James and Hilde Kirsch, Kieffer Frantz, and Max Zeller with the primary purpose of setting professional standards and overseeing the training of candidates. A low-fee clinic, founded at the same time (cf. Kirsch, 17 March 1953, p. 162 and note), shared in training and supervision. The first director of the Los Angeles training program, 1953–56, was James Kirsch. He was followed by Kieffer Frantz, I. Jay Dunn, Margaret McClean, William Alex, and Malcolm Dana. After the Institute's official founding in 1967, its first president was Yechezkel Kluger (cf. Kirsch, 14 March 1954, p. 197 and note).

4   Kirsch's previous letter is missing. In the summer of 1951, according to Kirsch's later memory, a handful of analysts were asked to preview the newly completed *Antwort auf Hiob*: "[Jung] had had six copies typewritten and had given some of them to the Zürich analysts, wanting to know their opinions about it. I was lucky enough in that Jung gave me one of those copies. I read it at once. My opinion was that *Answer to Job...* could and should be published as it was, as personal as it was.... But Dr. Rivkah Schärf found that the book was too subjective in character, that it would be rejected as being 'unscientific'" (James Kirsch, "C. G. Jung's Individuation as shown especially in 'Answer to Job'," undated typescript, written after Jung's death in 1961; ETH Library archive, p. 1).

5   Several corrections suggested by Kirsch were incorporated by Jung into Hull's translation of *Job*, which was published first in London, 1954.

I am slowly recovering, but I'm positively better now. Today I finished a fairly long article about the "philosophical tree,"[6] which has accompanied me during my illness. In the process I've discovered a few interesting matters. I entertained myself excellently with it as a compensation for the fact that so few of my contemporaries can understand what is meant by the psychology of the unconscious. You should have seen the reviews of *Job* in the press! How much naïve stupidity showed up there, you can't imagine.

Again please accept heartiest thanks and best greetings

From yours truly, C. G. JUNG

Figure 7.1 **Marie-Louise von Franz in Los Angeles.** *Photo: ©1953, Max Zeller. Courtesy Jacqueline Zeller-Levine.*

---

6   Revised and expanded from Jung's paper "Der philosophische Baum," orig. pub. in *Verhandlungen der Naturforschenden Gesellschaft Basel* [Activities of the Society for Natural Research, Basel], Band LVI (1945). Also published in *Wurzeln* (1945) and in CW 13, ¶304–482. Kirsch later recalled: "Jung had spent most of 1952 upstairs in his house, after a heart attack, writing his article 'the philosophical tree', using slips of paper he had stored up over years of research" (Countway Interview, p. 20). This anecdote may be accurate in its outlines but misdated. In 1944, when "Der philosophische Baum" was originally written, Jung spent much of the year recovering from a serious cardiac episode in February (cf. Jung, 25 July 1946, p. 107 and note). In late 1952, after his heart trouble recurred (cf. Jung, 18 November 1952, p. 141 and note), he revised the paper.

El Paseo Inn
51 Olivera Street
Los Angeles 12, California

22 February 1953[7]

Prf. Carl G. Jung
Küsnacht – Zch
Seestr. 228
Switzerland

Dear Professor Jung:

We had to celebrate Marlus'[8] big success in L.A.[9] And see where we landed!

Yours sincerely, JAMES KIRSCH and
HILDE KIRSCH
GERDA LORRIGO
MARIAN REITH

Viele herzliche Grüsse![10] MARIE-LOUISE V. FRANZ[11]

(Gene Thessin!) SHERRY PETICOLAS[12]

---

7   Handwritten postcard, in English. Mailed from Pasadena, California. Postmark gives date of mailing. Front of card shows the inn's list of wines, "Prices de la casa." It is signed by each sender individually.

8   "Marlus" was a nickname of Marie-Louise von Franz, who stayed at the home of James and Hilde Kirsch during her visit (cf. Kirsch, 17 March 1953, p. 162).

9   A fund had been established in 1951 to invite leading representatives of Jung's circle to come to Los Angeles for several weeks at a time. Rivkah Schärf (cf. Jaffé, 22 November 1952) visited in 1951 and 1952. Next came Marie-Louise von Franz; then Jolande Jacobi (cf. Kirsch, 18 October 1953). Other visitors included Barbara Hannah (cf. Kirsch, 11 February 1954), C. A. Meier (cf. Kirsch, 27 November 1954), and later Gerhard Adler, Michael Fordham, and Margaret Ostrowski. Cf. Paul Bäuml Turner, "The Development of Jungian Psychology in California and the Components of a Jungian Theoretical Orientation" (Doctoral dissertation for the Pacific Graduate School of Psychology, 1981; typescript, VADL archive), p. 25.

10 Many cordial greetings!

11 Marie-Louise von Franz, Dr. phil. (1915–1998): Swiss Jungian analyst, born in Munich. Her father was a colonel in the Austro-Hungarian military. In 1919 the family moved to Switzerland, and in 1938 she was granted Swiss citizenship. Von Franz met Jung in 1933 when she began analysis, for which she exchanged her translations of Greek and Latin alchemical texts. From being his patient, she became Jung's research assistant and for 28 years his trusted colleague. In 1940 she earned her doctorate from the University of Zurich, with a dissertation on classical philology. Her visit to Los Angeles in 1953 was the first of three such visits (Gilda Frantz, "A Reminiscence," *The Fountain of the Love of Wisdom: An Homage to Marie-Louise von Franz*, ed. E. Kennedy-Xypolitas, Chiron, 2006, pp. 250ff). Von Franz published 30 volumes on the interpretation of fairy tales, myths, dreams, alchemy, synchronicity, and the *puer aeternus*. She taught for many years at the Club and the Zurich Institute. Later in life she founded the Zentrum für Tiefenpsychologie (Research- and Training Centre for Depth Psychology according to C. G. Jung and Marie-Louise von Franz), to emphasize the symbolic and archetypal dimensions of the psyche. Through her long, final battle with Parkinson's Disease, she continued to see analysands, to research and to write.

12 Signed sideways to other signatures. Sherry Peticolas was a longstanding member of the Los Angeles APC, who served on its Executive Committee (Peticolas to Kirsch, 5 June 1949, Kirsch archive). He attended many of Kirsch's dream seminars, as well as those on *Job* and *Aion*.

6120 Barrows Dr.
Los Angeles 48
Calif.

17 March 1953[13]

My dear Professor!

For a long time I have been meaning to write you, but I have to admit quite frankly that your high praise[14] was a great shock to me, from which I haven't really recovered yet, because my guilt feelings about systematic research work are enormous. Again and again I've lost the momentum of steady, ongoing work. Even though I fully recognize and know deep down that you are by no means the "owner" of Jungian psychology, I still need to express the fact that you have worked incredibly hard, with concentration and a secure instinct, on behalf of the secular movement of the spirit. Yesterday, after concluding the *Job* seminar, I looked up something in the *Association Studies*[15] and could finally comprehend what an extremely long way you have traveled. From several experiences I've had recently, and many passages I've found in *Job*, I can fully appreciate the meaning of "glad serenitas."[16] I believe that I perceived and absorbed what is living and working within you, even while I was asking you about personal problems. Today the personal problems have receded, and I am seized and possessed by something hard to name, about which I can only pray that I'll endure the tension and have the intelligence to comprehend and integrate it.

That so few of our contemporaries are able to understand what is meant by the psychology of the unconscious does not surprise me, when I see what difficulties of understanding are experienced even by people who, based on their own analysis and their attendance at seminars, should understand quite a bit. For instance, the lady who is translating *Job* with me and thus should really know it very well, had a great shock today when I explained to her what it means, on pages 125–126,

13 Handwritten in German, on plain paper. Note on top, handwritten in English: "Answered personally by C. Jung 30/3/53." Jung's letter of 30 March 1953 is unfortunately missing.
14 Cf. Jung, 29 January 1953, p. 157.
15 Jung's early papers on his word association experiments appeared originally in two volumes, each titled *Diagnostische Assoziationsstudien: Beiträge zur experimentellen Psychopathologie* [Diagnostic Association Studies: Contributions to experimental psychopathology] (Vol. I, Leipzig: Barth, 1906; Vol. II, Leipzig: Barth, 1909). The first included four papers, one written with Franz Riklin (cf. CW 2, *Experimental Researches,* trans. by Leopold Stein with Diana Rivière, Parts 1, 2, 3, 5). The second comprised two papers: "Assoziation, Traum und hysterisches Symptom" [Association, dream and hysterical symptoms] (cf. CW 2, Part 7); and "Über die Reproduktionsstörungen beim Assoziationsexperiment" [On disturbances in reproduction in the association experiment] (cf. CW 2, *Experimental Researches,* Part 9).
16 Cf. Jung, 29 January 1953, p. 157.

where you say, "John's unconscious personality is closely identified with Christ; that is, he is born in similar circumstances and for a similar destiny."[17]

I also have a practical problem with the translation. In San Francisco, New York, and even I think in Zurich, it's apparently being rumored that I have a translation of *Job*. The need to have this book, and soon, is really great. Up to now only a few typed copies exist in the hands of the local analysts and three others, who are correcting the text during the seminars. Aside from my hand-written text, only one corrected version exists. If it were possible, without violating the copyrights,[18] to send copies to Dr. Whitney[19] and others, I could have the text duplicated on an offset press. At the beginning, of course, I would insert the same proviso about citation and publication as is found on the English Seminars.[20] In addition, I would only distribute the text to people to whom you (or someone you would authorize) give permission to read it.

It is truly a difficult situation, which arises from the fact that your books are in such great demand, especially *Job*, and on the other hand the Bollingen Foundation is withholding your books. You know more about this than I do!

My lawyer assures me that I have a perfect right to hand out the book to my students. Giving it to others would also have no consequences, since the Bollingen Foundation "does not supply this demand."[21] For many reasons, however, I would not want to do that. But I'd like to find a way that makes it accessible to a small number of people. Can you perhaps help me with this?

The C. G. Jung Clinic already has a long waiting list. But we're having difficult problems where the doctors are concerned. Whereas my wife, Ph.D.s, and lay analysts can work there, I am not allowed to do so, because my M.D. degree is from

---

17 This passage reads, in Hull's translation: "In this case it is John himself whose unconscious per-sonality is more or less identified with Christ; that is to say, he is born like Christ, and born to a like destiny" (CW 11, ¶713, p. 441).

18 In consultation with John Barrett, the copyright question was resolved (cf. Kirsch, 9 May 1953, p. 168 and note).

19 Elizabeth Goodrich Whitney, MD (1888–1966): American psychiatrist and Jungian analyst. With her husband, James G. Whitney, MD, she analyzed with Jung in the 1920s and opened an analytic practice in San Francisco in 1927. James G. Whitney was secretary of the MSAP from 1943 until his early death. Elizabeth Whitney played an important role for decades, mainly behind the scenes, fostering cooperation among the diverse branches of the San Francisco analytic commu-nity (cf. *Jungians*, p. 77). Their son, James Whitney, Jr., MD, was the first analyst trained in San Francisco.

20 C. G. Jung, "The English Seminars." At the time available only as typewritten, mimeographed transcriptions, based on listeners' handwritten notes, circulating privately in Zurich. All have since been published by PUP. In 1953 the available transcriptions of Jung's English Seminars consisted of the following: "Analytical Psychology, 1925" (PUP, 1989); "Dream Analysis, 1928–30" (PUP, 1984); "The Kundalini Yoga, 1932" (PUP, 1996); "Interpretation of Visions, October 1930–March 1934" (*The Visions Seminars*, Zurich: Spring, 1976; PUP, 1997); and "Psychological Interpretation of Nietzsche's Zarathustra, 1934–39" (PUP, 1988). Cf. Jung, 6 June 1932, p. 28 and note; cf. also Kirsch, 28 May 1935, p. 68.

21 Phrase orig. in English.

another state.[22] The professional organizations have now informed the two M.D.s (Dr. Kieffer Frantz[23] and Dr. Peggy McClean[24]) that it is "unethical"[25] to work together with osteopathic doctors.[26] This means that the doctors want to exclude them from all professional organizations, prevent them from working in hospitals, and even withdraw their "Board,"[27] i.e. take away their specialist's certification for which they worked very hard. In addition, this would mean that they could not teach at universities under any circumstances. And reaching out to young people would mean a great deal to us! How this conflict that the two are burdened with (which is, of course, an expression of a strongly functioning archetype), I don't know.[28] Thus far they are not willing to agree to a compromise with the doctors. But in America as a whole there is a general tendency to declare as "unethical"[29] any collaboration between M.D.s and osteopaths, and consequently to aim these heavy guns at M.D.s who collaborate professionally with O.D.s.

Dr. von Franz's visit[30] was a great experience. She was far better in all respects than I have ever experienced her in Zurich. She was much freer, more concentrated, and she made a profound impression with her personality, knowledge, integrity, and humor. She was generally accepted without any reservations. Only I was asked repeatedly: Why isn't she married? In the seminars I asked her about the unio mentalis, corporalis, and the unus mundus. I'd have liked to hear more on these subjects, and I hope you'll make them accessible soon.

22 Kirsch had been licensed as a doctor in New York State since 1943. He never obtained his medical license in California, since that state required that he complete a year-long medical internship. His application for permission to practice at the C. G. Jung Clinic (cf. Kirsch, 9 May 1953, p. 169, note 65) included a questionnaire recounting his medical education and analytic training through late 1952 (undated document, Kirsch archive). California did permit him to practice as an analyst, but he was forbidden to represent himself as a licensed physician. As a result, Thomas Kirsch recalls, after the mid 1950s his father seldom wrote "MD" after his name; or if he did, he added "(NY)."

23 Kieffer Evans Frantz, MD (d. 1975): American psychiatrist and Jungian analyst, practicing in Los Angeles. At the founding of the low-fee C. G. Jung Clinic in 1953, Frantz became its first director. It was later renamed the Kieffer Frantz Clinic. He directed the analytic training program in Los Angeles, 1956–58.

24 Margaret McClean, MD: American psychiatrist and Jungian analyst, practicing in Los Angeles. Co-founder and staff member of the C. G. Jung Clinic. She directed the analytic training program in Los Angeles, 1960.

25 Word orig. in English.

26 I. Jay Dunn, whose medical licence was in osteopathy (cf. Kirsch, 29 September 1948, p. 118 and note), was on the staff of the newly founded C. G. Jung Clinic. He directed the analytic training program in Los Angeles, 1958–60.

27 Word orig. in English.

28 Incomplete sentence in original: *Wie dieser Konflikt, der den beiden aufgebrummt ist (natürlich als Ausdruck eines stark funktionierenden Archetypus) weiss ich nicht.*

29 Word orig. in English.

30 Cf. Kirsch *et al.*, 22 February 1953, p. 159 and note.

In the "pamphlet"[31] regarding the Collected Works I saw an announcement of the *Mysterium Coniunctionis*.[32] In 1951 I had the privilege of reading two chapters of that work. Will it be published soon?

May I tell you about a recent dream of mine? I don't expect you to discuss it but would like to show you how much the creative problem is occupying my mind – and torturing me:

> In the first part of the dream I had suddenly been elected as President of the U.S. But then I slept in the same room with you. During the entire time melodies went through my head, but I had no chance to write them down, because I did not know how. Waking up I noticed that you had written melodies. It was news to me that you are also a composer.
>
> Then you went with me into a neighboring room and, sitting at a round table, explained to me how you write your books. You said a mouse would always be running around in circles in your belly.[33] I interrupted you and wanted to tell you that I had the same experience, but then I thought that just such an interruption may be the reason why I am not writing. Instead, I should be listening!

In your letter you wrote that you are positively feeling better. But then I heard that after seeing your students, you took to your bed again. I'm so sorry about that. I can well imagine that you must have become very sensitive to the unconscious of other people. The meaning of this is of great concern to me, and I wonder how you may be doing. In July I'd like to come to Zurich for about ten days but scarcely dare to hope I'll see you then.

Cordial greetings and all good wishes,

Your very much indebted JAMES KIRSCH

---

31 Word orig. in English.
32 Cf. Kirsch, 23 November 1952, p. 147 and note.
33 Jung's reply is missing. He evidently interpreted this image on the subjective level, i.e. as referring to the dreamer. Cf. Kirsch, 14 April 1953, p. 165 and 9 May 1953, p. 169.

[draft of Kirsch's 18 April 1953 letter]

14 April 1953[34]

Dear Professor!

First I'd like to thank you most sincerely for your letter, written in such personal terms.[35] *You'll understand very well how I'm feeling, since I've known you now for 24 years. Partly I am identified with you (and thus also inflated), to a large extent I know you from your books, and to a great and undefined degree my image of the Self is blended with the image of you, and I find it very difficult to separate these two from each other. In that regard, such a letter from you is helpful to me.*

You wrote me a detail about Toni's death which nobody else had reported to me, and which completes the medical picture. The American physicians, with their rationalism and their mechanistic conception, yet practical attitude, would have handled the case differently; not better, certainly, but differently. What kind of physician one has is definitely part of one's fate. I'm thinking of Toni a lot. It hurts me deeply to think of her lonesome death, as I experienced Toni as a very solitary person in the last years. In February I had a brief correspondence with her about her health, with regard to cortisone.[36] *But I, too, had not the remotest idea she was so close to death. She herself probably didn't think of it either because Hilde received a letter from her, one or two days before she died, in which she said that as far as her health was concerned she was feeling particularly good!*

It strikes me as uncanny that you yourself had such dreams of Hades and the hereafter as well as of Dionysos Katachthonios.[37] *May I ask if the character of your dreams has changed now? They must have signified a new initiation? I'm so deeply involved in the process of individuation myself, it's difficult for me to imagine the psychic state that occurs when individuation is achieved, which is what the infinite "multiplicatio" actually represents. About death as a destination you've already written in earlier years. Gilgamesh sought for the plant of immortal life, found it, and lost it again. It is a theme, perhaps the theme in alchemy. You also wrote about the experience of immortality which results from the ego's contact with the Self. I have not had this experience. But I am continuously engaged with you and your work. For that reason this dream of Dionysos Katachthonios keeps going around in my head.*

---

34 Handwritten in German, in green ink, on letterhead, unsigned. This letter is found only in the Kirsch archive. It appears to be a first draft for Kirsch's letter of 18 April 1953, which follows. This draft contains personal details which he omitted from the sent version. It is printed here with permission from the Estate of Toni Wolff.

35 Jung's preceding letter is unfortunately missing.

36 Toni Wolff had written to Kirsch that she would not take cortisone for her arthritis pain, and that her physicians were doubtful about the use of wonder drugs in general (Wolff to Kirsch, 7 February 1953, Kirsch archive).

37 Cf. Kirsch, 18 April 1953, p. 166 and note.

Yesterday I gave a lecture with a subsequent hour-long discussion on "My understanding of religious experience"[38] at the School of Religion.[39] I found it extremely difficult to make these concepts clear to people who lack any experience of the unconscious. However, the questions revealed that a few people were open to them – and they want to hear more about Jung! For some of these young clergymen, science is identical with "predictability."[40] Responding to this question I mentioned – very cautiously – astrology. That was too much for them!

Last Saturday and Sunday we had our meeting[41] in Santa Barbara with the analysts from San Francisco. In every sense it was "successful."[42] We made altogether about 22 participants. The group functioned quite harmoniously. Dr. Dunn discussed a dream; Dr. Perry presented a case of schizophrenia; and Dr. Henderson spoke in detail about T. S. Eliot. All the lectures were of a high caliber and the discussions lively, general, and to the point.[43]

The most important thing for me was the clear realization that Jungian psychology here in Los Angeles positively doesn't depend solely on me any more, that it's alive, and that the exchange between S.F. and L.A. has proven to be productive. A closer collaboration between the two groups is being planned, in both scientific and practical respects. A larger meeting is contemplated for next year in Asilomar.

I wanted to ask you at this time about the peculiar addiction which I've often found in Jewish people and which creates a great difficulty for me, too. I connect it with the so common ego-weakness of the Jew vis-à-vis the anima.

I'd like to thank you especially for your remarks about my dream of the mouse circling in my belly. In an organic sense I'm certain that I'm not epileptic, but it is a fact that unconscious events often happen to me like attacks, that the invasions of the unconscious happen to me suddenly, and that I am preoccupied with the Self in a manner I can absolutely designate as possession, or morbus sacer.[44] The question of what I need to be released from, and for, is not answered by this, but it is made somewhat more definite.

[draft unsigned]

---

38   Title orig. in English.
39   Cf. Kirsch, 18 April 1953, p. 167.
40   Word orig. in English.
41   Word orig. in English.
42   Word orig. in English.
43   Phrase orig. in English.
44   sacred illness. In antiquity certain conditions were thought to be caused by divine possession.

Los Angeles 48, Calif.
18 April 1953[45]

Dear Professor,

It is very hard for all of us here to get used to the thought that Toni is no longer among us. For me she was so decidedly the woman in whom the Self had been realized, and to an extent I have never known elsewhere. Especially during the last sessions I had with her last year, I gratefully sensed the integrity of her creative intellect, which was inseparably linked to a warm humanity.

In the night of her death I could not sleep – without knowing why. Since then I have felt a great tension without comprehending what all this might point to. For some months, I have been preoccupied with an active imagination of an elephant who is my constant companion. Sometimes he becomes huge and sometimes tiny. The color of his hide has changed to golden yellow. What's extraordinary are his wise black eyes.

Your dream of Dionysos Katachthonios[46] keeps going through my mind again and again. Does it hint at a new initiation? I had to think of you so much, who have so deeply experienced the sea of mercy as well as the fire of his wrath, while you always held fast to his oneness.

Last Sunday we Los Angeles analysts held our first joint meeting[47] with the San Francisco analysts in Santa Barbara. In all respects it was a successful meeting.[48] The scientific lectures were of a high caliber. Dr. J. Dunn[49] discussed a dream in detail; Dr. John Perry[50] described a case of schizophrenia and its healing. It's

---

45 Handwritten in German, on plain paper. This version supersedes the draft of 14 April 1953.

46 *Katachthonios* (or *Kata Chthonios*): referring to the underworld aspect of a Greek god. Dionysos (Bacchus) is the god associated with wine, thus also with grape-growing and the earth; also with ecstatic states of intoxication and visions. Jung may have reported this dream in his first letter to Kirsch (now missing) about Toni Wolff's death.

47 Word orig. in English.

48 Phrase orig. in English.

49 Cf. Kirsch, 29 September 1948, p. 118 and note.

50 John Weir Perry, MD (1914–1998): American psychiatrist and Jungian analyst. The son of the Episcopal bishop at whose house C. G. and Emma Jung stayed in 1936 while visiting Providence, Rhode Island (cf. Jung, 3 January 1936, p. 77 and note), the young Perry met Jung on that occasion and talked with him about psychology. He earned his medical degree in 1941 and served as an ambulance corpsman in China during the Second World War. In 1947–49 he attended the newly founded C. G. Jung Institute, Zurich. In 1950 he opened his practice in San Francisco and began to lecture and write. For several years he ran a residential facility, Diabasis, for the non-pharmaceutical treatment of psychotic patients. In 1972, due to persistent boundary violations with patients, he was put on probation by the California State Medical Board. In 1981 the Jung Institute of San Francisco suspended him indefinitely as an analyst. Eventually his medical licence was also revoked. Perry's major published works include *The Self in Psychotic Process* (1953, Foreword by C. G. Jung); *Lord of the Four Quarters: Myths of the Royal Father* (1966, Foreword by Alan Watts); *The Far Side of Madness* (1974); *Roots of Renewal in Myth and Madness: The Meaning of Psychotic Episodes* (1976); and *The Heart of History: Individuality in Evolution* (1987).

also supposed to be published in the near future. Dr. Joe Henderson[51] spoke about T. S. Eliot's work as an expression of personal and collective significance. The discussions were lively and productive. The principal impression was that "Jungian psychology is here to stay"[52] and that the two groups function homogeneously despite all the individual differences. A meeting on a larger scale is being planned for next spring.

On Monday, I gave a 2-hour lecture at the School of Religion of the University of Southern California on the topic of "My understanding of religious experience."[53] I believe I was fairly successful in conveying something significant. Both the lecture and the discussion were recorded. Maybe a book can come out of it later.

In the *Job* seminar, we thoroughly discussed the parable of the dishonest steward[54] and also read your comments on the subject in your 1937 Seminar.[55] Even today I cannot say that I understood it fully. It reminds me of a "koan" where one stumbles on a sudden understanding after a long meditation. You indicate in *Job* that the moral criterion forms consciousness. In your Seminar of 1937, you find it important "that he saves face, his face and that of the Lord,"[56] and that "He muddles through, he survives – and that is the best he can do."[57] However, I am aware that there is still something irrational behind it, which is blocked by my spasm of consciousness.[58]

---

51 Joseph Lewis Henderson, MD (1903–2007): American psychiatrist and analyst, early friend and follower of Jung. Born in the tiny town of Elko, Nevada, Henderson met H. G. Baynes in San Francisco in 1927, and went to Zurich in 1929 to analyze with C. G. Jung and Toni Wolff. He studied medicine in London at St. Bartholemew's Medical College, until 1938, where he became friends with Joseph and Jane Wheelwright (cf. Kirsch, 27 June 1949, p. 125 and note). Henderson then left England with his wife, Helena, to settle first in New York and then in 1940 in San Francisco. There he opened a practice and became a central figure in the Jungian community of northern California. An early patron of the Jung Institute in Zurich, Henderson also helped to found the APC of San Francisco, the San Francsico MSAP, and later the San Francisco Jung Institute, where he taught for many decades. He was also an honorary founder of ARAS (The Archive for Research in Archetypal Symbolism). At age 99 he closed his practice in San Francisco but continued to work out of his home in Ross until age 102. He contributed a chapter for Jung's last book, *Man and His Symbols* (1964). His full-length works include *The Wisdom of the Serpent: The Myths of Death, Rebirth and Resurrection* (with Maud Oakes, 1963) and *Thresholds of Initiation* (1967).

52 Statement orig. in English.

53 Title orig. in English. The lecture has not been found.

54 Luke 16:1–9, discussed in Job, ¶696.

55 C. G. Jung, *Nietzsche's Zarathustra: Notes of the Seminar Given in 1934–1939* (Part II) (PUP, 1988), pp. 993ff. Jung's discussion of this theme occurred on 10 June 1936. (With thanks to Ulrich Hoerni.) The unjust steward was also a theme in Jung's 1941 Eranos lecture (cf. "Transformation Symbolism in the Mass," CW 11, ¶416).

56 Phrase orig. in English.

57 Phrase orig. in English.

58 *Bewusstseinskrampf.*

Dear Professor, my most affectionate wishes are always with you. I hope that the tachycardia is not tormenting you too badly.[59]

With cordial greetings, Faithfully yours, JAMES KIRSCH

P.S.   I wrote to Mr. Barrett.[60]

Los Angeles 48, Calif.

9 May 1953[61]

Dear Professor,

From my friends in Zurich I had heard that you were once again unwell, but that you are now recovering. With all my heart I hope that you are now feeling somewhat better. Now that my wife is again in Zurich, I hope to have news about you on a regular basis.

Recently I read your letter to Sinclair Lewis[62] in the "New Republic" wherein you briefly touch on the question of Jesus' personality which you discuss in much more detail in your *Antwort auf Hiob*. I actually finished the translation quite some time ago. A large part of it is already "mimeographed",[63] but a few details are still missing, and I have not been able to complete the task due to the great demands of my practice. If you wish, I could send Sinclair Lewis a copy of my translation.

I received a pleasant reply from Mr. Barrett so that I'll have nothing to fear there with respect to any violation of the copyrights.[64]

The convention of American Psychiatrists took place this week. A lot of "hot air" – few people who had anything to say. But one copy of *Alchemy and*

---

59   Jung's cardiac symptoms recurred after Toni Wolff's death. Cf. Jung, 28 May 1953, p. 170 and note.

60   Kirsch was concerned that copyright restrictions would limit the use of his translation of *Job*. Barrett reassured him on the subject (cf. Kirsch, 17 March 1953, p. 161).

61   Handwritten in German, on plain paper.

62   Kirsch's accidental substitution for Upton Sinclair (1878–1968), another American writer. Jung's letter to Sinclair, "The Challenge of the Christian Enigma. Letter to Upton Sinclair" (cf. *Letters II*, pp. 87ff), appeared in *The New Republic* (Washington, DC, Vol. 128, no. 17, issue 2004) dated 27 April 1953. In it Jung takes issue with Sinclair's book, *A Personal Jesus* (1952), which he says creates an over-rationalized, demythologized portrait of Jesus. He reproaches Sinclair for selecting only parts of the New Testament text, omitting all the parts conveying mystery and eschatology. Two years later Jung published a second letter to Sinclair: "The Christian Legend: An Interpretation" (*The New Republic*, 21 February 1955).

63   Word orig. in English.

64   Cf. Kirsch, 17 March 1953, p. 161 and note.

Psychology in English was already displayed there. So why we can't buy it in the bookstore is a mystery to me!

The first "staff meeting"[65] of our C. G. Jung Clinic took place on May 1. Besides analysts, the "psychologists"[66] and our social worker[67] participated (here only the individuals who give tests are called "psychologists"). The analysis of the Rorschach test was an outstanding achievement which surpassed everything I have seen otherwise in the field of the Rorschach. It showed that with a knowledge and experience of the ucs. one can indeed grasp the depth and characteristics of an individual's emotional situation.

It is certainly important and necessary to have this kind of possibility to discuss a case with several individuals and on the basis of different methods, as we did in our staff meeting. The attending analyst surely learned a lot. Nevertheless, I could not help feeling great unease that such an individual was discussed by a small collective. Of course, we had the patient's written authorization to do so.[68] We can depend on the discretion of those who were present, but I have a great concern about the effect on the patient, since one is dealing with numinous aspects.

Your remark about my dream of the mouse circling in my belly[69] stayed with me for a long time. In an organic sense, of course, I do not suffer from epilepsy, but since childhood I have repeatedly been exposed to invasions of the unconscious which led to attacks of all sorts. I am hoping and working to be able to integrate the latest invasion. I find my greatest difficulty in the still persisting identification with the anima.

Recently I had a dream about a dog who had to decide whether to return to his old master, who had raised him and had once saved his life, but for whom he had to work very hard, or to stay with his new master, who was friendly to him and with whom he had a comfortable life. After the dog resolved the conflict and decided to return to his old master, I was able to touch the white, round stone. It feels charged with electricity. When I touch it, I can discover what the Blessed Virgin (who hovers beside the stone) wants to reveal to mankind.

It was a numinous dream. I hope that touching the white stone was a "comprehension"[70] and not an identification. Even though I feel I've reached a certain level, I am by no means at the end of the opus psychologicum. Then, in the next dream, I participated in an experiment with the atom bomb, together with the anima, both as guinea pigs![71] In the process, models of the atom were thrown

---

65 Phrase orig. in English. The fact that Kirsch participated at this meeting suggests that, after the initial denial, he received the State's permission to practice as an analyst (cf. Kirsch, 17 March 1953, pp. 161f, note 22). He was also the director of the training program in which the C. G. Jung Clinic played an integral part.

66 Word orig. in English (here and following).

67 Phrase orig. in English.

68 A hand-drawn line in the left margin highlights this sentence.

69 Cf. Kirsch, 17 March 1953, p. 163.

70 *Be-greifen* (for *Begreifen*): lit. "grasping hold."

71 *Versuchskarnickel*: lit. "experimental rabbits."

to me; one of which was a square between two very beautiful wooden globes, but the other looked much more complicated, something like the models of the Self which you sketched in *Aion*.[72]

By the way, I am working on a story by Jack London,[73] "The Red One",[74] which actually is an active imagination, in which the Self appears as a red, resonating sphere. I hope to be able to publish it.

I very much hope and wish that God's grace will sustain your health and creative power.[75]

   With cordial greetings also to your wife. Faithfully yours, JAMES KIRSCH

Prof. Dr. C. G. Jung
Küsnacht-Zürich
Seestrasse 228

28 May 1953[76]

Dear Colleague![77]

At last I'm able to thank you personally for the kind letter you wrote me on the occasion of Toni Wolff's death. On the day of her death, even before I had received the news, I had a bad relapse of my tachycardia.[78] This has now subsided but it left an arrhythmia which very much impedes my physical capacities. Now I've risked going to Bollingen over Whitsuntide, and I hope to recover here a bit more.

T. W. died so suddenly and so entirely unexpectedly that one could scarcely realize her disappearance. I had seen her two days earlier – both totally unsuspecting. As early as mid-February I had Hades dreams, which I related entirely to

---

72 Cf. Jung, 28 May 1953, p. 171 and note. Jung's "models of the Self" (*Aion*, CW 9(ii), pp. 227, 231, 236, 238, 247) are derived from a single, large diagram of "four quaternios" which he enclosed in a letter to Fr. Victor White, 21 May 1948 (*Jung–White Letters*, pp. 118ff; pp. 122f).

73 Jack London (1876–1916): American author, pioneer in commercial magazine fiction, one of the first who made a career exclusively from writing. Major works include *White Fang* (1900); *The Call of the Wild* (1903); *Sea-Wolf* (1904). His story, "The Red One," was written in 1916, six months before his death, and published in a volume by the same name.

74 Cf. Kirsch, 7 June 1954, p. 199 and note. Cf. also Appendix C, p. 287.

75 Final paragraph and closing are written sideways in left margin.

76 Handwritten in German, on letterhead. Based on his first paragraph, Jung wrote this letter at Bollingen. Prev. pub. in *PP* and in *Letters II*.

77 *Herr Collega!* Jung's salutations alternate between Latin (*Collega*) and German (*Kollege*). In his early letters to Kirsch he often combines the two forms (*Herr College!*). The Latin spelling is commonly used between doctors.

78 Cf. Jung, 18 November 1952, p. 141 and note.

myself, because nothing pointed to Toni. None of the people who were close to her had any warning dreams, while people in England and Germany did, and in Zurich only some who knew her merely superficially.

At the beginning of my illness in Oct. 52 I dreamt of a big black elephant who uprooted a tree. (Since then I have written a rather long essay about the "philosophical tree.")[79] The primordial uprooting of trees can also mean death. Since that time I have dreamt several more times of elephants, whom I always had to go carefully around. Apparently they were occupied with road construction.

Your news interested me very much. The Ordinarius[80] for Old Testament at the university here is discussing my *Job* in a seminar. One can regard "Job" from different sides, of course. What mattered to me this time was the human relationship to God, that is, the God-image. If God's consciousness is clearer than human consciousness, then creation makes no sense and humanity has no purpose for existence. Then indeed God does not play dice, as Einstein says, but has invented a machine, which is even worse. In fact, the creation story resembles an experiment with dice more than anything intentional. These insights probably signify an enormous change of the God-image.[81]

"Synchronicity"[82] should appear in English soon. *Psych. & Alch.*[83] is finally out.

The clinical practice of psychotherapy is a mere expedient, which prevents numinous experiences as much as possible. To a certain extent things can also go all right this way. But there will always be cases which go beyond this, even among the physicians.

The "white stone" (*calculus albus*)[84] occurs in the Apocalypse as a symbol of election.

The model of the Self in *Aion* is based on Ezekiel's vision![85]

With best greetings, Yours truly, C. G. JUNG

P.S. Recently I saw your wife at the Club, when I went back for the first time to attend a lecture.

---

79 Cf. Jung, 29 January 1953, p. 158 and note.
80 In universities of German-speaking countries, title corresponding to the rank of full professor.
81 Cf. Kirsch, 14 September 1953, pp. 175f.
82 C. G. Jung and Wolfgang Pauli, "Synchronizität als ein Prinzip akausaler Zusammenhänge." Orig. pub. in *Naturerklärung und Psyche* (Studien aus dem C. G. Jung-Institut Zürich, 4, Zürich: Rascher, 1952. English version, revised: "Synchronicity: An Acausal Connecting Principle," trans. Hull, in *The Interpretation of Nature and the Psyche*, New York: Pantheon; London: Routledge & Kegan Paul, 1955. (Hereafter *Synchronicity*) (Cf. CW 8, ¶816–968.)
83 First English edition of *Psych & Alch*, CW 12, pub. 1953; 2nd ed. pub. 1968. (Cf. Jung, 3 January 1936, p. 77, note 39.)
84 In Kirsch's dream he was given a white stone (cf. Kirsch, 9 May 1953, p. 169). Jung refers the image to the white stone in Rev. 2:17 (*Letters II*, p.118, note).
85 Cf. Ezekiel 1:14. Cf. also *Aion*, CW 9(ii), ¶410f.

Los Angeles 48, Calif.
14 June 1953[86]

Dear Professor,

I was very pleased to read in your letter that you ventured out to Bollingen. Apparently it agreed with you, because my wife wrote that you and your wife are planning a reception for Friday. My most heartfelt wishes that you may spend a beautiful summer in your beloved Bollingen.

Habent sua fata libelli![87] The translation of your *Job* – which I completed several weeks ago and on which Mr. Barrett sent me congratulations – is encountering the strangest difficulties. The lady who was typing it suddenly took ill, abandoned the manuscript in mid-sentence, and had to leave town to recuperate. Then the lady who was mimeographing it also left me in the lurch for two weeks. Tomorrow it should finally be finished. I'll send you a copy at once.

Now I'm preparing for my trip and hope to be in Zurich by mid-July. Hoping I'll be allowed to see you for a brief time.

Yesterday I visited Dr. Ziskind.[88] I'd seen his manuscript twice already in recent years and corrected a number of things. I'd made him aware how impossible his attitude and conception are, but to no avail.[89] At that point I had to recall your opinion – which is certainly correct – that no one can help anyone else progress beyond where he is himself, and it's certain that nobody can understand you and your point of view unless he's experienced the unconscious at least to some degree. But I must acknowledge that he showed me his manuscript with your corrections, and the letter you had sent to him, a letter that, if I'd received it, I would have retreated behind the stove with. In our discussion he disputed the fact that you are an empiricist. He recognized, nevertheless, that the archetypes are a fact; but not the coll. ucs. For him there are only physical facts, while psychic facts exist only to the extent that they can be physically proven. He is trying to

---

86 Handwritten in German, on plain paper.

87 "Books (*lit.* little books) have their destinies!" A Latin saying, which Jung also quotes regarding the vicissitudes of his publications (cf. Jung, 11 September 1954, p. 206 and note). The saying is from a late third-century work on poetics by Terentianus Maurus, *De litteris, syllabis, metris*, where it is preceded by the words, *"pro captu lectoris"* ["depending on the capacity of the reader"] (Georg Büchmann, *Zitatensammlung: 'Geflügelte Worte',* München/Zürich: Droemer/Knaur, 1959, p. 99; with thanks to Ulrich Hoerni). *Libellus* [little book] also occurs in the title of an alchemical volume in Jung's library (cf. Kirsch, 25 July 1936, p. 87, note 82). The thought is echoed when Jung calls his 1937 Terry Lectures "my little book" (cf. Jung, 25 July 1946, p. 106), or writes that "a little book of mine [i.e. *Job*] will be published" (Jung to Priestley, *Letters II*, p. 192).

88 Eugene Ziskind, MD (1900–1993): Swiss-American psychiatrist, founder of the Gateways Psychiatric Hospital. Among the first American psychiatrists to treat mental illness through neurology, including ECT, insulin and lithium. At this date he was Professor of Psychiatry at the University of Southern California.

89 Ziskind's forthcoming book, *Psychophysiologic Medicine* (1954), included a section on Jung's contribution to the field, about which Kirsch repeatedly sent him polite but pointed criticisms (Kirsch to Ziskind, 8 March 1953 and 15 September 1954, Kirsch archive).

understand all forms of modern psychology, but simply can't do it. For that reason the Freudians call him "Re-sistkind."

At the same time, he is the psychiatrist who put my name forward at the University of Southern California[90] and continues to fight for "Jung" to be taught at the University. As a human being he is also very friendly and helpful. How such intellectual impudence, dishonesty, can co-exist with this unsentimental humanness is a psychological enigma to me. By the way, he's one of the most renowned representatives of the "psycho-biological school"[91] which was founded here in the U.S.A. by Adolf Meyer[92] – also a Swiss import!

My wife wrote me that she saw you recently at the reception for the foreign instructors. I was pleased to hear that you were well enough to see so many people.

With most cordial greetings, Faithfully yours, JAMES KIRSCH

From an unidentified secretary:

17 July 1953[93]

Dr. James Kirsch
Hotel Sonnenberg
Aurorastr. 98
Zürich 7/32

Dear Dr. Kirsch,

A line to tell you that I gave Dr. Jung your message and he said I should tell you how sorry he was that it was not possible for him to see you before he left on his holiday. However he expects to be back in Zürich very briefly probably at the end of next week and there is just a possibility that he might be able to fit it in then, if you are going to be in Zürich at that time. Perhaps you would be so kind as to ring me up next Friday or Thursday afternoon just to say what your plans are.

Yours sincerely, Secretary *[carbon copy unsigned]*

90 This possibility of a faculty appointment appealed to Kirsch greatly. He wrote to Liliane Frey-Rohn that he would be honored to represent Jung's psychology at the university level, and that the appointment would mean he would be able to obtain a California medical license (Kirsch to Frey-Rohn, 25 January 1953, Kirsch archive). Unfortunately, the university appointment failed to materialize.

91 Phrase orig. in English.

92 Adolf Meyer, MD, LLD (1866–1950): Swiss-American psychiatrist, who emigrated to the United States before the First World War. He became president of the American Psychiatric Association, carrying on extensive correspondence with Eugene Ziskind, 1935–38. His major publication, published posthumously, was titled, *Psychobiology: A Science of Man* (1957).

93 Typewritten in English, on plain paper; unsigned carbon copy. The writer may have been Una Thomas (cf. Thomas, 20 October 1952, p. 140 and note).

Prof. Dr. C. G. Jung
Küsnacht-Zürich
Seestrasse 228

6 August 1953[94]

Dear Colleague![95]

Many thanks for your kindness in making your translations of *Job* available to me. You've already set fires with them in various places in England.[96]

I was very sorry that I couldn't see you again. My work load reached the outer limits, which I'm no longer allowed to cross. I hope to be able to make up for this neglect next year – *Deo concedente!*[97]

With many thanks and collegial greetings, Yours truly, C. G. JUNG

James Kirsch
Analytical Psychologist
6120 Barrows Drive
Los Angeles 48, Calif.

Walnut 9229

14 September 1953[98]

Dear Professor!

Accept my most heartfelt thanks for your letter of 6 August. I know that at the end of July you were at the limit of your capacity for work and simply could not see any more people. You speak from your own experience when you describe John's exhaustion of old age. Nevertheless I hope – *Deo concedente* – to see you again next year.

As I already wrote you recently, Dr. Evans-Wentz has asked me to write a short preface to your Introduction to the "Great Liberation." It is enclosed herewith. Of course, I have some reservations about it, because in your Introduction you

---

94 Handwritten in German, on letterhead. First paragraph prev. pub. in *PP.*
95 *Collega!*
96 Kirsch had also sent his translation of *Job* to Michael Fordham in London. Fordham, an editor of the CW, replied: "I am enjoying it enormously, but further I think the translation is satisfying and I hope it will get published. I have a letter today from McGuire saying that the translation is in Hull's hands and he is going to decide so you may like to contact him in Ascona, but please use this information discretely" (Fordham to Kirsch, 17 July 1951, Kirsch archive).
97 God willing!
98 Handwritten in German, on letterhead.

say enough about your understanding of "Soul"; and because "Dharmakaya" and "Soul" are only identical in one particular aspect. Dr. Wentz was of the opinion, however, that the Eastern reader would lay aside and not even read a book which makes use of the intuitive concept of "Soul."[99] I can hardly believe that. From this viewpoint such a "preface" would not even be necessary.

What I think of the translation,[100] I had already written to you. I tested it on a few Americans, with the same effect. I mean just linguistically. Now I hear from Dr. Wentz that you OK'd the Introduction in its current form, and that it is already in press. Thus any changes will only be possible in the 2nd edition. A pity!

Here in our Club subtle changes are taking place which became evident at our last meeting. It seems that here in America people tend over and over again to forget the shadow, feeling suddenly very satisfied with whatever's been accomplished, patting themselves benevolently on the shoulder – while being cut off from everything real. Also, in the admission of new members, the Club has given preference to individuals with good external, "social" adaptation over others whose state of conflict was noticeable and who were deeply gripped by the numinosity of the individuation process. "Coincidentally," these were all patients of mine or Hilde's. At first I was quite dismayed that the Club was reacting in this manner. But then I realized that this situation in the inner circle ran parallel to changes in my own attitude to the collective, that other depths of the coll. ucs. are now touching me most profoundly, and therefore – synchronistically – the collective is reacting differently toward me.

In one of your letters to me[101] you wrote: "If God's consciousness is clearer than human consciousness, then creation makes no sense and humanity has no purpose for existence. Then indeed God does not play dice, as Einstein says, but has invented a machine, which is even worse. In fact, the creation story resembles an experiment with dice more than anything intentional. These insights probably signify an enormous change of the God-image."

---

99 Evans-Wentz had "asked Mr. Hull if it would be allowable in certain instances to use 'psyche' rather than 'soul' (which is, as doubtless you know, objectionable to the Buddhist)" (Evans-Wentz to Kirsch, 17 June 1953, Kirsch archive). In his next letter he adds, "In the eyes of the Buddhists, the 'soul' is a transitory thing. The word, to them, implies nothing of permanent character such as it does for most Europeans who have had their thinking confused by Christian dogmatics" (Evans-Wentz to Kirsch, 25 August 1953, Kirsch archive).

100 Two of Jung's writings appear to be confused here. One piece, "Psychological Commentary on 'The Tibetan Book of the Great Liberation'" (cf. CW 11, ¶759–830), was written in English in 1939 (cf. Jung, 2 October 1953, p. 177). Of this piece Evans-Wentz writes: "I surmise that the commentary was never in German, because Dr. Jung sent it to me, in English, soon after our Oxford conference" (Evans-Wentz to Kirsch, 25 August 1953, Kirsch archive). The other piece, whose English title is "Psychological Commentary on 'The Tibetan Book of the Dead'" (cf. CW 11, ¶831–58), was published in German in 1935 with a brief introduction by Jung, also written originally in German. Referring to this piece, Evans-Wentz writes to Kirsch, "You have greatly improved the translation of the German introduction" (Evans-Wentz to Kirsch, 27 August 1953, Kirsch archive).

101 Cf. Jung, 28 May 1953, p. 171 and note.

I can only concur with these statements of yours. If I may presume to say so: I can confirm them on the basis of my latest experiences. That God's consciousness is less clear than that of human beings seems, on that basis, to be irrefutable. I can also accept the image of the dice game, as long as it is presented in contrast to something intentional. But I cannot conceive of the creation as a game of dice after all, because a Dike or Moira would have to rule over it, i.e. something that would "arrange" the creation synchronistically, and not teleologically.[102]

Into my thoughts on this problem there falls an image or saying which was once given me by the unconscious, "that the creation was generated once and is recurring again and again." This 2nd sentence would correspond to mutations which can be observed in biology. Such acts of creation generally happen in a meaningful order, even though the "trickster" also appears to play his special tricks right here. But how I should visualize the history of creation, I don't know. I'm familiar with a multitude of creation myths, my favorite and nearest being from the "Zohar."[103] Recently there came to me, as a nocturnal impression, the image of the double pyramid, which was hurled at me from an explosion of an atomic bomb. On its sides, the triangles, were transfer pictures such as we had as children. After putting water on them, colored pictures appeared. That is also what I did in my dream image. But what occurred inside the pyramid, I did not see. Do we have to content ourselves with these pictures? My active imagination has been greatly engaged with this pyramid.

Psychologically I feel much better. The violent, inner altercation has simultaneously brought a great calming. I am reflecting – something new for me.

Gratefully and faithfully yours, JAMES KIRSCH

Enclosure in Kirsch's letter of 14 September 1953:

Preface to the Eastern Reader[104]

This book addresses itself in the first place to the Western reader and attempts to communicate important Eastern experiences and conceptions to the Western mind. Prof. Jung tries to facilitate this difficult undertaking by his 'Introduction' and 'Psychological Commentary'. It is therefore unavoidable that, in so doing, he speaks in images and uses concepts which are familiar to the Western mind, but which are objectionable to the Eastern mind.

---

102 A hand-drawn line in the left margin highlights this sentence.

103 *Zohar*: Hebrew (lit. "radiance"). A central work of Kabbalah, it is a mystical commentary on the Torah (the five books of Moses), written in medieval Aramaic and Hebrew.

104 Typewritten in English, on plain paper. A copy of this preface had been sent to Evans-Wentz, who wrote, "It is very appropriate for use, as intended, in the forthcoming edition of *The Tibetan Book of the Dead*" (Evans-Wentz to Kirsch, 27 August 1953, Kirsch archive).

Such a term is the word "Soul". According to Buddhistic belief, the 'soul' is ephemeral, is an illusion and therefore has no existence at all. The German word 'Seele', which by no means is the same as the English word 'Soul', is an old word, sanctioned by Tradition, used by the greatest German mystics like Eckhart and poets like Goethe to signify the Ultimate Reality, but experienced under a feminine aspect. Prof. Jung uses it frequently as a poetical term for 'psyche', the collective psyche. In scientific language, it represents the *Collective Unconscious* as the matrix of everything. It is the birthplace of everything, even of the Dharmakaya. It is the Dharmakaya itself.

I beg therefore of you, my Eastern reader, to put your understanding of 'soul' aside for the time being, to accept Prof. Jung's use of this word, and to follow him with an open mind into the depths when he tries to build a bridge from the Eastern to the Western shore and to describe the different paths to the Great Liberation, the Una Salus.[105]

2 October 1953[106]

Dr. James Kirsch,
6120 Barrows Drive,
Los Angeles 48,
California.

Dear Kirsch,

Thank you very much for kindly sending me your "Preface to the Eastern Reader".[107] I quite agree with it. I am aware of the fact that the style of my contribution to Evans-Wentz's book is questionable, and I had hoped that Evans would be reasonable enough to smooth it out. I wrote it originally in English. I have not heard of its fate for ages and I am quite astonished to hear that it is now already in the printer's press. I thank you very much for your "editorial note". I assume that Evans is bristling with resistances against my psychological point of view because, as every true Easterner, he believes that he has produced an eternal truth, but, with the whole of the East, he has, of course, never heard of a theory of cognition and of Immanuel Kant, just as little as the Catholic Church. On the pre-Kantian level there is no such thing as psychology, only metaphysics.

I was pleased to hear that your translation of *Job* had been accepted. It is nice to know that the book can thus soon appear.

I am awfully sorry that I did not send you my original text of the commentary to Evans-Wentz's book. There is no German original and as far as I remember I wrote the thing rather hurriedly, being pressed by other work. I also do not

105 One Salvation (cf. Jung, 18 November 1952, p. 143 and note).
106 Typewritten in English, on letterhead. Prev. pub. in *PP*.
107 Cf. Kirsch, 14 September 1953, "Preface to the Eastern Reader" (enclosure), above.

know what, in the long time that has elapsed since I wrote it, has happened to my manuscript. I wondered whether you had the original typescript. As far as I remember, it was all perfectly simple and clear, but of course I would not claim to write a perfect English style.

Synchronicity means a factor inherent in Nature. It is a factor accounting for the existence of teleological arrangements, which does not mean that the whole of creation is premeditated, or in any way conscious. It only indicates the fact that there are chance groupings that make sense. I assume that the existence of this factor accounts for the fact that man forever thinks in terms of gods. Well, this is a problem which I do not claim to have solved.

The American tendency to let the unconscious slip by is not specifically American. It happens with us too. No sooner do you have a certain collectivity than people try, in the ratio of its increase, to emancipate themselves from the shadow. Look what happened to Christianity when it became a church.

With best wishes, Yours sincerely, C. G. JUNG

Los Angeles 48, Calif.

18 October 1953[108]

Prof. Dr. C. G. Jung
Küsnacht-Zürich
Seestrasse 228

Dear Professor,

Please accept my most heartfelt thanks for your letter of 2 October.

I read the "Introduction" to the "Great Liberation" in the galley proofs and made only a few linguistic corrections. In addition, off and on, I replaced the word "soul" – which so disturbed Evans-Wentz[109] – with "psyche" or "psychic life" in a few places, but mostly I let it stand. I believe I haven't changed anything in the sense of your Introduction, but have only brought it out more clearly. A number of passages still remain which would benefit from "editing."[110] I'm enclosing a finished copy, typed by my secretary, which already includes the passages I corrected.

p. 3, 2nd line – I would suggest replacing "unwarrantable" with "improvable."

p. 10. I believe that the sentence referring to the center, in its current wording, contradicts your teachings about the Self, centering events in the individuation process, etc. and therefore that the thoughts here hinted at should be amplified further.

---

108 Handwritten in German, on plain paper.
109 Cf. Kirsch, 14 September 1953, p. 175 and note.
110 Word orig. in English.

p. 14. "gratuitously offensive" makes no sense here. Perhaps you could say instead: "it is considered an insult to say.…"

p. 14. "Anfractuosities" is such a dictionary word[111] that I have not yet found anyone who knows it. This fact certainly does not speak against this word, but would "deviousness" not perhaps be preferable?

p. 14A. In English, the word "constellate" only means "to unite stars in a cluster." For that reason it is never understood here. Perhaps a footnote here about the meaning of this word would be appropriate, although the subsequent sentence explains what's meant to some extent.

I immediately wrote to Evans-Wentz and asked him whether small changes would perhaps still be possible, but as yet I've had no answer from him.

At the present time I'm giving a small seminar attended by 4 analysts, in which we're reading and discussing your book *Aion*. A great debate[112] resulted from your statement on page 67: "The psychological equivalent to it (Christ's descent into hell) constitutes the integration of the coll. ucs. which represents an essential component of individuation."[113] Seen rationally, this statement contradicts what you say, for instance, on page 29 of this manuscript: "It (i.e. the Mind) can never be realized completely. This is certainly true of the unconscious."[114] I believe I know what you mean. There is also a distinction between "integration" and "realization." But how does one explain this to someone who has not had the experience of a descent into hell? In a certain way, your entire work deals with these things, and yet I would be grateful if you could write something on the subject to this small but lively group.[115]

When I wrote that in our local Club the shadow – and thus the unconscious – is being forgotten, I referred to the fact that, after we'd resisted it for many years, we've now decided to invite Frau Jacobi[116] to visit here. Now she's here, and we

---

111 Phrase orig. in English.

112 Cf. Kirsch, 1 January 1954, p. 186.

113 Quoted sentence orig. in English (i.e. Kirsch's translation). In the CW this passage reads: "The God-image in man was not destroyed by the Fall but was only damaged and corrupted ("deformed"), and can be restored through God's grace. The scope of the integration is suggested by the *descensus ad inferos,* the descent of Christ's soul to hell, its work of redemption embracing even the dead. The psychological equivalent of this is the integration of the collective unconscious which forms an essential part of the individuation process" (*Aion,* CW 9(ii), ¶72, p. 39).

114 Quoted sentence orig. in English (Kirsch's translation). In Hull's translation: "The unconscious as we know can never be 'done with' once and for all" (ibid, ¶40).

115 As his initial reply, Jung sent a copy of his letter to a Catholic priest, Fr. Victor White, OP, about the validity of the Christ-symbol (cf. Kirsch, 1 January 1954, p. 186, note 7).

116 Jolan (Jolande) Jacobi, Dr. phil. (1890–1973): Jungian analyst, born to a prominent Jewish family in Budapest. She moved to Vienna in 1918. In 1928 she became vice-president of the Austrian *Kulturbund*, where Jung lectured. Jacobi traveled to Zurich frequently for analysis with Jung. In 1938 she fled Austria to settle in Zurich. She returned to Vienna the next year, at great risk because of the German occupation, to receive her doctoral degree in philosophy and psychology. For the rest of her life she practiced and taught in Zurich. She wrote several books on analytical psychology, including *The Psychology of C. G. Jung* (Routledge, Kegan Paul, 1943), a classic which is still in print. One of Jung's trusted colleagues and friends until his death, she was also one of the leading exponents of his work in German.

can survey the result in some measure. I wrote about this in detail to your wife – and I'm wondering very seriously how it is even possible for such a woman to go out into the world as your messenger (or even as *the* messenger). I'm sure I cannot tell you anything new about her. I can also imagine your reaction to her. Maybe she's worse here than in Zurich because your "restraining influence"[117] is missing. I can also see how she bears your work into the world, and that it has to be this way. She is even OK (with some reservations), as long as she speaks theoretically. But when she analyzes dreams or images, she is so irreverent and Freudian that she comes across as destructive. She is a true antimimos… an imitative spirit.[118]

Please excuse me for asking you the question, why such a woman has to go into the world in your name – and to teach students (at the Institute). You present me with a large problem, how one must or should handle the devil when he appears not in one's own psyche but personified externally.

Frau Jacobi's appearance in L.A. has had far-reaching consequences, in the sense that minds are divided, and that many projections we had onto Zurich and the Institute[119] are being withdrawn, and we will absolutely become more self-reliant.

There are even a few things about her that I like well enough. It would even be fine with me if she took personal responsibility when releasing her opinions to the world. I saw her here with her old teacher, Dr. Charlotte Bühler from Vienna;[120] and I became aware how much Frau Jacobi represents the Viennese Freudian school. But you, dear Professor, have separated from Freud! Why then must Freud come in again through the back door and declare, in your name, that the complexity of the soul is only an illusion?

With cordial greetings, a deeply shocked JAMES KIRSCH

---

117 Phrase orig. in English.

118 Kirsch had more than one episode of conflict with Jacobi. Correspondence from the summer of 1949 shows his suspicion that Jacobi, who had been raised by assimilated Jewish parents in Hungary and who became a convert to Catholicism, was "not at home with herself" and had a "Jewish problem." Jacobi replies that she prizes her Jewish heritage and defends her spiritual choice in the light of personal experience. She also quotes Jung (cf. CW 11, ¶167), on the inviolability of individual convictions (Jacobi to Kirsch, 1 July 1949, Kirsch archive).

119 Kirsch's accusations against Jacobi became generally known, leading to polarization among the Institute's Curatorium (Meier to Kirsch, 29 January 1954, Kirsch archive), and Jacobi's demand for a public apology (cf. Jung, 16 February 1954, p. 192; Kirsch, 11 June 1955, p. 220).

120 Charlotte Malachowski Bühler, Dr. phil. (1893–1974): Berlin-born developmental psychologist, educated in Munich. She and her husband, Karl Bühler, accepted teaching positions in Vienna in 1922, where Jolande Jacobi received training from them both. Charlotte Bühler, who admired Sigmund Freud's emphasis on early childhood and Anna Freud's close observation of infants, founded a child-study laboratory in Vienna. Until 1939 she was a member of the AAGP, then of the IAAGP. The Bühlers emigrated in 1940 and settled in Los Angeles, where Charlotte Bühler taught clinical psychology at the University of Southern California. In 1962 she founded the American Association of Humanistic Psychology. With Abraham Maslow she played a major role in launching the human potential movement, with its hub at Esalen in Big Sur. Bühler returned to Germany in 1972 and died two years later, in Stuttgart. Among many publications, her major works include *The First Year of Life* (1930) and *From Birth to Maturity* (1937).

Hotel Sonnenberg
Zürich 32

12 December 1953[121]

Dear Fräulein Gautschi![122]

Prof. Jung told me that perhaps he may be able to see me one more time before Christmas. Would you be kind enough to ask him during the next scheduling session?

He also mentioned the *7 Sermones*.[123] May I perhaps call you next Tuesday between 2 and 4 p.m.?

With warm regards, Yours truly, JAMES KIRSCH

---

121 Handwritten in German, on plain paper.
122 One of Jung's secretaries after the departure of Marie-Jeanne Schmid.
123 Cf. Jung, 13 February 1931, p. 14 and note.

1954

HABENT SUA FATA

6120 Barrows Dr.
Los Angeles 48, Calif.

1 January 1954[1]

Dear Professor!

This trip to Zurich and now also the return home were filled with wonderful and unusual experiences. Our airplane flew over Iceland, about which I've often dreamed, and also over the southernmost point of Greenland. The clear moonlight gave both these islands a ghostly appearance. New York was a great shock as always, with its gigantic scale and masses of people.

There I had a half-hour meeting with Mr. Barrett. *Answer to Job* (in English) should already be published by March.[2] Mr. Hull wrote to me, though, that he will still be making a number of changes.[3] It's very good, then, that you'll see it before publication, and that decisions about certain terms in the text will be yours to make.

I also spoke with Mr. Barrett about the translation of *Aion*. He told me that after the publication of *Job* they'll continue with publication of the Collected Works. I mentioned specifically that it is of great importance to you to have your most recent works, particularly *Aion*, published in English as soon as possible. But he gave his opinion that you were a "lucky author" anyhow[4] and that *Aion* would have to wait a while longer. I pointed out that *Aion* and *Answer to Job* belong together for internal reasons. But it appears that the Bollingen Foundation wants to proceed with the Collected Works. They consider the book *Aion* a bit too "heavy." Perhaps you yourself could communicate your wishes to Mr. Barrett and also to *Adler*[5] in London.

---

1   Handwritten in German, on plain paper.
2   In 1954 Hull's translation was published, but not in the United States. It appeared in London (Routledge & Kegan Paul, 1954), incorporating several of Kirsch's corrections (cf. Jung, 29 January 1953, p. 157 and note). Of this edition Jung wrote, "Soon a little book of mine will be published in England which my publishers in the USA did not dare to print" (Jung to J. B. Priestley, 8 November 1954, *Letters II*, p. 192); adding, "Sir Herbert Read, who is informed about its contents, wisely said, 'You certainly understand how to put your foot in it'" (ibid. p. 193). An American edition of *Job* appeared in 1956 with the Pastoral Psychology Book Club, Great Neck, New York. The Bollingen edition of *Job* was delayed on both sides of the Atlantic until 1958, with the publication of CW 11, *Psych & Rel.* Cf. also Jung to H. A. Murray, August 1956, *Letters II*, p. 323.
3   Soon after their work together in Ascona, Hull wrote to Kirsch: "Yes, despite the occasional collisions, I feel sure the collaboration has been fruitful, and I am most grateful for your help. There are of course a number of passages where I have not followed you verbatim; these I will mark in the galleys and let Jung decide" (Hull to Kirsch, 19 December 1953, Kirsch archive).
4   Phrase orig. in English.
5   Gerhard Adler (cf. Jung, 2 July 1934, p. 58 and note) was one of the editors of the Collected Works. Kirsch underlines his name.

I'll be very glad, in any case, if *Answer to Job* comes out and the English translation renders the German text as accurately as possible.

The small seminar about *Aion*[6] already took place last Tuesday. We're very grateful that you allowed us to read and discuss the letter on "Christ as a valid symbol."[7] The English edition of Schweitzer's autobiography[8] also includes a brief summary of the results of his "Leben Jesu"[9] research, which we're also reading. We had a very stimulating discussion about all that.

On page 67 of *Aion* is the second part of a sentence I mentioned to you recently,[10] i.e. "The psychological equivalent to this is the integration of the collective unconscious, which represents an indispensable component of individuation."[11] Since none of us can claim to have integrated the collective unconscious, we are of course rather puzzled,[12] especially since you say at a different juncture that of course one cannot ever integrate the *entire* collective unconscious.[13] This integration may well be the same as "the dark night of the soul?"[14]

---

6 Cf. Kirsch, 18 October. 1953, p. 179. The "Aion" seminar members next wrote to Jung to ask his opinion on the doctrine of Christ's resurrection and received a substantial answer (cf. Jung, 19 May 1954, p. 198 and note).

7 Jung had sent Kirsch a lengthy excerpt from his letter to Fr. Victor White, 24 November 1953 (cf. Kirsch, 23 January. 1955, p. 216 and note), which begins: "Forget for once dogmatics and listen to what psychology has to say concerning your problem: *Christ as a symbol is far from being invalid …*" (*Jung–White Letters*, pp. 218–23). In his holograph of this letter, Jung directed his secretary to create extra carbon copies of the bulk of the text (ibid., p. 223 n. 61), which he then shared with selected colleagues.

8 Albert Schweitzer (1875–1965): Alsatian-born theologian, musician, philosopher, and physician; winner of the 1952 Nobel Peace Prize. As a medical missionary in west central Africa, Schweitzer founded and sustained the Lambaréné Hospital, Gabon, to which he devoted the second half of his life. In English his autobiography is titled, *Out of My Life and Thought: An Autobiography* (trans. C. T. Campion, New York: Henry Holt, 1933, 1949) (orig. *Aus meinem Leben und Denken*, Leipzig: Felix Meiner, 1931).

9 "Life of Jesus": an approach to Christology developed by liberal German theologians in the late nineteenth century, about which Albert Schweitzer wrote a penetrating historical-critical analysis, *The Quest of the Historical Jesus: A Critical Study of Its Progress from Reimarus to Wrede* (trans. W. Mongomery, London: A & C Black, 1910) (orig. *Von Reimarus zu Wrede: Eine Geschichte der Leben-Jesu Forschung*, Tübingen: J. C. B. Mohr, 1906). Schweitzer's reputation as a theologian rests largely upon this work.

10 A heavy pencil line in the left margin, presumably drawn by Jung, highlights the following two sentences.

11 Cf. Kirsch, 18 October 1953, p. 179 and note.

12 Word orig. in English.

13 ibid., note 113.

14 Phrase orig. in English. Familiar term derived from a poem by the Spanish Carmelite mystic, St. John of the Cross (San Juan de la Cruz) (1542–1591). Jung refers to this image when discussing mystery and darkness as positive aspects of the individuation process, e.g. in his Eranos lecture of 1946, "Der Geist der Psychologie" [The Spirit of Psychology]. Later revised, republished as "Theoretische Überlegungen zum Wesen des Psychischen" in *Wurzeln* (cf. Jung, 28 November 1952, p. 149 and note); in English, "On the Nature of the Psyche," CW 8, ¶431.

Quite a lot happened here during my absence. The argumentation concerning the Jacobi matter – which was carried out on my back – led to a deep clarification for most and cleansed the entire atmosphere.[15] All is well that ends well![16] Now we are looking forward to Dr. Meier's visit to Los Angeles.[17]

It's very difficult to express in words how many riches were bestowed on me in Zurich on this visit, and I would like to thank you and your wife once again for the wonderful hours I was privileged to spend at your house. Special thanks also for the "Sermones ad mortuos".[18] I hope very much that your wife will decide to publish the lectures about the Anima in book form.[19]

With most cordial greetings and best wishes for a happy New Year,

Faithfully yours, JAMES KIRSCH

Los Angeles 48
Calif.

5 February 1954[20]

Dear Professor!

From my friends in Zurich I heard that you were in the Ticino and did not feel very well there. I can only hope that you're somewhat better now.

A few days ago, we received your new book *Von den Wurzeln des Bewusstseins*.[21] It's delightful that I can have a thorough conversation with you in this manner. I also read the "Sermones" several times and am gradually beginning to understand them. They are very exciting. I have to think of your remark that there are so few people who really know how to read a book.

---

15 Cf. Kirsch, 11 June 1955, pp. 220f.
16 This and following sentence orig. in English (quotation from Shakespeare).
17 C. A. (Fredy) Meier (cf. Kirsch, 21 September 1948, p. 116 and note). In the autumn of 1954 Meier lived in the Kirsch household for a month, while lecturing at the Los Angeles Institute and other settings (cf. Kirsch, 27 November 1954, p. 209 and notes).
18 Cf. Jung, 13 February 1931, p. 14 and note.
19 Emma Jung wrote two important papers on animus and anima. In 1931 she delivered a long lecture to the Club, "Ein Beitrag zum Problem des Animus" (trans. Cary F. Baynes, "The Nature of the Animus"). It was included in Jung's *Wirklichkeit* (1934). In 1955 her paper, "Die Anima als Naturwesen" (trans. Hildegard Nagel, "The Anima as an Elemental Being") was included in the Festschrift for Jung's 80th birthday, *Studien zur analytischen Psychologie C. G. Jungs* (Zürich: Rascher, 1955). The two translated papers were then published together as a book: Emma Jung, *Animus and Anima*, New York: Spring, 1957. Cf. Kirsch, 11 September 1936, p. 91 and note.
20 Handwritten in German, on plain paper.
21 Cf. Jung, 28 November 1952, p. 149 and note.

In my seminars I'm reading several chapters of *Aion* and thus am making good progress. Just translating the relevant chapters forces me to enter into them with deep feeling and a most precise understanding.

In our analyst seminar we read the letter to the Catholic priest[22] (three evenings). The discussion was very far-reaching and profound, and on behalf of the small group I would like to express our heartiest thanks for your great kindness. There was one question which, of course, we had to leave unanswered: "How would your letter have been written if, instead of a Catholic priest, I (or a modern Jew) had asked you the question, 'Is Christ still a valid symbol?'"[23] For, as I've observed, Christ is only now emerging in the Jewish unconscious as a living symbol. As far as I can see, it does not lead to an imitatio Christi (and this not only out of fear) but to parallel processes. A. Schweitzer's book was very helpful in clarifying these matters for me. Also the books by C. F. Burney[24] and Prof. Schaeder[25] concerning John the Presbyter[26] as the author of the Fourth Gospel and the Epistles, the Apocalypse and possibly the Odes of Solomon. Therefore, how would you answer the question posed by a Jew in whose history the incarnation has become a repressed complex, even though, as you demonstrated in *Answer to Job*, his history has most thoroughly prepared him?

From the sublime to the ridiculous: I just saw in the February 1954 issue of the astrological magazine *Horoscope* that a Mr. Sydney Omarr[27] discussed astrology on the Radio (CBS) on 5 September 1953 and mentioned you extensively. In addition, he mentioned that he'd had a conversation with Dr. Jolande Jacobi, "a top-row disciple of Dr. Jung, a member of the staff of the Institute of Analyt. Psychology, Zürich", and "She said that the eminent doctor enjoys almost nightly discussions with one of his leading students on the subject of astrology."[28]

When I was in Zurich just now I told you that I have gout. Up to now the attacks have been mild and passed rather quickly. But two weeks ago I had a very painful and long-lasting attack (9 days) which only got better after taking the strongest medication (ACTH injections). This caused a shock to my system.

---

22 In a slip of the pen, Kirsch wrote, *"Brief an den katholischen Brief"* ("letter to the Catholic letter"). Cf. Kirsch, 1 January 1954, p. 186 and note.

23 Question orig. in English.

24 The Rev. Charles Fox Burney (1868–1925): English Hebrew scholar, Oriel Professor of Interpretation of the Holy Scriptures, Oxford. Author, *The Aramaic Origin of the Fourth Gospel* (Oxford, 1922).

25 Hans Heinrich Schaeder: early twentieth-century German Islamist and Iranist; Professor at the University of Berlin and the University of Göttingen. With R. Reitzenstein, author of *Studien zum antiken Synkretismus aus Iran und Griechenland*, in which "Son of Man" is studied in its christological usage, based on comparative religions and citing the work of Burney. Jung quotes Schaeder's work in *Aion* and *Mysterium Coniunctionis*.

26 Phrase orig. in English.

27 Sydney Omarr (1926–2003): American astrologer, CBS radio newscaster, columnist and consultant to Hollywood stars, author of thirteen publications.

28 Quoted sentences orig. in English.

Of course, I can take it as a precedent that my grandmother suffered from severe gout, but even the Journal of the American Medical Association maintains that it is a consequence of unbalanced emotional tensions. So much for the etiology of this metabolic disturbance! I freely admit it. I know I have enormous tensions within me. For the first time, the unconscious also reacted to the gout.

The first dream during the attack was simple: That a "non-such problem"[29] becomes physical is a terrible thing.

(2) A June bug with feelers, looking like blossoms or eyes, now becomes the ucs. which is being realized. Two "feelers" were on the head of the June bug and two on the wings.

(3) The earth circles in its orbit, followed by another planet that's like a giant cloud. It explodes and discharges itself as fruitful rain on the earth.

(4) A brother and sister are meeting secretly at night in an apartment in Paris in order to have intercourse. I go there: a holy-gruesome atmosphere. In the second room of this apartment there is a large wall-mirror.

(5) As a result of Dream 3: A lot of water on the earth which can thus now be moved. It is not too dangerous. The pair of opposites is on the water; on the left the coat of arms of Zurich, and on the right the "Round One".[30]

(6) An active imagination which I started on the basis of No. 5: My elephant enters the room where the brother and sister are united. On the back he's carrying a shallow, elliptical wash-bucket full of water; he circumambulates the pair. Suddenly he pours all the water on the pair.

(7) The next day: An enormous tree grows up from below, grows around the pair, which is now a sphere, a gigantic tree-top.

Without your books I would never understand these dreams and active imaginations. I am surprised that I rarely play a role in them. Consciously I'm aware of great resistances, I'm full of affects that I'm not releasing. My physician asked if I was particularly "irascible",[31] because that's supposed to be a characteristic of gout patients. He also confirmed that he has never seen a case where gout disappears again. "Physician heal thyself" has become a necessity for me.[32]

Most cordially, Faithfully yours, JAMES KIRSCH

---

29 Phrase orig. in English.
30 *das Runde.*
31 Word orig. in English.
32 Sentence orig. in English.

6120 Barrows Dr.
Los Angeles 48, Calif.

14 February 1954[33]

Dear Professor!

I'm enclosing herewith a copy of a letter which I received from Mr. Hull a few days ago, and a copy of my answer to it.[34] I had been wondering why I hadn't received the galley proofs that had been promised to me. I am very sorry that I am not mentioned as "joint translator" of your Job book, which I love so much; but I can also understand Mr. Read's[35] standpoint.[36] It may be best to leave it as it is and not to be further involved.

With cordial greetings, Faithfully yours, JAMES KIRSCH

Enclosure in Kirsch's letter of 14 February 1954:

11 February 1954[37]

Mr. R. F. C. Hull
Casa Sulzer A
Ascona, Switzerland

Dear Mr. Hull:

The long delay in answering my letter gave me some warning of what I had to expect. I also noted that I did not receive the galley proofs of *Answer To Job.* Quite frankly, your letter means a great disappointment to me, since in your letter of November 21st, 1953, you wrote that you "took the liberty of acknowledging my help by naming me as joint translator".[38] It was this letter and this fact that

---

33 Handwritten in German, on plain paper. With two enclosures.

34 Essential points from Hull's letter are covered in notes below.

35 Sir Herbert Read (1893–1968): English poet and author, best known as a critic of literature and art. He published nearly 100 titles in his lifetime. Professor of fine arts at Edinburgh University in 1931–33. From the inception of the Collected Works in 1947, he was Senior Editor of the Collected Works, together with Editors, Gerhard Adler and Michael Fordham, and the Executive Editor, William McGuire. In 1953–54 Read was living in the United States, serving as Norton Professor at Harvard University.

36 Read had declined to list Kirsch as joint translator with Hull (cf. Kirsch to Hull, 11 February 1954, p. 191 and note).

37 Typewritten in English, on plain paper, with signature.

38 Hull had written, "In the typescript [recently sent to Bollingen Foundation] I took the liberty of acknowledging your help by naming you as the joint translator" (Hull to Kirsch, 21 November 1953, Kirsch archive).

caused me to interrupt my work in Zurich and work through your translation with a fine comb, and further to make the trip to Ascona.[39]

I have no intention to press the financial point any further. In view of the circumstances it does not seem to make any sense to argue the point whether my work with you should be classed as consultation or hauling through the mirror.[40] I regret that your opinion on our work is now such, in contrast to your opinion expressed in your letter of November 21st. My attitude was certainly that of a translator who accepted full responsibility for his work.

I can understand Sir Herbert Read's attitude[41] though I cannot approve of it. Mr. Barrett appeared to have a different opinion when I talked with him in New York.

Frankly, I feel that Miss Hannah's[42] and Dr. von Franz' share in the translation of *Psychology and Alchemy*[43] have deserved much more acknowledgment than they actually received, but this is not my business.

---

39 Cf. Jung, 28 November 1952, pp. 149f, note 73.

40 Explaining why Kirsch should not, in fact, be named as a joint translator, Hull wrote: "The work we did together in Ascona could reasonably be classed with the consultation, or hauling through the mirror, which I enjoy periodically with Miss Hannah and Frl. v. Franz." (Hull to Kirsch, 4 February 1954, Kirsch archive). The image of "hauling through the mirror," probably not original with Hull, suggests a transformative process, involving inspiration as well as skill.

41 According to Hull, Read and Barrett had written to him that they would not like to introduce a second translator or joint translator, as Hull had been designated from the beginning as sole translator of the CW (ibid.). This judgment is consistent with Barrett's original reply to Kirsch: "It is our plan to have the Collected Works entirely translated by Mr. Hull in order to achieve uniformity in interpretation, terminology, etc. It would, therefore, appear unlikely that we could make use of your translation. However, we are grateful for your suggestion that you might make it available to us for consideration" (Barrett to Kirsch, 16 December 1952, Kirsch archive).

42 Juliet Barbara Hannah (1891–1986): English Jungian analyst and writer. She lived most of her adult life in Switzerland, where she studied and analyzed with Jung. In the 1930s and early 1940s she translated transcriptions (collected from listeners' notes) of his lecture courses at the ETH: *Modern Psychology, Vol. 1 and 2: Notes on Lectures given at the Eidgenössische Technische Hochschule, Zürich, October 1933–July 1935; Modern Psychology, Vol. 3 and 4 [...]: October 1938–March 1940; Alchemy Vol. 1 and 2, The Process of Individuation [...]: November 1940–July 1941.* (Jung's lecture "Exercitia spiritualia of St. Ignatius of Loyola" is found in Vol.4.) Hannah's published works include *Striving Towards Wholeness* (1971, 1973, 1987); *Jung: His Life and Work* (1976, 1977); and *Encounters with the Soul: Active Imagination as Developed by C. G. Jung* (1981). Hannah shared a house and many intellectual interests with Marie-Louise von Franz.

43 In 1946 Hannah and von Franz had worked together to correct the first edition of Jung's *Psych & Alch* (cf. *Jung–White Letters,* pp. 344ff). They also consulted with Hull on his translation of that and other works (cf. note 40 above).

But things are as they are, and powers and principalities that be must be acknowledged, and the only important thing is that Jung's books are published in readable English and also express what he meant to say.[44]

We had quite a hot spell here for nine days, the hottest February in fifty years, you know. . . I cannot check up on this. Anyhow, it was very pleasant and for two weekends about a million people swarmed the beaches. I would have loved to spend my time in snow-covered Ascona, without translating work of course.

Give my kind regards to Mrs. Hull and the kids.

Yours, JAMES KIRSCH

Prof. Dr. C. G. Jung
Küsnacht-Zürich
Seestrasse 228

16 February 1954[45]

Dr. J. Kirsch,
6120 Barrows Drive,
Los Angeles 48, California

Dear Kirsch,

Many thanks for your kind letter! The gouty "irascibility"[46] appears to manifest itself in a general emotional lack of control. With Dr. Jacobi you have "mis le pied dans le plat"[47] in a most imprudent way. In your very own interest, you should pay more attention to your affects, otherwise you become too godlike. That's why strict observance of the law was the guiding principle of your ancestors.

Your dreams are impersonal to compensate for your consciousness being at the mercy of affects. For the same reason they're also so archetypal. Sprinkling

---

44 In a lecture delivered after Jung's death, Kirsch described his translation of *Job* and his consultation with Hull, omitting any mention of misunderstandings or disappointments. He recounts that after reading Jung's newly written *Job* in 1951, he started work at once on an English translation. "As it happened, Mr. R. F. C. Hull, as the official translator of the English edition of Jung's collected works, had also made a translation. At Jung's suggestion, we compared our translations. I think we spent three days, from morning to night, carefully going over every sentence and word. We agreed on almost everything except three words which we submitted to Jung as our ultimate arbitrator" ("C. G. Jung's Individuation as shown especially in *Answer to Job*," typescript, c. 1962, ETH Library archive, p. 2).

45 Typewritten in German, on letterhead. Jung's hand-written draft of this letter, dated 13 February 1954, is in the ETH Library archive. Part of letter prev. pub. in *PP* and *Letters II*.

46 Word orig. in English.

47 "put your foot in it" (Kirsch's behavior toward Jacobi had seriously upset her.)

with rain or other water signifies primarily a cooling (of affects) and, as a further consequence, fertility. Affects are actually volcanic: with the lava they bring nutritious minerals to the surface of the earth.

I hardly believe that the Jews have to accept the symbol of Christ. They only have to understand its meaning:

Intending to transform Yahweh into a moral God of goodness, Christ had torn apart the united (in God) but unharmonious and unreflected opposites (Satan falls out of heaven, Luke 10:18), thus the suspension between the opposites in the crucifixion. The purpose of the Christian Reformation was to remove the bad moral consequences which are caused by the amoral divine model. One cannot simultaneously "strain at gnats and swallow camels" (Matt. 23:24), or "serve two masters" (Matt. 6:24), etc.

This moral differentiation is a necessary step on the path of individuation. Without thorough knowledge of "good and evil," of the ego and the shadow, there is no recognition of the Self, but at most an involuntary and therefore dangerous identification with it.

The Jew has approximately the same moral development behind him as the Christian European; therefore he has the same problem. As well as I, or perhaps even better, in the hostile pair of brothers – Christ-Satan – a Jew can recognize the *Self*, and with that the incarnation, or Yahweh's assimilation to man. Through which, of course, the status of humanity is profoundly changed.

The Jew has the advantage of already having anticipated the development of human consciousness in his spiritual history. By that I mean the Lurianic[48] level of the Kabbalah, the breaking of the vessel, and human help in its reconstitution.[49] Here for the first time the idea emerges that man must help God to repair the damage which creation has caused. Here for the first time the cosmic responsibility

---

48 The radical formulation of Kabbalah by Isaac Luria (1534–1572), a Kabbalist in Palestine. His ideas came to Europe with his disciples, and became the basis of the Sabbatean heresy (cf. Kirsch, 8 June 1934, p. 51 and note) and of Hasidism. Cf. Sanford Drob, *Kabbalistic Visions: C. G. Jung and Jewish Mysticism*, New Orleans: Spring Journal, 2010, p. 10.

49 This passage in Jung's letter is quoted at length by Jaffé in her essay "C. G. Jung and National Socialism" (*Life and Work*, p. 102). She writes, "It meant so much to Jung when he found that the idea of a collaboration between Man and God was also contained in the writings of the cabalist Isaac Luria… According to Luria, in the act of creation, God formed vessels to contain the light but they proved too weak and broke apart. Thus evil entered the world and since that time all things have contained the defect of the split. Man is called upon, however, by virtue of his consciousness, to use his deeds and thoughts, and also his prayers, to help the Creator overcome the split and re-establish unity" (*Life and Work*, p. 102). In a footnote Jaffé adds that Jung had learned of Lurianic Kabbalah from Gershom Scholem's *Die jüdische Mystik in ihren Hauptströmungen* (German ed., 1957) (cf. Jung, 18 November 1952, p. 142 and note), which he also owned in its English edition (1941), and to which he often referred (*Life and Work*, p. 102, n. 59).

of man is acknowledged. Naturally it is a question of the Self and not of the ego, although the latter will be strongly affected.[50]

This would be my answer to a Jew.

Best greetings from
Yours truly, C. G. JUNG

Prof. Dr. C. G. Jung
Küsnacht-Zürich
Seestrasse 228

5 March 1954[51]

Dr. James Kirsch,
6120 Barrows Drive,
Los Angeles 48, Cal.

Dear Kirsch,

Many thanks for forwarding your exchange of correspondence with Hull. I cannot intervene in this matter, of course, as little as with regard to your suggestion re: *Aion*. I have to be careful not to thrust myself too much into view, because I made a great many recommendations earlier and now consider it advisable to keep somewhat in the background.

The integration of the collective unconscious means about the same as taking note of and adapting to the world; but that doesn't mean that one would have to become acquainted with the whole world, or that one must have lived in all climates and continents of the world. The integration of the unconscious is of course always only a very relative matter, and affects only the constellated material, not the theoretical totality. John of the Cross's "Dark Night of the Soul"[52] has nothing to do with it. Rather, integration is a conscious working through,[53] a dialectical process, as I have described it in *Beziehungen zwischen dem Ich und dem Unbewussten*.[54] It seems that a lot of fog has spread here.

With best greetings, Yours very truly, C. G. JUNG

50 *obschon letzteres schwer in Mitleidenschaft gezogen wird*: lit. "although the latter will be strongly drawn to share in suffering."
51 Typewritten in German, on letterhead. Second paragraph prev. pub. in *PP* and *Letters II*.
52 Cf. Kirsch, 1 January 1954, p. 186, note 14.
53 *Auseinandersetzung*: cf. Jung, 3 February 1933, p. 35.
54 Jung's book, *Die Beziehungen zwischen dem Ich und dem Unbewussten* (Rascher, 1928). Cf. "The Relations between the Ego and the Unconscious" in CW 7, *Two Essays on Analytical Psychology*, Part II (1953/1966).

6120 Barrows Dr.
Los Angeles 48, Calif.

14 March 1954[55]

Dear Professor!

Many heartfelt thanks for your two letters of February 16 and March 5. They were extremely helpful. The group of analysts with whom I'm working through *Aion* also asked me to express all our thanks to you. Your explanations with respect to the integration of the collective unconscious contributed a lot toward transforming some of the fog which had spread over us into therapeutic water.

Your remarks on the "general emotional lack of control" did me a lot of good. In particular it made me look carefully at a dream where I sat with a stoker in a locomotive, while the engine driver was separated from it. In the dream, of course, I did not reach my destination. I hope I've now overcome this situation to some extent. Nevertheless, I have to admit that "godlikeness" continually presents the greatest difficulties for me. For instance, I am now again accepted more fully in the group, and also in my practice I've had a number of really remarkable successes. At once, the anima shows up and tries to make me believe what a "devil of a fellow"[56] I am. At the same time there were enough objective factors involved which had nothing to do with me.

I can only hope that my affects in the Jolande case have also brought about something positive – in spite of everything.[57]

I did not think at all that you should do anything in relation to Hull. I only wanted to inform you about it. Yesterday I received a very friendly letter from Hull, together with the "Translator's Note," with which I am perfectly happy and which entirely ends the matter for me.[58]

Today I'd like to tell you about another case of synchronicity – at least I look at it that way. In 1950, at a time when I was not doing well and – as you later interpreted from a dream – the Self was constellating itself, I had the crazy "hunch"[59] to buy oil leases very cheaply in Nevada, where thus far no oil has been found. A few weeks ago, we decided to buy a new house in a much more desirable area. The very evening when the purchase of the house was concluded, I noticed

---

55 Handwritten in German, on plain paper. Handwritten note at top of page: "to file." A second handwritten note, in different handwriting (possibly Adler's): "not answered?"

56 *Teufelskerl.*

57 Phrase orig. in English.

58 Hull's "Translator's Note" acknowledges help from several sources on various parts of the book, including "Dr. James Kirsch, for making available to me his private translation of 'Answer to Job,' prepared for members of a seminar he conducted at Los Angeles, 1952–53, and also for his helpful criticism during personal discussions" (*Psych & Rel*, CW 11, p. vii).

59 Word orig. in English.

a wide column in the paper: "Gold rush in Nevada – Black gold (oil) found in Nevada."[60] The oil which was found in Nevada is near the property I own, and my land has the same geological structure. Of course, up to now that oil is only potentially there, it's not a reality yet.

Ever since buying that land, doubt has been gnawing at and in me: Does it concern external or internal oil? At least some real oil has now been found in the neighborhood, which corresponds to my inner situation. I have also dreamed about it: "A married couple is searching for oil. I say, I have a great deal of oil deep under my property. It isn't funny. It is such a burden.[61] Then I walk with my friend on a path through a dark forest. A frightful noise like a jet plane, but then a different sound like the rustle of the wind. I see the moon (full moon) veiled by a light haze."

Now I can only hope that – *Deo concedente* – the oil will soon "flow," inside as well as outside.

Figure 8.1 **Zurich Club, Carnival party, 1954.** Persons mentioned in this volume: C. A. Meier (floor, center); Kurt Binswanger (first row, left of center); Rivkah Schärf-Kluger, Emma Jung, C. G. Jung, Jolande Jacobi, Liliane Frey-Rohn (first row, center to right); Lena Hurwitz-Eisner (first row, extreme right); Barbara Hannah (second row); Yechezkel Kluger, Aniela Jaffé (second row, far right). Also present: Katie Hillman (floor, left); Franz Riklin (first row, far left); James Hillman (second row, third from right). Others unidentified. *Photo ©1954, Oskar Hofstetter. Courtesy Robert Hinshaw.*

60 Headline orig. in English.
61 Previous two sentences orig. in English.

Recently, Dr. Kluger[62] sent me a picture of the Zurich carnival group.[63] I was delighted to see you and your wife in the picture. I hope you're doing well now.

I am very concerned about Dr. Frey's state of health.[64] Psychologically she has developed greatly in recent time.

With cordial greetings, especially also to your wife,

Faithfully yours, JAMES KIRSCH

James Kirsch
906 Thayer Avenue
West Los Angeles 24, Calif.
Arizona 3–7903

7 May 1954[65]

Dear Professor!

I just wanted to let you know that our move went well. My wife, of course, was burdened with most of the work. Even though it all went smoothly, I find the change of location "rather unsettling."[66]

Also, I wanted to tell you that I read the only book which exists in the Library of Congress under the name of Freud's son, the lawyer. It doesn't contain one

---

62 Yechezkel Harold Kluger (1911–1995): Jewish-American psychologist and Jungian analyst, born in New York. Kluger and his first wife, Tovah, lived on a kibbutz in Israel, where their daughter Nomi was born. His first profession was optometry. Living in Los Angeles in the 1940s, Kluger analyzed for several years with James Kirsch and two more with Hilde, before moving to Zurich to begin analytic training (Kirsch to Jaffé, 27 January 1952, unpub. corresp., Kirsch archive). In 1954 he helped to found AGAP (the Association of Graduate Analytical Psychologists). He returned to California and earned a PhD in psychology from Claremont College. In 1954 he married Rivkah Schärf (cf. Jaffé, 22 November 1952, p. 145, note 50), and they taught at the Los Angeles Jung Institute, while maintaining close ties with Jung's community in Zurich. In 1969 they moved to Haifa, where Kluger established the Israel Training Program for Analytical Psychology. His published works include *Dreams and Other Manifestations of the Unconscious*, and *A Psychological Interpretation of Ruth*, (with Nomi Kluger-Nash, 1999).

63 Two group photographs were taken by Oskar Hofstetter at the Zurich Institute *Fastnacht* party, spring 1954 (cf. Figure 8.1, p. 196), showing C. G. and Emma Jung, broadly smiling, in the middle of the first row.

64 Kirsch and Liliane Frey-Rohn carried on a voluminous correspondence. Her ill health (narrowing of the coronary arteries) was a theme in their letters in late 1952 and early 1953 (Frey-Rohn to Kirsch, 13 November 1952; Kirsch to Frey-Rohn, 10 January 1953, Kirsch archive). Despite medical concerns, she lived to the age of 89.

65 Handwritten in German, on two sides of half-sheet letterhead.

66 Phrase orig. in English.

word about his father. It's nothing but the love adventures of an Austrian officer during the first World War![67]

With cordial greetings, also to your wife,

Faithfully yours, JAMES KIRSCH

Prof. Dr. C. G. Jung
Küsnacht-Zürich
Seestrasse 228

19 May 1954[68]

Dr. James Kirsch
6120 Barrows Drive
Los Angeles 48, Calif.

Dear Kirsch,

Enclosed I'm sending you your ominous wish-fulfillment, namely, a short answer to the seminar question.[69] I send this piece of writing to your address, with the request that you forward it with my kindest greetings to the three ladies named in it.

With best greetings, Yours truly, C. G. JUNG

P.S.[70] Many thanks for your letter. For the oil adventure one can only wish the best of success. Ordinarily such things are "empty nuts." Considering my age, some days I feel worse and sometimes less bad. Nevertheless, I've just turned out a short commentary to Radin's[71] Trickster.[72]

---

67 (Jean) Martin Freud (1889–1967): eldest son of Sigmund Freud, a lawyer, born in Vienna, died in London. His novel about an Austrian officer is *Parole d'honneur* [Word of Honor] (London: V. Gollancz, Ltd., 1939). Later he published a work about his father: *Glory Reflected: Sigmund Freud, Man and Father* (London: Angus & Robertson, 1957).

68 Typewritten in German, on letterhead.

69 Jung's letter to the members of Kirsch's *Aion* seminar, dated 19 February 1954, is published under the title "On Resurrection," *The Symbolic Life: Miscellaneous Writings*, CW 18, ¶1558–74. Members of the seminar who wrote to Jung were Martha Dana, Peggy Gerry, and Marian Reith. Kirsch later summarized their request: "While the seminar was in progress, [they] became curious about the fact that in all the writings of Jung, they had not found any commentary on the idea of Resurrection… which seemed to be the central event in the Christ story, and they therefore wondered why Jung had not said anything about it" (CW 18, p. 692n).

70 The postscript is handwritten.

71 In Jung's letter, Radin's name is underlined.

72 "Zur Psychologie der Schelm-Figur" ("On the Psychology of the Trickster Figure," CW 9(i), ¶456–88). Cf. Jung, 11 September 1954, pp. 205f, note 108.

James Kirsch
906 Thayer Avenue
West Los Angeles 24, Calif.
BR0–4067

7 June 1954[73]

Dear Professor!

On May 22 and 23, the Los Angeles and San Francisco groups held a joint meeting in Carmel. The scientific portion consisted of two lectures: one by me, about a story by Jack London,[74] and one by Joseph Henderson on "Transference."[75] Under separate cover I'll send you a copy of my lecture,[76] and Henderson will present his lecture again, in a somewhat altered form, this summer in Zurich at the International Congress. Essentially the meeting served to let the members of both groups get to know each other and discuss organizational questions. The result was a significant rapprochement of viewpoints, even if no agreement was reached, since our attitudes are so diverse. If I may say it in somewhat simplified terms, what's essential for L.A. is the attitude to the unconscious, while S.F. hopes to be accepted someday as the Jungian group in the AMA (American Medical Association) and in the APA (American Psychological Association). These vastly divergent attitudes make it finally impossible, in my opinion, to unite the two groups organizationally.[77] Nevertheless, here in Los Angeles we became aware

---

73 Handwritten in German, on letterhead.

74 Cf. Kirsch, 9 May 1953, p. 170 and note. Kirsch first lectured on Jack London's major story "The Red One" on 22 May 1954, at the initial joint meeting of Jungian analysts from northern and southern California. Drawing on alchemical parallels in several of Jung's works, he interprets London's story as an active imagination based on the author's encounter with the Self. The lecture was later published as "Jack London's Quest: 'The Red One'," in *Psychological Perspectives*, Vol. 11, No. 2, The C. G. Jung Institute of Los Angeles, Fall 1980. Kirsch attached great importance to this paper, one of his major explorations of the Self archetype. It is reprinted in this volume, with permission, in its original version, as Appendix C, "'The Red One': A Psychological Interpretation of a Story by Jack London" (pp. 287–303).

75 Title orig. in English.

76 Kirsch's lecture, "The Red One," is no longer found among Jung's papers. Because Kirsch also sent it to the New York APC, however, the 25-page typescript was saved at the KML archive. That version is published here.

77 As Kirsch predicted, the relationship between Los Angeles and San Francisco Jungians continued to undergo strains due to differences in theoretical orientation, despite which they have continued to work fruitfully together. I am thankful to Marianne Morgan of the VADL archive, who sent me the typescript of a historical study: Mel Kettner, "Orthodoxy, Heresy, and Shadow Projection: A brief history of the Los Angeles/San Francisco collaboration" (typescript, California Spring Conference of Jungian Analysts and Control Stage Candidates, 4–7 March 1993, Carmel, CA; now in progress toward publication as a book).

of how inadequate our attitudes are to the local collective, e.g. medical and psychological organizations.

While everyone praised my paper highly, I was the only one who was dissatisfied with it. I want to amplify it and, if possible, develop it into a book. Above all I want to work out the collective and archetypal aspects more clearly. For instance, if you'll give me permission, I'd be interested in including the synchronistic phenomenon[78] in a somewhat more explicit way. I am encouraged to do this, because I see that you authorized Prof. M. Eliade[79] to publish the visions from 1914[80] (page 24 in my paper).[81]

I just heard that you recently succumbed to the flu. I only hope that by now you're fully recovered. I'm very sorry that I cannot come to Zurich this year; I'll greatly miss the direct contact, especially with you. With great hesitation I'm

---

78 Kirsch notes that around 1916 Jung and London each experienced an archetypal encounter with the Self. London symbolized this experience in "The Red One" and Jung in his mandala paintings. Kirsch, who had seen Jung's paintings (cf. Sonu Shamdasani, "Introduction," *Red Book*, p. 215), implies that Jung should allow him to discuss them in print, supporting his thesis of a synchronistic occurrence. Permission to use this material was evidently not given.

79 Mircea Eliade (1907–1986): Romanian historian of religion, novelist, philosopher, and an international authority on yoga. For his doctoral study, Eliade devoted himself to yoga in India, 1928–31. He taught in Bucharest, 1933–36, then for three decades in Paris. In 1950 he began to attend Eranos, where he collaborated with Jung, Radin and Scholem. Moving to Chicago in 1956, Eliade taught at the University of Chicago until his death. He was a member of the American Academy of Arts and Sciences and editor-in-chief of the Macmillan *Encyclopedia of Religion*. A few of Eliade's best-known works in English are *The Myth of the Eternal Return* (1949, 1954); *Yoga: Immortality and Freedom* (1936, 1954); and *The Forge and the Crucible* (1956, 1962).

80 In August 1952 Eliade had interviewed Jung at Ascona. In Eliade's report, "Rencontre avec Jung," published in a French periodical, *Combat: de la Résistance à la Révolution* (Paris, 9 October 1952), he comments: "Finally, in 1914, still on the track of a series of dreams and waking dreams, he [Jung] came to understand that the manifestations of the collective unconscious are, in part, independent of the laws of time and causality. *Since Professor Jung has kindly given me permission to speak of these dreams and waking dreams* which have played a capital role in his scientific career, here is a summary of them" ("Eliade's Interview for 'Combat'," trans. Hull, *C. G. Jung Speaking*, p. 232; emphasis added).
    Jung's "visions of 1914" are explored in detail in *Red Book*, pp. 202, 231. Cf. also *MDR*, Ch. VI. His discovery of the mandala, in relation to the collective unconscious, is also cited by Eliade in a work which appeared in a Bollingen edition in 1954: *Yoga: Immortality and Freedom* (trans. Willard R. Trask, Princeton University Press). Here Eliade cites the mandala images which Jung had published in CW 12, ¶122ff, and CW 9(i), ¶627ff (*Yoga: Immortality and Freedom*, pp. 226, 409). With thanks to Prof. Bryan Rennie, who drew my attention to this source.

81 Citing this passage: "Jack London was not the first one, as he believed, to whom this lordly fortune [a vision of archetypal power] was vouchsafed. Nietzsche was probably its first tragic victim in modern times. It is worth noting that Jung's great development and discovery of the Collective Unconscious took place in just these same years. In a commentary on Zimmer's book, 'Art-Form and Yoga', he mentions the fact that it was at about this time that he discovered the mandala and essential facts about the archetype of the Self" (cf. Appendix C, p. 304). Cf. also Jung, "The Psychology of Eastern Meditation" (CW 11, ¶908–49); and *MDR*, Ch. VI, "Confrontation with the Unconscious," esp. pp. 195ff.

sending you a few of my dreams. I am doing quite well at this time. Only the contents of these dreams are strange and unfamiliar to me, and force me into an entirely new kind of reflection:

1) "Being is the father (Eupator) of the One Who Is."[82] The sentence came through exactly like this, so to speak, without any preceding or following statement. Also, the word "Eupator" as such is unknown to me, even though I am aware of similar word formations from Gnosticism.

2) The male and female are uniting and becoming "Isness."[83] I say to Mary W.[84] (one of my wife's patients): "Strange, the Self in a woman often adopts a male form and is frequently immersed in the filth of the earth or is covered by earth." At the same time, I see an oblong iron bomb (similar to an oxygen container) with a stopper at the end.

3) I was on a large ship; an extended ocean trip lay before me. I knew the destination, and yet it was unknown to me. We sailed along the west coast of South Africa.

All of a sudden there was a young black woman on the ship who possessed all the movements of a South African prairie antelope. She had not learned them from the antelope or was not imitating one, rather the movements had been impressed on her by the earth. I approached her, and she spoke to me in a very friendly way. She had black and white stripes wound around her forehead.

As I heard, my friend-enemy, Dr. Klopfer, visited you recently. He spoke here very enthusiastically about his meeting with you. I sincerely hope that his visit in Zurich will contribute to an easing of the tension between us. For years I haven't had any antagonistic feelings toward him, and our mutual work would only benefit from it.

I understand that Dr. Werner Engel,[85] my best friend, is currently in Zurich or on his way there. I'd be extremely pleased if you could see him. Under the difficult circumstances in New York, he has accomplished extraordinary things on behalf of psychology. In view of the fact that he is an exceptionally competent and conscientious physician and dearly loves general medicine, the choice of psychotherapy was especially hard for him. I sincerely hope that in Zurich he'll experience some essential insights into the unconscious.

---

82 *"Das Sein ist der Vater (Eupator) des Seienden."* Cf. Jung, 23 June 1954, p. 204, note 97.

83 Word orig. in English.

84 American body-therapist, long-time friend of both James and Hilde Kirsch and an integral part of the Jungian community in Los Angeles. Her last name is concealed in Kirsch's letter.

85 Werner Engel, MD (1901–1991): German-Jewish psychiatrist and Jungian analyst, part of the circle of Berlin Jungians, which had included Adler, Sussmann, and Kirsch. He analyzed with Kirsch in Berlin, 1930–33, as well as with Jung. Engel left Berlin in the late 1930s to settle in New York City (cf. Kirsch, 19 November 1940, p. 95 and note). There he helped to found the New York C. G. Jung Foundation, directed its clinic, and served as president of the New York Association of Analytical Psychology (NYAAP). In 1950 he defended Jung in the *American Journal of Psychotherapy*, after a columnist in that journal wrote that Jung was a "fascist." The still-existing Kirsch–Engel correspondence dates from 1943 to 1987 (Kirsch archive).

May I take another moment to return to a problem of which I once again became highly conscious during my work with the very rich material in Jack London's story "The Red One"?[86]

Unfortunately, I was interrupted at this point, and can continue writing this letter only today. What concerns me is that, whenever I need amplifying material here in Los Angeles, for the most part I have to refer to your books. Of course, you brought forth a lot of material, especially from Gnosticism and Alchemy, so that it is not lost and others can make use of it. But to the extent that I'm doing it, I can't help but have a guilty conscience and I feel like a thief.

"The Red One" contains enormously rich archetypal material, about which I could only include some essentials in my lecture. He knew very thoroughly your only book (*Psych. of the Ucs.*)[87] published at that time. Nevertheless, it[88] contains ideas which you described only much later. The breakthrough of the unconscious must have happened at about the same time for you and Jack London. My American audience was greatly surprised to learn that such material was available in Jack London.

Meanwhile your letter to the group of the *Aion* seminar[89] arrived and was deeply appreciated. Without boasting – *cum grano salis* – I had said, or tried to say, similar things in my psychological interpretation. The question that remains unanswered, for the ladies who grew up in Protestant, strictly evangelical[90] surroundings, is this: What is the significance of the resurrection as a unique historical event (e.g. Acts 17:31). Since you wrote in detail about the crucifixion as a unique and unparalleled event in history,[91] they would also like to hear about Christ's resurrection in this respect. In my opinion, this emphasizes the irrationality, the uniqueness of the Self, the ability of the coll. ucs. to relativize time and space, and possibly changes in the structure of the Self.

In any case, the ladies were not satisfied with my answer. Since I had recently heard a series of lectures by an outstanding, and free, and very learned Christian

---

86 Cf. note 74 above.
87 *Psychology of the Unconscious*: i.e. *Wandlungen*, in the early translation of Beatrice Hinkle (cf. Jung, 12 August 1931, p. 21 and note). Kirsch repeats the commonly held notion that London had read Jung's *Psychology of the Unconscious* before writing "The Red One." Recent scholarship has shown that, remarkably, London did not begin reading Jung's work until August 1916, four months after finishing "The Red One" (cf. Jay Williams, Review of "Jack London: One Hundred Years a Writer," *Studies in the Novel*, vol. 36, 2004, pp. 278–83).
88 From context, "it" refers to London's story.
89 Cf. Jung, 19 May 1954, p. 198 and note.
90 Phrase orig. in English.
91 Beside this sentence in the right margin are a hand-drawn line and a question mark.

theologian about the Fourth Gospel,[92] I've asked him to lecture in my seminar about the resurrection.[93]

By the way, he is of the opinion that the author of this gospel in no way intended to write a story, but used the existing gospels to present and teach his gnostic conception of Christ, the Son of Man. The author was a poet who also invented things when it suited his purposes. For instance, it appears that the story of the Samaritan Woman never happened. I am deeply interested in this conception, because then I can accept sayings like, "I am the true vine, etc." (15:1). He also views the story of Lazarus, for example, as symbolic. In addition, he maintains that Mary of Magdala, who is mentioned in John, has nothing to do with the one who is cited in Luke. We know nothing else about her, he says, except that she is "a lady from Magdala."[94]

This series of lectures and Schweitzer's studies have very much helped me to better understand the question of Christ, even if, as you say, one will never achieve a clear concept of the historical Jesus on account of the enormous projections. But it was very important for me to see John as a product of Gnosticism (the Jewish school, even, and not the Greek, according to the latest discoveries in the Jordan Valley).

***

These oil stories are not very important, as long as the inner sources of oil open up, of which I now and then get "glimpses."[95]

Dear Professor, I only hope that your age is not causing you too many difficulties. I hope that your sleep isn't too much disturbed.

With most cordial greetings and best wishes also to your wife,

Faithfully yours, JAMES KIRSCH

---

92 Possibly John Sanford (1929–2005), American Episcopal priest and Jungian analyst, who thereafter corresponded with Kirsch and who was living in Los Angeles at the time. Sanford held a Master of Divinity from the Episcopal Theological Seminary, Cambridge, Massachusetts, and an honorary Doctor of Divinity from Kenyon, based on his work in psychology and religion. He later published a book on the Fourth Gospel.

93 In a reply to Jung's letter, a member of the *Aion* seminar writes about the visiting theologian: "As it happened, he had written his doctors dissertation on the resurrection and he found your letter to be a further confirmation and extension of everything that had taken shape and form in his research in this area. He shared with us the evidence that underlaid his own conviction, that the bodily resurrection of Jesus, as an historical event, had little if any validation but that the return of the Christ as a moving and incontrovertible vision – a psychic experience – had gripped and transformed the disciples in much the same way as had the later appearance of Christ to Paul on the Damascus road" (Marian Reith to Jung, 21 June 1954, Kirsch archive). This document was kindly provided by Deborah Wesley, archivist of the C. G. Jung Institute of Los Angeles.

94 Phrase orig. in English.

95 Word orig. in English.

Prof. Dr. C. G. Jung
Küsnacht-Zürich
Seestrasse 228

23 June 1954[96]

Dr. James Kirsch,
906 Thayer Avenue
West Los Angeles 24
Calif.

Dear Kirsch,

Many thanks for your detailed letter. Up to now, unfortunately, I haven't been able to read your manuscript because I'm overwhelmed with work and should not tire myself too much. On the dreams:

1) The phrase could also be restated as that which exists through itself, the Increatum.[97]

2) The union of opposites: Both these dreams contain unconscious thinking – hence the oxygen bomb which contains compressed pneuma. The thinking venture is understood as a night sea journey[98] leading to South Africa, i.e. into the sphere of sensation (your thinking contaminated with sensation, compensatory for intense attitudes of consciousness). The informant[99] on this journey is the Anima Psychagogo.[100]

Once I briefly met Dr. Engel[101] after he had been to see my wife; but he has not contacted me up to now.

I'm curious about Jack London. It's completely natural for you to take amplifying material from my books; for in the end, why else did I write them; but if you wanted to write a scientific work yourself, you would of course have to go back to the sources, and that you can only do in a place with a very large library.

Concerning the problem of resurrection, the uniqueness of the event obviously serves the purpose of emphasizing this quality of the Self-experience. The "historic" uniqueness has to be understood *cum grano salis,*[102] of course, because such postmortal events frequently arise as mythological facts. Otherwise I wouldn't

---

96 Typewritten in German, on letterhead. Final paragraph prev. pub. in *PP*.
97 Uncreated. The reference is to Kirsch's dream-text: "Being is the father (Eupater) of the One Who Is" (p. 201). Cf. also Jung's statement in "The Spirit Mercurius": "It is therefore only logical when Paracelsus and Dorn state that the prima materia is an 'increatum' and a principle coeternal with God" (CW 13, ¶283).
98 Phrase orig. in English.
99 *Informatorin.*
100 Jung's invented phrase: "Soul-Guide Anima."
101 Cf. Kirsch, 7 June 1954, p. 201 and note.
102 "with a grain of salt".

have anything more to say about it. Your theological authority seems to have quite a liberal attitude: it's beyond me how one can determine the historicity of different gospel stories.[103] To be sure, the Gnosticism of which John the Evangelist is a descendent is certainly Jewish, but in its essence Hellenistic, in the style of Philo Judaeus,[104] who also originated the Logos doctrine.

Meanwhile with best greetings, Yours truly, c. g. JUNG

Prof. Dr. C. G. Jung
Küsnacht-Zürich
Seestrasse 228

11 September 1954[105]

Dr. James Kirsch,
906 Thayer Avenue
West Los Angeles 24
Calif.

Dear Kirsch,

My silence[106] is mainly due to the fact that, as much as possible, I've been refraining from dealing with my mail: for once I really needed to take a vacation. Unfortunately, our summer was horribly rainy; only now is the weather decent, and I can truly recover. My correspondence long ago got completely out of hand.

My essay about the Trickster really was a preface to Radin's new version of the "Winnebago Trickster Myth."[107] Since then, Brody – who is publishing the book – has also included Kerényi, who writes about Hermes and related subjects.

---

103 Jung dismisses the "liberal" Protestant schools of biblical theology which came to prominence in the nineteenth and early twentieth centuries. The use of literary-historical tools in the interpretation of biblical texts, he suggests, drains them of their archetypal (symbolic) meaning and severs them from the living experience of the psyche.

104 Philo Judaeus (c.20 BCE–c.50 CE): First-century Hellenistic Jewish philosopher, born in Alexandria, Egypt. Educated in Greek philosophy, Philo readily applied Hellenistic thought to his interpretation of the scriptures. His doctrine of the Logos is thought to have influenced the writer of the Fourth Gospel.

105 Typewritten in German, on letterhead. Parts of letter prev. pub. in *PP*.

106 Kirsch's previous letter is missing. He later summarized parts of it for the benefit of Gerhard Adler, who was editing *C. G. Jung Letters*. In relation to this passage he writes: "In August, 1954, I had visited the Hopis in Arizona and had seen the snake dance and some other dances in which katchinas (representing ancient spirits) were employed. I had told Jung about my experience" (Kirsch to Adler, 28 September 1967, Kirsch archive).

107 Conclusion of sentence orig. in English.

Unfortunately the book's now been retitled: *Der göttliche Schelm*.[108] I resisted this designation; it really is about the divine fool, and originally I wrote my essay only about this figure which – as I said – has absolutely nothing to do with a "scoundrel."

The purpose of this publication is not quite clear to me; the book is presented in an incredibly expensive and luxurious edition, with no relation whatever to its content.

I am glad you've had the experience of the primitive ceremonies; I never saw the katchina, only the buffalo dances of the Pueblo Indians of Taos, where I made friends with the old Locotenente Gobernador,[109] Ochwiä Biano.[110] The clowns whom you saw are the famous "Delight Makers,"[111] about whom some hundred years ago Bandelier wrote a charming book of the same name. They are relatives of the trickster figure.

Of my two writings, *Synchronicity*[112] and *Job*, I can say: "Habent sua fata libelli."[113] In America no one except Knoll of Princeton[114] has properly understood what I mean by it;[115] especially the statistics have just driven people crazy. Therefore I decided to take all tables out of the book and have replaced them with a description in words, probably with the same result, that people cannot get away from their causalistic thinking habits. It won't come out until next spring. In contrast, *Job* will be printed in England in short order, though significantly not in America; the Bollingen Press prefers to keep its distance, because *Job* could be misunderstood as "unamerican activity"![116] The other day I received a manuscript

---

108 lit. "The Divine Scoundrel." C. G. Jung, Paul Radin and Karl Kerényi, *Der göttliche Schelm: Ein indianischer Mythen-Zyklus* (Zürich: Rhein Verlag, 1954); *The Trickster: A Study of American Indian Mythology* (New York: Philosophical Library; London: Routledge & Kegan Paul, 1956). For Jung's contribution, "Zur Psychologie der Schelm-Figur," cf. "On the Psychology of the Trickster Figure," CW 9(i), ¶456–88.

109 Deputy Governor, or Governor *Locum Tenens*. Members of Jung's family recall that he enjoyed the Spanish title.

110 Cf. *MDR*, Ch. IX, "Travels," under "America: The Pueblo Indians," pp. 246–53.

111 Phrase orig. in English. Kirsch notes in his letter to Adler: "The book he mentions is Adolf F. Bandelier's charming one, *The Delight Makers*, of which I have a first edition (1890)" (Kirsch to Adler, 28 September 1967, Kirsch archive).

112 C. G. Jung, "Synchronicity: An Acausal Connecting Principle," first chapter in *The Interpretation of Nature and the Psyche* (with Wolfgang Pauli; trans. Hull, New York: Pantheon, 1955).

113 "[Little] books have their destinies" (cf. Kirsch, 14 June 1953, p. 172 and note).

114 Max Knoll, professor at Princeton University, whose lecture, "Transformations of Science in Our Age" (in *Man and Time: Papers from the Eranos Yearbooks, 3*, 1957) is twice cited by Jung (cf. CW 8, ¶875n, ¶987).

115 In his translation (*PP*) Kirsch here inserts *Synchronicity*.

116 Phrase orig. in English. The caution of the Bollingen Foundation was not necessarily unfounded. Anxiety was pervasive in the United States in the early years of the Cold War, during what became known as the McCarthy Era (cf. Kirsch, 27 November 1954, pp. 210f, notes 135, 136). Publishers and writers were among those being tarred by the proliferating suspicion of "un-American" (Communist) affiliations. Hull wrote to Kirsch at about this time: "Revised proofs of [*Job*] were sent me already at the end of January. At that stage someone thought it expedient

by Progoff,[117] in which he discusses the question of synchronicity very skillfully, especially under the aspect of archetypes. In Europe there are a few people who understand synchronicity: among them, it seems, some young physicists who are interested in it. It's especially not understood what an excellent joke was made with the astrological statistic;[118] people have even thought I wanted to prove something in favor of astrology. It's hardly worthwhile to go on any more about all these stupidities.

Mysterium Coniunctionis is currently in press, but I haven't received any proof-sheets yet.

It will perhaps interest you to learn that hardly were my letters published in the *Weltwoche*[119] when the "saucers"[120] also appeared above Zurich. One of the first was observed by my own physician, the second by a military flying officer. A whole squadron was seen near Lake Constance, as well as in Southern Germany. I have received a whole series of letters with further observations; consequently we are obviously not dealing only with American phenomena. I then received further information which could be very interesting, but I must wait until I have seen the eyewitness myself, for which there's some possibility. You are quite right:[121] McCarthy[122] is an exponent of American one-sidedness, which is what gives him the fanatical, paranoid character. It's probably not a genuine paranoia; he gives me more the impression of being an instrument of the American collective.

to submit the book to the Trustees for perusal. The verdict was that it might be considered too 'blasphemous' for publication in the USA in these stormy times, so it was decided to publish it in England under the R & KP imprimatur and to distribute it in that form in America" (Hull to Kirsch, 24 August 1954, Kirsch archive).

117 Ira Progoff, PhD (1921–1988): American psychotherapist and writer, best known for his development of the Intensive Journal Method. Progoff was interested in adapting the ideas of depth psychology, particularly Jungian, to people's ordinary lives. The manuscript to which Jung refers may have been an early version of Progoff's *Jung, Synchronicity and Human Destiny* (New York: Julian Press, 1973/1987). Another of his major works is *The Death and Rebirth of Psychology: An Integrative Evaluation of Freud, Adler, Jung and Rank and the Impact of their Culminating Insights on Modern Man* (New York: Julian Press, 1956/1974).

118 That is, the CW editors have failed to understand Jung's "excellent joke with the astrological statistic" in the second chapter of *Synchronicity*; cf. CW 8, ¶816–968. (A later, slightly condensed version appears in CW 18, ¶1174–92.)

119 Two letters, under the title "C. G. Jung zu den fliegenden Untertassen" [C. G. Jung on Flying Saucers], had appeared in the newspaper *Weltwoche* (Zürich, Jhg. 22, no. 1078, 9 July 1954; CW 18, ¶1431–44). Cf. Jung, 11 January 1955, p. 215 and note.

120 Word orig. in English.

121 Reference to Kirsch's missing letter. Cf. Kirsch, 27 November 1954, pp. 210f.

122 Joseph Raymond McCarthy (1908–1957): a United States Senator from Wisconsin, 1947–57. From February 1950 until December 1954, when he was formally censured by the Senate, McCarthy carried on a demagogic campaign against Americans with alleged Communist affiliations. He attacked government officials, politicians, members of the armed forces, and a wide array of intellectuals, clergy, and artists. McCarthy's popularity fell in 1954 and his campaign ended, after his methods were publicly exposed by the Army-McCarthy Hearings and two TV newscasts by Edward R. Murrow.

The difficulty you're encountering with the authorities in connection with your seminar seems completely incomprehensible to me. After all, you can receive anyone you want in your house, it seems to me.[123]

With regard to your essay "The Red One" I'll report at a later date; I haven't yet had a chance to read it.[124]

Meanwhile I remain, with best greetings, Yours truly, C. G. JUNG

Figure 8.2 **C. A. Meier, Zurich.** *Photo: ©1958, James Kirsch. Courtesy Thomas B. Kirsch.*

123 Kirsch had written to Jung about a conflict that arose with his neighbors, and eventually with the City of Los Angeles. He later summarized for Adler: "The 'difficulties' referred to… were due to my having about 40 people at my seminar and, correspondingly, about 38 cars parked on my small street. Thereupon, the City forbade me to continue using my home for any professional purpose, due to zone regulations." He adds, *"Please omit this paragraph* – I do not want to draw the attention of the authorities to me again!" (Kirsch to Adler, 28 September 1967, Kirsch archive).

124 This lecture, which Kirsch sent to Jung, is no longer among Jung's papers. A copy is found at the KML archive. It is printed below as Appendix C, pp. 287ff.

139 So. Beverly Drive
Beverly Hills, Calif.

27 November 1954[125]

Dear Professor!

I'm very sorry that I haven't written to you in such a long time. During the time Meier was here[126] – we now jokingly refer to it as the "Meier month" – there was simply no time for writing. He had to keep an enormously full schedule. Of course, I also accompanied him on all his excursions into the countryside and to the ocean. My kind neighbor never even called the police on me. So it all came out well. Meier also weathered it very well.

His visit was a great success. The essential factor was his personality, with which he doubtless made a deeper impression on all who came into contact with him than any of our earlier visitors. Whether or not he was also accepted is a completely different question. What so much distinguishes him, besides his enormous scholarship, is his ability to let the ucs. speak and his respect for the numinosity of the ucs. Especially in this respect he was well accepted by some in the Club, and rejected by others. The latter found particular fault with the fact that he never really "analyzed" the dreams and never really rounded them off by stating: "The dream means such and such."

Also his public appearance may have had a different effect than he perhaps expected. As a condition of his visit he had stipulated that he wanted to lecture at universities and medical schools. His greatest success – also his best lecture – was at the Mental Hygiene Society, where 600 people, mostly "laymen", were present.[127] He found the most limited response with the psychiatrists,[128] and that's where he was also most reticent.

We also had him as a guest in our house and enjoyed his company. In private we never spoke a word about psychology. I was deeply impressed by his ability to experience music, and that he lived his shadow so consciously.

This intensive, extraverted way of life brought my inner process almost to a standstill. But then we continued just as intensively, and in the end something like a temporary inner unification occurred. While I have not been sleeping well for years and have often been plagued by my gout attacks, my sleep is now much better, and the gout has left me in peace. (Toi! toi! toi!)

---

125 Handwritten in German, on plain paper.

126 Cf. Kirsch, 1 January 1954, p. 187 and note.

127 Meier lectured at the Southern California Society for Mental Hygiene, Los Angeles, 29 September 1954, on "Applying the Theories of Jung to Emotional Problems" (printed announcement, Kirsch archive).

128 Meier gave a guest lecture at the Department of Psychiatry, School of Medicine, UCLA, and accepted other invitations in New York, San Francisco, and Fresno (Meier to Kirsch, 18 March 1954, Kirsch archive).

What keeps disturbing me, though, is the fact that this process is interrupted again and again by intensive affects. None of them manifest outwardly, but the process is interrupted again and again, sometimes for days. Then it costs me a great effort to re-direct the intensity of these affects to the process.

Recently I had a mental picture before falling asleep: Someone who is coming to see me brings along a horse. I know he knows how he can water the horse at the large, round trough that I own. Then I see the trough before me, filled with water.

A week later I had a dream in which a woman enters a room and ignites the spirits(!)[129] with which the same round trough is filled. I clearly see the colorless, little flame flickering in the middle of the trough. Then she laughs mockingly, sarcastically, as if to say: "Now a great explosion will occur." However, nothing happens, and the flame continues to burn peacefully.

This sarcastic attitude of the anima points to a similar attitude in my consciousness, of which however I'm not really conscious. To that extent this dream is compensatory. I am also glad that the vessel[130] is now whole, and I notice from other, external things that there is a relative wholeness. I have a lot of dreams and images but cannot get close to active imagination.

In the meantime, I was unfortunately unable to continue writing this letter. In a subsequent dream I was conversing with you, and your figure transformed into that of a boy who was your nephew. Since that time an intensive soliloquy has been flowing. Despite some suffering I am doing quite well. Also in the outer world a number of changes for the better have taken place.

The only trouble I'm having is that I no longer have any need to work with Meier and (or) Liliane Frey. I don't have a negative attitude toward them, but simply feel a need to keep working by myself. Only with you I'd like to discuss a great many things – and here I'm very conscious of your work overload. I would like to come to Zurich again in the summer of 1955 – *Deo concedente* – and hope to be able to see you then.

Before closing, I'd like to say something briefly about McCarthy.[131] In the *Gestaltungen des Ubw* (p. 54),[132] you write: "I do not want to promise[133] to define

---

129 *Spiritus(!)*: i.e. alcohol.

130 *das Gefäss.*

131 Cf. Jung, 11 September 1954, p. 206, note 116.

132 C. G. Jung, *Die Gestaltungen des Unbewussten* [The Creations of the Unconscious], with a contribution by Aniela Jaffé (Psychologische Abhandlungen 7. Zürich: Rascher, 1950). The quotation comes from the second chapter, "Über Wiedergeburt" [Concerning Rebirth]. The book is not published as a whole in English, but chapters appear in various volumes of the CW: in CW 9(i), parts 5 ("Concerning Rebirth"), 11 ("A Study in the Process of Individuation"), and 12 ("Concerning Mandala Symbolism"); in CW 15, Part 7 ("Psychology and Literature"); and in CW 18, Part 56 ("Foreword" to *Gestaltungen des Unbewussten*).

133 *mich anheischig machen*: lit., obligate myself, make myself accountable; assert, claim.

an absolute boundary between possession and paranoia."[134] McCarthy is certainly an exponent of American one-sidedness. I just wanted to say that while observing his conduct on the television screen I received the impression that he personally has already crossed this boundary. To make sure I have no illusions that we Jews are free of this collective phenomenon, I've learned that his "evil spirit" is a Mr. Cohn,[135] and his closest collaborator is Rabbi Benjamin Schulz.[136] But I believe that remarkable changes are taking place in the American unconscious. Whether they will be strong enough to prevent the threatening war, with its apocalyptic consequences, is difficult to predict. I have a whole series of dreams, esp. of young people, in which the hydrogen bomb plays a part.

Dear Professor, to conclude I would like to send you and your wife my most heartfelt wishes for Christmas.

With most cordial greetings, Faithfully yours, JAMES KIRSCH

Enclosed is a photograph[137] which I took during Meier's seminar on 25 October 1954.

---

134 The full statement reads, in Hull's translation: "I am not prepared to lay down any hard and fast line of demarcation between possession and paranoia. Possession can be formulated as identity of the ego-personality with a complex" (*The Archetypes and the Collective Unconscious,* CW 9(i), "Concerning Rebirth," ¶220, p. 122).

135 Roy Marcus Cohn (1927–1986): American lawyer, prominent during McCarthy's investigations of alleged Communists in the United States government, who temporarily exercised great political power.

136 Rabbi Benjamin Schultz: As director of the American Jewish League Against Communism, Schultz influenced blacklisting decisions by the film and television industry and publicly supported McCarthy and Cohn (e.g., "Opinion: One Enchanted Evening," *Time Magazine,* 9 August 1954).

137 Enclosure not found.

1955–1958

ZURICH/TOKYO

pro tem. Ascona

11 January 1955[1]

Dear Colleague![2]

Many thanks for kindly forwarding the Saucer news![3] I always wonder why almost no photographs are taken, even though every trifle gets photographed! Some very good observations have also been made here recently, but again no photos! Something is being seen, but what?

The English *Job* has now been published,[4] although with some printing errors, e.g. "childish" instead of "childlike." Otherwise good. The printing of "Synchronicity" gives endless difficulties, which are principally due to the fact that the editors hardly understand what it's about; e.g. they don't grasp the astrological experiment.[5] They think one would have to *believe* in astrology in order to make such an experiment!! One founders on the rock of stupidity and ignorance, against which nothing can be done.

I'm trying to relax here in the south. But even here it's difficult to guard against visitors. Also, the weather leaves something to be desired. My *Mysterium Coniunctionis*[6] is now being printed – finally! But no proof-sheets yet. Around here we still don't know whether and how America has affected C. A. Meier.

Thank you kindly for all the news you sent to me. I hope you're doing well.

With the best wishes for the New Year, Yours truly, C. G. JUNG

Beverly Hills, Calif.

23 January 1955[7]

Dear Professor!

It was a great pleasure to receive your letter from Ascona. Also, I was very glad to hear that you were again able to take a short vacation. I assume that your wife

---

1   Handwritten in German, on undated airmail letter. The envelope, found with the original letter in the Kirsch archive, bears a postmark: "11.1.1955." Several copies and partial copies of this letter also exist. One photocopy is hand-dated "1954." Another is hand-dated "Summer 1957"; this date is mistakenly assigned to the letter in *PP*.

2   *Herr Collega!*

3   Kirsch's letter is missing.

4   Cf. Kirsch, 1 January 1954, p. 185 and note.

5   This paper, published in 1954 in *The Interpretation of Nature and the Psyche* (cf. Jung, 11 September 1954, p. 206 and note), was later republished, slightly revised, in CW 18. Cf. "An Astrological Experiment," CW 18, ¶1174–92.

6   Cf. Kirsch, 23 November 1952, p. 147 and note.

7   Handwritten in German, on plain paper.

was there with you and can thus conclude that she has finally recovered from her sciatica, or whatever it was.

I can easily imagine that even in Ascona the visits don't leave you in peace. What an evil guard dog it would be, who could successfully keep visitors away from you! To a small degree I'm experiencing something like that here, as if people had become aware of the changes in me without anybody talking about it. Recently I had a dream that my son was killed; his body was macerated, and then his golden head was placed in a shrine in my study. I can interrogate him anytime.

But I always have to think of the Hasidic story about why so few find the truth: "Nobody wants to stoop so low."

I'm surprised to hear you complain about the stupidity of humankind, you of all people, who have given your best to humankind again and again, literally[8] risked your skin, doing so much pioneer work, and you continually ran into the resistance, inertia, and hostility of the masses. Especially in "Synchronicity" there are so many new ideas and attitudes, which flowed from the experience of the archetype, that the masses cannot comprehend it at all. And a great many of our "educated" people belong to the masses.

I also want to tell you that during the 1¼ hours I observed the "flying saucer" my camera – loaded with film – was in the adjacent room, and the idea never occurred to me to photograph it! For this unconsciousness on my part, I have no explanation.

In the meantime, Father White[9] gave a lecture here about "Good and Evil."[10] You know his ideas, of course. The audience highly respected his "Sophistry"[11] but rejected his principles. During the discussion I addressed the main question, i.e. whether good and evil are equivalent or "privative"[12] opposites and elaborated

---

8   Word orig. in English.
9   Rev. Victor White, O.P. (1902–1960): English Dominican priest and theologian, Jung's colleague and friend since August 1945, at this time living in Oakland, California. He visited the Los Angeles C. G. Jung Clinic in December 1954 and again in January 1955 (White to Kirsch, 6 December 1954, Kirsch archive). White collaborated with Jung for ten years, until their falling-out in 1955. Their break was due partly to White's hostile review of *Job* ("Jung on 'Job'," *Blackfriars*, March 1955), but more fundamentally to their underlying conflict about the nature of God and the reality of evil (cf. note 10 below). White's published works include *God and the Unconscious* (London: Harvill, 1952; rev. ed. Dallas, Texas: Spring, 1982); *God the Unknown* (London: Harvill, 1956); and *Soul and Psyche: An Enquiry into the Relationship of Psychotherapy and Religion* (New York: Harper, 1960). Cf. *Jung–White Letters;* cf. also Ann Conrad Lammers, *In God's Shadow: The Collaboration of Victor White and C. G. Jung*, Mahwah, NJ: Paulist, 1994 (hereafter *IGS*).
10 White's lecture "Good and Evil" was first delivered to the London APC on 21 November 1953. With case material, including illustrations from his own analysis, he argues that no contradiction exists between Jung's understanding of the opposites of good and evil and the Catholic ("privative") theory of evil (cf. note 13, below). Perhaps because of its personal content, this lecture remained unpublished until six years after White's death (*Harvest*, Vol. 12, 1966) (*Jung–White Letters*, p. 230n, p. 245n). Cf. also *IGS*, pp. 215–20.
11 Word orig. in English.
12 Word orig. in English.

on your idea that the privatio boni[13] leads to an undervaluation of the soul and cuts off the creative process. Afterwards I was privately asked how it was possible for someone to know you for such a long time without ever experiencing the essential.

Of course, it is obvious that Father White has suffered a lot. In personal relations he is very friendly, and I like him very much. But as a Catholic and a servant of the Church, it's obvious that he can never go beyond a certain limit. The question whether Christ is a symbol of the Self, or the Self a symbol of Christ, and the one about the privatio boni are closely connected and appear to be an insurmountable obstacle for a Catholic person, insofar as their experience of the Self is concerned. You may possibly believe that this could change for Catholics in the future. But Father W. can never belong to himself, but finally only to Mother Church. In any case, his contact with you has caused a dreadful conflict for him, which is plainly visible.

From Feb.[14] 20 to 22 our Los Angeles group and the one from San Francisco held a convention in Palm Springs. There were three lectures: One by Dr. Marg. McClean about the treatment of a case of schizophrenia in analytic practice, which was quite outstanding and surely reached the standard of presentations in Zurich. I hope she will publish it. I spoke about "active imagination." A lady from San Francisco presented the third lecture which – in the common opinion of both groups – was very bad. The intellectual difference between the two groups was really striking – without boasting[15] – and I started to ask myself what the San Francisco Group was seeking and expecting from us here. Most of the time during the 2½-day meeting was spent discussing questions of organization, training, and qualifications.[16] Of course, these are important matters and need to be clarified nowadays, but on closer scrutiny, despite its ambitious demands on M.D.s and Ph.D.s, San Francisco has not attracted any M.D.s; and this attitude toward the existing association (if I may tell you my confidential opinion on the subject) has led to noticeable intellectual superficiality. Henderson and Perry are the only ones who even have a real relationship with the ucs.

This yearly convention has now become an established tradition and serves its function. The article about you in *Time*[17] has made us "respectable"[18] at a single

---

13 privation of good. The term, which stems from ancient and medieval church writings, is basic to Catholic (esp. Thomistic) discourse about the nature of evil (cf. *IGS*, pp. 206–12; also *Jung–White Letters*, pp. 182–84, 188–89, 190–92).

14 Probably a slip of the pen for January. (The letter, dated January 23, reports a meeting that had just taken place.)

15 Phrase orig. in English.

16 Word orig. in English.

17 A fine photographic profile of "Psychiatrist Carl Jung" was shown on the cover of the 14 February 1955 issue of *Time*, with a banner heading: "Exploring the Soul: A Challenge to Freud." The long lead article, by Boris Artzybasheff, bore the title "The Wise Old Man" (*Time Magazine*, Vol. LXV, No. 7, 14 February 1955).

18 Word orig. in English.

stroke and has already had its consequences. We now have to earnestly consider the establishment of an Institute,[19] which is difficult because our group is so small.

Your book *Answer to Job* has been sold out here for weeks, even though no newspaper has reviewed it.

There would be so much more to write to you, dear Professor, for instance about the devil without whom[20] there is no hope, according to one of my dreams. So I'd better stop here.

Most cordially, Faithfully yours, JAMES KIRSCH

Figure 9.1 **C. G. Jung at 69, after illness, Küsnacht, 1944.** *Photo: ©1944, Margareta Fellerer. Courtesy Franziska Fellerer/Interfoto/Andreas Jung.*

139 So. *Beverly Drive*
Beverly Hills, Calif.

11 June 1955[21]

Dear Professor!

I'm afraid it's been a long time since I heard from you directly, but from my friends in Zurich and also from my wife I understand that you are doing quite well

19 The Jung Institute of Los Angeles was officially founded in 1967. Until that time, the Society of Jungian Analysts of Southern California continued to provide analytic education, and the C. G. Jung Clinic of Los Angeles (later the Kieffer Frantz Clinic) oversaw practical training.
20 From here to end, handwritten sideways in left margin.
21 Handwritten in German, on plain paper.

but that your wife hasn't been so well and has had a stomach resection.[22] With all my heart I hope that her vacation at Lake Constance will be good for her and that the disease is completely removed from her organism.

About four weeks ago I experienced a terrible shock. My son's best friend was one day found lying dead on his bed. At first even an autopsy did not reveal a cause of death. I felt very close to this 19½-year-old man, to a degree that I was completely unconscious of at first. Only from my deep grieving did I recognize how much this young man had meant to me. He was not only enormously intelligent but had such a clear, pure soul, wrote incredibly good poems, and showed an incredible understanding for psychology. He was doing pre-med studies at Harvard and wanted to become a Jungian analyst.

Naturally he was closely identified with his mother. The mother told me: He was my breath, he was my life,[23] but nevertheless he wasn't really the typical puer aeternus, for he'd gone to Harvard against his mother's will, and also had relationships with girls.

Only now, three weeks later, the cause of death has been established.[24] In the chem. lab. some cyanide got under his fingernail. When playing ball he hurt a finger, then sucked at it.

The mother, who knew about the injury to his finger, had a dream about a week after his death, that a black dog bit her son in the finger, and that this was the cause of his death. I was so disconcerted by his death that I dreamt you could tell me something with respect to his death. Unfortunately I did not know him very well and really only spoke to him once at length. But naturally I perceived the very timid anima, the God-seeking of this young Jew, who was alienated from anything religious. But now I hear that after our discussion he read the Bible (including the N.T.) from the first to the last line. I also know that he avoided all contact with anything dark, coarse, or ugly.

It is always a great pleasure for me to be together with the young men my son brings to our house. He surpassed them all by far.

After gaining some understanding about this death, I feel better again. I'd like to ask you for advice with regard to a dream that I had a few days ago:

> You gave a seminar about the Old Testament here in Los Angeles. (In it you were much older, more than 100 yr., and something like the prophet Elijah.)

---

22 Emma Jung had begun to be ill in 1954 and was diagnosed with inoperable cancer in the spring of 1955. In July 1955 she took part in Jung's eightieth birthday celebration, but her condition quickly worsened in the autumn, and she died on 28 November.

23 Sentence orig. in English.

24 According to Thomas Kirsch his friend's death was understood by his contemporaries to have been a suicide.

Then came an intermission. I approached 'you' but somehow was unable to formulate my questions properly. They fell flat.[25] But then I was able to ask you whether it was all right to question you about individual words or letters as symbols in the kabbalistic sense, e.g. about that *[drawing: Shin with three branches]* (which would only begin to have four branches in the Messianic era *[drawing: Shin with four branches]*). You responded hesitantly: 'Yes. – Because it was said: "He is so familiar with the primitive spirit of the Old Testament that he is past master."'[26]

Now came two female analysts I know (who are lesbians), and you received them in an adjoining room (in order to discuss their homosexuality with them analytically). I thought, there he's exhausting his strength. Then someone like Dr. L. Frey said it doesn't matter, because for the things he says about the O. T. he doesn't need any strength. I added that it was refreshing to have such a long intermission (½ hour), because a cool breeze was coming in.

By ordinary mail I am sending you an article from the "New Yorker" that gives a summary report about the Scrolls from the Dead Sea.[27] On pages 105 and 107 you'll find a confirmation of the hypothesis that the Fourth Gospel is purely Jewish.[28] In no way do I wish to deny that even the Essenes were influenced by the Greek spirit. These documents, for instance, also strongly show the influence of Pythagoras, the fact that the number 50 was very important; even the calendar of the Essenes differed from that of others on the basis of Greek astronomy. It was holy – and justifiably so.

Now I'd like to come back briefly to the business with Frau Jacobi. I really want to lay it to rest. Under today's circumstances, I certainly would not have come near her and would never again accuse anyone. You know that my difficulty grew out of the fact that I did *not* speak up here in Los Angeles. What I did say, unfortunately, was correct.[29] My affects were also factually grounded.

I also know that I owe her an explanation or apology which will reach the collective. But I cannot do this from here, for once again she goes way too far in what she asks of me.[30] I cannot subscribe to lies. My Self does not allow it. I hope the business can be cleared up in October, when I come to Zurich. I'm extremely

---

25 Sentence orig. in English.
26 Phrase orig. in English.
27 Edmund Wilson, "The Scrolls from the Dead Sea," *The New Yorker*, May 14, 1955, pp. 45ff. Later revised and published as a book, *The Dead Sea Scrolls – 1947–1969* (1969).
28 Wilson's article suggests that the first Christians borrowed ideas from the Jews at Qumran, the Essenes, who created the Scrolls.
29 Cf. Kirsch, 18 October 1953, pp. 179f and notes; cf. also Kirsch, 16 February 1954, p. 192 and note.
30 Evidently Jacobi was asking for a public apology.

sorry that I cannot be at the Dolder Hotel on July 25 and that this business prevents me from being present on your day of honor.

Very cordial greetings to you and especially to your wife,

Faithfully yours, JAMES KIRSCH

From Aniela Jaffé

11 September 1955[31]

Dear Dr. Kirsch,

May I ask for your advice as to whether or not Jung should publish an article in this collection at all? If affirmative, I would appreciate your mailing my letter,[32] but otherwise throw everything in the wastebasket. Or better yet, bring it back to me so that I can send a letter of refusal. Perhaps it would do no harm if Jung were better known in this way. It just can't be something absolutely obscure.

With many thanks for your help, and see you soon![33]

Cordial greetings, Yours, ANIELA JAFFÉ

From Aniela Jaffé

31 October 1955[34]

Dear Dr. Kirsch,

You're now written down for Saturday, 12 November, at 11:15. Since you said that Friday morning is the only time when you're busy, I very much hope that this date is convenient. Again, my apologies for having forgotten about your lecture.

It was very pleasant to chat with you yesterday afternoon.

With best greetings, Yours, ANIELA JAFFÉ

---

31 Typewritten in German, on plain paper; signed carbon copy.
32 Reference unclear. Enclosure not found.
33 In September and October 1955 Kirsch was in Zurich. Cf. Jaffé, 31 October 1955, below.
34 Typewritten in German, on plain paper; signed carbon copy.

From Aniela Jaffé

20 December 1955[35]

Dear Dr. Kirsch,

Prof. Jung gave me the task of returning precious manuscripts which have been languishing in our bookcases to their authors. The reason for this is not only a tremendous overflow in our storage areas, but also the fear that valuable material could be lost here.

I hope that you had great success in London!

Are you staying on longer in Zurich?

Cordial greetings and wishes for the year's end and for 1956.

Yours, ANIELA JAFFÉ

James Kirsch
Analytical Psychologist
139 So. Beverly Drive
Beverly Hills, Calif.
CRestview[36] 1–6034

10 January 1956[37]

Dear Frau Jaffé!

After a pleasant trip I arrived here safely but do not feel quite at home yet. I wonder whether that will ever be the case again?

A lot has actually happened here. It's really a lively group.

For the Professor I'm enclosing an article by a theologian about *Answer to Job*.[38]

Most cordially, Yours, JAMES KIRSCH

From Aniela Jaffé

1 February 1956[39]

Dear Dr. Kirsch,

Thank you very much for forwarding the article regarding *Answer to Job* which Prof. Jung appropriated at once. (I'll steal it from him later, in order to

---

35 Typewritten in German, on plain paper; signed carbon copy.
36 Standard American usage of the period. Phone numbers were now normally dialed, rather than spoken to an operator, but they were not yet fully numeric. They still included a word, whose first two letters, customarily printed in capitals, were dialed.
37 Handwritten in German, on half-sheet letterhead.
38 Reference unclear, as Kirsch's enclosure is missing.
39 Typewritten in German, on plain paper; signed carbon copy.

read it!) – I'd like to use this opportunity to thank you especially warmly for the delightful photos, which made me laugh out loud. They are a precious reminder of that memorable day with the fabulous lunch. – I look forward enormously to the music.

With all your allusions[40] to things that occurred in L.A. during your absence, you're making a curious nature like myself most anxious to hear more. – Maybe that will be our next talk[41] at Streulistrasse.[42]

Under the circumstances, Prof. Jung is doing – touch wood – reasonably well. Last Saturday he held a discussion with young psychiatry assistants which lasted three hours and was a very great success.

Also last week he visited the Indian Embassy in Berne where he was invited to a festivity. Despite the exertion (overnight stay, train journey, etc.) it agreed with him. And – last but not least[43] – he wrote a preface to the new edition of *Discourses of the Buddha*[44] for Artemis Press, Zurich. All that in one week is really quite extraordinary, in my opinion (besides seeing people,[45] etc.).

Please give your wife my affectionate greetings. Best greetings to you, and a thousand thanks for the great fun.

Yours, ANIELA JAFFÉ

James Kirsch
Analytical Psychologist
139 So. Beverly Drive
Beverly Hills, Calif.

7 June 1956[46]

Dear Professor!

I seem to remember that many years ago you asked my opinion about the significance of the rib from which Eve was created. I also believe that – on a tentative basis – you gave a psychological interpretation in one of your books. Today I found a philological explanation in an otherwise rather rationalistic book

---

40 Word orig. in English.
41 Phrase orig. in English.
42 Jaffé's home address.
43 Phrase orig. in English.
44 "On the Discourses of the Buddha" (cf. CW 18, ¶1575–80). Promotional copy written by Jung for Karl Eugen Neumann's translation, *Die Reden Gotamo Buddhos* (Zurich & Stuttgart: Artemis; Vienna: Paul Zsolnay, 1956).
45 In addition to his patients, Jung always had many visitors.
46 Handwritten in German, on half-sheet letterhead.

by a "cuneiformist"[47]: Samuel Noah Kramer,[48] *From the Tablets of Sumer,* The Falcon's Wing Press, Indian Hills, Colorado, p. 171.

He writes:[49] "Why a rib? Why did the Hebrew storyteller find it more fitting to choose a rib rather than any other organ for the fashioning of the woman whose name, Eve, according to the Biblical notion, means approximately 'she who makes live?' The reason becomes clear if we assume that a Sumerian literary background, such as that represented by the Dilmun poem, underlies the Biblical paradise tale. In the Sumerian poem, one of Enki's sick organs is the rib. The Sumerian word for rib is *ti.* The goddess created for the healing of Enki's rib is called *Nin-ti,* 'the lady of the rib'. But the Sumerian word *ti* also means 'to make live'. The name *Nin-ti* may therefore also mean 'the lady who makes live'. In Sumerian literature, 'the lady of the rib' came to be identified with the lady who makes live through what may be termed a play on words. It was this, one of the most ancient literary puns, which was carried over and perpetuated in the Biblical paradise story, although here, of course, it loses its validity, since the word for 'rib' and that for 'who makes live' have nothing in common."

All this for what it's worth![50]

Hoping that you're doing well.

With cordial greetings, Yours truly, JAMES KIRSCH

I'll send you the book.

Prof. Dr. C. G. Jung
Küsnacht-Zürich
Seestrasse 228

21 June 1956[51]

Dear Colleague,[52]

My sincere thanks for the explanation of Adam's rib! By this representation, what the woman apparently originated from was an illness in the male; yet she is destined to heal this illness.

With best greetings, Ever yours truly, C. G. JUNG

---

47 Word orig. in English.
48 Samuel Noah Kramer (1897–1990): One of the world's leading Assyriologists and an expert on Sumerian history and language. Kirsch cites one of Kramer's many published works, *From the Tablets of Sumer: Twenty-five firsts in man's recorded history* (1956).
49 Following paragraph orig. in English.
50 Sentence orig. in English.
51 Typewritten in German, on letterhead.
52 *Herr Collega!*

Prof. Dr. C. G. Jung
Küsnacht-Zürich
Seestrasse 228

25 July 1956[53]

Dr. J. Kirsch
139 So. Beverly Drive
Beverly Hills, Calif.

Dear Colleague,[54]

I'm especially indebted to you for taking the great trouble to send me evidence of the American literature concerning double-bodied vessels.[55] I was certain that numerous references could be found in the American literature. By the way, the same motif exists in Europe: it's the double-bodied drinking vessel known in Croatia, which is called "Bilekum" and used to pledge close friendship.[56] The word "Bilekum" is definitely derived from the Old High German "Willekum." It's a double-bodied vessel made of clay or even porcelain.

With best greetings, Yours ever, C. G. JUNG

Probably from Aniela Jaffé

4 January 1958[57]

Dear Dr. Kirsch,

For eight days I am in Minusio near Locarno and am enjoying rest, sunshine, and mellowness. The mail was forwarded to me, including your letter regarding Mr. Jewell.[58] I am sorry to tell you this, but Jung refuses categorically to see him. Jung has not been feeling well as of late and has reduced his program to such

---

53 Typewritten in German, on, letterhead.
54 *Herr Collega.*
55 Kirsch's previous letter is missing. Jung returned to him one of the documents in question: a letter in English, dated 7 July 1956, from Bernice Johnston of Los Angeles. It opens, "Dear Dr. Kirsch, Dr. Dixon sent me this material from his dissertation on Double-Bodied Communicating Vessels. I checked his source from the Chicago Museum in our library and made a sketch of the specimen he referred to in his bibliography" (addendum, Jung–Kirsch correspondence, ETH Library archive). Materials from Dr. Dixon's dissertation were not found.
56 *Bruderschaft trinken*: lit. "drink brotherhood."
57 Typewritten in German, on plain paper; unsigned carbon copy. This letter closes a 17-month gap in the record of the Jung–Kirsch correspondence. From context, the writer is Aniela Jaffé.
58 Apparently a traveler who had hoped to visit Jung. (Kirsch's previous letter is missing.)

Figure 9.2 **First meeting of IAAP delegates, Hotel Sonnenberg, Zurich, August 1956.**
Gerhard Adler, Hilde Kirsch and Liliane Frey-Rohn; Adler's daughter Miriam
is to his left. *Photo: ©1956, James Kirsch. Courtesy Thomas B. Kirsch.*

an extent that visits of this kind will probably have to be discontinued – if not
permanently, at least for the time being. He sees 4–5 people per week![59] And so
you can imagine how difficult things are. – I myself suffer greatly, because I feel
for all those who are losing out. On the other hand, I think Jung is right to be very
sparing with his energies. In a way I go through it with him every day, seeing him
so quickly exhausted.[60]

Perhaps you could perform a kindness and explain the situation to Mr. J., in
case he needs such an explanation, which naturally I can't judge.

To you and your wife all good wishes for the New Year: good health and
everything else!

Cordial greetings, Yours, *[carbon copy unsigned]*

59 A low number, given the demands on Jung's time from patients and visitors. In 1952 Jung had
stopped accepting new patients. Analysands of long standing – including James and Hilde Kirsch
– continued to receive occasional sessions.
60 *Ich erlebe es ja sozusagen täglich mit, wie rasch sie [seine Energien] verbraucht sind.*

From Aniela Jaffé

20 March 1958[61]

Dear Dr. Kirsch,

Many thanks for your card[62] with the interesting news about Jung's double. I don't know anything about him, and neither does Prof. Jung whom I asked.

I won't travel to Ascona: it's much too tiring, and I prefer to read the volume[63] later.

To enrich your stay in Zurich[64] – if all goes well – I can tell you that a kind of discussion session[65] with Jung and the graduating candidates is scheduled to take place on Saturday afternoon, 14 June.[66] Such discussions are usually very stimulating and productive.

Now it's almost time to say: "Auf Wiedersehen!"[67]

Please give my regards to your wife.

With best greetings, Yours, ANIELA JAFFÉ

---

61 Typewritten in German, on Jung's letterhead, and signed.

62 Kirsch's card is missing.

63 i.e. *EJ 1958*.

64 Kirsch spent much of the summer of 1958 in Switzerland. The first Congress of the International Association for Analytical Psychology (hereafter IAAP), at which he delivered a lecture on Melville's *Moby-Dick,* took place at the ETH in early August (cf. Jung, 12 November 1959, p. 250 and note).

65 These conversations were tape-recorded. In 2004 they were published under the title, *Ueber Träume und Wandlungen* [On Dreams and Transformations], Walter/Patmos Verlag, Düsseldorf.

66 Kirsch's presence at this session is indicated in a typed, two-page document, *Fragen für den Empfang vom 14. Juni* [Questions for the June 14th reception]. Based on handwritten notes, it was prepared for Jung's use by Liliane Frey-Rohn, then secretary of the Club. A handwritten line of instruction appears below the heading: *"Anordnung nach Ihrem Belieben!"* [Organize as *you* see fit!] The first of five typed questions, bearing the name Dr. Kirsch, refers to a picture by Birkhäuser and asks Jung to explain the 4th dimension in the unconscious (undated typescript, Kirsch archive, kindly provided by the Stiftung der Werke von C. G. Jung).

67 "See you soon!"

Prof. Dr. C. G. Jung
Küsnacht-Zürich
Seestrasse 228

29 April 1958[68]

Dear Kirsch,

Thank you for your letter[69] and the additional information about the Guatemala UFO! I am glad at least to have made an understatement and not the contrary.[70] (Here I notice that I'm answering you unnecessarily in English, which is due to the fact that recently I've been speaking more English than German.) *O quae mutatio rerum!*[71]

It is characteristic that in your dream it's the Russians who are sending the UFOs (white discs), because Russia represents the other side which complements the West.

The concreteness of the God-image in your dream is somewhat alarming[72] – evidently a war god (helmet) with the "horns of power," at once a Celtic-Germanic combination, an Ares or Mars, eager to fight and stirring up conflict. Viewed collectively: a reason for war; individually: a menacing germ of strife. The concreteness of the image points to a certain identity of the subject with the God-image. Seen from the side of the coll. unc: a fall of the archetype into the three-dimensional world. Seen by the subject: an inflation by the archetype, or concretizing of the Self in the empirical human being. One reaches involuntarily beyond oneself, with all the inherent dissociative consequences. The god must not enter too far into matter, or the human being perishes. A human being has to walk the narrow path:[73] "erit via et semita sancta."[74]

I wish you good luck and patience for your theological talks.[75] I know only few theologians who take the difference between *image* and *original* seriously

---

68   Handwritten, mainly in German, on letterhead. Prev. pub. in *PP* and *Letters II*.

69   Kirsch's previous letter is missing.

70   Greeting through second sentence orig. in English.

71   From the refrain of a drinking song: "*O jerum, jerum, jerum, O quae mutatio rerum!*" [Oh sorrow, sorrow, sorrow! Oh, what a change in things!]. The song, "*O alte Burschenherrlichkeit*" [Oh, former boyhood splendor], would have been familiar to Jung and Kirsch, as "old boys" from their respective university fraternities. With thanks to Ulrich Hoerni.

72   *gibt zu denken*: lit., gives cause for thinking. The connotation, however, is of concern, even a feeling of shock.

73   *auf dem schmalen Pfade*: "on the narrow path" (Matt 7:14). In Luther's translation: "*Und die Pforte ist eng, und der Weg is schmal, der zum Leben führt; und wenige sind ihrer, die ihn finden*" [And the gate is small, and the way is narrow that leads to life, and few are those who find it].

74   "There will be a way and a sacred path." Paraphrasing Isaiah 35:8a, Vulgate: "*Et erit ibi semita et via, et via sancta vocabitur*" [And a path and a way shall be there, and it shall be called the holy way]. This biblical citation appears on the title page of the *Red Book* (cf. Kirsch, 7 June 1954, p. 200, note 78).

75   Probably a reference to Kirsch's radio lectures on psychology and religion (cf. Jung, 12 November 1959, p. 250 and note).

and understand it. Too little humilitas and too much hybris! And what about the psychologists? Vae scientibus![76]

I am feeling reasonably well and getting increasingly older.

With best greetings, Faithfully yours, C. G. JUNG

From an unidentified secretary:

2 July 1958[77]

Herrn
Dr. James Kirsch
Plattenstrasse 46
Zürich 7[78]

Dear Doctor,

Enclosed I am sending you the letter of recommendation, signed by Professor Jung, to Prof. Hisamatsu.[79]

With warm regards, *[carbon copy unsigned]*

---

76 Woe to the wise!
77 Typewritten in German, on plain paper; unsigned carbon copy. The writer may be Magda Pestalozzi, who served as Jung's secretary from time to time in his final years.
78 Kirsch was now in Zurich (cf. Jaffé, 20 March 1958, p. 227 and note).
79 Hosekei Shin'ichi Hisamatsu (1889–1980): Japanese philosopher and Zen Buddhist scholar. Hisamatsu served on the Kyoto University faculty, 1932–49, teaching Philosophy of Religion and Buddhism. A colleague of D. T. Suzuki (cf. Kirsch, 2 December 1958, p. 237 and note), Hisamatsu's special interest was the integration of Eastern and Western philosophies. In 1958 he received an honorary doctorate from Harvard and made a European lecture tour. On 16 May 1958, he visited Jung in Küsnacht. Their conversation, as recorded by Jaffé, is printed as "Gespräch mit einem Zen-Meister," *C. G. Jung im Gespräch: Interviews, Reden, Begegnungen* [C. G. Jung in Conversation: Interviews, talks, encounters] (Zürich: Daimon Verlag, 1986, pp. 186ff). (This conversation does not appear in *C. G. Jung Speaking.*) Six weeks later Jung wrote to Hisamatsu, recommending Kirsch to him: "He intends to spend 2 months in Japan, and I should be much obliged to you if you could help him to find his way in your country" (Jung to Hisamatsu, 1 July 1958, ETH Library archive; orig. in English). Cf. Kirsch, 9 October 1958, pp. 233f and notes.

Zürich 7/32
Plattenstr. 46

8 July 1958[80]

Dear Professor!
Would you be so kind as to give me permission to read the letters of your correspondence with Freud[81] which, as I understand, are being kept at the Jung Institute?[82]

With cordial greetings, Faithfully yours, JAMES KIRSCH

Küsnacht, 12 July 1958[83]

Dr. James Kirsch
Plattenstr. 46
Zürich 32

Dear Colleague,
Herewith I grant you permission to read my correspondence with Freud, which is located at the Jung Institute.

With best greetings, C. G. JUNG

---

80 Handwritten in German, on plain paper. Note at top by Jaffé: *"mit Karte Erlaubnis erteilt"* [permission given by card].

81 Cf. William McGuire, ed., *The Freud-Jung Letters*, trans. Ralph Manheim & R. F. C. Hull, PUP, 1974 (hereafter *FJL*). Cf. also Kirsch, August 1958, p. 231 and note.

82 As of 1958, the originals of Freud's letters to Jung were located at the C. G. Jung-Institut Zürich, to which Jung had given them in 1952 for safekeeping (Introduction, *FJL*, pp. xxif). Originals of Jung's letters to Freud were in the care of Freud's heirs; but copies had been given to C. A. Meier in 1954, who brought them back to Zurich (ibid., p. xxiv). Around 1970, when the correspondence was being prepared for publication, the two sides of the correspondence were formally exchanged. Originals of Freud's letters to Jung are now at the Library of Congress, and originals of Jung's letters to Freud at the ETH Library archive.

83 Typewritten in German, on postcard.

Hotel Fuji
Honmura-cho
Minato-ku
Tokyo
Tel. 45–8301 – 3

[August 1958][84]

Dear Professor!

I would like to thank you again most sincerely for granting me the great privilege of reading your entire correspondence with Freud. It aroused the most peculiar and very mixed emotions in me, and simultaneously I felt close to you in an entirely new way. At the same time my respect for Freud increased greatly and also an understanding of the enormous human tragedy which was summed up in the fact that he valued his authority higher than the truth. The most contradictory emotions quarreled within me because I experienced you in your letters both as the man in the 1930s and now also in your advanced age, alone and among your numerous students during the congress. To some extent I was able to take account of the enormous path of self-discovery you have traversed in these fifty years.

I would consider it a great mistake to publish these letters in their entirety and at an early date, serving no useful purpose.[85] Your judgments of people at that time, for instance, were certainly often harsh and unfair. Some "editing"[86] would probably be appropriate, which could be accomplished by the Institute together with a Freudian. Such "editing" would have to spare neither you nor Freud but perhaps third parties, such as Bleuler.[87]

With[88] most cordial greetings and best wishes for your good health,
Your deeply indebted and faithful, JAMES KIRSCH

---

84 Handwritten in German, on hotel letterhead, undated. From context the letter dates from August 1958. Kirsch's two-month visit to Japan ended in mid October (cf. Kirsch, 9 October 1958, p. 232).

85 Phrase orig. in English.

86 Word orig. in English.

87 Paul Eugen Bleuler (1857–1939): eminent Swiss psychiatrist, director of the Burghölzli clinic when Jung worked there, 1900–09. Bleuler, who coined the term schizophrenia, was never wholly convinced by Freud's theories of sexual etiology. He is mentioned over 100 times in Jung's letters to Freud, sometimes with admiration but also as the object of intense annoyance (e.g. Jung to Freud, 20 February and 19 June 1908, *FJL*, pp. 124, 157). In later years, Jung would express respect and warmth toward his former teacher (Jung–Bleuler correspondence, 1900–37, ETH Library archive).

88 Remaining lines written sideways in left margin.

906 Thayer Avenue
Los Angeles 24
Calif.

9 October 1958[89]

Dear Professor!

My sojourn in Japan is nearing the end, and now I would like to tell you about some of my experiences in this beautiful and very strange land.

As chance would have it, a few days after my arrival in Tokyo an international congress (Congress for the History of Religions)[90] was held here. I was lucky enough to get permission to attend. It lasted about three weeks, of which five days were dedicated to lectures and discussions. As usual, not much is accomplished during these scientific gatherings. This congress made no exception to that rule; in all the lectures one noticed the absence of psychology. What was significant for me, however, was that I became acquainted with a number of well-known scholars, specialists of all sorts, mythologists, historians of religion from many countries, from whom I learned a lot about the current situation in their fields. In the lectures your name was expressly mentioned twice – once by a Mrs. Block[91] of Columbia University, and once in an entire lecture on archetypes by a professor from Geneva, a student of Beaudouin's,[92] which unfortunately was not very good and elicited no discussion.

The second part of the congress consisted of the so-called "research tours"[93] which were magnificently organized tours, actually, and acquainted us with this country and its incredible number of religions,[94] and we got to see all sorts of Shinto shrines, Buddhist temples, religious dances, tantric fire rituals. On these occasions I discovered some of our specialists who explained these things especially for my benefit. And, of course, there were many discussions on the

---

89 Handwritten in German, on plain paper.
90 Title orig. in English. Cf. *Proceedings of the IXth International Congress for the History of Religions, Tokyo and Kyoto, 1958*, xiv, 914pp. Edited by Congress Organising Committee. Tokyo: Maruzen, 1960.
91 name unidentified.
92 = Charles Baudouin (1893–1963): French-born Swiss psychoanalyst; associate professor of philosophy at the University of Geneva. Baudouin founded the International Institute of Psychagogy and Psychotherapy and directed the review *Action et Pensée*. He had analyzed with a Freudian and two Jungians, and in his theoretical and clinical work he combined Freudian with Jungian psychology. He was particularly interested in the relation between psychoanalysis and education. In 1957 he published *Psychanalyse du symbole réligieux* and *Y-a-t'il une science de l'âme?* [Is there a science of the soul?]. Baudouin's student, who lectured on this occasion, is unidentified.
93 Phrase orig. in English.
94 Kirsch's footnote: *Es gibt einen Verband neuer Religionen!* [There is an association of new religions!]

subject of the ucs. with American scholars, such as Joseph Campbell[95] or Eliade,[96] or the Frenchman Dupont-Sommer[97] and even Massignon,[98] etc. This part of the trip into the countryside was certainly enormously fruitful, both humanly and scientifically.

Since then I've stayed in Kyoto, to study Zen. Prof. Hisamatsu,[99] whom I met thanks to your letter of recommendation, says that "to study Zen" means "to practice *Zazen* (Zen meditation)".[100] I had the greatest resistances against it, but my dreams spoke for it without reservation. So I began,[101] and subsequently my dreams assimilated the Zen meditation in a most positive way. I encountered things (which are well known to you), slept outstandingly, and generally felt very well. So far it was probably alright.[102] Then followed the discussions, during which I certainly learned a lot about Zen, and now and then I was asked questions concerning the Self and the coll. ucs. in a Jungian sense, but the discussions really led to nothing. The trump card was always that in your conversations with Hisamatsu[103] you had supposedly said that one could get rid of the coll. Unc.![104] I responded that such an assertion on your part seemed highly unlikely to me, especially as a "parting shot."[105] So Hisamatsu produced the minutes of your talk with him in German, and it became very clear what you said and intended to say (liberation from the "must" of the unconscious and the 10,000 things). All in all I clearly realized how much Eastern thinking differs from Western, and how what

---

95 Joseph John Campbell (1904–1987): American professor of comparative mythology and comparative religion at Sarah Lawrence College, Bronxville, New York, and at the Foreign Service
   Institute of the US State Department. A multi-lingual scholar, Campbell studied with Heinrich
   Zimmer (cf. Jung, 25 June 1932, p. 29 and note) and edited his papers for publication. Having
   studied both Freud and Jung, Campbell gravitated to Jung's theory of archetypes. In later life
   he lectured widely on comparative mythology and his own theory of the monomyth. Among
   Campbell's best-known works are *The Hero with a Thousand Faces* (1949) and *The Masks of
   God* (four volumes, 1959). His first trip to Asia was in 1955–56. He attended the 1958 conference
   with two friends from American universities, Mircea Eliade and Joseph Kitagawa.

96 Cf. Kirsch, 7 June 1954, p. 200 and notes.

97 André Dupont-Sommer (1900–1984): French orientalist and Aramaicist, professor at the Sorbonne
   and the École de France. Dupont-Sommer's commentaries on the Dead Sea Scrolls (cf. Kirsch, 11
   June 1955, p. 220 and note), e.g. *The Jewish Sect of Qumran and the Essenes: New Studies on the
   Dead Sea Scrolls* (1954), draw a connection between the Essenes and the early Christians.

98 Louis Massignon (1883–1962): French Islamist, professor at the Collège de France, 1926–54. A
   believing Catholic, working to create openness to Islam in the Catholic Church and the West. His
   pioneering work is reflected in *Nostra Aetate*, a pastoral declaration of Vatican II.

99 Cf. secretary, 2 July 1958, p. 229 and note.

100 Phrases orig. in English.

101 Kirsch later wrote: "I was doing eight hours of Zen meditation daily and saw my Zen-master once
    or twice a week. His name was Prof. Hisamatsu" (Kirsch to Adler, 28 September 1967, Kirsch
    archive).

102 Word orig. in English.

103 Hisamatsu had visited Jung in May 1958.

104 Paraphrase orig. in English.

105 Phrase orig. in English.

we call consciousness is not at all what Zen means by it, and that Hisamatsu and perhaps all Zen people are possessed by the idea of the Self in a metaphysical sense, make promises about the Awakening (Satori)[106] and generally extol Zazen as a panacea. We parted in good friendship but with a certain tension, especially since in Japan anything like "privacy" apparently does not exist.

The remark you allegedly made about "getting rid" of the coll. ucs.[107] has already been repeated publicly, not by Hisamatsu but by the Japanese professor[108] who accompanied Hisamatsu and was functioning as an interpreter at the time. I hope that my correction and explanation will help somewhat. No doubt, in the course of your life you have become used to being quoted wrongly – or in a distorted way – but the thinking process is so different here that they have the greatest difficulties to accept your ideas which you developed on the basis of your own experience. An additional difficulty probably is the fact that these scholarly Japanese have apparently read *everything*. On account of their feelings of inferiority they boast about it, but they can't possibly have digested everything – Jaspers, Heidegger, and the various American schools. (Hisamatsu does not boast; he is humanly very warm and related, even if naive.)

Hisamatsu is of course not married, has been living for 40 years in a house which is part of a temple district, although he is not a Zen monk or priest. He takes care of his own garden and writes books about "Zen and the arts."[109]

Generally speaking, even after a week-long acquaintance, I can't find out whether a Japanese is married or not. If it happens, by way of an exception, that a woman comes along to the station or even to a restaurant, she always walks three steps behind and never participates in conversation.

The young Japanese, esp. the psychiatrists, were very eager to hear more from me about you and with joy and enthusiasm soaked up everything I had to say about dreams, etc. – much in contrast to the Zen philosophers.[110]

There would be an awful lot more to say. Each day brings new impressions, but I am now ready to return to Los Angeles, to my work and my writing (and to sit in a room with furniture and chairs!).

---

106 Word orig. in English. *Satori*, the spiritual goal of Zen Buddhism, is generally described as a flash of sudden awareness, realigning consciousness and the unconscious.

107 Phrase orig. in English.

108 Possibly Masao Abe (1915–2006): Japanese Buddhist scholar and student of Hisamatsu, with special interest in Buddhist-Christian dialogue. Abe took part in Hisamatsu's conversations with Kirsch, as Kirsch later recounted: "I told [Jung] about discussions I had with Hisamatsu and a Dr. Abe, about their insistence on achieving an imageless state of mind and their statement that the ego could and should completely disappear, which of course was not acceptable to me" (Kirsch to Adler, 28 September 1967, Kirsch archive).

109 Phrase orig. in English.

110 Jung's response to this news reached Kirsch through Jaffé: *"Er hat mir dann auch davon erzählt und war erfreut über die 'Propaganda', die Sie unter den jungen Japanern für seine Psychologie gemacht haben"* ["Then he told me about it, too, and was happy about the 'propaganda' you made for his psychology with the young Japanese"] (Jaffé to Kirsch, 17 October 1958, Kirsch archive).

I hope that you have been well and that this letter will reach you in the best of health.

Perhaps with new meaning I can say: Faithfully yours, JAMES KIRSCH

Prof. Dr. C. G. Jung
Küsnacht-Zürich
Seestrasse 228

3 November 1958[111]

Dr. James Kirsch,
Thayer Ave 906
Los Angeles 24, Calif.

Dear Kirsch,

Many thanks for your kind letter from Japan. Everything you reported to me interested me very much. Mrs. Jaffé apprized me of the letter she received.[112] What shed the most light for me was your remark that Zen meditation could also represent a kind of dumbing-down yoga.[113] This is indeed the case with anyone who has some intellectual development. One needs to be of an unusual mental simplicity in order to become a once-and-for-all Enlightened One as a result of a broken foot. Satori experiences occur for us as well. I remind you, e.g. of Jakob Böhme,[114] who enters his workshop; on his table is a flat pewter plate in which a ray of sunlight is reflected; it hits Böhme in the eye, and with this he's "enraptured[115] into the innermost of Nature." Even my Somali headman[116] in Africa chose a similar metaphor to describe his meeting with Chadir.[117] He picked up a blade of grass from the ground and said, "Chadir can appear to you in this way too."[118]

---

111 Typewritten in German, on letterhead. Prev. pub. in *PP*.

112 At the same time as his last letter to Jung, sent from Japan, Kirsch had sent Jaffé a card, for which she thanked him (Jaffé to Kirsch, 17 October 1958, Kirsch archive).

113 *Verdummungsyoga* (invented word).

114 Jakob Böhme (1575–1624): German Christian mystic, to whose works and thought Jung refers repeatedly in his CW. A self-taught cobbler, influenced by Paracelsus, Kabbalah, astrology, alchemy, and the Hermetic tradition, Böhme coined the word "theosophy." His theophany, which Jung discusses here, occurred in 1600.

115 *"entzücket"*: lit. "delighted, charmed." Jung quotes Böhme's phrase in full: *"entzücket bis ins Innerste der Natur."*

116 Word orig. in English.

117 As noted by Adler, "Chadir (or Khidr) is the enigmatic, immortal knower of divine secrets, who figures in the 18th Sura of the Koran and plays an important role in Sufism. Cf. 'Concerning Rebirth,' CW 9(i), ¶240ff" (*Letters I*, p. 346 n. 3).

118 In another context, Jung tells the story in nearly identical terms (Jung to Neal, 9 February 1952, *Letters II*, p. 40).

Someone with a more lively spirit won't be satisfied with such impressions for very long, because unfailingly he'll think about them and in doing so dissolve them. Here one needs firmer foundations, that is, a real understanding.

Hisamatsu is without a doubt a genuine but somewhat simple mind who over-values his simplicity as generally valid. May it be preserved for him without restriction!

With best greetings, Yours truly, C. G. JUNG

James Kirsch
906 Thayer Avenue
West Los Angeles 24, Calif.
GRanite 7–3110

2 December 1958[119]

Dear Prof. Jung:

Please permit me to write to you in English although, as you know, I am very happy to receive letters from you in German.

I was profoundly interested in your remarks on Satori or illumination. I had practically no books in Japan but during all that time I had vividly in my mind two examples you discussed in *Psychological Types*.[120] One was Buddha's Fire Sermon[121] and the other was the wonderful chapter on Meister Eckehart.[122] The gist of these two commentaries helped me to maintain my viewpoint as against that of Zen, which tried to exclude any sort of image from meditation.

---

119 Typewritten in English, on letterhead, with hand-corrected phone number. An almost identical earlier version of this letter has been preserved, dated 25 November 1958 (typewritten in English, on plain paper, unsigned; Kirsch archive). The later version is clearer and slightly more complete than the draft, but otherwise identical.

120 Cf. Jung, 23 May 1932, p. 27 and note. *Types* had been one of the first works of Jung's to come to Kirsch's attention. It influenced his decision in 1922 to enter analysis with a Jungian, and later with Jung himself (cf. Preface, p. xii).

121 After a summary of this famous sermon, in which the Buddha warns, "the whole world is consumed by fire," Jung adds: "It is this fearful and sorrowful vision of the world that forces the Buddhist into his abstracting attitude" (CW 6, ¶494f).

122 Meister Eckhart, OP (c. 1260–1328): Eckhart von Hochheim, German theologian and mystic, professor of theology, a leader in his Dominican Order. He earned the Magister in theology at the University of Paris. Late in life Eckhart was charged with heresy by the Inquisition and became famous for his reasoned defense. In *Types*, Jung devotes part of a chapter to "The Relativity of the God-concept in Meister Eckhart" (CW 6, ¶407–33). The interiority of the God-image in Eckhart's mystical writings represents for Jung a medieval foray into psychology.

The attempt in Zen meditation is to get at the "formless" and therefore image-less Self, whilst any sort of Satori with which I was acquainted was always accompanied or expressed by some image. For example, in the case of your Somali headman it is accompanied by the blade of grass. This blade of grass is not the mystery, but it is needed to point to the mystery, just like the ear of corn in the Eleusinian mysteries.

There was only one Japanese who actually admitted to me that he himself had a Satori. Significantly enough, he did not claim it to be *the* one and only Satori, but this Satori was expressed by a circle of Buddhas in the center of which was a golden Buddha. And it was the sun-like radiation from the Buddha-head which had the numinous effect upon him. But, characteristically, this man is a doctor and a psychotherapist (not a philosopher like Suzuki)[123] who besides daily "sitting" (zazen = Zen-Meditation) also pays close attention to his own dreams. He naturally, as you say, reflects about his experiences and by that dissolves them. He was also the only one with whom for me from the very first moment a genuine friendship existed and developed during my stay in Japan. (Dr. Akihisa Kondo)[124]

I would be very grateful to you if you could comment on this question of whether Satori, or any form of sudden widening of consciousness, could exist without some image, and also what this image-less state is to which Zen and also Indian Yoga so often refers. I can only conceive that if there is an experience there must be an ego which experiences and that whatever is experienced has something of an image or at least a tone, a blade of grass or a ray of light.

In January I am going to give a seminar on *Ein Moderner Mythos*[125] and I am now terribly sorry I did not talk more with you about this book. Being one of "those who have seen a UFO, dreamt about them and spread the rumor about them," I have to make the best attempts possible to "transform it into an integrated content of consciousness." I am sure it will be a pretty lively seminar.

---

123 D. T. [Daisetz Teitaro] Suzuki (1870–1966): eminent Japanese philosopher, teacher and author on Zen Buddhism. His home was Kyoto, but he taught for long stretches at Western universities. Suzuki's acquaintance with Jung began as early as 1933 (cf. *Letters I*, pp.127f). At this date Kirsch had studied Suzuki's *Zen Buddhism* (1956), and *Mysticism: Christian and Buddhist* (1957), in which Suzuki shows a connection between Zen and Meister Eckhart.

124 Name added in handwriting. Akihisa Kondo, MD (1911–1999): Japanese psychiatrist and Zen Buddhist, student of D.T. Suzuki. Kondo, who had analyzed with Karen Horney in New York, "spoke a flawless English" (Kirsch to Adler, 28 Sept. 1967, Kirsch archive) and was a highly respected clinician. Kirsch later described him as "my closest friend in Japan" (Kirsch to Meier, 17 March 1970, Kirsch archive). Kondo's work focused on person-centered psychotherapy, Morita therapy, psychoanalysis, and the relation of Christian and Buddhist spirituality. One of his best-known English-language publications is "Zen in Psychotherapy: The Virtue of Sitting" (*Chicago Review* 12, No. 2, 1958).

125 C. G. Jung, *Ein moderner Mythus: Von Dingen, die am Himmel gesehen werden* [A modern myth: Of things seen in the sky] (Zürich: Rascher, 1958). A small volume (122 pages), later republished, with additions, as GW 10, ¶589–824; and in English, as "Flying Saucers: A Modern Myth of Things Seen in the Skies," CW 10, ¶589–824.

Hoping that you are in good health.[126]

With cordial greetings, Yours faithfully, JAMES KIRSCH

From Aniela Jaffé

6 December 1958[127]

Dear Dr. Kirsch,

My best thanks for your letter of 30 November 1958.[128] I find it simply touching that you are taking such great pains on account of Freud's "sex life."[129] A thousand heartfelt thanks! "My" chapter, i.e. Jung's chapter, on Freud is complete in its structure. For the time being it lacks indiscretions of this kind, but maybe it would be important to know more about it and, if it were permissible, to say something about it.[130] It fits tremendously well[131] with what Jung is saying about him. But of course I must cite a third person.

With regard to the Colin Still,[132] I immediately questioned Miss Bailey.[133] Unfortunately, we have not yet been able to locate the book. Please do not worry about this, as this is a common pre-condition here, until things suddenly turn up in unsuspected places. Thus, I shall push and pester relentlessly until it turns up. So I ask for further patience.

Cordial greetings, Yours, ANIELA JAFFÉ

126 Final three lines handwritten in German: *Mit herzlichen Grüssen, Ihr getreuer James Kirsch.*
127 Typewritten in German, on plain paper; signed carbon copy.
128 Kirsch's previous letter to Jaffé is missing.
129 Hilde Kirsch had told Jaffé about a lecture, "Sigmund Freud als Jude" [Sigmund Freud as a Jew] by Ernst Simon (Jaffé to Kirsch, 17 October 1958, Kirsch archive). Simon, a Freudian working at the "Leo Baeck Institute of Jews from Germany" in Jerusalem, was Kirsch's old friend and fellow member of the Blau-Weiss Society (cf. Kirsch, 19 November 1959, p. 251 and note). Jaffé hoped for permission to quote a passage from Simon's lecture, in which he stated that Freud's sex life had had a tragic aspect. She asked Kirsch to ask Simon to send Jung a copy of the lecture (Jaffé to Kirsch, 28 October 1958, Kirsch archive); this Kirsch promptly did, and Simon agreed (Simon to Kirsch, 12 December 1958, Kirsch archive).
130 Freud's sex life was largely unstudied at this point, and the subject was felt to be taboo. Jung seriously considered including this material in his chapter on Freud (cf. *MDR*, Ch. V, pp. 146ff), but decided against it. Jaffé wrote: *"Ich habe lange mit Jg. gesprochen und wir sind zu dem Resultat gekommen, die Anspielung auf die Sex-Frage nicht zu bringen. Jg. erwähnt Fr's 'Neurose', ohne sie weiter zu beschreiben."* ["I talked with Jung for a long time, and we came to the conclusion to refrain from alluding to the sex question. Jung mentions Freud's 'neurosis' without describing it further."] (Jaffé to Kirsch, 17 February 1959, Kirsch archive; trans. ACL).
131 *ungeheuer gut*: The term reflects Jaffé's excitement on receiving Kirsch's information.
132 Colin Still (1888–1973): English writer and literary advisor and editor, author of several works on Shakespeare, including *Shakespeare's Mystery Play: A Study of the Tempest* (1921, 1973). As Kirsch had begun to be engrossed in a study of Shakespeare's plays (cf. Jaffé, 3 October 1960, p. 264 and note), this may have been the book in question.
133 After Emma Jung's death, Ruth Bailey lived as a caregiver in Jung's household. She and Jung first crossed paths in Africa in 1925, and at his invitation she joined his expedition. Thereafter she sometimes visited him for a few weeks at a time.

From Aniela Jaffé

10 December 1958[134]

Dear Dr. Kirsch,

à propos of the Colin Still: You gave it to Jung, Jung gave it to Miss Bailey, Miss Bailey gave it to Barbara Hannah! And *she* – I learned yesterday – has read it, found it very interesting, and will return it to you and also write about it!

Thank God! This puzzle has been solved. Now I am hunting for two other books!

Cordial greetings, Yours, ANIELA JAFFÉ

Prof. Dr. C. G. Jung
Küsnacht-Zürich
Seestrasse 228

10 December 1958[135]

Dr. James Kirsch
906 Thayer Avenue
West Lost Angeles 24, Calif.

Dear Colleague,

Many thanks for your kind and interesting letter of December 2. The satori experience of your friend Dr. Kondo[136] is a typical mandala vision. If there are people in the East who assert that they've had an imageless experience, one must always remember that as a rule the report is supremely unpsychological. It's the tradition that such an experience is imageless, and therefore they say that the experience has been imageless. Not because they experienced it as imageless but just because it is the tradition. That it cannot possibly be imageless is proven by the fact that they remember something definite. Had it been totally imageless, they could never say that they remember something. For memory is an image of something that has been. This simple reflection however does not occur to the Eastern person, as little as when he asserts that he has come into an imageless state when he received an illumination. He knows, of course, that it was an imageless state, and that in itself is already an image, which however these people cannot understand. I've never really succeeded in convincing an Indian that if no conscious ego is present, no conscious memory can be present, either. The comparison they

---

134 Typewritten in German, on letterhead, and signed.
135 Typewritten in German, on letterhead. Prev. pub. in *PP* and *Letters II*.
136 Cf. Kirsch, 2 December 1958, p. 237 and note.

always make with a deep sleep, in which no memory at all exists, is just a state in which no memory can come into being, because nothing is perceived. But in a satori experience something is perceived; namely, that an illumination, or something like it, has taken place. But that is a definite image which can even be compared with tradition and brought into harmony with it. Thus I consider this assertion of an imageless state as an uncritical and unpsychological assertion, which originates from a lack of psychological differentiation. This lack also explains why we find it so difficult to have real contact with such people, and it is no accident that the only one who could give you a satisfactory explanation was an observing psychologist.[137] It is utterly incomprehensible how an event can be registered, if no one is present who has had it. This someone who registers is always an ego. If no ego is present, absolutely nothing can be perceived. We find similar assertions among us also, e.g. a Christian can assert that he has been redeemed by Christ, although one can prove to him without difficulty that fundamentally he has been redeemed of nothing. He has only experienced a change in the disposition of his mind and looks at certain things differently from before. In principle, however, the situation is essentially the same as it was.

It interested me to hear that you want to give a seminar on the "Modern Myth."[138] As you will have noticed, I left open the question of the reality of UFOs. Recently I saw photographs that were taken in the area of the Bernina, showing a landed saucer. According to the opinion of all, including that of experts, these photographs seem to be genuine, as strange as it may sound. The only thing one can establish with certainty is that a phenomenon which was already observed in past centuries has in our own day, for the first time, given rise to a myth. What this phenomenon is, however, appears to me for the present still utterly unclarified.

With my best wishes for the New Year, I remain

Faithfully yours, C. G. JUNG

---

137 *beobachtender Psycholog.*
138 Cf. Kirsch, 2 December 1958, p. 237 and note.

Greetings on a Christmas party menu
from the Psychological Club, Zurich[139]

Menu[140]

Oxtail clair au Porto
Sacristains

*

Jambon de campagne braisé
Epinards à la crème
Pommes fines herbes
Salade

*

Parfait glace aux framboises
ou
Corbeille de fruits

---

139 Undated document found at the James Kirsch archive among miscellaneous letters from 1959. It almost certainly dates from December 1958. Inscriptions are handwritten in ink on the reverse side of a handmade Christmas dinner menu by members of the Zurich Club. Such greetings would not likely have arisen at the Club's 1959 Christmas party, which was described by the Club secretary, Liliane Frey-Rohn as, "rather depressing.... *Jung wird leider sehr alt, er zieht sich mehr und mehr zurück, schränkt alles ein, um immer mehr in sich zu versinken"* [Jung is unfortunately getting older and older, he withdraws more and more, curtails everything in order to sink further into himself] (Frey-Rohn to Kirsch, 20 December 1959, Kirsch archive).

140 Handmade menu, typewritten on beige construction paper. On each side of the list of courses are pasted-on decorations, also made of construction paper: two red candles with yellow flames, standing on green pine sprays.

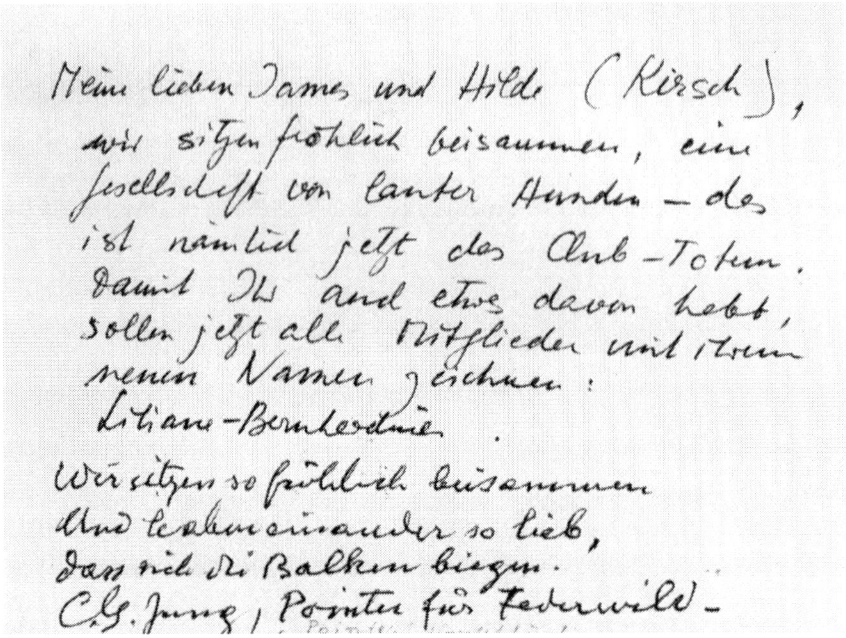
Meine lieben James und Hilde (Kirsch),
wir sitzen fröhlich beisammen, eine
Gesellschaft von lauter Hunden – das
ist nämlich jetzt das Club-Totem.
Damit Ihr auch etwas davon habt,
sollen jetzt alle Mitglieder mit ihrem
neuen Namen zeichnen:
Liliane-Bernhardine.
Wir sitzen so fröhlich beisammen
Und haben einander so lieb,
dass sich die Balken biegen.
C.G. Jung, Pointer für Federwild –

Figure 9.3 **1958 "Christmas menu" card (excerpt), Psychological Club, Zurich.** *Photo: ©2010, Ann Lammers. Courtesy Kirsch archive/Stiftung der Werke von C. G. Jung/Estate of Liliane Frey-Rohn/Robert Hinshaw.*

My dear *James and Hilde (Kirsch),*

- we're sitting joyously together,[141] a society of nothing but dogs – which is now the Club totem. To share the experience with you, all members shall now sign with their new names:

LILIANE[142] – St. Bernard

- We're sitting so joyous together
And loving each other so much[143]
that the rafters are bending.[144]

C. G. JUNG, Pointer for wild fowl[145]

141 *Wir sitzen fröhlich beisammen:* partial quotation from song, quoted by Jung at greater length.

142 Liliane Frey-Rohn (cf. Kirsch, 20 May 1951, p. 138 and note), currently the Club secretary. Signers of the card are identified where possible; all are members of the Club.

143 *Wir sitzen so fröhlich beisammen / und haben einander so lieb*: Jung quotes the first two lines of a folksong (Kotzebue, 1761–1819), which continues: *"Erheitern einander das Leben; / Ach wenn es doch immer so blieb!"* [We make each other so happy; / Oh, if we could stay like this forever!].

144 Recalling a proverb, *"Er lügt, dass sich die Balken biegen"* [He lies so much, the girders are bending].

145 Penciled below, in different handwriting: " Pointer (*Vorstehhund*)."

- In this feeling-situation I am naked and helpless as a Chihuahua.

  M.-L. VON FRANZ[146]

  (i.e. naked and bare he'll depart from hence, if possible in the diligence.
  A Commentator.)[147]

- After these intelligent epigrams, there is nothing left for the poor Pomeranian
  to bark.

  M. PESTALOZZI[148]

- As a Cairn-Terrier (house-angel – street-devil)
  I send warm greetings

  DORA MARIA KALFF[149]

- Hunting dog BAUMANN[150]

- Warm regards, J. KUNZ

- Cordial greetings, H. BINDER

- Most cordial greetings from the "innocent lamb in dog's clothing" (Bedlington
  Terrier)

  Alias EDITH REICHSTEIN

- Cordial greetings and good wishes for the New Year.

  Yours, PETER WALDER

- S. TAUBER

- We're getting more and more cheerful – until it is almost too late to go home.
  Sending all good wishes "towards you"[151]

  K. STEIGER

- N. STAUFFACHER

---

146 Marie-Louise von Franz (cf. Kirsch *et al.*, 22 February 1953, p. 159 and note).
147 Addendum to von Franz's greeting, in Jung's handwriting.
148 Magda Pestalozzi (cf. secretary, 2 July 1958, p. 229 and note).
149 Dora Maria Kalff (1904–1990): Swiss Jungian therapist, specialist in the therapeutic use of sand
   trays and miniatures. She studied with Margaret Lowenfeld in London before developing her own
   method, Sandplay Therapy, based on Jung's theories. In 1969 Kalff came to Los Angeles as a
   visiting lecturer (Kirsch to Meier, 28 January 1969, Kirsch archive).
150 Fritz Baumann-Jung, the husband of Jung's daughter Gret Baumann Jung, was a member of the
   Club.
151 Quoted words orig. in English.

- Cordial greetings, ALICE CROWLEY[152]

- We are all "dogs" together this Xmas – Pity you can't be with us.

  UNA G. THOMAS,[153] Airedale

- ANIELA[154] – Schnauzer: good kernel in clean shell sends greetings (bow-wow!)

- Warm wishes and greetings

  HANNA KUMMERLÉ

- Most cordial greetings to both of you

  LENA[155]

- E. SCHLEGEL

- With warmest greetings from – the Scottish Terrier – BARBARA[156]

- Best of wishes, we wish you were among us – ELIZABETH WELSH[157]

- Best regards K. BINSWANGER[158] – Fox Terrier

---

152 Signature illegible; name penciled above the line in different handwriting.
153 Cf. Thomas, 20 October 1952, p. 140 and note. Greeting orig. in English.
154 Cf. Jaffé, 22 November 1952, p. 145 and note.
155 Lena Hurwitz-Eisner, wife of Dr. Siegmund Hurwitz (cf. Thomas, 20 October 1952, p. 140 and note) was one of the early editors of the GW.
156 Barbara Hannah (cf. Kirsch to Hull, 19 February 1954, p. 191 and note). Greeting orig. in English.
157 Elizabeth Welsh: Englishwoman living in Zurich since the 1930s. She attended Jung's ETH seminars, 1933–35, and translated notes from his lectures and other early writings (cf. Kirsch, 29 September 1948, p. 118, note 34; Thomas, 20 October 1952, p. 140 and note). Greeting orig. in English.
158 Kurt Binswanger, Dr. med.: Swiss psychiatrist; son of Ludwig Binswanger (1881–1966), who served with Jung at the Burghölzli clinic and founded existential psychotherapy; great-nephew of Otto Binswanger (1852–1929), professor of psychiatry at Jena University.

1959–1961

MYSTERIUM

James Kirsch
906 Thayer Avenue
West Los Angeles 24, Calif.
GR7–3110

15 March 1959[1]

Dear Professor!

I'm just now realizing how much time has gone by since I wrote to you. Your letter of Dec. 10 was very helpful in my coming to terms with Japan and especially with Zen. Right now Prof. Chang[2] from New York is here. He gave a lecture at our Club on the subject of "Tao and Transformation"[3] and, fortunately, he is staying with us, so we have many opportunities to talk about Zen and other questions of Eastern and Western psychology. To look at Zen and Japan now from a Chinese vantage point has very much assisted me in sorting out this problem. The Japanese unconscious burdened me to a much greater extent than I anticipated and perceived. But my ship is now sailing much more smoothly with all this assimilated material.

The 10-hour seminar on your "Flying Saucer"[4] book was very well attended. I also believe that the announcement concerning coming events and the problem of individuation was largely well understood. From time to time I find it on the whole quite amazing that – here in the American desert – such a group exists, where a number of people are seriously gripped by the unconscious and are seriously working through your books. My wife contributes very seriously to this. She gave an 8-hour seminar for the training candidates[5] on your book *Psychologie der Übertragung*,[6] in which eight analysts participated. The entire book was discussed, chapter by chapter. I was astonished to see how well the young candidates (all in their mid thirties) had grasped this very difficult problem. In addition, she is reading through this book sentence by sentence with another group. Inasmuch as a mythological theme like the *coniunctio* has become the subject of a discussion, a spiritual center is again being established, such as had not existed here for many years. Of course, there are also some here who prefer to occupy themselves with

---

1 Handwritten in German, on letterhead, with hand-corrected phone number.
2 Chung-Yuan Chang, PhD: Chinese Taoist scholar. Chang received his doctorate from Columbia University in 1943 and served as Professor of Chinese Philosophy at the Asian Institute, New York, 1947–53. He lectured on Taoist philosophy at Eranos, 1955, 1956, 1958, and at the Zurich Jung Institute in 1956 and 1957. He taught at the Buddhist Society, London, in 1955, and at the Society of Analytical Psychology, London, in 1957. His lecture for the Los Angeles APC, 13 March 1959, was titled "Self-Transformation and Tao" (typed announcement, Kirsch archive). In April and May 1963 Chang returned to Los Angeles to give a six-week APC workshop, "Tao and its Reflections in Poetry, Painting, and Movement" (typed announcement, Kirsch archive).
3 Title orig. in English.
4 Title orig. in English. Cf. Kirsch, 2 December 1958, p. 237 and note.
5 Phrase orig. in English.
6 Psychology of the Transference. Cf. Jung, 25 July 1946, p. 107 and note.

individual clinical cases, but it is also becoming clear to what extent this clinical attitude leads to intellectual constriction, impoverishment, and rationalism.

By the way, Erich Fromm[7] quotes a letter to Jones about you (January 22, 1911!),[8] from Jones's *Life and Work of Sigmund Freud*:[9]

> "I am more than ever convinced that he is the man of the future. His own investigations have carried him far into the realm of mythology, which he wants to open up with the key of the libido theory. However agreeable all that may be, I nevertheless bade him in good time to return to the neuroses. There is the motherland where we have first to fortify our dominion against all things and everybody."[10]

Freud was quite a good prophet, after all! This conflict between the one-sided attitude to the individual clinical case and the one that includes mythology in the broadest sense is thus very old and will probably endure for ever.

May I tell you a dream I had after Prof. Chang's visit, and after he spoke with high praise about an article I wrote on "Zen and the Process of Individuation?"[11]

> I was in New York; crossed the street with someone. At some distance I saw a blue streetcar (like the ones in Zurich). Said to my companion:

7 Erich Seligmann Fromm, PhD (1900–1980): German-Jewish social psychologist, psychoanalyst, humanistic philosopher, and democratic socialist. In 1922 Fromm earned a doctorate in sociology from Heidelberg University, where he and Kirsch were fellow members of the Blau-Weiss student union (cf. Kirsch, 19 November 1959, p. 251 and note). He received psychoanalytic training in Heidelberg and at the Frankfurt Institute for Social Research, and opened his practice in 1927. In 1933 he fled Germany, moving first to Geneva, then to Columbia University. In New York he was a close colleague of Karen Horney. He taught at Bennington College, 1941–50, and at the University of Mexico, 1950–65. There he established a psychoanalytic department at the medical school. In 1957–61 he was a professor of psychology at the University of Michigan. His many published works include *Escape from Freedom* (1941), *The Art of Loving* (1956), *Beyond the Chains of Illusion: My Encounter with Marx and Freud* (1962), and *Greatness and Limitation of Freud's Thought* (1979).

8 Erich Fromm, *Sigmund Freud's Mission: An Analysis of his Personality and Influence* (New York: Harper, 1959; p. 91 and note). Kirsch follows Fromm in mistaking the source and date of the quoted passage.

9 Ernest Jones, *The Life and Work of Sigmund Freud, Volume II: 1901–1919, Years of Maturity*, New York: Basic Books, Inc., 1955, p. 140.

10 The actual source of this passage, as cited by Jones, is Freud's letter to Ferenczi, 29 December 1910 (ibid., p. 471, note 47). Jones adds that Freud had issued the same warning to him, i.e. not to become distracted by an interest in mythology (ibid., p. 140).

11 At this date Kirsch's article bore the working title, "Zen and the Process of Individuation." It was based on his earlier lecture, "The Role of the Analyst in Jung's Psychotherapy," delivered on 6 August 1957 at a conference on "Zen and Psychotherapy" in Cuernavaca, Mexico (Kirsch sent a typescript of the lecture to C. A. Meier, and it is found among Meier's papers, ETH Library archive). The revised version shown to Chang in 1959 was thereafter published under a more neutral title: "Affinities between Zen and Analytical Psychology" (*Psychologia: An International Journal of Psychology in the Orient*, vol. III, no. 2, June 1960, Kyoto, Japan, pp. 85–91).

"What makes me so 'mad'[12] in New York is that once a streetcar gets stuck, it has to wait ten minutes until the tracks are cleared before it can keep going."

Then I'm inside a building. There is a celebration in your honor. A Chinese delegation is also present and commends you especially for your work with the I Ching, and as a sign of gratitude they are presenting you with a large blue cane or wand.

I say to you: You have been richly rewarded by the I Ching. Your work expressed your thanks to the I Ching, and now this reward! You nod in agreement.

Things are unchanged as far as the Klugers are concerned, but they've definitely improved their manners in public meetings and discussions. I cannot say that I've personally found a way to give my "fighting cock" nature a creative expression. I'm finished now with the *Moby-Dick* seminar.[13] A lot of it was captured on tape. I hope to be able to finish the book about Melville this year.[14]

Dear Professor, I hope you're doing well and enjoying the spring, which has already arrived in full splendor here. In the last few days I had a mild gout attack, the first one in 5 years, but couldn't find a satisfactory psychological explanation for it. Inwardly, I find the transference problem and the Mysterium Coniunctionis the most difficult of all, and almost impossible to master.[15]

With most cordial greetings and all good wishes, Faithfully yours, JAMES KIRSCH

Prof. Dr. C. G. Jung
Küsnacht-Zürich
Seestrasse 228

12 November 1959[16]

Dear Kirsch,

Many thanks for the pleasant news![17] I am particularly pleased to hear that you met again with G. Adler. He is indeed a very solid person with an unqualified

---

12 Word orig. in English.
13 Kirsch's seminar built on many months of research. Two years earlier, in March 1957, he had delivered a long paper, "The Enigma of Moby-Dick" (typescript, KML archive) to the Los Angeles APC. On 11 August 1958 he lectured at the first congress of the IAAP on "The Problem of Dictatorship as Represented in *Moby-Dick*" (mimeographed typescript, KML archive).
14 Kirsch never wrote the projected book on *Moby-Dick*, but he published his second paper (cf. Kirsch, 19 November 1959, p. 252 and note).
15 *das Allerschwierigste und kaum-zu-Bewältigende*. In context, Kirsch's use of technical terms from Jung's corpus is meant as an abstract reference to his own interior struggle (cf. Kirsch, 31 January 1960, pp. 254ff; Jung, 12 February 1960, pp. 259f).
16 Typewritten in German, on letterhead. Second paragraph prev. pub. in *PP* and *Letters II*.
17 A letter from Kirsch is missing.

sense of responsibility. It is a pity that the universities are so far behind the times. He would deserve a professorship.

I'm also glad to hear about your activity on the radio.[18] Today that's the way to reach the public. For me personally it goes against the grain, but increasingly I belong to the past and can no longer adapt to the restlessness and superficiality of present-day life. It's beyond my comprehension how one can talk about "Job" on the radio without causing misunderstandings, since its argument[19] is one of the most subtle I've encountered, especially if such a banal brain as a Fromm[20] precedes you onstage as a premise, so to speak. I therefore wish you much luck on such an incalculable undertaking. I don't underestimate one thing, however, and that is the to me amazing and unexpected *intuition* of the American public, of which I had an impressive example on the occasion of my lectures at Yale University. The little book[21] has a limited but constant market in the USA. I am anxious to hear your experiences. Possibly you'll start a "war," which will certainly erupt one day, the more darkly the political sky becomes overcast.[22] My appearance on British television[23] appears to have been a considerable and unexpected success.

My best wishes, Always yours truly, C. G. JUNG

18 In 1958 and 1959, at the invitation of a public radio station, KPFK, Los Angeles, Kirsch prepared three lectures for broadcast under the collective title "Psychology and Religion," and a fourth lecture, "Job." When he sent these writings, in carbon copy, to the APC of New York, the first page of each document was altered (probably by Kirsch) to serve as a title page. The date for all four lectures is given as "April, 1960" (typescripts, KML archive). Cf. Kirsch, 19 November 1959, p. 251.

19 Referring to the text of the biblical book, or to Jung's own argument in *Job.*

20 Cf. Kirsch, 15 March 1959, p. 248 and note.

21 Probably *Psychology and Religion*, Jung's 1937 Terry Lectures, which had continued to be sold in the original paperbound edition (Yale University Press, 1938). It had also been republished in 1958 as the first part of CW 11, *Psych & Rel.*

22 Jung's references to "war" and the darkening "political sky" may refer to divisions which had come to the surface in the international Jungian community. At the first congress of the IAAP, August 1958, tensions between the archetypal and developmental Jungian schools played a prominent role, as reported in a contemporary *Time Magazine* article (25 August 1958) (cf. *Jungians*, Ch. 18, esp. p. 224). In this ongoing contest among Jungians, Kirsch could be counted on to take the archetypal side (cf. Kirsch, 26 December 1948, p. 122 and note).

23 Jung was interviewed on BBC television by John Freeman, 22 October 1959. Cf. "'Face to Face' Interview," *C. G. Jung Speaking*, pp. 424–39.

James Kirsch
906 Thayer Avenue
West Los Angeles 24, Calif.
GR 3–4143

19 November 1959[24]

Dear Professor!

Your prompt answer encourages me to answer you at once, too. The fact is, I don't feel at all comfortable with this radio work,[25] and I had to overcome the greatest inner difficulties before agreeing to do these radio lectures. And then, the strangest and most irrational things keep happening. At first I was strongly urged to have the lectures ready by a certain date, as they were supposed to be broadcast in the middle of November. Then I hear nothing from the station for months, and the lectures don't appear on the program. The lecture on "Job" is actually more a commentary or an introduction to your book, because I've encountered the most remarkable misunderstandings, contradictions and affects with regard to it. So I'm trying to clear things up a bit, to let people read your book with less prejudice.

In the meantime, I presented my lecture[26] here to a Jewish group. It was a complete failure, inasmuch as the "chief"[27] of this group felt it necessary to "translate" what I had said, that is, to make intellectual and ethical rubbish of it. From the questions I was asked privately by individual members, however, I could tell they had grasped some essential points. Under these circumstances, I have the strongest misgivings about airing these lectures on the radio and now wish to cancel them. What you call "the restlessness and superficiality of present-day life" is definitely also a problem for me. I wonder if it would not be preferable to write down what I have to say and publish it in a book.

Fromm is doubtless a banal intellect, as you say. He's a friend of mine from our student days at Heidelberg.[28] I've had a number of conversations with him in New York and Mexico[29] about the ucs. He has learned a lot and stolen a lot from you, but he'd never admit it. His great difficulty is that he cannot comprehend

---

24 Handwritten in German, on half-sheets of letterhead, with hand-corrected phone number.
25 Cf. Jung, 12 November 1959, p. 250 and note.
26 Probably Kirsch's long lecture, "Job" (ibid).
27 Word orig. in English.
28 Kirsch and Fromm had been graduate students at Heidelberg University in the early 1920s. There they knew one another through Blau-Weiss, the Zionist society which Kirsch had joined in high school. Kirsch felt a lifelong friendship with his Blau-Weiss brothers. With some he had voluminous correspondences and family ties. With Ernst Simon (cf. Jaffé, 6 December 1958, p. 238, note 129), he maintained a warm collegial connection, despite professional differences. His attitude toward Fromm, as he explains to Jung, had changed over the years. They were now rarely in contact.
29 The dates of these contacts are hard to determine. Fromm was a professor at the University of Mexico from 1950 to 1965. In August 1957 Kirsch attended a conference, "Zen and Psychotherapy," in Cuernavaca (cf. Kirsch, 15 March 1959, p. 248, note 11).

that the objective psyche exists. When it suits him, or when things get dangerous, he feels free to revise dreams. He truly believes that dreams are produced by the ego. He comes from an orthodox Jewish family, is enormously learned in Jewish subjects, but doesn't believe in God. Right now he is totally fascinated by Zen and Suzuki.[30] It's really too bad for him, because as a young man he was very promising. He's completely cut off from his instincts.

In the "war" which will unavoidably break out,[31] I have only been injured so far. I also don't know what methods I ought to use. I am very anxious about it – not for myself, but I wonder if I'm the right man, or how I can become the right man, and whether I am using the right methods.

In any case I promised Adler that I'll submit my book on *Moby-Dick* at the congress in 1961.[32]

Hoping that you are doing very well, Faithfully yours, JAMES KIRSCH

Prof. Dr. C. G. Jung
Küsnacht-Zürich
Seestrasse 228

10 January 1960[33]

Dear Mr. Kirsch!

Your news impressed me very much. Please convey my expression of sympathy to your dear wife![34] In 1944[35] I also suffered a broken foot because I did not want to submit to a "higher" will. I had to change my "standpoint"; I was still too high up, i.e. not "humble" enough to accept my life in all its forms. I knew better and for that reason could not touch the real ground. I was – so to speak – *thrown* down the steps because I did not want to *go* down. Where did your wife not want to go down, and where does she want to reserve power for herself? The wiser one yields in time, even when he does not, i.e. not yet, understand it. At that time, I also had

---

30 Fromm's *Psychoanalysis and Zen Buddhism* was published in 1960.

31 Cf. Jung, 12 November 1959, p. 250 and note.

32 *Jedenfalls habe ich Adler versprochen, dass ich beim Kongress im Jahre '61 mein Buch über Moby-Dick vorlege.* By his "book on Moby-Dick," Kirsch evidently means his paper from the first IAAP congress, "The Problem of Dictatorship in Moby-Dick." It was published in 1961, with other lectures from the congress of 1958, in a volume edited by Gerhard Adler: *Current Trends in Analytical Psychology* (London: Tavistock Publications, 1961, pp. 261–74).

33 Handwritten in German, on half-sheets of letterhead. Final paragraph prev. pub. in *PP*.

34 A letter from Kirsch is evidently missing. On a walk in the forest, Hilde Kirsch had broken both ankles (cf. Kirsch, 31 January 1960, p. 256; cf. also Appendix B, p. 284).

35 In Jung's German original he substitutes an English usage, "in 1944."

no idea what it was about. However, these things are positively dangerous; for heaven's sake no inflation, unless one wants to risk a *casus ab alto*.[36] One has to be extremely liberal in assuming that one is blind somewhere and thus impatient. It's right to be in doubt about oneself, dangerously wrong, though, to believe one can be sure of oneself.

Once I also gave up smoking for a quarter of a year without noticing much difference. Was it the cigarettes?[37] I only smoke pipes & 1 cigar in the evening. Your reaction is amazing.[38] The nicotine seems to have held down a great many things.

With best greetings and wishes, Faithfully yours, C. G. JUNG

Prof. Dr. C. G. Jung
Küsnacht-Zürich
Seestrasse 228

20 January 1960[39]

Dear Kirsch,

Recently I received a letter from Ruth S. White, CAPRICORN RECORDS.[40] This lady proposes to make several phonographic recordings either of a lecture of mine, or an interview concerning my ideas. I would be very grateful if you could give me some information with respect to this lady as well as the referenced company CAPRICORN RECORDS.[41] She informed me that she's a member of the Analytical Psychology Club of Los Angeles. Her idea is certainly a good one, but I don't know the company's reputation.

With many thanks in advance, Yours truly, C. G. JUNG

---

36 fall from the heights.

37 Obscure reference in the original. Possibly Jung is wondering whether his exposure to second-hand cigarette smoke reduced his benefit from giving up smoking.

38 Cf. Kirsch, 31 January 1960, p. 255.

39 Typewritten in German, on half-sheet letterhead.

40 Every effort was made to locate Ruth S. White or her heirs. No information was found, beyond what Kirsch reports to Jung in his reply (cf. Kirsch, 26 January 1960, p. 254). The fact that Ruth White has been in analysis appears to be mentioned only to support Kirsch's recommendation of her, and her proposed recording of Jung's speaking voice. Her business firm and her partner are also named, which means that, to conceal her identity entirely, further textual cuts would be required. After consultation, the editor takes full responsibility for letting her name stand.

41 Although Jung became interested in the proposed project and even entered into detailed negotiations about it (cf. Jaffé, 3 February 1960, p. 256; Kirsch, 10 February 1960, pp. 258f), in the end he was unable to make the planned recording (cf. Jaffé, 15 February 1960, p. 261).

James Kirsch
906 Thayer Avenue
Los Angeles 24, Calif.
GRanite 7–3110

26 January 1960[42]

Dear Professor!

Very confidentially I would like to pass on some information to you about Miss Ruth White. She has worked with me for about a year and about 2 years with my wife. She is extremely gifted musically, a really creative composer, approx. 34 years old. For about 6 years she has been producing "educational records"[43] which are of the highest quality and are "collectors' items". All the records she has issued to date deal with music. Her reputation is "above reproach", about the best and most solid one can desire in business and artistic matters. For about a year now she's also had a business alliance with her friend, Marg. McClean, M.D., who is one of our training analysts, and founded the company called Capricorn Records. The two ladies now intend to record the voices, teachings, and personalities of important persons of our time. For this purpose they want to use the best technical means. Both are very deeply committed indeed to analytical psychology. I'm convinced that, technical conditions aside, they would arrange everything as you wish.

Briefly, I would be very happy if it came to fruition: a recording without stupid questions, in which you could express what is close to your heart.

Most cordially, Faithfully yours, JAMES KIRSCH

James Kirsch
906 Thayer Avenue
West Los Angeles 24, Calif.
GR 3–4143

31 January 1960[44]

Dear Professor!

Your letter touched me deeply, and I thank you with all my heart for taking such deep interest in Hilde's and my fate.

The fact that something is not quite right with me has been evident to me for a long time, and I am also aware that a major change is necessary and close at

---

42 Handwritten in German, on letterhead.
43 Quoted phrases throughout letter orig. in English.
44 Handwritten in German, on letterhead with hand-corrected phone number.

hand, but without knowing in what direction it's going. For quite some time[45] I have been meaning to mention in my letters to you a visionary dream which has been on my mind ever since: "Suddenly I saw Christ in front of me. But he was an angelic being – a girl. He-she gave a brief, friendly laugh and said: How can one really doubt that he is the essence, the foundation of the world, the sole reality."

Consciously at the time I wasn't preoccupied with Christ. On the other hand, I had very carefully read your books on the subject and had given a long seminar about the chapter in *Aion*, "Christ, a Symbol of the Self."[46] I had also reflected at length on the "Anthropos" as a union of opposites. I could not comprehend in what sense this dream referred to me.

When I decided not to send you this dream, so as not to burden you, I had additional dreams about Christ, and others where deities made personal appearances. In retrospect, I realize that this was also the time when suddenly a lot of water collected in my body.

Viewed strictly organically, it was an endocrine disturbance that afflicted me for decades and because of which I was very heavy. In 1950 I started taking thyroid medication and went on a strict diet which changed me very much in every respect. During the past few years, however, I stopped taking the thyroid medication and developed all kinds of symptoms, which I attributed to smoking (heart pain, glossitis, etc.), on account of which I once even consulted a specialist in Zurich. Here, too,[47] the doctors didn't understand the condition properly, until the major edema occurred when I gave up smoking. I've had all kinds of examinations, including the most modern ones, but they did not result in an unequivocal picture. The thyroid gland functions normally. My doctor attributes the general disturbance to the aldosterones which retain 30 times more salt in the body than other sterones. In any case, the thyroid medications are helping, and I am back at my normal weight; the glossitis and the heart symptoms have disappeared, and above all the enormous exhaustion is gone. That a strong psychic factor plays a role in this became clear when, from one day to the next, even before taking the thyroid medication, I lost seven (!) pounds.

The whole thing has a terribly close connection to my relationship with my wife, or the lack of relationship, that's gone on for the last nine years, and very generally to the difficulties I experience in relating to others. I would very much like to discuss this with you in April when I'll be in Zurich.

Repeatedly and very plainly I've experienced the "higher will" as blows and as miracles, and I am very conscious of my unconsciousness in so many things and

---

45 Based on what follows, the dream may have occurred six years before Kirsch reported it.

46 Ch. V of Jung's *Aion* (1951), "Christus, ein Symbol des Selbst" (CW 9(ii), ¶68–126), is a revised, expanded version of the second half of his 1948 Eranos lecture, "Über das Selbst" (cf. Jung, 16 May 1951, p. 138 and note). Kirsch's seminar on *Aion* took place in1953–54 (cf. Kirsch, 1 January 1954, pp. 186, 188 and notes; also 7 June 1954, p. 202).

47 i.e. in Los Angeles.

relationships. Where "it" wants to go from here, I don't know. Many years ago, for instance, I definitely decided to stay here in Los Angeles. But just a few days ago I had a dream that I was in New York and was asked whether all the things that have happened to me here recently were not unconscious preparations for New York? To what extent do I have to view such a dream in a concrete manner? In New York I am a physician, here I am not.

My wife is also doing much better. She walks quite well with her crutches, sees her patients, cooks, etc. The X-rays show that the bones are healing well. The physician maintains that her feet will be as good as they used to be.

We'll understand soon, we hope, what all this means.

With cordial greetings, Faithfully yours, JAMES KIRSCH

From Aniela Jaffé

3 February 1960[48]

Dear Dr. Kirsch,

On Prof. Jung's behalf I would like to thank you kindly for the information you supplied regarding Miss Ruth White.

In theory, the following has resulted: Prof. Jung agrees in principle to produce a spoken record.

He would be recorded in a conversation with you. Specifically he says that he always needs someone to throw him a ball so that he can then play with it, i.e. speak about it. (Congratulations!)

Mrs. White has made him an offer: Either an accounting per record sold, or an outright sale of the material at $500.00.

Prof. Jung would prefer a one-time payment so that he does not have to deal with any accounting business, which is understandable. He is now asking you whether in the U.S.A. a price of $500.00 would be adequate. (May I admit that to me personally it seems rather low, taking into consideration the amount of profit made on gramophone records. But of course I am not informed and am only taking the liberty of voicing to you a totally unofficial viewpoint.)

Prof. Jung would appreciate receiving a brief description of how the session will be planned; also, when you'll be in Zürich.

One difficulty is the fact that he does not yet know what his program for the spring will look like. He experienced a light indisposition, felt weak, and his physician prohibited all visits for the entire month of February. However he already looks much better, sleeps fairly well, and personally I find that he is doing better than before. Nevertheless, I do not know whether he'll be out of town in

---

48   Typewritten in German, on Jung's letterhead, and signed.

March, and he doesn't know either. Everything is still up in the air in this respect. That doesn't prevent making plans, though, especially for something so beautiful. That's my opinion; don't you agree?

I heard that Hilde broke her ankle. I was very shocked and sorry to hear it. In the meantime, I hope she's already made a full recovery. Please give her my kindest regards.

The biography[49] is finished. To "recuperate" I am toying with a new topic. But actually I am still far too tired for that.

With very cordial greetings to you both, Yours, ANIELA JAFFÉ

Figure 10.1 **Aniela Jaffé at 80**. *Photo: © c.1983, Robert Hinshaw. Courtesy Estate of Aniela Jaffé/Robert Hinshaw.*

---

49 Although *MDR* continued to undergo discussion and revision for some time after Jung's death, at this date Jaffé viewed the memoir as finished. Similarly, in July 1960 she wrote privately to Kirsch: *"Die Auto- oder Biographie ist jetzt beim Uebersetzer. Das MS ist fertig!"* ["The autobiography or biography is now with the translator. The ms is finished!"] (Jaffé to Kirsch, 30 July 1960, Kirsch archive; trans. ACL).

James Kirsch
906 Thayer Avenue
West Los Angeles 24, Calif.

10 February 1960[50]

Dear Frau Aniela!

I did not respond to your letter by return mail because I had to make some inquiries, and discreet ones at that. I myself know awfully little about "business" but I try my best.[51]

The amounts paid as honorarium for such a spoken recording depend first of all on the size of the recording company and secondly the "stature"[52] of the personality speaking on the record. Miss White's company is very small and thus has limited capital. She wants to come to Zurich in order to arrange all the details personally for the recording session. These expenses & honorarium will stretch her budget almost to the limit.

I could expect to receive about $250 for such a recording (as I learned by asking around). But what multiple of that sum would have to be paid to someone of Jung's "stature"? Who knows? She (Miss White) would probably pay a little over $500, or possibly $600. But under the circumstances, might it be best to ask for $500 plus such-and-such royalties after more than x-100 recordings are sold?

Miss White intends to use the capital at her disposal for this "venture" to produce an outstanding recording, technically and in all other respects. How successful all of this may be, in a commercial sense, is hard to predict.

Of course, I would be very happy to participate as the "interviewer" on this recording. When I first read that, I became slightly frightened and had to put down the letter for a few minutes. I have more confidence now; my illness has disappeared almost entirely, my memory is restored, and I believe that my perceptive faculties function well. In other words, both Hilde and I are doing much better. Hilde's cast has already been removed from her left foot. She walks very well with a cane, and in the kitchen even without it, which I find to be amazing.

Therefore I'm now able to make more definite travel plans. I will arrive in Zurich the afternoon of March 23, and on March 25 I plan to join the Kerényi trip to Greece, which is expected to last till about April 10. I then plan to stay in Zurich until the end of May (*Deo concedente*).

Miss White visualizes things as follows: She will come up with a number of questions and topics, which she'll use to create a script. She will then submit it to Prof. Jung, and he can accept, reject, or propose how he would like to shape the recording. Her preference would be a discussion of material which he has not yet

---

50   Handwritten in German, on letterhead, with phone number crossed out.
51   Quoted word and following phrase orig. in English.
52   Quoted words throughout letter orig. in English.

published, or published in a different form, perhaps new thoughts about UFOs, or something new on the subject of Job, or the political situation. I have full confidence that Jung will instinctively hit on the right topics.

To prepare everything properly will probably take until the end of March or early April, so a date after April 10 is most likely.

I was sorry to hear about Jung's indisposition.[53] No one told me about it. I'm glad that he is making travel plans.

Recently I attended two seminars by Y. Kluger.[54] I was surprised how good they were in every respect. In human terms, too, he had changed very much for the better. Rivkah has also changed for the better and talks much less. So I wrote him a nice letter and hope with that the situation is improved. It is curious that the Ks are now best friends with those who attacked them earlier most viciously, and against whom we defended them – the *mysterium iniquitatis*.[55]

Please excuse my claw.[55] The fact that it is so "spasmodic"[56] has to do with the medications I am taking.

Perhaps Hilde will also come to Zurich in April.

Most cordially, Yours, JAMES KIRSCH

Prof. Dr. C. G. Jung
Küsnacht-Zürich
Seestrasse 228

12 February 1960[57]

Dr. J. Kirsch
906 Thayer Avenue
West Los Angeles 24, Calif.

Dear Kirsch!

You should have sent me the visions of the androgynous XP[58] before anything else, because he holds the key to your situation. Not only this vision but also the fact that you gave a seminar about XP as a symbol of the Self shows that you

---

53 Remainder of letter handwritten on half-sheet of letterhead, with phone number printed on the left.
54 Yechezkel Kluger's seminar at the Los Angeles Institute, on the subject of Old Testament myths (cf. Kirsch, 21 February 1960, pp. 262f and note).
55 *die Klaue*: a self-mocking colloquialism, apologizing for his handwriting.
56 *"ausfahrend"*: used here in its medical sense, referring to sudden involuntary movements.
57 Typewritten in German, on letterhead.
58 Christ (using the first two letters of the name in Greek): a habitual abbreviation in Jung's letters.

are being confronted inwardly by the Anthropos. This is indeed a *fact*, not just an opinion. It's supported by your own testimony, the seminar, and the vision. What's going on is therefore a confrontation with the Anthropos.

What does this mean? It means that on the one hand you are the empirical person, Dr. Kirsch, your own familiar ego. On the other hand, you are also the Anthropos. The XP of your dream teaches you that he is "the foundation of the world, the only reality," thus what we commonly designate as "God."

This is an extremely critical situation, a dangerous paradox, which usually leads, if conscious, to megalomania; if unconscious, to micromania (inferiority). The historical parallels to this are: 1) the XP who says, "I and the Father are one," "who sees me, sees the Father." 2) The suffering, godforsaken servant of God on the cross. 3) An even stronger example of 1) is the "godless" Buddha, the exalted, perfect one, the all-knowing, all-conquering, the leader of human beings *and gods*, the one who no longer has any God above himself, but is himself the world-being, without sorrow or joy.

XP is the Anthropos, the man of sorrows and joys, who suffers from his divinity, because he *cannot differentiate himself from it sufficiently*. To be sure you will not be nailed to the cross but instead be inundated by the flood of the ucs, because you do not differentiate sufficiently between the Self (the world-being) and the ego, because you are not logically thinking the problem through. Your values are too undefined. The question: Do *I* want this, or am I unable to resist a stronger will? must be decided again and again in hundreds and thousands of cases and indeed with unrelenting severity. Often questions must be held *in suspenso* for a long time, until they are decided beyond a doubt. Pretexts, false reasons, illusions must be recognized and eliminated. There are no approximate solutions. "Le vrai, en forme brute, est plus faux que le faux".

Your situation is the confrontation[59] with the Anthropos. Hence, when you occupy yourself with explanations, such as the relationship to your wife or other people, whether you should go to New York or stay in Los Angeles, etc. you play with symptoms and are on the wrong track and the downward path, fleeing backward, and thus you drown in the great waters of inflation.

A thorough reflection upon motives, consideration and review of values, no hasty ego-decisions, no escape from unpleasant insights! The solution lies in stepping forward, not in a retreat into minimization.

With cordial greetings, also to your wife, Yours truly, C. G. JUNG

---

59 *Auseinandersetzung.*

From Aniela Jaffé

15 February 1960[60]

Dear Dr. Kirsch,

I send you many, many thanks – and Prof. Jung also sends his best thanks – for the detailed information with regard to the gramophone record.

Prof. Jung asked me, however, to tell you that at the moment he cannot make any definite plans –I would even say: isn't allowed to. He would like to go away and doesn't know at all yet what his program will look like, i.e. whether he'll see visitors, how many visitors, which visitors, etc. We can, of course, be certain that he'll do the right thing instinctively, but he'll always know it only at that moment. You can imagine what kind of nightmare I experience whenever I entertain any thoughts about a program!

Most cordial greetings, in haste, ANIELA

I was very pleased to hear the Kluger news.[61]

James Kirsch
906 Thayer Avenue
West Los Angeles 24, Calif.

21 February 1960[62]

Dear Professor,

I hasten to thank you heartily for your letter of 12 February. It was enormously comforting for me to have my nose pushed into the center of the problem! Many years ago you already called my attention to my "godlikeness," but I also remember that as early as 1929 you noticed my puffy and pale face, a symptom which my American doctor considers characteristic for a lack of thyroid hormones. At this time my skin color is very good, even though I don't spend much time in the sun. I have no more excess water in my body, but I still have to be very careful with salt, because the physiological problem persists as before and probably can only be solved psychologically.

For years I've been aware of the fact that I am internally confronted with the Anthropos. My fear and flight reactions have been quite terrible. But I've also

---

60 Typewritten in German, on plain paper; signed carbon copy.
61 Cf. Kirsch to Jaffé, 10 February 1960, p. 259.
62 Handwritten in German, on letterhead, with phone number crossed out. Handwritten note at top, "To file!"

become very bewildered, because I did not understand the nature of my dreams. For instance: one night Y. was in the Synagogue with his horror; the next night I was present when Shiva and Shakti were united. Then there was a dream in which a French painter had painted a picture of an ordinary person sitting on a bench in a Zurich forest and then the Light Being[63] sat down beside him.

The worst was the forever recurring projection of the Anthropos on the female patient and into sexuality. I believe that I have finally succeeded in freeing myself from this aspect of the projection. Even here, of course, it's better to hold onto my doubts, so that it won't attack me again from behind.

My words are much too ambiguous. I hope that my ego has now gained enough insight and humility to enable me gradually to come to terms with this problem.

My greatest difficulty and also my greatest fear concerns the Jews. They have, as the N.T. declares, always killed their prophets.[64] Not that I would like to be a prophet, but without fail I have to deal with sacred things.

One of the dreams was as follows: "I'm in a large room. At the same time it is the desert. There is a group which represents the entire Jewish people. They went to the KZ[65] or are about to go there. They received the government contract. A Jew (a rich one) walks by the group with his nose high in the air. He has rejected his people. The question is asked whether I have refused the government contract. Oh no, I've accepted it!"

What a question! And what consequences! To descend psychologically into the hell of such an introversion, then to accept such a commitment, and at the same time there is the collective shadow of the rich, i.e. materialistic Jew whom I well know in myself.

You are so right, I'm not thinking logically through all these questions. But to tell me that the Anthropos is also within me, this I've often done myself; but only now, after your letter, has it become a reality.

It has only now begun to dawn on me how I can write the book about *Moby-Dick*.[66] As the basis and introduction I'll take the Jonah myth, and then I'll move to Melville's real problem. That way I'll get to an objective and creative confrontation with the Anthropos.[67]

I am so very grateful for your closeness and interest in my problem. By the way, I am now regularly attending Yechezkel Kluger's seminar on the subject of myths in the Old Testament.[68] It is quite extraordinary in every respect: the depth of his conceptualization, his perfect mastery of the material, the way he works

---

63 *der Lichtmensch.*
64 e.g. Matthew 23:29ff.
65 Abbreviation for *Konzentrationslager* [concentration camp].
66 Cf. Kirsch, 19 November 1959, p. 252 and note.
67 Following paragraphs, through to the closing, are written on a half-sheet of letterhead.
68 Cf. Kirsch to Jaffé, 10 February 1960, p. 259 and note.

with the trainees, and the tight rein he keeps on Rivkah.[69] I wrote to him about this and thus broke the ice. It was a great surprise for me to see how much he's changed. Rivkah's demeanor is also much more civil in discussions. Of course, not all tensions are resolved.

My wife is feeling much better, although just now she is experiencing more pain. But she is already able to go up and down the stairs.

With best wishes for your good health. Faithfully yours, JAMES KIRSCH

From Aniela Jaffé

26 February 1960[70]

Dear Dr. Kirsch,

Just now your letter with the postal stamp of 22 February arrived. Prof. Jung has left for the Ticino and gave the order: "Do not forward any mail." For your information, I just wanted to let you know about this so that you won't be waiting in vain for an answer. Your letter will safely await Prof. Jung's return.

With best greetings, Yours, ANIELA JAFFÉ

James Kirsch
906 Thayer Avenue
Los Angeles 24, Calif.
GR 4–5210

4 May 1960[71]

Dear Aniela:

Our plans for the summer are pretty much made now. We shall be in Switzerland from approximately August 15th on. I suppose you will be on a vacation then. I will write to you and hope to be able to see you – maybe in September.

My talks have gone over the radio[72] now three times. There is one more to follow. The reception has been very good, the response most favorable. KPFK is a small FM station. It does not reach the same public as AM stations do, but

---

69 Cf. Jaffé, 22 November 1952, p. 145 and note.
70 Typewritten in German, on plain paper; signed carbon copy.
71 Typewritten in English, on half-sheet of letterhead, with corrected phone number typed in.
72 Cf. Jung, 12 November 1959, p. 250 and note.

it is listened to by a good deal of the intelligentsia. Nevertheless, it is of course difficult to find out who has heard them – but I know of a number of people who have taped these talks. On the basis of that, I have been asked to discuss my talks with two different groups.

Please give my kind regards to Jung.

Yours, JAMES K.

From Aniela Jaffé

3 October 1960[73]

Dear James,

Via express mail, I am sending you the letter from Los Angeles about which I advised you,[74] so that you can read it here together with a copy of J's reply.

Jung sends his best regards and asked me to convey his regret that he was not able to see you this time. The fact that you lectured and will lecture about King Lear[75] was also of great interest to him.

May I ask you to have Hilde return the L.A. letter to me here c/o Jung? Many thanks to both of you.

Auf Wiedersehen! Yours, ANIELA

---

73 Typewritten in German, on plain paper.
74 Jaffé's previous letter, with enclosures, is missing. The "letter from Los Angeles," and Jung's reply, may have reflected on events within the Los Angeles analytic community. A few months later, writing privately, Jaffé urged Kirsch not to be discouraged about Los Angeles; even if "the Ks" should leave, the "plowed land" would endure (Jaffé to Kirsch, 14 March 1961, Kirsch archive).
75 Kirsch's lecture "'King Lear' as a Play of Redemption" was delivered to the APC of Los Angeles in January 1961 (typescript, KML archive). His next lecture on Shakespeare, "Hamlet: A Drama of Haunted Man," delivered at the Club on 23 September 1961, was published by *Harvest* (vol. 8, London APC, 1962). His third paper on a Shakespearean tragedy, "The Sleepwalking Scene in 'Macbeth'," also appeared in *Harvest* (vol. 10, London APC, 1964). Kirsch's first published book, *Shakespeare's Royal Self* (Zürich: Daimon, 1966), focuses on these three tragedies.

From Aniela Jaffé

3 March 1961[76]

Dear Dr. Kirsch,

Thanks so much for sending your very interesting essay about Zen.[77] It is now on the little table next to Prof. Jung's chair. But at the present time he's sharply limited in any kind of reading: he is totally absorbed by his writing and not interested in anything else.

I can't even remember anymore where I left off in my last letter. I don't know whether I wrote to you that he did not feel very well, but after a six-day stay at the hospital he returned home not only rested but reassured and with prescriptions for a helpful course of treatment. The spring "Föhn"[78] has tired him, and writing both exhausts him and gives him pleasure at the same time. Riwkah and Yechezkel will arrive here in June for a year.[79] You know this. Perhaps such an opportunity is required, not only to feel but also to acknowledge what you and Hilde have accomplished as "pioneers."[80] Almost like clearing a primeval forest. And you persevered. Isn't that worth everything?

Currently I'm tormenting myself with an essay about art,[81] because I don't have enough time and space. Nevertheless I hope that one way or another I'll be able to get it done.

Cordial greetings to you both, Yours, ANIELA

---

76 Typewritten in German, on CGJ letterhead, and signed.
77 Cf. Kirsch, 15 March 1959, p. 248 and note.
78 *Föhn*: powerful, warm wind which sometimes blows for days, and is often blamed for changes in mood and energy.
79 The Klugers arrived in Zurich earlier than planned. Learning of Jung's death on 6 June 1961, they broke off teaching in Los Angeles and flew to Zurich. With other close colleagues, they were welcomed into Jung's home to view his body, then attended his burial and memorial (Y. Kluger to B. & E. Klopfer, 11 June 1961, Kirsch archive). (This document was kindly provided by Deborah Wesley, archivist of the C. G. Jung Institute of Los Angeles.)
80 For several years James and Hilde Kirsch had been called "pioneers" by members of Jung's circle, and thought of themselves as such. In 1952, when Kirsch was contemplating a move to New York, Liliane Frey-Rohn protested: "*Sie sind* unser *Pionier in California, und ich kann Sie nicht dort wegdenken*" ["You are *our* pioneer in California, and I can't think of you away from there"] (Frey-Rohn to Kirsch, 22 March 1952, Kirsch archive).
81 Jaffé's essay "Symbolism in the Visual Arts" was published with five other essays, by Jung and followers, in *Man and His Symbols* (ed. by C. G. Jung and after his death by M.-L. von Franz; coordinating ed. John Freeman. London: Aldus Books; Garden City, NY: Doubleday, 1964). Erich Neumann had first been asked to write the essay on the arts but after his death in late 1960, the assignment fell to Jaffé (Jaffé to Kirsch, 5 December 1960, Kirsch archive).

From Aniela Jaffé

27 May 1961[82]

Dear James,

Best thanks for your letter of May 17th.

I'm very happy that you're so immersed in Shakespeare. Probably it's the same for you as for me: sometimes stupid ~~letters~~ books(!) are more help than scholarly works.

From here, I'd like to let you and Hilde know that Jung is not feeling especially well. I ask you urgently to keep this news to yourselves, under strict discretion. I've also written about it to Rivkah, with the same warning. No one else knows. Even in Zurich not everyone is aware of it. (The Hurwitzes, for instance, don't know.) About 10 days ago Jung suffered a small stroke (or whatever it may have been in medical terms). Since then he has had serious aphasia. Perfectly lucid, but can't find his words. Yesterday and today I spent a few minutes with him looking over the mail. He was using a mixture of French, English, German, always in fragments. And always with torment. Then would come an unbroken series of four or five short sentences. Then once again, the "BLOCK." Very upsetting. He is patient, probably all the more because he's feeling extraordinarily weak. Unfortunately, or thank goodness!

Sleep and appetite are better. I believe the few real friends in the world[83] should know; that's why I'm writing you about it.

The doctor thinks a regenerative process is still possible, but at this age it's a fragile chance, or that's my feeling. And what should one really hope for?

Only this much for today. As soon as something happens that's worth telling,[84] positive or negative, I'll let you know. The fact that the Hurwitzes, for example, don't know is because I'm caught in the middle.[85] The family[86] absolutely don't want me to say anything, and I'm also ~~somewhat~~ obligated to them!

Warmest greetings,

Yours, Aniela

The official diagnosis, given out by the family, is "circulatory problems."

---

82 Typewritten in German on plain paper. The letter, evidently written in haste, included three errors, two of which Jaffé hand-corrected.

83 *"... die wenigen echten Freunde in der Welt":* The possessive pronoun is less frequently used in German than in English. Lacking a possessive pronoun, we cannot be sure whether "the few real friends in the world" refers to Jung's friends or the writer's.

84 Here Jaffé typed: *"... irgend etwas Erwählenswertes"* (lit. "something worth choosing"). The intended word may have been *"Erzählenswertes"* (worth telling) or *"Erwähnenswertes"* (worth mentioning).

85 *"... dass ich zwischen zwei Feuern stehe.":* Lit., "because I am standing between two fires."

86 It is unclear, here and below, which family members are referenced.

APPENDIX A

"THEN HE WILL OPEN
THE EARS OF MEN"[1]

James Kirsch, Tel Aviv, spring 1934[2]

It is widely understood in medicine at this time that neuroses are functional in nature, meaning that certain pathological symptoms cannot be traced back to anatomically identifiable organs or organ systems. There are no localized seats of disease in neuroses; instead there is "a certain something" which is ill or suffering and cannot be readily named.

The first investigations by Charcot and Bernheim showed very clearly that it was possible to plant symptoms by means of hypnosis – i.e. through mental influence – just as one could make them disappear again. Thus the facts seemed to indicate that certain mental phenomena – thoughts, words, feelings, affects, or experiences – evoke neurotic symptoms, i.e. changes, which also have an impact on physical well-being.

As important as these discoveries undoubtedly were, therapeutically they were totally unsatisfactory. For it was soon recognized that the individual symptom did indeed disappear, but another took its place. It is to Freud's indisputable credit that he found an alternative way. With his wonderful intuition, as if by chance, he discovered that when one causes a patient to speak in detail about himself,

---

1 אז יגלה אזן אנשים: The title, handwritten in Hebrew, is a phrase from the biblical Book of Job (Job 33:16). The passage from which it comes can be rendered: "In a dream, in a vision of the night, when deep sleep falleth upon men, in slumberings upon their bed; Then he openeth the ears of men and sealeth their instruction" (Job 33:15–16, KJV). A modern translation, revocalizing the final verb, concludes: "then he opens their ears and he terrifies them with warnings" (Job 33:16, NRSV). Kirsch's reading of the verse adheres to the unaltered Hebrew text (cf. p. 278). With thanks to Dr. Corney, here and elsewhere, for his linguistic assistance.

2 Undated document, stamped with Kirsch's address in 1934: Tel Aviv, Hayarkonstr. 101. The German typescript is among Kirsch's letters to Jung at the ETH Library archive. The *Signatur* number assigned by the archive (HS 1056 2817) places it first among Kirsch's 1934 documents. It is contextually related to Kirsch's letter of 7 May 1934 (cf. p. 42 and note), but it may not have been mailed until 8 June 1934 (cf. p. 50 and note).

the symptoms also disappear; especially if a patient relates pertinent experiences with appropriate affect, the experiences will be, as it is called in medical terms, abreacted.

On such occasions, patients often also related dreams. Here again, the imp "Chance" led a highly gifted individual to a crucial discovery.

Freud soon recognized that dreams elicited vitally important material from the deeper layers of the psyche.[3] Long-forgotten experiences which may have adversely affected a person's health came up from the depth of the unconscious. With the discovery of dreams, Freud found a new instrument for treatment which – in contrast to the coarse and violent method of hypnosis – originated in the patient's own psyche. The first dream analyses deeply impressed Freud and moved him to call the dream the *via regia* to the unconscious.[4]

On the basis of these surprising new impressions, Freud very quickly felt the need to establish a theory about dreams – the famous wish theory – and with it began Freud's unending tragedy. Unexpectedly, by way of dreams, Freud had encountered the creative depth of the human psyche. In the final analysis, every psychological theory originates out of the experience of whoever creates it. It always depends on the subject and is capable, at best, of explaining the psychology of its creator or human beings similar to him. It is either a fine- or a wide-meshed net, which indeed can pull much from the deep seas of the soul and bring it to light. One cannot claim, however, that all organisms living in the seas of the soul have been caught with this net. It is far more likely that huge numbers of living things of great diversity exist in regions where the net will never reach. The distressing but inevitable fact is that the creator of a psychological theory catches himself in his own net and loses sight of the vastness of the soul.

An excellent example of the way Freud deals with the unconscious is his analysis of a dream which he published in his work *Märchenstoffe in Träumen:*[5]

> She [Freud's patient] is in an entirely brown room. A small door opens to a steep staircase where a strange, little man ascends and enters the room. He is small, has white hair, a bald spot, and a red nose. He dances in front of her around the room and acts comically. Then he withdraws and descends the stairs. He is dressed in a gray, tight-fitting garment. (Correction: He wears a long, black coat and gray pants.)

3 *Seele*: The word can mean either soul or psyche. In this translation, *Seele* is rendered "soul" when the context is biblical, spiritual, or figurative. It is translated "psyche" when the context is clearly scientific. In Kirsch's writing, where these contexts tend to merge, "soul" is often the translation of choice.

4 In 1944 Kirsch borrowed material from this portion of his lecture for his inaugural address to the APC of Los Angeles ("Presidential Address," 6 October 1944, typescript, KML archive, pp. 2f).

5 Sigmund Freud, *The Occurrence in Dreams of Material from Fairy Tales* (1913). The Standard Edition of the Complete Psychological Works of Sigmund Freud, Volume XII (1911–1913), pp. 279–88.

Here I cannot enter into all the details of Freud's proposed interpretation and his odd use of associations but would like to emphasize one point which has methodological importance. He writes: "The personal description of the little man fits her father-in-law without alteration." However, his annotation already indicates that the description of the person does not entirely fit the father-in-law. Also, it is not clear why the dream did not mention the father-in-law if it referred to him. The patient doubtless brings up the father-in-law as an idea that suddenly occurs to her. The question is whether the little man explains the father-in-law or, conversely, the sudden idea of the "father-in-law" explains the little man. What should be considered as real? To whom does the dream actually refer? The simple question, how the associative material is to be used, shows clearly that the interpreter can bring his own attitude into a dream. In general, Freud tends to relate and reduce all dream figures to real persons. Also, in this case, Freud says: This is the father-in-law; then, without further justification, the father; finally also the penis.

The second association is to the German fairy tale "Rumpelstiltskin." Freud comments, "'Rumpelstiltskin' also facilitates the access to deeper, infantile layers of dream-thoughts. The droll little fellow (Rumpelstiltskin, father-in-law, or penis?) whose name is unknown, whose secret one would like to discover, who performs such extraordinary feats (in the fairy tale he turns straw into gold) – the rage one feels toward him, etc. – these are elements whose relationship to the fundamentals of the neurosis can only be touched upon here."

I ask for the reader's indulgence for my dwelling on these details. However, it is really necessary to ascertain, for once, on precisely what facts Freud bases his theories and to what extent he does violence to the dream with his "interpretation." Actually, he does not interpret the dream but only provides a number of "symbol" translations, so that nobody has truly understood the dream, but only receives, at best, some references to Freud's well-known theories about infantile sexuality, the castration-complex, etc.

Rumpelstiltskin also does not merit further consideration after being recognized as the "penis." Is that what he really is? Or is there again a confusion between the Phallus and the penis, the creative principle and the visible expression on the human body? Inasmuch as this physical part is also comprised in the Phallus, Freud's theories may be accurate. However, they cover only one aspect, and Freud does not recognize the larger and more essential one, which – with his oft-repeated phrase, "this is nothing but" – is at first unconsciously and later, in *Future of an Illusion*, fiercely rejected. Anyone who appreciates the fairy tale atmosphere of "Rumpelstiltskin" may prefer to perceive the little fellow who lives in the woods and spins gold from straw at night as the *soul,* or perhaps the nightly creative activity of the soul, manifested in dreams. Is it not the soul which confers value on everything we are, think, feel, and believe, and which transforms an event into an experience, turning straw into gold? Since I do not know the lady who had the dream and have no additional associations from her, I can only presume this interpretation, basing it on my knowledge of the fairy tale. But isn't it at least just as possible as Freud's view, based on the associations he mentions, as his conception of the little man as father-in-law, father, penis? Would my conception provide a new understanding of the dream? For example, the soul as the creative principle comes to her (by means of analysis) at night, in a dream, dressed in gray theory, and leaves her again when it is not understood.

As I said before, I cannot give an exact proof of this interpretation, but the allusion to Rumpelstiltskin, who after all is able to turn straw into gold, is certainly more than the male sexual organ. Thus the tragedy of the Galut Jew[6] has been realized once again in Freud's psyche. Fate led him into the creative depth of life, but at that moment he closed it off with a theory conditioned by his uprooting and his childhood experiences of the Galut. "He roused the unconscious so that it gushed forth powerfully, but not in order to honor it as his superhuman, eternal part, but instead to obtain information and to give his children contemptuous names."[7]

Therefore, it is no surprise that strong oppositions arose against Freud and his theory. Freud overlooked the fact that this resistance emanated not only from individuals who did not want to become conscious of their infantile shadow side, and so, for instance, did not wish to admit their perverse sexual fantasies. There were also people who espoused an entirely different psychology and who lived, as it were, on a different island in the ocean of the soul.

The great Zurich psychologist C. G. Jung – upon whom, in his personal relations, Freud had made a great impression – grasped this great aspect of the unconscious and with it the huge importance that exploration of the unconscious could have for human intellectual development. On the basis of his experiences he could not concede that the psychology of all people could be explained with a view from only one corner. He therefore avoided establishing one theory that should be viewed as the one and only solution. When he casts his net into the sea of the soul, he remains cognizant of the fact that there is an infinite diversity of additional life in that ocean. Consequently he avoids theories as such, preferring to leave the images of the unconscious in their natural state, pregnant with possibility. For this reason, he has to live with reproaches of being "mystical," unclear, and difficult to understand, which really bears witness to the fact that he recognizes the difficulty, complexity, and liveliness of psychic material. These things can easily be destroyed with words, concepts, and intellectual haste.

With this attitude, Jung left behind the atmosphere of the sick-room. He is no longer treating the neurosis but instead the suffering human being. A neurosis is not a localized illness but rather a sickness affecting the whole human being – often without symptoms. The person, the entire person, is suffering, perhaps because he has not found meaning in life, or the meaning of his life.

6   i.e. the Jew in exile (cf. Kirsch, 7 May 1934, p. 42 and note.)
7   Source unclear. In Kirsch's typescript a faint handwritten note follows this quotation. It appears to be a name, perhaps that of Heinrich Zimmer (cf. Jung, 25 June 1932, p. 29 and note).

Everyone has dreams, and the unconscious has much to say to everyone. The dream itself is never a neurotic symptom, but it has something to add to the consciousness of the patient, something he does not know, or something he is not sufficiently aware of. Thus, Jung perceives the unconscious not only as the center of repressions, a rubbish heap of perverse fantasies, but instead as the *creative life* within us. The unconscious is not neurotic. Our attitude to the unconscious determines whether we are neurotic or not. Therefore, Jung strives to lead human beings to the experience of the unconscious; whether or not they succeed is a question of fate. Jung often experienced that a patient's contact with the unconscious affected the individual in a way which can only be characterized as "transformation."

The unconscious is a part of nature, and like all of nature it is true; it is not hypocritical, it does not lie. Consequently, the dream *does not have a façade*. It represents the text of the unconscious, and it is a text which wants to be read, and read according to what the writer wished to convey. It can be compared to a letter somebody writes to us, which we should understand as much as possible as the writer intended it. Perhaps the most distinctive characteristic of the dream and of all messages from the unconscious is its strangeness from the point of view of consciousness. It is as if we had nothing to do with the creation of the dream, but it was sent to us. So in German we often say, *"Es träumte mir."*[8] In ancient times, the dream's strangeness in relation to consciousness was clearly perceived, and so it was said that a god or goddess had sent the dream.

This coincides with one of Jung's fundamental conceptions. He recognizes a higher force, greatly surpassing the human ego, an all-knowing force beyond time and space. Within the unconscious he distinguishes two layers: (1) a *personal* layer containing memories, experiences, feelings, affects, etc. which originate in the *personal* life of the individual; and (2) the layer of the *collective* unconscious storing all experiences, images, possibilities, instincts, etc. acquired and developed by human beings in the course of millions of years. They are embedded in a layer of guessed-at possibilities in the depths, ready to well up in an individual whenever his life encounters a dead end, or when his suffering cannot be alleviated by the limited means and experiences of the human mind. For that reason, primitive people made a clear distinction between "small" and "big" dreams. The small dream is of importance only to an individual, while the big dream is significant for the tribe or the general public. On the basis of such big dreams, the fate of entire peoples has been decided.

For Europeans who are reasonably well informed about the life of primitive peoples, it is astonishingly impressive to experience how far-reaching the influence of a dream, a vision, an inner voice, and all manifestations of the unconscious can be on the lives of primitives. However, we do not even have to go that far. We merely have to turn our attention to our own early history, as it is recorded in

---

8   Lit. "*It* dreamed to me."

the Bible, in order to be aware of the decisive importance of the dream, and the unconscious in general, for the life of our people.

For instance, I would like to cite a passage in The First Book of Moses[9] 20:3–6: "At night, God appeared in a dream to Abimelech and said to him…" It is self-evident that God comes to human beings in their dreams. The voice which speaks in a dream is not the voice of the ego. It has information to convey which is not known to the ego and which the ego cannot know on its own. Naively, and without the slightest doubt, Abimelech is guided exactly by what the dream proclaims. This brief example shows that the ancient people, unlike us moderns – *"Träume sind Schäume"*[10] is the ridiculous opinion of enlightened people – attributed great significance to their dreams and regarded them as the source of God's revelations. (Similarly in The First Book of Moses 31:24.)

The same is true in Jacob's dream in The First Book of Moses 28:10–22. A big dream, without doubt! It shows in a splendid way how Jacob's soul initiates a relationship to the Highest and how an intimate exchange with the Eternal takes place. "God's messengers[11] ascend and descend." The experience touches Jacob in the depth of his soul. He experiences the sublimity of the place and is deeply frightened: "He was afraid and said: how awesome is this place! It is none other than the house of God and the gate of heaven."

In this dream, we find three characteristic elements: (1) the imagery of the dream; (2) the direct language; and (3) the emotional affect of the dream experience. It is generally known that dreams occur in images. How these images are to be interpreted, however, is a problem that has been on people's minds since prehistoric times. Freud was not the first who thought these images speak a language. The question is, of course, what language they speak. Such a classic dream shows clearly the absurdity of a merely sexual interpretation. In Jacob's dream, an interpretation is initiated within the dream itself, through the prophecy of a blessing. As a consequence, Jacob is quite certain that he did not invent the dream but that it originated in exalted spheres, where one also has to search for its meaning. As he awakes, he is overcome by an overwhelming emotional impression that the Absolute, the Irrational, has spoken to him. He knows that he has had a *big* dream, and he vows that the place where he had the dream is a *holy* place. We sense the effect of the dream on Jacob and how he has been transformed by it. For the future, this dream will have the greatest significance for the entire people of Israel and its history.

Joseph's dreams have a different character. Of course, they are also immediately recognized for their importance, and it is interesting to note that they were understood the same way by his brothers (The First Book of Moses 31:5–8).

---

9 i.e. Genesis. The first five books of the Bible (Genesis, Exodus, Leviticus, Numbers, Deuteronomy) are traditionally ascribed to Moses.

10 "Dreams are bubbles."

11 *die Boten Gottes*: in Hebrew, the word for "messenger" is also that for "angel."

Here again, God's messenger is speaking, and so the dreams confer importance and distinction to Joseph. He feels like a special person, and his legitimacy is confirmed by these dreams.

The voice of the unconscious was not always heard. An excellent example is the passage in Samuel: "And God's word was precious in those days" (I Samuel 3:1). It is wonderful to note the reverential attitude with which Eli and Samuel accept this voice. More often than dreams, we find "visions" in the Bible, a vision in connection with a voice, and also apparitions where it is not at all clear whether they originated in a dream or a vision. As varied as their content is, it is all the more essential to be clear about their structure and psychological construction. In the vast majority of cases, not only the vision is communicated, but also the individual's reaction to it. A human being responds to the inner apparition, and often there is a continuing conversation between the ego and the absolute "Other," e.g. The First Book of Moses 15:1 and Isaiah 6.

The vision of Isaiah's call contains the primal experience.[12] It is recounted with the lively power of the great visionary. It begins with a simple description of the magnificent experience (Isaiah 6:1–2): "I saw God sitting on a huge, raised throne, and his robes filled the temple. Seraphim stood above him, and each had six wings. With two wings the Seraphim covered his face, with two wings they covered his feet,[13] and with two they flew." In the third verse, a voice is heard: "Holy, holy, holy," and with that the interpretation and comprehension of the marvelous happening has begun. The enormous psychic upheaval of seeing God himself, even veiled by the wings of the Seraphim,[14] is indicated by the shaking of the foundations of the threshold. But he remains differentiated from what is happening within him. He says, "Woe is me, I am undone! I am a man of unclean lips" (Isaiah 6:5a). The fact that he is not devoured by this vision shows the strength of his conscious personality. In the subsequent verses the contact with the vision is fully resumed. The Seraph touches him with the burning coal. He is cleansed. With this he is called, but also *transformed.*

When we submit such dreams and visions to a psychological analysis, there is no mention of the divine content itself. Such an approach to things we are familiar with does not offend religious feelings. On the contrary, it gives us as human beings a new understanding of the Immensity[15] and its effects on the soul.

---

12 *das Urerlebnis.*

13 In the canonical version of the Hebrew text, the Seraphim use their wings to cover their own faces and bodies. ("Feet" is a euphemism commonly used in Hebrew.) According to Dr. Corney, this part of the verse may be literally translated, "with two they covered their face, with two they covered their feet, and with two they flew" (Isaiah 6:2c). In Luther's translation, which was known to Kirsch (cf. Kirsch, 28 July 1931, p. 20 and note), the same meaning is given: "*mit zweien deckten sie ihre Antlitz, mit zweien deckten sie ihre Füsse, und mit zweien flogen sie.*" Kirsch may have found a variant Hebrew version; or he may have relied on his own reading of the verse.

14 Please see preceding note.

15 *das Ungeheure.*

Certainly, Freud saw in the "unconscious" only repression and rejected contents of all sorts; but the *consensus omnium*,[16] and also that of our Bible, knows it as the Highest speaking to human beings through the soul.

The Bible has various views of the expressions of the unconscious. Originally dreams were considered to have originated self-evidently from God; this is especially clear in The Fourth Book of Moses[17] 12:6: "And he said, Hear my words, when a prophet of God appears to you, I will make myself known by visions, I will speak to him through dreams." In contrast to this, Moses was deemed worthy of direct and sustained revelation: "I speak to him from mouth to mouth and show my face, and he will not see the image of God through riddles."[18] He appears to other prophets mostly in dreams. And as we know, dreams speak a language which is difficult to understand; they pose riddles.

How to understand these riddles, and who is a *"poter,"*[19] have been questions throughout time. How could a prophet prove his identity? Certainly, not every dream was sent by God. Two personal prerequisites were necessary: spiritual purity and the absence of self-interest. "Otherwise you will have night without vision, darkness without prophecy" (Micah 3:6–8): "Indeed, it will be night for you; you will no longer have visions. It will be dark, and you will be unable to do divination. The sun sets for the prophets, the day is dark for them."[20] The third prerequisite consists of an entirely irrational moment, a choice which occurred before the human being comes into existence. Jeremiah 1:5: "Before I formed you in the body, I chose you, and before you emerged from your mother's womb, I ordained you and appointed you as the prophet for all peoples."

But also, the content of the prophecy is the Shibboleth, to show whether they were sent by God, whether they are authentic or not. This is the sign, whether or not what they prophesy is a vision of their hearts. Inauthentic prophecies have an entirely personal character and reflect the human ego with its desires and impulses. The experience is missing that something objective, something other than "I," has spoken. This experience of the non-ego, the certainty that "It" is happening within me, and that the ego assumes a relationship with "It," this is the characteristic of a true prophet. If anyone has an authentic primal experience, like Jeremiah, that individual has a fine power of discernment between the genuine and the false. Referring to the fact that a dream has spoken is not sufficient.

---

16 the universal consensus.

17 i.e. the Book of Numbers (cf. p. 274, note 9).

18 The quote is from Numbers 12:8. Dr. Corney translates the full passage: "(6) If there is a prophet among you, I, YHWH, will be known to him in a vision; in a dream I shall speak to him. (7) Not so my servant Moses. With all my house he is entrusted. (8) Mouth to mouth I shall speak to him, [omitting the next word "vision" as an error] and not in riddles, and he shall look upon the likeness of YHWH."

19 (Hebrew) "interpreter of dreams" (Gen 40:8; 41:8,15).

20 The preceding lines appear to be Kirsch's paraphrase of Micah 3:6 (not 6–8).

There is something special about genuine inspiration, unlike the claims of other prophets. Jeremiah 23:25: "I hear the words of the prophets who prophesy lies in my name. I have dreamed, I have dreamed!" Only images can convey this unspeakable truth. Jeremiah 23:29: "My word is fire, says the Lord, a hammer which blasts boulders."

This power of discernment for true dreams, in comparison to lying dreams (*chalomot sheker*)[21] was lost soon after the appearance of the great prophets. Since it was no longer possible to tell who had the real inspiration, dreams and prophets were rejected. Amos, the most powerful of the early prophets, had said (Amos 3:8): "The lion has roared; who should not be afraid? God has spoken; who should not prophesy?" But Zechariah judges the prophets with contempt, resulting in a tremendous social decline, from adviser to the king and leader of the people (even if not always welcome as such), down to the lowest level of society. Prophets and a spirit of uncleanness were now viewed as one and the same. Zechariah 13:2–6: "I will also remove the prophets and the unclean spirits from the land. If anyone should still make prophecies, his father and his mother, his own parents will tell him: You shall not live, because you have told falsehoods in the name of God. And his own parents, his father and his mother, shall pierce him through as soon as he prophesies. On that day, the prophets will be ashamed of their prophetic vision whenever they prophesy. They will no longer put on a hairy mantle to tell lies. Each one will say: I am not a prophet, I am a farmer; or, from childhood I was raised to be a cattle-breeder."

The same as 2,000 years ago, we again stand at an important turning-point in our history. The entire world finds itself in an era of enormous upheaval. The old values and forms of religious and social ideology have little meaning for the psyche. At best, religion is a "private matter." It is stored in a more or less hidden corner of our life. In any case, religion is not the whole of life. Life yearns for a new experience, for an attitude which embraces the entire life. At this critical stage, many sufferers turn to physicians who are supposed to heal such conditions. Were the physicians equal to that task? Did the physicians understand the suffering of the soul, which was manifested in the strangest forms of neurosis? Did they know that the problems of the time and the eternal human question expressed themselves in the individual as depression? Our hygienic era could not have responded in any other way than to label these phenomena medically as neurosis, illness. And yet, fundamentally, these are very old experiences and have eternal answers. The writer of Job, for instance, knew very well that the human soul is the place where supernatural powers, God and Satan, do battle. He was also aware of their effect on human beings. Job 3:11–13: "Why did I not die at birth? When I came out of my mother's womb, I should have died at once. Why did the lap receive me, why

---

21 (Hebrew) "lying dreams." The phrase occurs in Jeremiah 23:32. In Dr. Corney's translation: "Behold, I am against ones prophesying lying (or false) dreams – oracle of YHWH – and they recount them and they lead my people astray with their lies and with their recklessness, and I have not sent them and I have not commanded them, and they profit not this people."

did I suck from the breasts? Then I could lie still and rest, I would sleep and be at peace." Job 33:20–21: "All food disgusts him, even the most desirable delicacy." Is this not neurosis and depression?

How does Job find a way out of this depression? "In a dream, in a vision of the night, when deep sleep falls on people, in a light slumber on their bed, at that time he (God) opens the ear of the people and seals it with their teachings."[22] Also for us, who experience people's suffering and see how individuals express the radically shifting times as neurosis, the dream and all manifestations of the unconscious have proven – not by chance – to be a fruitful path toward the patient's healing. With this we also have rediscovered an old path that leads the individual to the experience of the ancient fire, the *"esh kedoshah."*[23] And thus we have come to what we know, glancing at the *Tanakh*,[24] as the essential, to that which made Jacob into Israel, to the primal experience of religion. For us, of course, in contrast to him, these experiences take entirely different forms and produce different effects; but what we experience is always the One, the Unchangeable, at all times and in all places.

With the return to our own land it is necessary to remember our own essence, the special character of our existence. Everything will depend on whether our heart will harden, our ears go deaf and our eyes blind, or whether this time our eyes will see, our ears will hear, and our heart will understand (Isaiah 6:10). Whether we can give the true name to that which speaks to us through dreams and visions: "This is a holy place." "Then he will heal us."

The way such things are happening to us now as Jewish people, and what response the unconscious is giving to the Jews' state of distress, may be illustrated by the following dream of a woman who heretofore was totally estranged from anything Jewish until awakened by events of the Hitler era:

> Now I was crossing K. Street with Dr. S. and entered a store. There was a large exhibit of books and pictures. I descended further down a flight of stairs to the basement where especially rare and valuable books were stored. It was very dark there, and each book had additional lighting which was only visible as one stood directly in front of it. In the basement there was another room from which I heard voices, and I asked what was going on there. A small, bent-over man appeared, wearing a cap on his head and a heavy coat, with a large bunch of keys. He opened the door and pointed to a table, a large, round table, where ten men with long beards and caps were seated, holding prayer books. In the middle of the table was a silver box, lined with velvet, in which lay a diamond that sparkled so brightly, the table was lighted by it.

22 Cf. note 1, p. 267.

23 (Hebrew) "holy fire."

24 The Hebrew Bible. An acronym, formed from the initials of its three major sections: *Torah, Nevi'im, Kethuvim* [Torah, Prophets, Writings].

To comprehend the essential components of this dream, one only needs to extract what it contains. The dream tells us that the lady goes into a store where all kinds of spiritual and artistic works are exhibited. On the floor below especially rare and valuable things are stored, which require special illumination which is only visible when standing directly in front of them. In addition, something extraordinary is happening, and a peculiar man is leading her to it. This man we can consider to be the guardian of the threshold, the keeper of the keys, and – in keeping with the entire atmosphere of the dream – a *meliz*,[25] a religious figure who opens a spiritual room which is different from everything purely intellectual and artistic, as valuable as these may be. It is the religious community of Jews, and it is united and illuminated by the rays of a great gem.

So this dreamer, to whom until now Palestine and Judaism had consciously meant very little, found a very old truth. She did not read or learn about it, but by experiencing the unconscious, she discovered the old Jewish idea that community can only be established with the help of the radiant force of a great symbol; the idea that the meaning and value of being a Jew and a human being are bestowed by this diamond, which is separate from all and yet unites all.

For this woman, and for psychotherapy, the same thing has happened through dreams as happened for Saul. He went out to search for female donkeys and instead found a kingdom. She was looking for medication to treat a neurosis and instead found the royal diamond which heals the soul. So I believe that dreams, visions, and other emanations of the unconscious can lead us Jews back to creativity, to humanness, and thus to Judaism and its lively further development. We only have to learn, with the help of modern and exact science, to let the unconscious speak to us in its own language and to understand it. Intellect, art, and technology cannot save us, only the path that can revive the primal experience. Then Israel – God's warrior – could once again raise its full voice in the chorus of the great religions of the East.

---

25 (Hebrew) interpreter, interceder. In the Hebrew Bible the word occurs only in Gen 42:3, where it refers to a Hebrew-Egyptian interpreter. In later usage it can also mean "interceder, advocate."

APPENDIX B

LETTERS OF C. G. JUNG
AND HILDE KIRSCH

The documents of the C. G. Jung–Hilde Kirsch correspondence, found at the Kirsch archive and the ETH Library archive, are not numerous and are of varying degrees of interest. The following letters exchanged by Jung and Hilde Kirsch (Hildegard Silber) are selected for their intrinsic value, and because they may cast important side-lights on the main text of this volume.

Dr. C. G. Jung
Küsnacht-Zürich
Seestrasse 228

11 June 1934[1]

Frau Hildegard Silber
Gordonstr. 2,
Tel Aviv.
Palestine.

Dear Mrs. Silber,

    The problem you present to me concerns the religious meaning of the transference, which is still apparently unresolved for you. As long as the transference is active in the essentially instinctive realm, it's like an ape with

---

1   Typewritten in German, on letterhead, this is the first known letter from Jung to Hilde Kirsch. It was enclosed in Jung's letter to James Kirsch, "your treating physician," on 11 June 1934 (p. 57). At the time, Hildegard Silber (widowed by the death of Hermann Silber in Berlin, June 1933) was living in Tel Aviv and seeing James Kirsch for analysis. She had met Jung at the Berlin Seminar in June/July 1933, and at Eranos in August 1933, when the Kirsch and Silber families spent two months in Ascona.

the sun in its head.[2] This ape searches instinctively for the ideas that are buried in Egypt, from whence comes Mosaic wisdom. It must be rediscovered, that which Egypt originally taught the children of Israel through Moses. The image in your dream of the Jewish second-hand shop then changes into the unappetizing pancake, which you make yourself. One must eat what one cooks in one's own kitchen; that is, when the traditional symbols have lost their magical power. Since I would not want to correspond behind the back of your treating physician, I have taken the liberty of sending this letter to Dr. Kirsch, so that he will be informed about our correspondence.

Very respectfully yours,[3] C. G. JUNG

Dr. C. G. Jung
Küsnacht-Zürich
Seestrasse 228

8 February 1935[4]

Frau Hildegard Silber,
Gordonstr. 2
Tel Aviv,
Palestine.

Dear Mrs. Silber,

Since I am now in the middle of the semester and must go on a trip at the end of March, it is entirely impossible for me at the moment to accept further patients. I'll get back to my practice on the first of May at the earliest, and then, too, I'll be so busy that I can't promise anything for the time being. I'm giving so many lectures that I have to reduce my practice in any case. Before I'd have time for a new patient, one or another patient would have to drop out.[5]

Very respectfully yours, C. G. JUNG

---

2   *ein Affe, der die Sonne im Kopfe hat.* Reference uncertain. Possibly an allusion to the sight of great apes watching the sunrise, which impressed Jung during his visit to East Africa in 1925 (cf. *MDR*, pp. 268f, p. 274).

3   *Mit vorzüglicher Hochachtung.*

4   Typewritten in German, on letterhead.

5   In spring 1935, Hildegard Silber was living alone in Zurich (cf. Kirsch, 19 June 1935, p. 70, note 15). A woman in the same boarding house – one of Jung's patients – was taken sick. Learning of this, Hilde asked for and was given the vacant hour. She later wrote to Jung's secretary, seeking confirmation of her training hours with Jung and Toni Wolff. She stated that she had worked with Jung from March through June 1935, two to three times per week, and equally often with Wolff ("*regelmaessig 2–3 mal die Woche bis Ende Juni, desgl. 2–3 mal in der Woche mit Fraeulein Wolff*"). In May to June 1937, she wrote, she again worked five weeks with Jung, two to three times per week (H. Kirsch to M.-J. Schmid, 8 August and 30 September 1949, ETH Library archive).

Notwithstanding Jung's refusal, Hildegard Silber began to work with both him and Toni Wolff in the spring of 1935, and returned for five more weeks' work in 1937. In June 1936, writing from London, she tried to schedule future sessions with Jung. That letter, the earliest that now exists from Hilde Kirsch to Jung, can be roughly translated as follows:

London

3 June 1936[6]

Dear Professor Jung!

I recently *[wrote?]* to Fräulein Wolff, so you may perhaps know that I've been through a very hard time. I wouldn't like to make *[illegible word]* demands on your time, and inquire only if you might have time for me in the winter. I could make myself free here for only about 3 weeks and would have to arrange it carefully with my *[enormously?]* large household. This month I'm expecting the baby, and I have the feeling that with this pregnancy a great inner process, as well, has been set in motion. I'm very isolated here, since the Jungian analysts who have now come here have so much to do with transplantation and outer reality, they aren't adapted to *[illegible word]*. I'd be very grateful to you if you could make time for me in November or January. I hope *[illegible word]* practice allows *[illegible word]* with you *[after?]* January 1.

With respectful greetings, Yours, HILDE KIRSCH

On 15 December 1936 Hilde Kirsch wrote to request a letter of recommendation (eine Empfehlung), *which she could show to the Home Office. She explained that Dr. Michael Fordham was seeing her for analysis, but that without Jung's recommendation she was not permitted to work analytically.[7] Jung's reply has unfortunately been lost, but evidently he sent the needed letter.[8] and in 1937 Hilde Kirsch became, officially, an analyst.*

Some of Hilde's letters between 1937 and 1939 contain urgent requests for additional analytic sessions, to which Jung replies with regret, pointing to his own full schedule, his health, and the political events of the time. In July 1938 he wrote that he would be unable to give her an hour during his trip to England, either on his way to Oxford or on his way back (Jung to H. Kirsch, 2 July 1938,

---

6   Handwritten in German, on plain paper. There are several illegible words in the original.

7   Hilde Kirsch to Marie-Jeanne Schmid, 15 December 1936, ETH Library archive.

8   Later Jung confirms, "In 1936 I authorized her to work as an Analytical Psychologist" (C. G. Jung, certificate for Hilde Kirsch, 18 March 1959, p. 283).

ETH Library archive). In the spring of 1939, however, he wrote that, although he had intended to schedule no consultations during his short stay in London, he would make an exception in her case. He offered her a session on 3 April, 4 pm, at the Montague Hotel (Jung to H. Kirsch, 20 March 1939, ETH Library archive).

Four months later she wrote to schedule further sessions. By the time Jung answered, the war had broken out.

London

13 August 1939[9]

Dear Professor Jung,

May I remind you of our conversation in London in April, when you promised to grant me a few hours after the summer. As you know, I have a huge household and many other responsibilities as well, and I can only get free for 14 days.

I'd be very grateful if you could tell me quite soon when you can take me. I'd like to see you more than once during the 14 days.

Hoping you're otherwise well.

With respectful greetings, Yours, HILDE KIRSCH

Küsnacht

2 September 1939[10]

Dear Mrs. Kirsch,[11]

Under the circumstances our appointment will have to be cancelled. We also have a general mobilization here.

With warm greetings, Yours truly, C. G. JUNG

Jung sent very few letters to James and Hilde Kirsch during the war. The following appears to be his reply to a letter from Hilde (now missing), about the family's move to Los Angeles in 1940.

---

9   Handwritten in German, on plain paper.
10 Typewritten in German, on a plain postcard.
11 *Liebe Frau Doktor.*

Prof. Dr. C. G. Jung
Küsnacht-Zürich
Seestrasse 228

5 May 1941[12]

Frau Hilde Kirsch,
6621 Drexel Avenue,
Los Angeles, Calif.

Dear Mrs. Kirsch,[13]

This is a time when millions of people are threatened by catastrophes and perhaps must be destroyed by these catastrophes. In Germany the catastrophe came to you. You had to leave Germany. Then you arrived in England, where the catastrophe again reached you. You did not have to leave England, but you were unable to do otherwise. No one can say that you should have stayed in the London raids. But when suffering comes to human beings, it is always better to stay with the first suffering where one can remain. For this suffering is still comprehensible. The second, which comes anyway, is usually incomprehensible, and that is worse. In America you have landed on virgin ground,[14] where everything begins again from below. You must begin there from below, in order to live; otherwise it won't work.

For this I wish you the necessary insight and patience!

With cordial greetings, C. G. JUNG

Küsnacht

15 October 1954[15]

Dear Mrs. Kirsch,[16]

Excuse me for writing to you as briefly as possible, since I'm very pressed by work. Your dream is extraordinarily clear and simple: If you think about the meaning of Christ as a Jewish reformer, who tried to resolve the demonic contrast between good and evil in Yahweh by setting up an exclusively positive or "good"

---

12 Typewritten in German, on letterhead.
13 *Liebe Frau Kirsch.*
14 *In Amerika sind Sie auf primitiven Boden gekommen*: Jung's use of "*primitiv*" has a positive connotation.
15 Typewritten transcription, in German, on plain paper. This letter may have been transcribed with the intention of including it in the *C. G. Jung Letters*. The original is missing.
16 *Liebe Frau Doktor.*

God-concept, then you can easily recognize the analogy, that in "Job" once again a peculiar rectification of the God-concept takes place. Not only I, but also you, become symbolically transformed, inasmuch as you quite obviously assume the role of the Mother of God and the Queen of Heaven. This is naturally to be understood in the sense of individuation, and then no misfortune has occurred. It just shows you, in complete clarity how we, as correct personalities, participate in the life of the archetypes, and how they attempt to realize themselves in ordinary human life. Everything else you can easily interpret for yourself.

With best greetings, Yours truly, [no signature in transcription]

In early 1959 Hilde Kirsch wrote to Aniela Jaffé, requesting a certificate from Jung. She needed the document urgently, to make it possible for her to continue practicing as a psychologist in California. She apologized for making a demand on Jaffé's time but asked her to write a letter certifying her training and experience. Her deadline with the State of California was rapidly approaching. The letter ends, "I thought I had at least come far enough so that my whole existence wouldn't be called into question again"[17] (H. Kirsch to A. Jaffé, 18 February 1959, ETH Library archive). Jung sent her the following certification.

18 March 1959[18]

To whom it may concern:

I have known Mrs. Hilde Kirsch, 906 Thayer Avenue, Los Angeles, California, since 1933. Mrs. Kirsch attended my seminar on clinical material in 1933 in Berlin. She came to Zurich, Switzerland, in 1935, had 4 months of intense training with me and attended my private seminar and the lecture course I gave at the Eidgenössische Technische Hochschule (Swiss Federal Institute of Technology), Zurich. Mrs. Kirsch returned in 1937 for additional training with me, personal as well as clinical. In 1936 I authorized her to work as an Analytical Psychologist.

In 1939 Mrs. Kirsch attended a seminar I gave in London at the Institute of Medical Psychology, Malet Place, London, England. After the war she returned again to Zurich in 1950, 1951, 1953, 1955 and 1958, to continue her training.

---

17 *"ich dachte, dass ich wenigstens so weit gekommen bin, dass nicht wieder meine ganze Existenz in Frage gestellt ist."*
18 Typewritten in English, carbon copy on plain paper, unsigned.

Los Angeles

31 Jan. 1960

Dear Professor,[19]

I'd like to thank you sincerely for the letter you wrote to James,[20] regarding my broken legs. I've reflected on it very similarly to the way you described it, but for the moment I still don't know at all how I'm supposed to arrive at these changes and what it's all about.

It may interest you to know, I was especially conscious that I might fall, because for a year I've been in a depression. So I was wearing my Swiss mountain boots and carrying a hiking stick from Zermatt. I was in the desert with my children, and we were walking into a very archaic palm forest. I was just saying to my children, "I wonder how and what the Zermatt stick will reach towards this opposite landscape," when I fell and broke both ankels.[21]

Everything seems to be healing well, and next week the cast will be taken off one leg.

I do hope you are coming through the winter well, and that you don't feel too tired. I hope to be able to see you again this year.

Once again many thanks, Yours truly, HILDE KIRSCH

Mrs. Hilde Kirsch
906 Thayer Avenue
Los Angeles 24, California

Hotel Sonnenberg, Zürich

31 October 1960[22]

Dear Professor,

I am endlessly thankful that you are feeling better, though it hurts very much, of course, that I can't see you. But I cannot depart without wishing you, in this manner at least, all that is good and increasing strength, and I hope that the enclosed small items will also help a little with that.

Yours truly, HILDE KIRSCH

19 *Sehr verehrter Herr Professor.*
20 Cf. Jung, 10 January 1960, p. 252 and note.
21 Quoted sentence and following words orig. in English; "ankels" for "ankles."
22 Handwritten in German, on letterhead. A photocopy of this letter was kindly provided by the Stiftung der Werke von C. G. Jung.

Figure 12.1 **Hilde Kirsch at 70.** *Photo: ©1972, James Kirsch. Courtesy Thomas B. Kirsch.*

Prof. Dr. C. G. Jung
Küsnacht-Zürich
Seestrasse 228

2 November 1960[23]

Frau Dr. Hilde Kirsch
906 Thayer Avenue
West Los Angeles, 24
Calif.

Dear Mrs. Kirsch,
    Please accept my sincere thanks for the tasty gift with which you remembered me.

---

23 Typewritten in German, on letterhead. Letter prev. pub. in *PP*. It is the last letter the Kirsches received from Jung, and the final document published by Kirsch in the series he titled, "Letters from a Friend."

I deeply regret that circumstances were so unfavorable this time that I couldn't receive you. Such incidents[24] are unfortunately to be expected at my age. One becomes unreliable.

I can only thank you warmly, once again, and wish you a good trip home.

With best greetings to your husband and to you, I remain

Yours truly, C. G. JUNG

---

24 *solche Zwischenfälle*: probably health-related. Jung mentions it with mild irony, not specifying the problem.

APPENDIX C

"'THE RED ONE': A PSYCHOLOGICAL INTERPRETATION OF A STORY BY JACK LONDON"[1]

LECTURE GIVEN ON THE 22ND OF MAY, 1954, AT CARMEL, CALIFORNIA

By James Kirsch, MD

Ladies and Gentlemen:

I consider it a happy coincidence that we are meeting in Carmel today, and that I have the great privilege to speak here on one of California's great sons. Jack London loved Carmel. It was during the summer of 1913 that he spent happy weeks in Carmel – visiting his lifelong friend George Sterling, "swimming in the surf and sunbathing on the sand, hunting for abalones and eating abalone steaks

---

1 A typescript of this lecture, 25 pages long, orig. in English, is located at the KML archive. An inscription at the top right corner of the first page, in Kirsch's handwriting, reads, "Presented to the Library of the Analytical Psychology Club of New York, Inc., with the author's compliments." A slightly revised version, "Jack London's Quest: 'The Red One'," was later published in *Psychological Perspectives*, Vol. 11, No. 2, Fall 1980, pp. 137–54 (© the C.G. Jung Institute of Los Angeles). Except for its title and introductory paragraphs, the 1980 version is identical with the text of the original lecture. Permission to republish the lecture was kindly given by Christophe Le Mouël, Executive Director of the C. G. Jung Institute of Los Angeles, on behalf of Gilda Frantz, Co-Editor-in-Chief of *Psychological Perspectives*. The 1954 version is printed here, with corrections of spelling and punctuation. Footnotes have been added, giving full citations for quotations from published works.

cooked over a wood fire on the beach" (Irving Stone).[2] It was a happy and creative time, but a time in which the great conflicts of his life had reached a climax. He was writing stories such as "Valley of the Moon,"[3] was active in the Socialist movement of his day and was building his magnificent Wolf House, into which he poured his seemingly inexhaustible creative powers – and all his money; a house to which everyone referred as a castle, resembling "a palace of Justinian or Caesar."[4]

Fate had, however, determined that he should never live in it. On August 19th of the same year, the Wolf House went up in flames. "Something in his soul burnt out that night," says Irving Stone.[5] The Jack London of "Call of the Wild"[6] and many other great stories died in that inferno. A new one was born, but Jack London's vitality was spent, and thus the new personality never had a chance to develop. It died in the bud.

Was this conflagration which destroyed Jack London's dream house a symbol or an event synchronistic with that conflagration which only one year later should engulf more than half of the world? There have always been human beings who, seized by an archetype, experience in their individual life that which happens to the collective or even to the whole of mankind.

Jack London was certainly such a man. I cannot give you here a biography of this extraordinary man who, in spite of the fact that his books were widely read all over the world, has not yet been understood and accepted in his full significance. His life and personal history have been adequately, candidly, and with loving sympathy, described by Irving Stone in his book, *Sailor on Horseback.*[7]

He was born on January 12th, 1876, in San Francisco, California. His real father, Professor W. M. Chaney, a full blooded Irishman, by profession an itinerant astrologer, always denied his fatherhood. So Jack London grew up in the family of John London. He suffered extreme poverty throughout his childhood. At a very early age he had to work, and his wages, at many times during his youth, represented an important part of the family income. At one time, for instance, he worked in a cellar shoveling coal for $30 a month, with one day off a month.

---

2 Irving Stone, *Sailor on Horseback*, Doubleday, 1939; reprinted and copyright renewed by Signet, New American Library, 1965, p. 248. In the lecture typescript, Kirsch occasionally uses passages from Stone's life of Jack London (later subtitled "a biographical novel") without the formality of quotation marks and page citations.

3 Jack London, *The Valley of the Moon*, orig. copyright 1913 by *Cosmopolitan Magazine* and Macmillan. New York: The Review of Reviews Company, 1917. This long (530-page) novel, in a working-class setting, a love story told from the woman's perspective, has a socialist thematic.

4 Irving Stone, *Sailor on Horseback*, op. cit., p. 249, partially paraphrased.

5 ibid., p. 250.

6 Jack London's long story, "The Call of the Wild," orig. pub. 1903, was the first of his stories to be a bestseller.

7 The title of Stone's book had been London's own title for a never-written autobiography.

He never received a formal education. There was nothing in his surroundings which, at any time, could have stimulated him to develop his mind, but the flame of the spirit was burning in him. With iron energy he taught himself. For a time he went to school, and even took classes at Berkeley. It is one of the sagas of modern American life how this poverty-stricken youth, with no formal education, acquired a profound, comprehensive and thorough grounding in many fields. He was a voracious reader in the fields of history, social science, literature, philosophy and psychology. Very early he made up his mind to write a thousand words a day. He was always sure that he was a great writer. Success was bound to come his way – and it did in great measure.

He was deeply and wildly in love with life. He lived it to the full, always risking himself and giving himself fully to life as he found it on the outside. And with the same devotion, he gave himself to writing almost every day of his life. The conflict which necessarily arose in himself due to this powerful extraversion, as well as this introversion, reflected in many of his books as well as in the stories themselves.

But it becomes clear that after the fire of his dream house, which symbolized to him his conquest of the world, Jack London was finally captured by the inner world. A profound and complete introversion began just when he was thirty-seven years of age, which was only occasionally interrupted by heavy drinking bouts and a few trips.

Another pair of opposites was clearly evident in the fact that on one side he embraced Nietzsche's ideas of the Superman. He identified the ego with the Self. He said, for instance,

> I have always inclined toward Haeckel's position[8]. In fact, 'incline' is too weak a word. I am a hopeless individualist. I see a soul as nothing else than the sum of the activities of the organism plus personal habits, memories, experiences, of the organism. *I believe that when I am dead, I am dead. I believe that with my death I am just as much obliterated as the last mosquito you or I smashed.*
>
> I have no patience with fly-by-night philosophers such as Bergson. I have no patience with the metaphysical philosophers. With them, always, the wish is parent to the thought, and their wish is parent to their profoundest philosophical conclusions. I join with Haeckel in being... "a positive scientific thinker."[9]

---

8 Ernst Haeckel (1834–1919): German biologist, naturalist, philosopher, and artist, who popular-ized Darwin's work in Germany. His books, widely translated, were used as textbooks in schools and universities around the world.

9 Letter from Jack London to Ralph Kasper, 25 June 1914, quoted by Charmian Kittredge London in *The Book of Jack London* (New York: Century Co., Inc., 1921), Vol. 2, p. 363. (A photograph of the typewritten letter is also found in Vol. 1 at p. 304.)

On the other hand, he wrote the most imaginative and lively stories we have known in American literature. He writes, for instance, in "The White Silence":

Nature has many tricks wherewith she convinces man of his finity – the ceaseless flow of the tides, the fury of the storm, the shock of the earthquake, the long roll of heaven's artillery – but the most tremendous, the most stupefying of all is the passive phase of the White Silence. All movement ceases, the sky clears, the heavens are as brass; the slightest whisper seems sacrilege, and man becomes timid, affrighted at the sound of his own voice. Sole speck of life journeying across the ghostly wastes of a dead world, he trembles at his audacity, realizes that his is a maggot's life, nothing more. Strange thoughts arise unsummoned, and the mystery of all things strives for utterance. And fear of death, of God, of the universe, comes over him – the hope of the Resurrection and the Life, the yearning for immortality, the vain striving of the imprisoned essence – it is there, if ever, man walks alone with God.[10]

How great the conflict is we can see from these two quotations. On one side he was a staunch materialist of Haeckel's persuasion, so characteristic of the end of the 19th century; on the other hand, he was a poet, living with incorruptible sincerity and unquestioned devotion in the service of his inner voice. As this quotation from "The White Silence" shows, the numinous experience of the Unconscious reached and seized him. This pair of opposites, the scientific materialist and the poet, open to thoughts of God and yearning for immortality, is difficult to carry for any human being.

As one of his obituaries said, "The inner struggle of London is the key to his work. His biography is a record of privation in its first phase, and a diary of individual daring in its second and last phase. He died at the age of forty – left his playground of the world at large as he had lived his short life – left at full speed – took ill in the morning and crossed the tall hill as the sun went down on his mountain ranch."[11]

We could of course deduce from the outer events of his life, his marriages, for intance, his friendships, his monetary problems, his relationship to his publishers or to the Socialist movement of his day, what his fundamental problem was, but we are enabled to see the development and dénouement of his fate from the rich material of the Unconscious which he left us in his writings. Unfortunately, we know only two dreams of Jack London, but practically every story which Jack London ever wrote is "active imagination" and therefore a vivid self-representation of the Psyche. They allow us an amazing insight into his psychological problems,

---

10   Jack London, "The White Silence" (orig. pub. 1913), in *The Call of the Wild and Other Stories*, New York: Dodd Mead & Co., 1960, pp. 140f.
11   Reference unclear. Thousands of obituaries appeared after London's death, worldwide.

and also into the problems of his time. Let us turn first to these two dreams. The first is a childhood dream, which throws significant light on Jack London's outstanding character traits. It is told by George Wharton James. He says that Jack London told him:

> My other childish victory was over a peculiar nightmare. I have lived in the country and was one day brought to town and stood on a railway platform as a railway engine came in. Its ponderous size, its easy and resistless onward movement, its panting, its fire and smoke, its great noises, all impressed me so powerfully that that night I dreamt of it, and when the dream turned to a nightmare I was filled with the dread and horror at what seemed to be the fact that this locomotive was pursuing me and that I could not get out of its way. For weeks thereafter I was haunted by this dreadful fear, and night after night I was run down. But, strange to say, I always rose up again after suffering the pangs of horrible death, to go over it all again. The tortures those nightmares gave me none can understand except those who have gone through a similar experience. Then one night came release. In the distance, as the mighty modern juggernaut came towards me, I saw a man with a stepladder. I was unable to cry out, but I waved my hand to him. He hailed me and bid me come. That broke the spell. I ran to him, climbed to the top of the stepladder, and thereafter lost all terror at the sight of a locomotive. But the victory gained in climbing the ladder was as real as any I ever had in my waking life.[12]

This dream, as a frequently recurring dream, is very important. It indicates young Jack London's fear of the Unconscious. The locomotive symbolizes the tremendous energy which is contained in the Unconscious. It comes as a terrific threat against him. For a certain time the conflict continues and no solution seems possible, but at last he succeeds in climbing on top of it. In other words, his solution is getting on top of it, a mastering of the Unconscious – and thereby achieving a complete identification with it. The fruit of it is an increase of libido and power of imagination. It was this tremendous energy which moved him throughout the first phase of his life. The energy which radiated from him through his work, in his actions, in his many, many ideas, in his working out of new plans and strivings in many fields was characteristic for him throughout his life. It was only through the burning of the Wolf House that this enormous vitality received a shock, and that his libido definitely turned inward.

The other dream we know is reported by Charmian Kittredge, his second wife, in *The Book of Jack London*. She says there:

---

12 Jack London, as quoted by George Wharton James in "A Study of Jack London in His Prime," *Overland Monthly*, Vol. 68, May 1917, p. 393. Thanks to Jay Williams for locating this passage.

In Jack's dreams, at widely separated intervals, appeared the Man who would contest Jack's self-mastership, to whom he would eventually bend a vanquished intelligence. He never saw such a one in the flesh, yet that entity stalked through more than the hallucinations of sleep. It was long ago he first told me of this ominous figure in his consciousness. The last manifestation was within a very few years of his death. The man, imperial, inexorable with destiny, yet strangely human, descended, alone, a vast cascade of stairways, and Jack at the foot looked up and waited as imperially for the meeting that was to be his unknown fate. But the Nemesis never, in that form at least, overtook him.[13]

Charmian spoke very true words in saying this. This figure, as we understand it today, was certainly the archetype of the Self, and Jack London was a man who, through his constant active imaginations and the writing of his many books, was confronted with the Self – had called up the Self. It is sad to think, but it was tragically unavoidable, that Jack could not find any positive aspect in this figure. We don't know how much he realized that the archetype of the Self had established itself in him. We know that in the story "The Red One" he certainly describes in large details his meeting with the Self. We don't know, however, how much he realized that in writing the story he was writing all about himself and that he had met the objective Psyche.

He died at the age of forty under circumstances which never made it quite clear whether he had committed suicide or died from natural causes. There is, however, no doubt that toward the end of his life he was a very sick man.[14]

On one of his trips to Hawaii in May of 1916, six months before his death, he wrote "The Red One," a story which I want to present to you here today. It was preceded by stories like "The Hussy," in which a man finds the Tower of Jewels, the gold of the Incas, on a high mountain, and is followed by a story called "Argus of the Ancient Times," in which an old man is in quest of the Great Treasure and finds it. He writes there,

It was in the dusk of Death's fluttery wings that Tarwater thus crouched, and, like his remote forebear, the child-man, went to myth-making, and sun-heroizing, himself hero-maker and the hero in quest of the immemorable treasure difficult of attainment.

Either he must attain the treasure – for so ran the inexorable logic of the shadow-land of the unconscious – or else sink into the all-devouring sea, the blackness eater of the light that swallowed to extinction the sun each night… the sun that arose ever in rebirth next morning in the east,

---

13   C. K. London, *The Book of Jack London*, (op. cit.), Vol. 2, pp. 343f.
14   London's death certificate indicates that he died of uremia, subsequent to kidney disease.

and that had become to man man's first symbol of immortality through rebirth.[15]

I will now give you a brief outline of his story, "The Red One." It is interesting to know that the first title he gave it was "The Message." It was written on the 22nd of May, 1916, exactly six months before his untimely death, and exactly thirty-eight years ago to the day. Bassett, the hero of the story, is a young English scientist and botanist who is in search of the mythical jungle butterfly – one which is more than one foot from wing-tip to wing-tip and lives in the roof of the jungle. In quest of this mysterious butterfly, he hears one day from the island of Ringmanu a marvelous sound, which he likens to the trump of an archangel. He determines at once to discover the mysterious instrument which creates this sound. Throughout the story Jack London gives abundant and beautiful descriptions of this sound: "sonorous as thunder, mellow as a golden bell, thin and sweet as a thrummed taut cord of silver." "Walls of cities might well fall down before so vast and compelling a summons." "It is like the mighty cry of some Titan of the Elder World vexed with misery or wrath."[16] In almost every word of this magnificent story one feels the extreme fascination which the mysterious Red One exerts on Bassett – pardon me, on Jack London. The Self truly inspired this story – there is not a superfluous word in it.

Fascinated by the magic of the tone, Bassett enters the jungle, accompanied by the boy, Sagawa, who carries the shotgun and all the naturalist's gear of his master. Immediately upon moving into the jungle, Sagawa is decapitated – and Bassett, in his fight with the primitive natives, has a terrible struggle to survive. He loses two fingers of his hand. He spends several nights in the jungle and is eaten up by the insects, becomes very sick, shaken with fever; but at last succeeds in getting out of the jungle into a wonderful grassland. He then enters a village and finds there a roasted pig – there he meets the Anima for the first time. He resolves to shoot her, but can never remember whether he had or not – any more than he could remember how he chanced to be in that village, or how he succeeded in getting away from it.

At last, however, he fights his way into another village. This one happens to be the principal village in a federation of twelve. Their god is the Red One whom all worship, and to whom they bring bloody sacrifices. He, the Red One, has subdued the gods of all the other tribes on the island of Guadalcanal. Vngngn is the weak chief, Ngurn is the medicine-man whose main occupation is the curing of heads

---

15 Jack London, "Like Argus of the Ancient Times," in *The Red One* (New York: Macmillan, 1918), pp. 89–141. Kirsch owned the 1918 Macmillan edition, which is still in his library. Passages quoted here are found on pp. 129f.

16 Jack London, "The Red One," in the Macmillan collection of 1918, *The Red One* (op. cit.), pp. 1–50. Lines quoted here are from the first two pages of the story. London's "The Red One" was originally published in *Cosmopolitan*, Vol. 65, Oct. 1916, pp. 34–41, 132–38. Unless otherwise noted, pages are cited hereafter from the Macmillan edition.

over a fire. The headhunters bring to him the heads of their victims, and through curing these Ngurn receives the wisdom contained in these heads.

Bassett is increasingly possessed by the magic peal of the Red One and now bends every effort to find out its secret and then bring it back to civilization. He is very sick, and the natives know that he will never be able to leave them. Therefore, they give him permission to roam in three quadrants of the compass; but the fourth quadrant, in which the Red One is located, is declared taboo to him. In order to satisfy his consuming curiosity imposed upon him by the numinous sound of the Red One, and to find a way to set his eyes upon it, he decides to make love to Balatta, the girl who has saved him and has herself fallen in love with the whiteness of his skin. She is just as frightened of breaking the taboo as he is attracted to it by the numinosity of its sound. He succeeds, however, in persuading her to lead the way to the mysterious Red One.

He discovers that the Red One is a perfect sphere, fully 200 feet in diameter, with the color quality of lacquer, brighter than bright cherry red. On closer investigation it appears that it is no lacquer, nor does the Red One have a smooth surface. The substance is metal, but of no metal or combination of metals he had ever known. On the slightest touch it quivered [with] a sound "so elusive thin that it was shimmeringly sibilant;... piping like an elfin horn,... like a peal from some bell of the gods reaching earthward from across space."[17]

Amongst its many names were The Loud Shouter, The God-Voiced, The Bird-Throated, the Sun Singer, and the Star-Born. The Star-Born was certainly the most fitting one. "It was a creation of artifice and mind,... [A] child of intelligences."[18] ... "Bassett laughed aloud... at the thought of this wonderful messenger, winged with intelligence across space, to fall into a bushman stronghold.... It was as if God's World had fallen into the muck mire of the abyss underlying the bottom of hell;... as if the Sermon on the Mount had been preached in a roaring bedlam of lunatics."[19] So Jack London describes this wonderful discovery.

"Who were they?" he asks. "What were they, those far distant and superior ones who had bridged the sky with their gigantic, red-iridescent, heaven-singing message?... [This] sounding sphere... contained the speech and wisdom of the stars.... [It could] contain vast histories, profounds of research.... It was time's greatest gift to blindfold, insatiable, and sky-aspiring man. And to him, Bassett, had been vouchsaved the lordly fortune to be the first to receive this message from man's interstellar kin!"[20]

After his return to the village, Bassett renews his plans for going back to civilization. Soon, however, he realizes that his fevers continue to weaken him, and that death is inevitable. He continues to make love to Balatta, but with utter

---

17   ibid., p. 16.
18   ibid., p. 34.
19   ibid., pp. 37f.
20   ibid., pp. 40–42.

reluctance and loathing. He escapes from her as much as possible into the hut of Ngurn, the medicine-man who spends his time with curing heads and incantations. He assures Bassett that it will not be very long before he will also cure his head, because Bassett will certainly die from his illness. On a day when his mind is unclouded by his fevers, Bassett therefore proposes a contract to Ngurn. He wants to see and hear the Red One once more and die with this wonderful peal in his ears. He will accept to be ritually killed by Ngurn while seeing and hearing the Red One. This is done. At the last moment, Bassett consideres that he still could kill Ngurn with his shotgun,[21] but he rejects this idea.

> But why cheat him?… Head-hunting cannibal, beast of a human…, nevertheless Old Ngurn had… played squarer than square…. [I]t would be a ghastly pity and an act of dishonour to cheat the old fellow at the last. His head was Ngurn's, and Ngurn's head to cure it would be.
>
> …And Bassett… bending forward his head as agreed,… forgot Balatta who was merely a woman… and undesired….And for that instant, ere the end, there fell upon Bassett the shadow of the Unknown…. [I]t seemed that he gazed upon the serene face of the Medusa, Truth – And… he saw the vision of his head turning slowly, always turning, in the devil-devil house beside the breadfruit tree.[22]

These almost literal quotations will convey to you the full poetry and inspired quality of this story. But behind this poetry the story of Jack London's tragedy appears in stark relief.

Let us remember that as a child he climbed on the locomotive, and carried by the magic power of the Unconscious, he developed a fascinating personality; he wrote an incredible amount of great and also mediocre stories, was always driven to over-demand himself, strove to achieve the impossible in many fields, always living life to the fullest and fearlessly, sometimes wantonly, risking more than even his powerful organism could stand. So illness overtook him, catastrophe broke upon him in the fire of his beloved Wolf House. His daughters from his first marriage refused to live with him. In the midst of thousands of friends, men and women, he was lonely. He did not and could not realize that by his daring adventures into the life of the spirit, he had come into the neighbourhood of the Self, nor could he realize that the might of his genius did not originate in his ego, but came from the Self. For a long time, he could afford to identify with the Self and feel himself as a superman. Sooner or later, the "Auseinandersetzung" between himself and the

---

21 Kirsch has misread this passage in London's narrative: "His shotgun lay beside him in the litter. All he had to do, muzzle to head, was to press the trigger and blow his head to nothingness" (ibid., pp. 48f). The choice Bassett considers, in "a quick flash of fancy," is to destroy his own head, thus denying Ngurn the promised payment.

22 ibid., pp. 49f.

Self had to begin. And that is what the second dream tries to tell him. The "Man," the ominous figure, the Anthropos who descended, was destiny and became his nemesis. As Ngurn says in "The Red One," paraphrasing the Old Testament, "No white man could see him – and live."[23] (Exodus 33:20: "No man shall see me, and live.") And yet Jack London, in the person of Bassett, looked upon him and lived. He was even able to touch it and to awaken its marvellous voice and then return to the village. This he was able to accomplish because he went down to see him accompanied by the primitive Anima, that Anima so despised by Bassett. He had actually acquired his fatal illness practically at the instant at which he entered the jungle. And yet he did not die from his illness. His illness rather gave him the chance to experience the miraculous sphere again, to expose himself once more to the greatest risk and grace which can be bestowed upon man. That is, to meet the Self in its fullness, whose other name is Truth. He was driven to it in the hopelessness of his psychic condition, but paradoxically enough he also volunteered. It was a contract he made with the Self. At the last moment he was indeed tempted to cheat God but rejected it, because he acknowledged that the Self had played squarer than square with him. This was different from Faust, the story of another man who was granted a meeting and association with the Self, and upon whom the Self bestowed its richest gift – and whom he cheated at the last. Jack London's hero, in contrast, was true to himself to the end. He recognized that the Self had given him both spiritual and material riches, had played squarer than square with him and he, Jack London, must needs play fair as well with the Self to the end.

In the case of Faust, Faust's "immortal" soul is carried to Heaven, and his redemption takes place in the beyond. His last achievement is the discovery of the moment in its fullness. But Jack London's fulfilment is the vision of Truth, the Zen experience at the moment of his death, and the slow turning of the head in the devil-devil house, in the post-mortal state.

While the Self is the all-pervading motif of the story, we actually discover all the classical archetypes of the collective unconscious in this story, and even in their classical sequence: Shadow, Anima, Old Wise Man and Self. By its very beauty of language, it is obvious that it is not thought out, but truly inspired. The patterns of the Unconscious themselves have dictated the story.

In Bassett we find the Ego, or to be more correct, the representative of Jack London's Ego. It is in Bassett that we see the scientist, the rationalist who however carries in himself the longing for the non-rational which is symbolized in his quest for the mythical butterfly, a fitting symbol for the psyche. In his quest he encounters

---

23 Kirsch quotes the passage as it was originally printed in *Cosmopolitan*, 1916, (op. cit.), p. 137. In the 1918 edition this passage reads: "No white man, much less no outland man of the other bush-tribes, had gazed upon the Red One and lived.... Only a man born within the tribe could look upon the Red One and live" (*The Red One*, 1918, op. cit., p. 42). I am grateful to Jean Kirsch, here and elsewhere, for her research into the early versions of London's story.

something that transcends by far the value and meaning of this butterfly. It is the magic sound of the mysterious Red One.

Just as a comparison, I want to show you this amusing picture from the "New Yorker" of October 3, 1953. Jack London did not take to his heels – as the entomologist does in this picture when confronted with the mysterium of the Soul, who holds on to his "scientific" conceptions, which cannot catch or hold the Psyche. Jack London, in contradistinction, is immediately captured by the sound of the Red One, and is poisoned by the dank and noisy jungle of the Unconscious.

Like so many classical journeys, this one also begins as an adventure of a hero and his companion. But in contrast, for instance, to Dante's journey with Virgil or Moses' with Dulquarnein,[24] this second figure – the servant – is described with a remarkable degree of contempt: "He has a queer little monkeyish face, eloquent with fear." Yet he is faithful and – as it turned out – he foresees that the adventure must have a tragic end. Though a companion on this quest, he is not invested with the qualities of a superior guide like Virgil in the Divine Comedy. He has much more the characteristics of Jack London's inferior personality – of his shadow. His advice is not listened to, his common sense is not appreciated, and actually this shadow figure has no chance to interact with the Ego. The Ego at this point has already fallen under the spell of the Red One, and there is nothing, not even a trace of common sense, which would give the Ego fair warning of the dangers awaiting it on this quest, thus permitting it to equip itself for the hazards of the journey.

Thus, poorly prepared Bassett enters the Unconscious like a curious adolescent, without much realization of the dangers of such a journey, and Sagawa is immediately killed – that is, he is decapitated, and the hero is assailed by primitives with poisoned arrows and falls victim to the insects of the jungle, thus acquiring his fatal illness.

He has irrevocably been captured by the process of individuation. The fascination issuing from the archetypes, and quite especially from the Self, has caught him; but the loss of the shadow, i.e. the lack of insight into his human limitations, has the effect that the Unconscious invades him as poison and infection. Thus the Ego is forced to fight a courageous battle, but without the possibility of an ultimate victory or accomplishment of the task. Translated into actual reality, this psychological condition in Jack London meant, for instance, that he built the "Snark" and made the famous journey to the South Sea islands. In this way he overestimated by far his stamina and powers, his physical and financial resources, and actually contracted the disease which fatally sapped his strength.

In this way, one could consider Jack London as a tragic victim of the process of individuation. He certainly is, but still not a failure – because he lived his life fully and without reservation, because like a man he courageously accepted the

---

24 Reference unclear. Printed thus in "Jack London's Quest" (*Psychological Perspectives*, 1980, op. cit., p. 147). Possibly refers to a figure in the Koran, Zulquarnein, though the connection with Moses is impossible to verify.

challenge of the Self, and as a human being he was granted the vision of God in his voluntary sacrifice.

The second of the classical figures, the Anima, actually saves his life; but nevertheless she is treated by him with an amazing hostility and loathing. In remembering his first encounter with her he cannot even make sure whether he killed her or not. In her second and more permanent form, he heaps contempt on her, calls her quite frankly the inferior sex, expresses the same sentiments as Nietzsche. Quite obviously this Anima is to a large extent contaminated with the shadow. Not only is she described as primitive in the sense of primeval or original, but more in the sense of being barbaric, dirty, ugly and smelly. Furthermore, she is predominantly Nature to him, in the sense of sex without any positive feeling tone attached to her. In order to make contact, he has to teach her how to bathe, even to the point of giving her frequent scrubbings. When he meets her for the first time, he tells that "her sex was advertised by the one article of finery with which she was adorned, namely a pig's tail, thrust through a hole in her left ear lobe."[25] His relationship to her is simply that of making use of her and of exerting power over her. He needs her because there is a taboo which forbids a stranger to see the Red One, and because the Red One is hidden in a gorge within the Fourth Quadrant. He can find this place only with the help of a native – and Balatta, because of her love for him, would break the taboo. For this reason only, he is forced to make up to her. He uses the charm of his white skin and his masculinity as assets in the deal to achieve his overriding ambition of gaining access to the mysterious Red One. At no point in the story is she treated as an equal, to say nothing of consideration or love. Therefore, we find in Jack London's hero qualities like fascination by the Red One to an unlimited degree: acknowledgment of its power, superiority, and transcendental quality. We find submission to it and ecstasy in completely surrendering to it – but never love. And this is probably one important reason why in the same way as the Anima was contaminated with the shadow, the Self appears contaminated with an important aspect of the Anima, i.e. why it has the transmundane color – this unearthly red.

As was to be expected, the third classical figure is that of the Old Wise Man. Bassett is genuinely attracted to Ngurn, the primitive medicine-man of the tribe, but he also spends as much time as possible with him in order to escape from the loathsome Anima. Again we find that this figure has a great many negative qualities. Though he is certainly very wise and conveys his wisdom to Bassett, he is after Bassett's head nevertheless; not in order to re-establish his health and return him to life, but to gain his head and cure it. This whole story occurs in the country of headhunting primitives. The atmosphere of headhunting and the curing of heads pervades it. All the long talks between Bassett and Ngurn take place in Ngurn's hut whilst he is curing heads. He is one of the best curers of heads, having inherited his art from his medicine-man ancestors, an art long lost in other tribes.

25 "The Red One," p. 14.

He promises Bassett to take good care of his head after his death and to make his head his masterpiece. A curious motive![26] True, Jack London, in his South Sea journey, came across some examples of hunting and curing heads, but that it turned up just in this story is most significant.

I have met this motif of the wise head in dreams of my patients. I have met it in dreams, for instance, as the head which continually spoke perfect wisdom[27] – in this way symbolizing the Logos principle of the Unconscious. I have encountered it in dreams also as the vessel which had to be prepared and worked upon in order to become the perfect vessel. I have most frequently found it as the Round One, in this way being a symbol of the Self, a most suitable symbol, since as head it represented the essential and concentrated substance of the human being.

In *Psychology and Alchemy* (pp. 431–2 of the English edition)[28] Jung refers to the "sixth parable" of the Splendor Solis, where a vision of a dismembered body is mentioned, whose head was of fine gold, but separated from the body. Jung also mentions that the Greek Alchemists styled themselves: "Children of the Golden Head."[29]

In his newest book, "About the Roots of Consciousness" (p. 269),[30] Jung speaks in detail about primitive beliefs and rituals in which animal and human sacrifices were made in order to gain a head and to make it white; he mentions other rather gruesome rituals, the purpose of which was to gain a specially prepared head giving forth great wisdom. According to Jung, the head can be interpreted as the so-called "round element," since the Liber Quartorum establishes a connection between the vessel and the head. Furthermore, Zosimos mentions several times "the extremely white stone which is in the head."[31]

In addition, he mentions the rumor that Gerbert of Rheims [may] have possessed a golden skull which revealed oracles to him.[32] According to rabbinical tradition, the "teraphim," the oracle mentioned in the Old Testament, was supposed to have been a cut-off head or skull. Jung also quotes M. I. Bin Gorion: *Die Sagen der Juden,*[33] in which it is said that these teraphim were made in the following way: the head of somebody who had to be a native was cut off, then the hair was plucked out. Then the head was sprinkled with salt and anointed with oil. After that a small tablet made of copper or gold was inscribed with the name of the god and put under

---

26 Error in original typescript. From context, "motif" is probably the word intended. See first line in paragraph below.
27 Cf. Kirsch, 23 January 1955, p. 216.
28 Cf. CW 12, ¶530.
29 ibid.
30 Jung's 1954 volume, *Von den Wurzeln des Bewusstseins* (cf. Jung, 28 November 1952, p. 149 and note), included his paper later published as "Transformation Symbolism in the Mass." The passage cited is found in CW 11, ¶363–73.
31 Cf. CW 11, ¶366.
32 ibid, ¶367.
33 ibid, ¶368.

the tongue of the cut-off head. The head was then placed in a room, candles were lit before it, and one bowed before it, and it happened that when one prostrated oneself before it, the head began to talk and to answer all the questions which one addressed to it.

These examples are a striking parallel to Jack London's story and show that an archetypal pattern imposed itself on Jack London when he wrote at some length about the curing of the head – and that he recognized its true purpose, which was to gain wisdom. It follows an archetypal pattern when, in the end, he sees his own head slowly turning as the serene face of Truth. It is the "veritas efficaciae" which, according to Dorn (*Psychology and Alchemy*, 256), is "the highest power and an impregnable fortress wherein the philosopher's stone lies safeguarded."[34]

Ngurn says to Bassett: "I will tell you many secrets for I am an old man and very wise, and I shall be adding wisdom to wisdom as I turn your head in the smoke."[35] And yet, there is a great difference between the motif of the teraphim or the old alchemists and the curing of the head as described in "The Red One." The Alchemists or the Hebrew priests gaining the head did not identify with it. They gained possession of the head and found means to communicate with it. In Jack London's story, it is Bassett's head which will be cured, and wisdom will accrue to it and issue from it only after his death. In other words, it will occur only in the postmortal state. That is: the wisdom will never serve life or Bassett's individual life, but will represent a terminal condition.

The head itself as the Round One certainly symbolizes the Self, as Jung has demonstrated in *Psychology and Alchemy*. In his new book, *About the Roots of Consciousness*, Jung quotes the Liber Quartorum: "*Vas... oportet esse rotundae figurae: ut sit artifex huius (aperis) mutator firmanenti et testae capitis, ut cum sit res qua indigemus, res simplex.*" (The vessel must be of round shape, just as the artist of this work is a transformer of the firmament and of the skull, and like the thing which we need is "a simple thing.")[36] As a vessel, however, it also has feminine characteristics and therefore has a certain Anima aspect. One can therefore conclude that it was more the instinctual and emotional aspect of the Anima which was so unacceptable to Jack London, whilst her more spiritual aspect, relating him to the Self, could be assimilated to Consciousness.

This head as a vessel of wisdom needing a great deal of work represents the alchemical or psychological process – the opus. Yet it has a rather lugubrious aspect in Jack London's story and casts its dark and fatal shadow on Jack London's experience. This is certainly essentially different in the great symbol of the Self which has given its name to the whole story, and of which we hear again and again on account of its all-encompassing numinosity.

---

34 Kirsch's variant translation of a passage from Gerhard Dorn, quoted by Jung in CW 12, ¶377.

35 "The Red One," op. cit., p. 45.

36 Cf. CW 11, ¶363.

The sphere as a symbol of the Self is one of the most familiar representations of the Self, as Jung has shown in *Psychology and Alchemy*. The cosmogony of Empedocles, for example, calls this spherical being *eudaimonestatos Theos* ("the most serene God"),[37] just as Jack London calls the Red Sphere the serene face of Truth. The curious thing about it in this story is that it is described as a metal, "though unlike any metal or combination of metals he had ever known." He observes that it shows "signs of heat and fusing." It is "a child of intelligences, remote and unguessable, working corporally in metals. It is a far-journeyer which was lacquered by its fiery bath in two atmospheres."[38] In the *Roots of Consciousness* Jung discusses the question why the inner man and his spiritual being happen to be represented by metals.[39] He anwers that Nature seems to be concerned to drive consciousness to greater clarity, and therefore uses man's constant desire for metals, especially the precious ones, to search for them and to examine its possibilities. In this occupation, it might dawn upon him that a dangerous demon or a dove of the Holy Ghost might be contained in lead.[40]

It has exactly this effect upon the hero of our story. Entranced by the wonder of the unthinkable and unguessable thing, it makes him reflect and meditate on it. Psychologically speaking, it means that he has become aware of a world of active intelligences beyond the narrow field of human consciousness, that the awe engendered by the archetypes has struck him, and that he who for so long identified with the archetype of the Self, at last recognizes the activity of the archetypes and asks himself: "Who are they?" and significantly, "What are they?" – those far superior ones who had bridged the sky with their gigantic, red-iridescent, heaven-singing message. It reminds us of Dorn, who says: "*Nemo vero potest cognoscere se, nisi sciat quid, et non quis ipse sit, a quo dependat, vel cuius sit... et in quem finem factus sit.*" ("No one can truly know himself, unless he knows what he is, and not who he is, on what he depends, or to what or whom he belongs, and for what purpose he was created.")[41] Jung comments that "this differentiation between 'quid' and 'quis' is extremely significant. Whilst 'quis' has an indubitably personalistic aspect and therefore refers to the Ego, the 'quid' is a neuter, and therefore presupposes nothing but an object of which it is not even sure that it has personality."[42] In this way, Jack London experiences the psyche as an objective reality, as a "quid" and not a "quis." It is even possible to gain its extraordinary wisdom. He realizes that it might contain "engines and elements and mastered

---

37 Cf. CW 12, ¶433, p. 325.
38 "The Red One," op. cit., p. 34.
39 Reference to a chapter in *Wurzeln*. English version, "The Visions of Zosimos," is published in CW 13, Part 2.
40 Paraphrasing from Jung, "The Visions of Zosimos," CW 13, ¶119.
41 Latin passage cited in a footnote in Jung's *Aion*, Chapter XI, "The Alchemical Interpretation of the Fish," rendered here in Kirsch's translation. Cf. CW 9.(ii), ¶252, p. 164 and note.
42 ibid. This is Kirsch's translation of Jung's original text.

forces,… lore and mysteries and destiny-controls."[43] What insight! What vision! In this way, Jack London recognized that the archetypes are the factors which arrange and control our fate, and that by contacting them, we establish a relationship to our destiny and no longer remain mere objects of Fate. In this way, he recognized his destiny, but also his inability to change his destiny at such a late hour. He, Jack London, was the one who was "vouchsaved the lordly fortune to be the first to receive this message from man's interstellar kin."[44]

On account of his unstinted devotion to life as he found it, and to the spirit as he experienced it, he was granted the great vision, and this was his fulfilment. His strength was spent, and he could not go beyond this intuition. All his life he was a seeker for the "immemorable treasure difficult of attainment." Through most of his life he had been seeking the progress and salvation of mankind in Socialism. Irving Stone said his mind completely surrendered to Karl Marx. But this is not the whole truth inasmuch as he, at the same time, was one of the great myth-makers of mankind.

So much for Jack London. We, the heirs of his message, must ask ourselves how much of all this is still our problem today. What Jack London observed in discovering the mysterious sphere, the Red One, was an event in the Collective Unconscious. The story, "The Red One," does not describe Jack London's personal psychology, but is an accurate picture of American psychology and of Western man as a whole. The Self has embedded itself not only on the mythical island of Guadalcanal, but everywhere in mankind. Jack London was not the first one, as he believed, to whom this lordly fortune was vouchsafed. Nietzsche was probably its first tragic victim in modern times. It is worth noting that Jung's great development and discovery of the Collective Unconscious took place just in these same years. In a commentary on Zimmer's book, *Art Form and Yoga*,[45] he mentions the fact that it was at about this time that he discovered the mandala and essential facts about the archetype of the Self.[46]

The world as a whole has been in constant unrest since. In the years that followed the writing of "The Red One," two world wars, revolutions of social, political and religious nature have been fought, and the discovery of the Hydrogen Bomb has been made. All this is due to the all-determining fact that, as Jack London describes it, the Self has embedded itself in our soil. But the soil in which it has been implanted is a "bushman stronghold." We are "man-eating and head-hunting savages." It is "as if God's World had fallen into the muck mire of the abyss underlying the bottom of hell,… as if the Sermon on the Mount had been preached in a roaring bedlam of lunatics."[47]

---

43 "The Red One," op. cit., p. 41.
44 ibid., p. 42.
45 Cf. Kirsch, 7 June 1954, p. 200, note 81.
46 ibid.
47 "The Red One," op. cit., pp. 37f.

Bassett's problem is our problem. We are in the same psychological boat. It is a general human attitude to forget the Shadow. We need a good and adequate knowledge of the Shadow to release his positive values. We cannot afford to maintain an attitude of contempt, hostility or loathing against the Anima, i.e. against the non-rational quality of the Unconscious. We would do better to accept it as it is, a world of images and of mysterious life. Such an approach will give us new strength and understanding to receive the Self in our midst and thus to release its unlimited resources of wisdom.

The changes necessary for the reception of the Self in our life cannot occur by means of political agreements or economic planning, they cannot take place in institutions or nations, but only through the work and experience of the individual human being to whom they occur in the stillness and storms of his soul. Only that civilization will survive which allows the individual to meet his Self in full freedom. Only thus, as Jack London says, can "man's life on earth, individual and collective, spring up from its present mire to inconceivable heights of purity and power."[48]

---

48   ibid, p. 41.

APPENDIX D

A BRIEF HISTORY OF
THE AAGP/IAAGP

The members, history and activities of the *Allgemeine ärztliche Gesellschaft für Psychotherapie* [General Medical Society for Psychotherapy], later the *Internationale¹ allgemeine ärztliche Gesellschaft für Psychotherapie* [International General Medical Society for Psychotherapy], an organization of medical psychotherapists, centered in Germany (referred to in these pages under the abbreviations AAGP and IAAGP), constitute an important part of the background for Jung and Kirsch's early letters to each other. The two writers make frequent, often cryptic, references to individuals and events related to this professional organization in which both of them were – for varying lengths of time and in varying degree – contributing members.

An outline of the history of the AAGP/IAAGP is provided here. This can be only a brief summary of the evolution of an organization which interacted with its political environment for nearly two decades in a complex period of history. For a fuller and deeper grasp of the story, the reader is referred to works by other scholars, particularly to the classic volume by Geoffrey Cocks, *Psychotherapy in the Third Reich*,² a nuanced examination of this period, placing the AAGP and IAAGP in their wider context.

In 1926 and 1927 two initial gatherings of physician-psychotherapists from several European nations, representing a diversity of theoretical schools, took place in Germany. At their third meeting, in 1928, the *Allgemeine ärztliche Gesellschaft für Psychotherapie* was founded. Its primary goals in the first five years, as Geoffrey Cocks observes, were "to minimize the dissension among the

---

1 In 1933–34, the restructured organization was often designated the *Überstaatliche* (rather than "*Internationale*") *allgemeine ärztliche Gesellschaft für Psychotherapie*. The term, "supranational," may have been a concession to German sensibilities at the time. The name quickly reverted, however, to the more commonplace "international." In correspondence in 1934, Jung mentions the "*Internationale Gesellschaft für Psychotherapie*" (cf. Jung, 26 May 1934, p. 44 and note). Official invitations to the Congress of 1935, too, referred to the "*Interntionale*" AAGP.
2 Geoffrey Cocks, *Psychotherapy in the Third Reich, The Göring Institute*. (2ⁿᵈ ed, New Brunswick and London: Transaction Publishers, 1997). Cf. esp. Chapters 2, 5 and 6.

various theories of psychotherapy and to encourage its practice in all branches of medicine, and to encourage research in the young field."[3]

In line with these goals, a research journal, *Zentralblatt für Psychotherapie und ihre Grenzgebiete* [Journal for Psychotherapy and Its Related Fields], was published quarterly, and every member of the AAGP was invited to subscribe. Surviving issues of the *Zentralblatt* are a primary source for research in the history of the AAGP. Another is the series of reports from annual meetings.[4]

Although Jung was not present at either the 1926 or 1927 Congress, his name and theories received positive mention from several speakers in 1927, and he attended the Congress of 1928, serving at the first session as *Ehrenvorsitz* (Honorary Chairman). In 1929 he joined the organization and gave the opening address. Kirsch also attended the 1929 Congress, where he first met Jung and heard him speak.[5] At the Congress of 1930, a German psychiatrist, Professor Ernst Kretschmer, was elected 1. *Vorsitzender* (President) and Jung 2. *Vorsitzender* (Vice-president) of the AAGP. Jung was also asked to organize the next congress and to give the opening address. Kirsch joined the AAGP in 1931 and lectured at that congress. (It is the only year in which he can be shown to have been a member.)

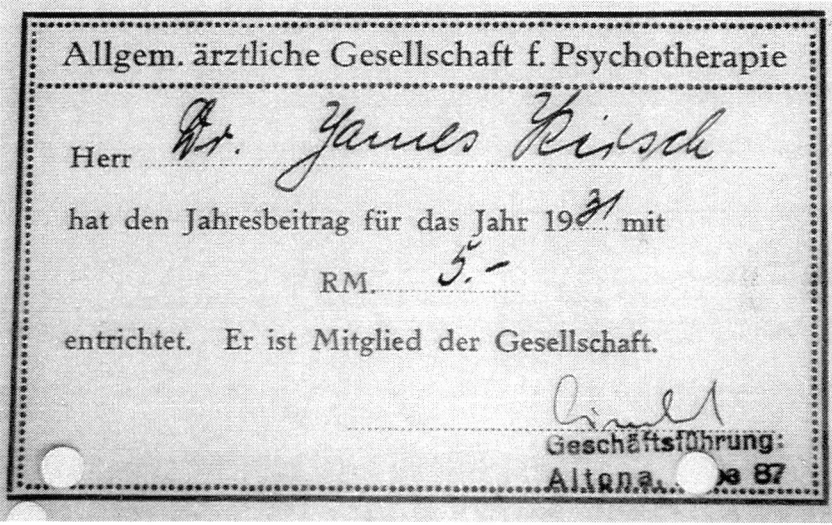

Figure 14.1 **Kirsch's AAGP member card, 1931, signed by Cimbal.** *Photo: ©2007, Ann Lammers. Courtesy Kirsch archive/Estate of James Isaac Kirsch.*

3 ibid., p. 24.
4 There being no published report for 1926, the first of these is titled, *Bericht über den II. Allgemeinen Ärztlichen Kongress für Psychotherapie in Bad Nauheim, 27. bis 30. April 1927.* Bound editions of these primary documents, dated from 1927 to 1940, are part of C. A. Meier's private collection, located now at the ETH Library archive.
5 cf. Kirsch, Countway Interview, p. 1.

In early 1933, immediately on Hitler's accession to power, the German state imposed the principle of *Gleichschaltung* (conformity to the principles of National Socialism) on all organizations in Germany. In late March the AAGP President, Ernst Kretschmer, cancelled that year's congress, which had been scheduled for April in Vienna, and a week later resigned the presidency, for reasons which were publicly stated to be health-related.[6]

As Vice-president, Jung was immediately and urgently asked to assume the post of President, to keep the organization intact and continue publication of the *Zentralblatt*. He agreed, but only on condition that the AAGP be legally reorganized, to create a neutral international organization. This change in structure was agreed upon in mid 1933 by the governing board, and Jung publicly accepted the presidency on 21 June 1933, when he was in Berlin to give a week-long seminar. In March 1934, with the intention of blunting the impact of Germany's anti-Jewish laws, Jung privately took responsibility for the legal structure of the *Internationale allgemeine ärztliche Gesellschaft für Psychotherapie*. He hired a young lawyer, Vladimir Rosenbaum, who agreed to redraft the organization's statutes.[7] In May 1934, at the Seventh Congress for Psychotherapy, the IAAGP was founded, and Rosenbaum's careful wordings were incorporated into its charter.

By restructuring the organization, Jung partly achieved his purpose. The IAAGP took over publication of the *Zentralblatt*, with Jung as editor. Both the IAAGP and its journal were now declared to be politically neutral. *Landesgruppen* (national sections of the IAAGP) were to have their own leaders and policies and could

6   Both at the time and later, rumors circulated depicting Kretschmer as a Jew whom Jung had dis placed in office. Finding this rumor still current in later years, Kirsch consulted with a colleague, Dr. Hans Dieckmann, in Berlin. Dieckmann consulted with Kretschmer's son, and confirmed, *"dass Kretschmer kein Jude gewesen ist. Er gehörte ganz sicher zu den Gegnern des Nazi-Regimes und hat sich nur auf Grund seiner prominenten Stellung während der Nazi-Zeit hier gehalten"* ["… Kretschmer was not a Jew. He certainly belonged to the opponents of the Nazi regime, and survived here during the Nazi era only because of his prominent position"] (Hans Dieckmann to Kirsch, 1 February 1980, Kirsch archive). The first statement is accurate. Contrary to the second, however, more recent research shows that Kretschmer was a sponsoring member of the SS in 1933 (Ernst Klee, *Das Personenlexikon zum Dritten Reich*, 2005, p. 339). Also relevant is a document I found in 2014 at the Bundesarchiv, Berlin: a piece of official Party correspondence dated January 1945, written to Kretschmer by "Der Bevollmächtigte für das Sanitäts- und Gesundheitswesen" [State Authority for Emergency Medicine and Health], which shows that he held a government position during the war years. Many thanks to Dr. Rasche for his invaluable research assistance. Cf. also Jörg Rasche, "C. G. Jung in the 1930s," *Jung Journal Culture and Psyche,* Fall 2012, Vol. 6, Number 4, p. 59.

7   The episode is reported by Peter Kamber in *Geschichte zweier Leben – Wladimir Rosenbaum & Aline Valangin* (Zürich: Limmat Verlag Genossenschaft, 2000). In a 1979 television interview Rosenbaum recalled: "Jung felt that, at the general meeting that would decide about the change in statutes [dictated by *Gleichschaltung*], an attempt should be made to push through a different, milder wording, a wording that would somehow offer Jewish colleagues the possibility to keep practicing their medical profession, [and that one should try] to build a sort of back door into the statutes, to find a wording open to several interpretations, that wouldn't mean an absolute negation of the Jewish colleagues" (Peter Kamber, *Geschichte zweier Leben*, pp. 169f, trans. ACL). I am indebted to Thomas Fischer for drawing my attention to the relevant passages in Kamber's book. (Cf. also Bair, *Jung: A Biography*, Boston, New York, London: Little, Brown & Co., 2003, pp. 448ff.)

publish their own *Sonderhefte* (special editions). The national groups and the international umbrella organization, while collegially aligned, were declared to be independent of each other. By this arrangement, the German section – by far the largest – could "conform" to the Nazi state, while the IAAGP could (in theory, at least, under its charter) retain political neutrality.

That this plan could be only imperfectly carried out is illustrated by features of the exchange between Kirsch and Jung in May and June of 1934. Jung may have overestimated the strength of the new structure against all the forms of pressure – in numbers, finances, manipulation, and will-to-power – that persistently worked to undermine the neutrality of the IAAGP, to make it (and Jung himself, if possible) conform, or at least appear to conform, with Nazi principles. The best example of this phenomenon is the public relations disaster that occurred in December 1933, when Jung's name, as Editor of the *Zentralblatt*, was tarred by association with M. H. Göring's official manifesto of Nazi loyalty.

Against the political neutrality of the IAAGP, the first issue of the newly reorganized *Zentralblatt* featured a message of Nazi conformity: *"Mitteilung des Reichsführers der 'Deutschen allgemeinen ärztlichen Gesellschaft für Psychotherapie'"* ["Statement of the *Reichsführer* of the 'German General Medical Society for Psychotherapy'"], by Matthias Heinrich Göring.[8] No explanation was ever given for the "mistake" of publishing a statement of *Gleichschaltung* in the first issue of the "neutral" IAAGP journal. The piece was inserted in the *Zentralblatt* by the secretary of the German *Landesgruppe*, either by mistake, as he claimed, or perhaps because the first issue of the German *Sonderheft* – where Göring's manifesto should properly have appeared – was delayed.[9]

The placement of a Nazi loyalty statement immediately after Jung's editorial not only violated the neutrality of the IAAGP but also cast doubt on Jung's own position. Jung protested to several people.[10] Cimbal, secretary of the German section, heartily apologized for his mistake;[11] but the damage to Jung's reputation was dramatic.

This is not the place for a detailed discussion of Jung's own writings at the time, or the degree to which they may have reflected a dubious attitude toward National Socialism. When considering how the *Zentralblatt* fared under his editorship, however, it should be noted that the first two issues contained statements by Jung himself for which he later found it necessary to apologize.[12] Gustav Bally's

---

8 *Zentralblatt*, Band 6.3, 1933, pp. 140f.
9 Walter Cimbal, *"Bericht des Geschäftsführers"* [Report of the General Secretary], ibid., p. 141.
10 E.g. Jung to Cimbal, 2 March 1934, *Letters I*, pp. 145f.
11 Cimbal to Jung, 4 March 1934, ETH Library archive.
12 Kirsch later described Jung's heartfelt apology to him in August 1947, the first time they met face to face after the war, for his ill-timed and ill-chosen words in the 1934 issue of *Zentralblatt* (Kirsch to Ernst Simon, 19 June 1962; similarly to Heinrich Fierz, 3 January 1983, Kirsch archive). The story of Jung's apology to Rabbi Leo Baeck, and its effect not only on Baeck but also on Gershom Scholem, can be read in Jaffé, *Life and Work*, pp. 99f.

outraged article, *"'Deutschstämmige' Psychotherapie?"* ["'German-born' Psycho-therapy?"],[13] was prompted by ambiguities in Jung's own words. In *"Geleitwort des Herausgebers"* ["Editorial"] in the December 1933 issue of the *Zentralblatt,* Jung emphasized the contrast between "Germanic" and "Jewish" psychology.[14] The idea of collective psychologies, which differ from one culture to another, was a well-established strand of Jung's thought. He vigorously denied, then and later, that his words had had any anti-Semitic implication. Whatever his intent, however, it was a moment in history when the use of such language had a profoundly troubling resonance. The impact of Jung's problematic writings at this time, both in the last *Zentralblatt* issue of 1933 and the first of 1934,[15] comes under discussion in the present volume, especially in May–June 1934.[16]

One positive achievement Jung claimed at this time was that, by the charter signed in May 1934 at Bad Nauheim, the IAAGP was legally defined as being "above" the policies of any of its national sections. In practical terms, this meant that German Jewish psychiatrists and psychotherapists could apply for individual membership through the IAAGP. This direct access helped some Jewish psychotherapists to continue to practice in Germany, at least for a time.[17] Jung points to this achievement

13 Gustav Bally, "Deutschstämmige Psychotherapie?", *Neue Zürcher Zeitung,* 27 February 1934 (cf. Kirsch, 7 May 1934, p. 40 and note).

14 C. G. Jung, "Geleitwort des Herausgebers," *Zentralblatt,* Band 6, Nr. 3, pp. 139f. Cf. CW 10, ¶1014ff.

15 C. G. Jung, "Zur gegenwärtigen Lage der Psychotherapie," *Zentralblatt,* Band 7.1 (Leipzig: Hirzel Verlag, 1934, pp. 1–16). Cf. CW 10, ¶330–70. Another piece of writing by Jung in the same year, discussed as problematic by Andrew Samuels in *The Political Psyche* (London & New York: Routledge, 1993, p. 298), is a birthday greeting to Dr. Robert Sommer, co-authored with M. H. Göring, in which Sommer's work on family, heredity and race (*Familienforschung, Vererbungs- und Rassenlehre*) is singled out for praise (*Zentralblatt,* Band 7.3, 1934, pp. 313f).

16 Cf. Kirsch, 7 May 1934 and 8 June 1934, pp. 40ff and 48ff; Jung, 26 May 1934, pp. 44ff.

17 Later, trying to persuade a friend in Jerusalem that Jung had made no compromise with Nazism, Kirsch praised Jung for arranging this individual membership in the IAAGP, by which Jewish psychotherapists could maintain their professional standing: "Jung made it possible for Jewish analysts (especially Freudians) to continue practicing in Nazi Germany – my first wife amongst them" (Kirsch to Ernst Simon, 19 June 1962, Kirsch archive).

in his letter to Kirsch, 26 May 1934. It often plays a part in the defenses mounted on his behalf, then and later, against imputations of anti-Semitism.[18]

Protected to some degree by Swiss citizenship, Jung could lead the newly restructured IAAGP. He could not, however, prevent the German chapter – the largest and most powerful national section under the "umbrella" – from intruding in the affairs of the IAAGP or attempting to control the editorial policy of the *Zentralblatt*. Documents of the time suggest that pressure from the German section to publish anti-Semitic writings and exclude the writings of Jews was constant and required constant negotiations. Some members of the German *Landesgruppe*, submitting papers to the *Zentralblatt* for publication, had fully embraced the Nazi ideology. Egregiously racist writings were rejected for publication. Others, however, with implicitly racial and nationalist themes, were sometimes accepted. Over against this, it must be said that the inclusion of writings by Jewish psychotherapists, and the refusal to publish the worst anti-Jewish offerings,[19] represent a solid achievement in the circumstances.

Looking back on the challenges of the era, C. A. Meier scoffed at the idea that Nazi colleagues ever really controlled the content of the journal:

> Where the *Zentralblatt* is concerned, there were never two editions. On the contrary, I made sure that even during the Nazi era we could publish works by Jewish colleagues. Also, I had to keep either correcting or suppressing critical and erroneous reviews of Jewish books and articles. This was all pretty easy, because up to the end I had a completely free hand. Officially, Jung was part of it until the end; but from the beginning

---

18 Jung's defenders over the years have pointed to this and to several other kinds of evidence, includ-
    ing his help to Jewish colleagues fleeing Germany, his increasingly dire warnings about Hitler
    and National Socialism over the 1930s, the fact that by 1940 he was himself on a Nazi black-
    list, and his work with Allen Dulles for American intelligence (Kirsch to Ernst Simon, 10 May
    1963, Kirsch archive). On the last point, cf. esp. Deirdre Bair, *Jung*, op. cit., pp. 486–95. Essays
    by Jung's first-generation Jewish colleagues include Jaffé's "Jung and National Socialism," in
    Life and Work; and Kirsch's "Reconsidering." In the past 20 years, members of the Jungian
    community have published historical studies on the topic, including two collections of essays:
    Aryeh Maidenbaum and Stephen Martin, eds., *Lingering Shadows: Jungians, Freudians, and
    Anti-Semitism* (Boston & London: Shambhala, 1991), and Aryeh Maidenbaum, ed, *Jung and the
    Shadow of Anti-Semitism* (Berwick, ME: Nicolas-Hays, Inc., 2003).
19 An example of editorial screening is found in a letter from Jung to the president of the German
    Landesgruppe, Matthias Göring, explaining that his review, of a book systematically demeaning
    toward Jewish history and religion, could not be printed in the *Zentralblatt* (Jung to M. H. Göring,
    16 November 1937, *Letters I*, p. 238). Göring's review was on *Der Mythus des 20. Jahrhunderts*
    (1930), by Alfred Rosenberg, which is described by Gerhard Adler as "the most egregious exposi-
    tion and pseudo-scientific foundation of the Nazi doctrines on civilization" (ibid., p. 238n).

he had left everything to me. In later years they forced a German co-editor on me. This was Curtius; but he never did anything either.[20]

(Meier to Kirsch, 28 February 1980, Kirsch archive)

Basic information about the AAGP/IAAGP will be difficult for many readers to locate, so it may be helpful here to provide a list of the Society's major meetings. Until the Depression and Hitler's rise to power, AAGP congresses were held annually. The annual congresses[21] are listed below, from the inception of the AAGP in 1926 through Jung's resignation in 1940.

Annual meetings of the AAGP/IAAGP
(Internationale) Allgemeine Ärztliche Gesellschaft für Psychotherapie

Date	Title of annual meeting; Official name of society	Location
1926	"Der Allgemeine Ärztliche Kongress"; die Kongress-Organisation für Psychotherapie.	Baden-Baden, Germany
1927 April	"Der 2. Allgemeine Ärztliche Kongress"; die Kongress-Organisation für Psychotherapie.	Bad Nauheim, Germany
1928 April	"Der 3. Allgemeine Ärztliche Kongress"; die Allgemeine ärztliche Gesellschaft für Psychotherapie.	Baden-Baden, Germany
1929 April	"Der 4. Allgemeine Ärztliche Kongress"; die Allgemeine ärztliche Gesellschaft für Psychotherapie.	Bad Nauheim, Germany
1930 April	"Der 5. Allgemeine Ärztliche Kongress"; die Allgemeine ärztliche Gesellschaft für Psychotherapie.	Baden-Baden, Germany
1931 May	"Der 6. Allgemeine Ärztliche Kongress"; die Allgemeine ärztliche Gesellschaft für Psychotherapie.	Dresden, Germany

20 *"Was das Zentralblatt betrifft, so hat es nie zweierlei Ausgaben gegeben, hingegen habe ich es durchgesetzt, dass wir noch während der Nazi-Zeit Arbeiten von jüdischen Kollegen publizieren konnten. Ich musste auch immer wieder beschimpfende und unrichtige Referate über jüdische Bücher und Artikel entweder korrigieren oder unterdrücken. Dies war alles relativ leicht, weil ich bis zum Schluss vollkommen freie Hand hatte. Offiziell war Jung bis zum Schluss dabei, hatte aber von Anfang an alles mir überlassen. In den späteren Jahren hat man mir dann einen deutschen Ko-Editor aufgedrängt. Dies war Curtius, aber auch er hat nie etwas getan"* (Meier to Kirsch, 28 February 1980, Kirsch archive; document kindly provided by Deborah Wesley, archivist of the C. G. Jung Institute of Los Angeles).

21 According to Geoffrey Cocks, the last international congress was held in Oxford in 1938.

(1932)	*[meeting postponed to avoid financial hardship for German doctors]*	
(1933) (April)	*[meeting cancelled by Kretschmer, who then resigned]*	(Vienna, Austria)
1934 May	"Der 7. Kongress für Psychotherapie." *[Jung presided at this meeting, at which the IAAGP was formally created, separate from the German AAGP.[22]]*	Bad Nauheim, Germany
1935 March	"Der 8. Allgemeine Ärztliche Kongress"; die Internationale allgemeine ärztliche Gesellschaft für Psychotherapie.	Bad Nauheim, Germany
(1936)	*[Congress scheduled to take place in the neutral Netherlands.[23] Dutch leadership cancelled the congress in December 1935, stating they feared that German politics would dominate the proceedings. Feeling that the purpose of the IAAGP was being undermined and his leadership questioned, and fearing that Germany would become the location for all subsequent congresses, in January 1936 Jung threatened to resign as president.]*	(Amsterdam, Netherlands)
1937	"Der 9. Allgemeine Ärztliche Kongress"; die Internationale allgemeine ärztliche Gesellschaft für Psychotherapie.	Copenhagen, Denmark
1938 29 July – 2 August	"Der 10. Allgemeine Ärztliche Kongress"; die Internationale allgemeine ärztliche Gesellschaft für Psychotherapie. *[At a special gathering, 1 August 1938, Jung met with English delegates and members to plan his resignation.]*	Oxford, England
1939 July	Delegiertenversammlung (Meeting of Delegates). *[Jung attended. The purpose was to arrange new leadership and to plan the Congress of 1940 in a neutral country.]*	Zurich, Switzerland

---

22 The German *Landesgruppe* kept the old organizational name as part of its new name, becoming officially the *Deutsche allgemeine ärztliche Gesellschaft für Psychotherapie*.

23 Many thanks to Thomas Fischer, who helped me to grasp this sequence of events in 1935–36, based mainly on the letters of Jung and J. H. Van der Hoop (ETH Library archive). (Cf. also *Letters I*, pp. 149ff, 184f.)

1940   Delegiertenversammlung (Meeting of Delegates).   Vienna,
September *[Jung had submitted his resignation in July 1940.*   Austria
             M. H. Göring, now president of both the German
             AAGP and the IAAGP, presided over this planning
             meeting in September, to which Jung sent C. A.
             Meier as a delegate and observer. After this, until the
             end of the war, the IAAGP and Zentralblatt were run
             from Berlin.]

Further details about Jung's role in the organization, and about various key participants – Cimbal, Kranefeldt, Kretschmer, Kronfeld, Künkel, Schultz and others – are found in the pages of this volume and in the annotations. Again, interested readers are referred to Geoffrey Cocks's thoroughgoing analysis, *Psychotherapy in the Third Reich*, cited above.

EDITOR'S NOTE

The primary text

Many steps are involved in transforming the raw materials of a correspondence – letters and enclosed documents – into a text suitable for publication. Once all the basic documents of the Jung–Kirsch correspondence were in hand, from whatever source and in whatever language, the first step was to transcribe them all. The transcriptions were then patiently double-checked against the originals. Many of the original letters are handwritten, and some passages are almost impossible to read. It soon became clear how fortunate we are that Ursula Egli's education equips her to decipher the handwriting of Swiss and German writers from the early years of the past century. Two readers, Ulrich Hoerni and I, then studied the transcriptions and compared them with the originals. Corrections were made as needed.[1]

After the text was established and the accuracy of the transcriptions confirmed, we were ready to begin the translations. Here the project took a turn we had not anticipated. Ursula Egli had been assigned the task of translating, while as editor I was mainly responsible for stylistic corrections. We discovered, however, as the months went by, that each of us brought a different and essential set of gifts to the process of translating. Eventually it became clear that the job called for nearly equal participation from us both. I can manage stylistic shadings in my own language, but I lack native facility with German, so I miss subtleties (and occasionally get the meaning absolutely wrong). Ursula, born in Zurich, has Swiss-German as her first language, and the variants of High German are no secret to her. English, in which she has excellent skills, is still a non-native language,

---

1 Details in the transcriptions continued to be corrected as long as research was going on. For example, a footnote required work, and research for this purpose led to the writings of a biblical scholar, referred to in a somewhat obscure source, whose work correlated exactly with the subject of the passage to which the problem footnote was attached. Suddenly, the hitherto illegible name in that handwritten passage was not "*Scholder?*" but Schaeder (p. 190).

with the result that her English versions tend toward more formality than one sees in the original texts.

At some point we began a mutual process of translation and correction. Ursula was usually the first translator. I studied her English versions, compared them with the originals, and revised for style. Where theological or psychological terms were involved, I sometimes also corrected for meaning. Then Ursula corrected my revisions, and together we resolved problem passages. As a final step, I sent our "finished" translations of all the letters to the representatives of the Jung and Kirsch estates. Ulrich Hoerni read through them on behalf of the Foundation of the Works of C. G. Jung and participated in the discussion of passages still in need of work. Thomas Kirsch, representing the Kirsch Estate, offered suggestions and clarifications. In their final form, the translations are the result of a team effort by Ursula Egli and Ann Lammers, approved by the heirs of James Kirsch and C. G. Jung.

Annotations

Since the great preponderance of letters in this volume are translations, which suffer inevitably from the losses, approximations and compromises that even the best translation process entails, many linguistic footnotes are included. These point out the writers' linguistic mistakes, ambiguities, and invented phrases. They also highlight words with historical connotations and other irreducible particularities of the original text.

Aside from commenting on issues of translation, in preparing this volume I may have erred on the side of what a friendly critic hinted was "too much of a good thing." I acknowledge the failing. I find, though, that when publishing letters from an earlier period and an unfamiliar culture, the editor should give enough background so that readers will know – if possible – what the original writer intended and the original reader understood. Jung and Kirsch didn't need to spell out their glancing references; each of them knew whereof they wrote. But to penetrate the distance which separates us from these writers' times and places, I've tried to give enough information so that, with patience and imagination, today's reader can enter into their world.

Privacy and confidentiality

Editorial policies for this volume, regarding privacy and confidentiality, are set by agreement with the Stiftung der Werke von C. G. Jung and with the Kirsch Estate, copyright holders for the letters of Jung and Kirsch, respectively. Their permission to publish the correspondence is foundational to the book. In addition, an initial agreement – signed by representatives of the Jung and Kirsch estates, an official of the ETH, and the book's editor and translator – refers to the careful treatment of "sensitive" passages. Later, contracts were signed with the publisher, which include specific guidelines for the protection of medical confidentiality and personal privacy.[2]

In most cases these guidelines have been followed without difficulty. For example, when a patient is named, in a passage concerning clinical diagnosis or treatment, permission has been sought from the patient's heirs. If the heirs cannot be found, or if permission is not forthcoming, the normal procedure is to conceal the patient's name. Fortunately, this has been necessary in only a few cases.[3] I am profoundly grateful to the heirs of patients who graciously gave permission to publish their family members' names in this volume.

Exceptionally, however, after careful consideration, the names of two identified patients have been allowed to stand, although it was impossible to locate anyone who could answer for their estates.[4] After consultation with all parties to the book's publication, I take full responsibility for letting their names appear in the text.

Ann Conrad Lammers, Editor

2 In Swiss and European law, the term *Persönlichkeitsschutz* (personality rights) is commonly used. It has no exact analog in English and US law, but combines elements of libel law and medical confidentiality, to which is added a somewhat flexible concept of individual and family privacy. Editorial guidelines, devised in 2002, help an American editor negotiate these boundaries while giving final authority to the holders of copyright (cf. "Editorial Note," *Jung–White Letters*, pp. 361f).

3 Square brackets and ellipsis– [...] –indicate where a name is concealed by the editor. Where a name is omitted or abbreviated by Jung or Kirsch, the lacuna is shown as in the original, usually with a first initial, sometimes with an ellipsis.

4 Cf. Kirsch, 25 December 1935, p. 75 and note; Jung, 20 January 1960, p. 253 and note.

TRANSLATORS' NOTE

Letters originally written in German – the main part of the correspondence – are translated in a style as close as possible to the style of the original. The writers' errors and verbal oddities (misspelled names, ungrammatical phrasings) are allowed to show in translation, with comments in the footnotes when needed. Their typical abbreviations are also carried over into English. For example, *das Ubw* (for *das Unbewusste*) is rendered "the ucs" (for "the unconscious").

Similarly, letters that were originally written in English are reproduced as written, without making improvements in the writers' non-native diction. This means there are contrasts in the text between the majority of the letters (translated from German) and the minority (originally written in English). The translated letters have, or are intended to have, the stylistic naturalness and fluidity of texts written in a native language. But occasional awkward or stilted phrasings can be expected when anyone, no matter how gifted, writes in a second language. So the handful of letters originally composed in English (a competent second language for both Jung and Kirsch) often convey hints of each writer's German or Swiss-German "accent."

When Gerhard Adler was editing the *C. G. Jung Letters* for publication, he asked R. F. C. Hull to "improve" Jung's English-language letters,[1] bringing them closer to standard English. The editorial decision to correct Jung's English may have made sense in context, but it sometimes led to changing the writer's meaning.[2] Rather than subjecting Jung's and Kirsch's English-language letters to a similar brushing-up, we have chosen to respect the original texts, even though it often meant leaving the edges rough. A benefit is that the reader has a clearer sense of Kirsch's growth as a writer. His later letters in English are noticeably more fluent than those he composed soon after his arrival in the United States.

Greetings and closings are famously hard to translate. Throughout their lives, Jung and Kirsch addressed each other with the polite form of *"Sie"* in German

---

1 Cf. G. Adler, "Introduction," *Letters I*, p. xviii. This editorial policy was consistent with the original intention for Jung's *Letters* (*Briefe*), which were expected, at first, to form part of the Collected Works.
2 Cf. A. Lammers, "Introduction," *Jung–White Letters*, p. xxix.

and never used first names. Consequently their use of language is conventional, even though their writing style is direct and at times quite muscular. Greetings and closings in their letters are rather formal, as was the custom in the middle of the twentieth century, and have been standardized in translation.

Idiomatic phrases are sometimes quoted in German in the text and translated and/or explained in a footnote. In other instances, especially where a term is invented, or idiosyncratic, or has a variety of connotations, the translated text is referenced with the original language in a footnote. Words in other languages – notably Hebrew and Latin – are treated similarly.

Because this is primarily a work of translation, we cannot pretend that most of the letters printed here are the ones Jung and Kirsch actually wrote to each other. We have tried to convey the energy and unconventionality that so often characterize Jung's writing, while maintaining the relative formality of a medical professional, writing in German, in the middle of the twentieth century. A similar balancing act was needed for Kirsch's letters. Any translation involves compromises, but we have stayed as close as possible to the sense and style of the originals.

Ursula Egli and Ann Conrad Lammers, Translators

LIST OF LETTERS

I. Letters to James Kirsch

Jung's letters to Kirsch, previously published*

19 Aug. 1929	*PP, L2*	29 Jan. 1953	*PP, L2*
15 Aug. 1930	*PP (excerpt)*	28 May 1953	*PP, L2*
12 Aug. 1931	*PP (excerpt)*	6 Aug. 1953	*PP (excerpt)*
12 March 1932	*PP (excerpt)*	2 Oct. 1953	*PP*
20 Jan. 1933	*PP (excerpt)*	16 Feb. 1954	*PP, L2 (excerpt)*
20 Feb. 1934	*PP (excerpt)*	5 March 1954	*PP, L2 (excerpt)*
26 May 1934	*PP, L1, and in*	23 June 1954	*PP (excerpt)*
	Psychiatric Quarterly	11 Sept. 1954	*PP (excerpt)*
16 Aug. 1934	*PP*	11 Jan. 1955	*PP*
29 Sept. 1934	*PP, LI (excerpt)*	29 April 1958	*PP, L2*
17 Feb. 1935	*PP (excerpt)*	3 Nov. 1958	*PP*
25 July 1946	*PP (excerpt)*	10 Dec. 1958	*PP, L2*
12 July 1951	*PP (excerpt)*	12 Nov. 1959	*PP, L2*
18 Nov. 1952	*PP, L2*	10 Jan. 1960	*PP (excerpt)*
28 Nov. 1952	*PP (excerpt)*		

* Prev. pub. in *Psychological Perspectives (PP); C. G. Jung Letters, Vol. 1, Vol. 2 (L1, L2).*

Jung's letters to Kirsch, previously unpublished

16 Nov. 1928	23 May 1932	31 July 1935	7 July 1948
9 Nov. 1929	6 June 1932	30 Aug. 1935	30 Sept. 1948
17 March 1930	25 June 1932	16 Sept. 1935	12 July 1949
14 April 1930	26 Sept. 1932	3 Jan. 1936	16 Oct. 1950
2 June 1930	28 Jan. 1933	27 Jan. 1936	16 May 1951
23 Sept. 1930	3 Feb. 1933	7 Feb. 1936	19 May 1954
27 Oct. 1930	17 Feb. 1933	19 May 1936	21 June 1956
13 Dec. 1930	28 Feb. 1933	25 June 1936	25 July 1956
6 Feb. 1931	6 May 1933	1 Aug. 1936	12 July 1958
13 Feb. 1931	31 Aug. 1933	12 Aug. 1936	Christmas 1958
20 July 1931	11 June 1934	19 July 1938	20 Jan. 1960
20 Feb. 1932	2 July 1934	6 Jan. 1941	12 Feb. 1960
6 April 1932	7 June 1935	3 Aug. 1945	

Jung's letters to Hilde Kirsch (Hildegard Silber), previously unpublished

11 June 1934	15 Oct. 1954
8 Feb. 1935	18 March 1959
2 Sept. 1939	2 Nov. 1960
5 May 1941	

Secretaries' letters to Kirsch, previously unpublished

From Marianne Jung

17 Nov. 1930   28 Nov. 1930

From Marie-Jeanne Schmid

21 Oct. 1947 *(unsigned)*

From Una Thomas

20 Oct. 1952

From Aniela Jaffé

22 Nov. 1952	4 Jan. 1958	15 Feb. 1960
11 Sept. 1955	20 March 1958	26 Feb. 1960
31 Oct. 1955	6 Dec. 1958	3 Oct. 1960
20 Dec. 1955	10 Dec. 1958	3 March 1961
1 Feb. 1956	3 Feb. 1960	27 May 1961

From unidentified secretaries

17 July 1953   2 July 1958

II. Letters from James Kirsch

Kirsch's letters to Jung, previously unpublished

Date	Location	Date	Location
Summer 1931 (paper)	Berlin	2 July 1949	Zurich
28 July 1931	Berlin	5 Aug. 1949	Los Angeles
20 Aug. 1931	Berlin	9 Sept. 1949	Los Angeles
28 Nov. 1932	Berlin	1 Oct. 1950	Los Angeles
7 May 1934	Tel Aviv	20 May 1951	Zurich
8 June 1934 (with	Tel Aviv	23 Nov. 1952	Los Angeles
"Schlusswort")		10 Dec. 1952	Los Angeles
26 Aug. 1934	Tel Aviv	28 Dec. 1952	Los Angeles
28 May 1935	Zurich	22 Feb. 1953	Los Angeles
19 June 1935	London	17 March 1953	Los Angeles
9 July 1935	London	14 April 1953	Los Angeles
Aug. 1935	London	18 April 1953	Los Angeles
25 Dec. 1935	London	9 May 1953	Los Angeles
14 Jan. 1936	London	14 June 1953	Los Angeles
1 Feb. 1936	London	14 Sept. 1953	Los Angeles
9 March 1936	London	(with"Preface to	
3 May 1936	London	the Eastern	
20 June 1936	London	Reader")	
25 July 1936	London	18 Oct. 1953	Los Angeles
4 Aug. 1936	London	1 Jan. 1954	Los Angeles
11 Sept. 1936	London	5 Feb. 1954	Los Angeles
13 July 1938	Los Angeles	14 Feb. 1954 (with Hull	Los Angeles
19 Nov. 1940	Los Angeles	correspondence)	
25 Nov. 1944 (with Hilde	Los Angeles	14 March 1954	Los Angeles
Kirsch's letter)		7 May 1954	Los Angeles
18 Nov. 1945	Los Angeles	7 June 1954	Los Angeles
22 June 1946	Los Angeles	27 Nov. 1954	Beverly Hills
5 July 1946	Guatemala	23 Jan. 1955	Beverly Hills
22 Dec. 1946	Los Angeles	11 June 1955	Beverly Hills
16 Sept. 1948	Los Angeles	7 June 1956	Beverly Hills
21 Sept. 1948	Los Angeles	8 July 1958	Zurich
29 Sept. 1948	Los Angeles	Aug. 1958	Tokyo
15 Nov. 1948	Los Angeles	9 Oct. 1958	Los Angeles
27 Nov. 1948	Los Angeles	2 Dec. 1958	Los Angeles
26 Dec. 1948	Los Angeles	15 March 1959	Los Angeles
28 May 1949	Zurich	19 Nov. 1959	Los Angeles
21 June 1949	Zurich	26 Jan. 1960	Los Angeles
27 June 1949	Zurich	31 Jan. 1960	Los Angeles
		21 Feb. 1960	Los Angeles

Kirsch's letters to other recipients

To Una Thomas

19 Nov. 1952   Los Angeles

To Frl. Gautschi

12 Dec. 1953   Zurich

To R. F. C. Hull

11 Feb. 1954   Los Angeles

To Aniela Jaffé

| 10 Jan. 1956 | Beverly Hills | 4 May 1960 | Los Angeles |
| 10 Feb. 1960 | Los Angeles | | |

Letters from Hilde Kirsch to C. G. Jung

3 June 1936	London	31 Jan. 1960	Zurich
13 Aug. 1939	London	31 Oct. 1960	Zurich
25 Nov. 1944	Los Angeles		

SELECTED BIBLIOGRAPHY

Note: This bibliography lists all the works of C. G. Jung and James Kirsch cited in the text and footnotes of this volume. Further information on Jung's writings may be found in *General Bibliography*, Collected Works, 19 (1979) and in *Bibliographie*, Gesammelte Werke, 19 (1983). Many of Kirsch's writings are unpublished, so certain titles under his name are listed as typescripts, with the names of pertinent archives. A brief list of secondary works is provided. For all other works cited in this volume, please consult the Index and annotations.

* * *

Primary Sources

"C. G. Jung – James Kirsch Correspondence" (HS 1056), C. G. Jung Archive, Department of Manuscripts and Legacies, Archive of the Swiss Federal Institute of Technology, Zurich. [Korrespondenz C. G. Jung – James Kirsch (HS 1056), C. G. Jung-Arbeitsarchiv, Hauptabteilung Handschriften und Nachlässe des Archivs der ETH Zürich.]

"C. G. Jung – James Kirsch Correspondence," Archive of James Isaac Kirsch (documents dating from 1928 to 1988), overseen by Dr. Thomas Kirsch, Palo Alto, California.

* * *

The Collected Works of C. G. Jung

The Collected Works of C. G. Jung. Edited by Herbert Read, Michael Fordham, and Gerhard Adler; executive editor (from 1967), William McGuire. Translated by R. F. C. Hull, except as noted. New York: Pantheon Books for Bollingen Foundation, 1953–60; Bollingen Foundation (distributed by Pantheon Books, a Division of Random House), 1961–67; Princeton University Press, 1967–68 (Bollingen Series XX). London: Routledge & Kegan Paul, 1953–78. The New York and London editions are identical except for title pages and bindings. Reprintings vary.

The volumes of Collected Works are listed below in numerical order, for reference. They do not contain all the works cited by Jung and Kirsch. (See detailed bibliography listings.)

Collected Works, 1, *Psychiatric Studies*, 1957/1970.

Collected Works, 2, *Experimental Researches*, translated by Leopold Stein in collaboration with Diana Riviere, 1973.

Collected Works, 3, *The Psychogenesis of Mental Disease*, 1960.

Collected Works, 4, *Freud and Psychoanalysis*, 1961.

Collected Works, 5, *Symbols of Transformation: An Analysis of the Prelude to a Case of Schizophrenia*, 1956/1967.

Collected Works, 6, *Psychological Types*, 1971.

Collected Works, 7, *Two Essays on Analytical Psychology*, 1953/1966.

Collected Works, 8, *The Structure and Dynamics of the Psyche*, 1960/1969.

Collected Works, 9(i), *The Archetypes and the Collective Unconscious*, 1959/1968.

Collected Works, 9(ii), *Aion: Researches into the Phenomenology of the Self*, 1958/1968.

Collected Works, 10, *Civilization in Transition*, 1964.

Collected Works, 11, *Psychology and Religion: West and East*, 1958/1969.

Collected Works, 12, *Psychology and Alchemy*, 1953/1968.

Collected Works, 13, *Alchemical Studies*, 1967.

Collected Works, 14, *Mysterium Coniunctionis: An Inquiry into the Separation and Synthesis of Psychic Opposites in Alchemy*, 1963/1970.

Collected Works, 15, *The Spirit in Man, Art and Literature*, 1966.

Collected Works, 16, *The Practice of Psychotherapy: Essays on the Psychology of the Transference and Other Subjects*, 1954/1966.

Collected Works, 17, *The Development of Personality*, 1954.

Collected Works, 18, *The Symbolic Life: Miscellaneous Writings*, 1975.

* * *

Die Gesammelten Werke von C. G. Jung

Die Gesammelten Werke von C. G. Jung. Herausgegeben von Marianne Niehus-Jung, Lena Hurwitz-Eisner, Franz Riklin, Lilly Jung-Merker, and Elisabeth Rüf, Zürich: Rascher-Verlag, 1958–70. Olten: Walter Verlag, 1971–81.

The volumes of the Gesammelte Werke are listed below in numerical order, for reference. They do not contain all the works cited by Jung and Kirsch. (See detailed bibliography listings.)

Gesammelte Werke, 1, *Psychiatrische Studien*, 1966.

Gesammelte Werke, 2, *Experimentelle Untersuchungen*, 1978.

Gesammelte Werke, 3, *Psychogenese der Geisteskrankheiten*, 1968.

Gesammelte Werke, 4, *Freud und die Psychoanalyse*, 1969.

Gesammelte Werke, 5, *Symbole der Wandlung: Analyse des Vorspiels zu einer Schizophrenie*, 1973.

Gesammelte Werke, 6, *Psychologische Typen*, 1971.

Gesammelte Werke, 7, *Zwei Schriften über Analytische Psychologie*, 1964.

Gesammelte Werke, 8, *Die Dynamik des Unbewussten*, 1967.

Gesammelte Werke, 9(i), *Die Archetypen und das kollektive Unbewusste*, 1976.

Gesammelte Werke, 9(ii), *Aion: Beiträge zur Symbolik des Selbst*, 1976.

Gesammelte Werke, 10, *Zivilisation im Übergang*, 1974.

Gesammelte Werke, 11, *Zur Psychologie westlicher und östlicher Religion*, 1963/1973.

Gesammelte Werke, 12, *Psychologie und Alchemie*, 1972.

Gesammelte Werke, 13, *Studien über alchemistische Vorstellungen*, 1978.

Gesammelte Werke, 14, *Mysterium Coniunctionis: Untersuchung über die Trennung und Zusammensetzung der seelischen Gegensätze in der Alchemie*, 1968.

Gesammelte Werke, 15, *Über das Phänomen des Geistes in Kunst und Wissenschaft*, 1971.

Gesammelte Werke, 16, *Praxis der Psychotherapie. Beiträge zum Problem der Psychotherapie und zur Psychologie der Übertragung*, 1958.

Gesammelte Werke, 17, *Über die Entwicklung der Persönlichkeit*, 1972.

Gesammelte Werke, 18, *Das symbolische Leben: Verschiedene Schriften*, 1981.

* * *

Note: The text and notes of this volume refer to various editions and translations of Jung's works. Early editions of Jung's works are often hard to find. Titles of later editions and English translations may depart widely from the originals. This bibliography accordingly lists multiple editions of many works. Titles mentioned by Jung and Kirsch in their letters appear as main entries, listed alphabetically. Later editions and translations, bracketed and indented as sub-entries, are listed in chronological order. Because Jung and Kirsch sometimes refer to the original edition of a work, as well as to later editions and translations, some works appear in this bibliography both as sub-entries (bracketed and indented) and as main entries. When a Collected Works edition contains the first published English translation of one of Jung's writings, that edition may be listed as the only sub-entry for the work in question.

Jung, C. G.

Aion: Untersuchungen zur Symbolgeschichte, Unter Mitarbeit von M.-L. von Franz, Psychologische Abhandlungen 8, Zürich: Rascher-Verlag, 1951.

[*Aion: Researches into the Phenomenology of the Self*, CW 9(ii)]

Antwort auf Hiob, Zürich: Rascher-Verlag, 1952.

[*Answer to Job*, translated by R. F. C. Hull, London: Routledge & Kegan Paul, 1954; Great Neck, New York: Pastoral Psychology Book Club, 1956]

["Answer to Job," CW 11, ¶553–758.]

"Der Aufgang einer neuen Welt', *Neue Zürcher Zeitung*, Bücher-Beilage, 7 December 1930, p. 6.

["The Rise of a New World," CW 10, ¶925–34.]

Aufsätze zur Zeitgeschichte, Zürich: Rascher-Verlag, 1946.

[*Essays on Contemporary Events*, translated by Elizabeth Welsh ("Preface," "After the Catastrophe," "Epilogue"); Barbara Hannah ("Wotan"); and Mary Briner ("Psychotherapy Today," "Psychotherapy and a Philosophy of Life"), London: Kegan Paul, Trench, Trubner, 1947.]

["Preface to 'Essays on Contemporary Events'," CW 10, pp. 177–78; "Wotan," CW 10, ¶371–99; "After the Catastrophe, CW 10, ¶400–43; "Epilogue to 'Essays on Contemporary Events'," CW 10, ¶458–87; "Psychotherapy and a Philosophy of Life," CW 16, ¶175–91; "Psychotherapy Today," CW 16, ¶212–29.]

"Die Bedeutung der Psychologie für die Gegenwart," *Wirklichkeit der Seele: Anwendungen und Fortschritte der neueren Psychologie, mit Beiträgen von Hugo Rosenthal, Emma Jung, W. M. Kranefeldt*, Zürich: Rascher-Verlag, 1934, pp. 32–67.

["The Meaning of Psychology for Modern Man," CW 10, ¶276–332.]

"Die Bedeutung von Konstitution und Vererbung für die Psychologie," *Die Medizinische Welt*, Vol. 3.47, Berlin, November 1929, pp. 1677–79.

["The Significance of Constitution and Heredity in Psychology," CW 8, ¶220–31.]

Die Beziehung der Psychotherapie zur Seelsorge, Zürich: Rascher-Verlag, 1932.

["Psychotherapists or the Clergy," *Modern Man in Search of a Soul*, translated by W. S. Dell and Cary F. Baynes, New York: Harcourt Brace; London: Kegan Paul, 1933, pp. 255–82.]

["Psychotherapists or the Clergy," CW 11, ¶488–538.]

Die Beziehungen zwischen dem Ich und dem Unbewussten, Zürich: Rascher-Verlag, 1928.

["The Relations between the Ego and the Unconscious," CW 7, Part 2, ¶202–406.]

C. G. Jung Speaking: Interviews and Encounters, William McGuire and R. F. C. Hull, eds, with various translators, Princeton, NJ: Princeton University Press, 1977.

"C. G. Jung zu den fliegenden Untertassen," *Weltwoche*, Zürich: Jg. 22, Nr. 1078, 9 July 1954, n.p.

["C. G. Jung on flying saucers," *Bulletin*, Analytical Psychology Club of New York, Vol. 16.7, October 1954, pp. 7–14.]

[In CW 18, 1975, ¶1431–44.]

"The Challenge of the Christian Enigma. Letter to Upton Sinclair," *The New Republic*, 27 April 1953, pp. 18–19.

[In *C. G. Jung Letters*, Vol. 2, Jung to Sinclair, 3 November 1952, pp. 87–91.]

"Christus, ein Symbol des Selbst," Ch. V, *Aion: Untersuchungen zur Symbolgeschichte*, Unter Mitarbeit von M.-L. von Franz, Psychologische Abhandlungen 8, Zürich: Rascher-Verlag, 1951, pp. 63–110.

["Christ, a Symbol of the Self," *Aion*, CW 9(ii), ¶68–126.]

"The Christian Legend: An Interpretation. Letter to Upton Sinclair," *The New Republic*, Vol. 132.8, 21 February 1955, pp. 30–31.

[In *C. G. Jung Letters*, Vol. 2, Jung to Sinclair, 7 January 1955, pp. 201–08.]

Contributions to Analytical Psychology, translated, mainly from *Über die Energetik der Seele* (1928), by H. G. and Cary F. Baynes, New York: Harcourt Brace; London: Kegan Paul, Trench, Trubner, 1928.

["On Psychic Energy," CW 8, ¶1–130; "Instinct and the Unconscious," CW 8, ¶263–82; "General Aspects of Dream Psychology," CW 8, ¶443–529; "The Psychological Foundations of Belief in Spirits," CW 8, ¶570–600.]

Diagnostische Assoziationsstudien: Beiträge zur experimentellen Psychopathologie, Vol. I, II, Leipzig: Barth, 1906/1909.

"Dr. Hans Schmid-Guisan: In Memoriam," *Basler Nachrichten*, 25 April 1932, n.p.

["Dr. Hans Schmid-Guisan: In Memoriam," CW 18, 1975, ¶1713–15.]

"Einführung," *Das Tibetanische Totenbuch*, W. Y. Evans-Wentz, ed., Zürich: Rascher-Verlag, 1932, pp. 15–35.

["Psychological Commentary on 'The Tibetan Book of the Dead'," CW 11, ¶831–58.]

"Einführung," W. M. Kranefeldt, *Die Psychoanalyse*," Berlin und Leipzig: Walter de Gruyter, 1930, pp. 5–16.

["Introduction to Kranefeldt's *Secret Ways of the Mind*," CW 4, ¶745–67.]

"The English Seminars": "Analytical Psychology, 1925"; "Dream Analysis, 1938–30"; "The Kundalini Yoga, 1932"; "Interpretation of Visions, 1930–34," typescripts, Zurich, 1925–34, ETH Library archive.

[*Dream Analysis: Notes of the Seminar Given in 1928–1930*, William McGuire, ed., Princeton, NJ: Princeton University Press, 1984.]

[*Analytical Psychology: Notes of the Seminar Given in 1925*, William McGuire, ed., Princeton, NJ: Princeton University Press, 1989.]

[*The Psychology of Kundalini Yoga: Notes of the Seminar Given in 1932 by C. G. Jung*, Sonu Shamdasani, ed., Princeton, NJ: Princeton University Press, 1996.]

[*The Visions Seminars*, Claire Douglas, ed., Princeton, NJ: Princeton University Press, 1997.]

"Die Erdbedingtheit der Psyche," *Mensch und Erde*, Hermann Keyserling, ed., Darmstadt: Otto Reichl Verlag, 1927, pp. 83–137.

["Mind and Earth," CW 10, ¶49–103]

["The Structure of the Psyche," CW 8, ¶283–342.]

Erinnerungen, Träume, Gedanken, aufgezeichnet und herausgegeben von Aniela Jaffé, Zürich: Rascher-Verlag, 1962.

[*Memories, Dreams, Reflections*, recorded and edited by Aniela Jaffé, translated by Richard and Clara Winston, New York: Pantheon (Random House), 1962/1973.]

[First paperback edition: New York: Vintage Books (Random House), 1965.]

ETH lectures: "Modern Psychology," Vol. 1 and 2, Notes on Lectures given at the Eidgenössische Technische Hochschule, Zürich, October 1933–July 1935; "Modern Psychology," Vol. 3 and 4: Notes on Lectures given at the Eidgenössische Technische Hochschule, Zürich, October 1938–March 1940; "Alchemy," Vol. 1 and 2, The Process of Individuation: Notes on Lectures given at the Eidgenössische Technische Hochschule, Zürich, November 1940–July 1941, unpub. typescripts from listeners' notes; translated by Barbara Hannah, Zurich, 1933–1941.

"'Face to Face' Interview" (Transcription of Jung's interview on BBC television by John Freeman, 22 October 1959), in *C. G. Jung Speaking: Interviews and Encounters*, William McGuire and R. F. C. Hull, eds, Princeton, NJ: Princeton University Press, 1977, pp. 424–39.

"Der Geist der Psychologie," *Eranos-Jahrbuch 1946*, Herausgegeben von Olga Fröbe-Kapteyn, Zürich: Rhein-Verlag, 1947. pp. 385–490.
["Theoretische Überlegungen zum Wesen des Psychischen," *Von den Wurzeln des Bewusstseins*, 1954, pp. 497–608.]
["On the Nature of the Psyche," CW 8, ¶343–442.]

"Geleitwort des Herausgebers," *Zentralblatt für Psychotherapie und ihre Grenzgebiete*, VI.3, December 1933, pp. 139–40.
["Editorial," *Zentralblatt*, VI (1933)," CW 10, ¶1014–15.]

"The German Seminars," "Bericht über das deutsche Seminar von Dr. C. G. Jung, 6.–11. Oktober 1930 in Küsnacht-Zürich," pp. 1–113; "Bericht über das deutsche Seminar von Dr. C. G. Jung, 5.–10. Oktober 1931 in Küsnacht-Zürich," pp. 1–153; unpub. typescripts, collected by Olga von Koenig-Fachsenfeld, Stuttgart, 1931, 1932.

Die Gestaltungen des Unbewussten, Mit einem Beitrag von Aniela Jaffé, Psychologische Abhandlungen 7, Zürich: Rascher-Verlag, 1950.

The Integration of the Personality, translated, mainly from *Wirklichkeit der Seele* (1934), and *Eranos-Jahrbücher* (1935, 1936), by Stanley Dell, New York: Farrar & Rinehart, 1939.

"An Interview on Radio Berlin, Conducted by Adolf Weizsäcker, June 26, 1933," *C. G. Jung Speaking: Interviews and Encounters*, William McGuire and R. F. C. Hull, eds, translated by R. F. C. Hull, Princeton, NJ: Princeton University Press, 1977, pp. 59–66.

Memories, Dreams, Reflections, recorded and edited by Aniela Jaffé, translated by Richard and Clara Winston, New York: Pantheon (Random House), 1962/1973.
[First paperback edition: New York: Vintage Books (Random House), 1965.]

Modern Man in Search of a Soul, translated by W. S. Dell and Cary F. Baynes, New York: Harcourt Brace; London: Kegan Paul, 1933.

Ein moderner Mythus: Von Dingen, die am Himmel gesehen werden, Zürich: Rascher, 1958.
["Flying Saucers: A Modern Myth of Things Seen in the Skies," CW 10, ¶589–824.]

Mysterium Coniunctionis: Untersuchung über die Trennung und Zusammensetzung der seelischen Gegensätze in der Alchemie, Psychologische Abhandlungen 10, Unter Mitarbeit von Marie-Louise von Franz, Zürich: Rascher-Verlag, 1955.

"Nach der Katastrophe," *Neue Schweizer Rundschau*, XIII.2, Zürich, June 1945, pp. 67–88.

["After the Catastrophe," CW 10, 1964, ¶400–43.]

Nietzsche's Zarathustra: Notes of the Seminar Given in 1934–1939, Part 2, Princeton, NJ: Princeton University Press, 1988.

Paracelsica: Zwei Vorlesungen über den Arzt und Philosophen Theophrastus, Zürich und Leipzig: Rascher-Verlag, 1942.

"Paracelsus: Ein Vortrag gehalten beim Geburtshaus an der Teufelsbrücke bei Einsiedeln am 22. Juni 1929," *Lesezirkel*, Vol. 16.10, September 1929, pp. 117–25.

["Paracelsus," CW 15, ¶1–17.]

"Der philosophische Baum," *Verhandlungen der Naturforschenden Gesellschaft Basel*, Vol. 56, 1945, pp. 411–23.

[Revised, in *Von den Wurzeln des Bewusstseins: Studien über den Archetypus*, Psychologische Abhandlungen 9, Zürich: Rascher-Verlag, 1954, pp. 351– 496.]

["The Philosophical Tree," CW 13, ¶304–482.]

"The Process of Individuation: Exercitia Spiritualia of St. Ignatius of Loyola," ETH Lectures 8–11, 1939; ETH Lectures 1–16, 1940, *Modern Psychology*, Vol. 4, translated by Barbara Hannah, privately published, Zurich: Karl Schippert & Co., 1940/1959, pp. 102–264.

"Psychological Commentary on 'The Tibetan Book of the Great Liberation'," CW 11, ¶759–830.

Psychologische Typen, Zürich: Rascher-Verlag, 1921.

[*Psychological Types*, translated by H. G. Baynes, London: Routledge & Kegan Paul, 1923.]

[*Psychological Types*, translation rev. (1923) by R. F. C. Hull, CW 6, 1971.]

Die Psychologie der Übertragung, Erläutert anhand einer alchemistischen Bilderserie, Für Ärzte und praktische Psychologen, Zürich: Rascher-Verlag, 1946.

["The Psychology of the Transference, interpreted in conjunction with a set of alchemical illustrations, for physicians and practical psychologists," CW 16, ¶353- 539.]

Psychologie und Alchemie, Psychologische Abhandlungen 5, Zürich: Rascher-Verlag, 1944.

[*Psychology and Alchemy*, CW 12, 1953/1968.]

Psychology and Religion (Terry Lectures, 1937), New Haven, Yale University Press, 1938.

["Psychology and Religion," CW 11, ¶1–168.]

"The Psychology of Eastern Meditation," CW 11, ¶908–49.

The Psychology of the Unconscious: A Study of the Transformation and Symbolisms of the Libido, A Contribution to the History of the Evolution of Thought, translated from *Wandlungen* (1912) by Beatrice M. Hinkle, New York: Moffat Yard, 1916, 1919; London: Kegan Paul, Trench, Trubner, 1917, 1921.

The Red Book: Liber Novus, Sonu Shamdasani, ed., translated by Mark Kyburz, John Peck, and Sonu Shamdasani, Philemon Series/Foundation of the Works of C. G. Jung, New York: W. W. Norton & Co., 2009.

"Religion und Psychologie," *Merkur* 6:5, May 1952, pp. 467–73.

    ["Answer to Buber," *Spring 1957*, translated by Robert A. Clark, New York: Analytical Psychology Club, 1957, pp. 1–9.]

    ["Antwort an Martin Buber," GW 11, pp. 657–65.]

    ["Religion and Psychology: A Reply to Martin Buber," CW 18, ¶¶1499–1513.]

"On Resurrection," letter to members of Dr. Kirsch's *Aion* seminar, 19 February 1954, CW 18, ¶¶1558–74.

Seelenprobleme der Gegenwart, Psychologische Abhandlungen 3, Zürich: Rascher-Verlag, 1931.

VII Sermones ad Mortuos, Die Sieben Belehrungen der Toten, Geschrieben von Basilides in Alexandria, der Stadt, wo der Osten den Westen berührt, Übersetzt aus dem griechischen Urtext in die deutsche Sprache, Printed for private circulation, Zurich, 1916, pp. 1–28.

    [*VII Sermones ad Mortuos. The Seven Sermons to the Dead, Written by Basilides in Alexandria, the City Where the East Toucheth the West*, translated by H. G. Baynes, Edinburgh: Neill, 1925.]

    ["Septem Sermones ad Mortuos," Appendix V, *Memories, Dreams, Reflections*, New York: Vintage/Random House (addition to paperback), 1966, pp. 378–90.]

Spirit and Nature: Papers from the Eranos Yearbooks, Joseph Campbell, ed., New York: Pantheon, 1954; London: Routledge & Kegan Paul, 1955.

Studies in Word-Association, Experiments in the Diagnosis of Psychopathological Conditions Carried Out at the Psychiatric Clinic of the University of Zurich, under the direction of C. G. Jung, New York: Moffat Yard, 1918; London: Heinemann, 1919.

    [In CW 2, ¶1–638; ¶660–727; ¶793–862; ¶918–38.]

Die Symbolik des Geistes: Studien über Psychische Phänomenologie, Psychologische Abhandlungen 6, Zürich: Rascher-Verlag, 1948.

"Traumsymbole des Individuationsprozesses: ein Beitrag zur Kenntnis der in den Träumen sich kundgebenden Vorgänge des Unbewussten," *Eranos-Jahrbuch 1935: Westöstliche Seelenführung*, herausgegeben von Olga Fröbe-Kapteyn, Zürich: Rhein-Verlag, 1936, pp. 13–133.

    ["Traumsymbole des Individuationsprozesses," *Psychologie und Alchemie*, Psychologische Abhandlungen 5, Zürich: Rascher-Verlag, 1944, pp. 69–305.]

    ["Individual Dream Symbolism in Relation to Alchemy," CW 12, 1953, ¶44–331.]

    [Rev. version in CW 12, 2nd ed., 1969, ¶44–331.]

Two Essays on Analytical Psychology, translated by H. G. and Cary F. Baynes, New York: Dodd, Mead; London: Baillière, Tindall & Cox, 1928.

"Über das Selbst," *Eranos-Jahrbuch 1948*, herausgegeben von Olga Fröbe-Kapteyn, Zürich: Rhein-Verlag, 1948, pp. 285–315.

["The Self," Ch. IV in *Aion*, CW 9(ii), ¶43–67.]

["Christ, a symbol of the Self," Ch. V in *Aion*, CW 9(ii), ¶68–126.]

"Über das Unbewusste," *Schweizerland*, Vol. 4.9, pp. 464–72; Vol. 4.11–12, 1918, pp. 548–58.

["The Role of the Unconscious," CW 10, ¶1–48.]

"Ueber die Archetypen des kollektiven Unbewussten," *Eranos-Jahrbuch 1934*, herausgegeben von Olga Fröbe-Kapteyn, Zürich: Rhein-Verlag, 1935, pp. 179–229.

["Archetypes of the Collective Unconscious," *The Integration of the Personality*, translated by Stanley Dell, New York: Farrar & Rinehart, 1939, pp. 52–95.]

["The Archetypes and the Collective Unconscious," CW 9(i), ¶1–86.]

Über die Energetik der Seele und andere psychologische Abhandlungen, Zürich: Rascher-Verlag, 1928.

"Über die Philosophie des Steins der Weisen," three papers read to the Psychological Club, January 1936, unpublished holographs, ETH Library archive.

Über psychische Energetik und das Wesen der Träume, Zürich: Rascher-Verlag, 1948. Revised and expanded from *Über die Energetik der Seele* (1928).

["On Psychic Energy," CW 8, ¶1–130; "Instinct and the Unconscious," CW 8, ¶263–82; "General Aspects of Dream Psychology," CW 8, ¶443–529; "The Psychological Foundations of Belief in Spirits," CW 8, ¶570–600.]

"Über den indischen Heiligen," Zimmer, Heinrich, *Der Weg zum Selbst*, C. G. Jung, ed., Zürich: Rascher-Verlag, 1944, pp. 11–24.

["The Holy Men of India," CW 11, ¶950–63.]

Über Träume und Wandlungen, Transcription of tape-recorded discussions with C. G. Jung at the C. G. Jung-Institut, Zürich, 1958; Düsseldorf: Walter/Patmos Verlag, 2004.

"Über Wiedergeburt," *Gestaltungen des Unbewussten*, mit einem Beitrag von Aniela Jaffé, Psychologische Abhandlungen 7, Zürich: Rascher-Verlag, 1950, pp. 37–91.

["Concerning Rebirth," CW 9(i), ¶199–258.]

"Vorwort," H. Schmid-Guisan, *Tag und Nacht*, Zürich und München: Rhein-Verlag, 1931, pp. vi-x.

["Foreword to Schmid-Guisan: *Tag und Nacht*," CW 18, ¶1711–12.]

"Vorwort," H. Zimmer, *Der Weg zum Selbst*, C. G. Jung, ed., Zürich: Rascher-Verlag, 1944, pp. 5–6.

["The Holy Men of India," CW 11, ¶950–63.]

Wandlungen und Symbole der Libido: Beiträge zur Entwicklungsgeschichte des Denkens, Leipzig and Vienna: Franz Deuticke, 1912.

[*The Psychology of the Unconscious, A Study of the Transformation and Symbolisms of the Libido, A Contribution to the History of the Evolution of Thought*, translated by Beatrice M. Hinkle, New York: Moffat Yard, 1916, 1919; London: Kegan Paul, Trench, Trubner, 1917, 1921.]

[*Symbole der Wandlung: Analyse des Vorspiels zu einer Schizophrenie*, vierte, umgearbeitete Auflage, Zürich: Rascher-Verlag, 1952.]

[*Symbols of Transformation: An Analysis of the Prelude to a Case of Schizophrenia*, translated by R. F. C. Hull, CW 5, 1975.]

"Das Wandlungssymbol in der Messe," *Eranos-Jahrbuch 1940/41*, herausgegeben von Olga Fröbe-Kapteyn, Zürich: Rhein-Verlag, 1942, pp. 67–155.

["Transformation Symbolism in the Mass," CW 11, ¶296–448.]

Wirklichkeit der Seele: Anwendungen und Fortschritte der neueren Psychologie, mit Beiträgen von Hugo Rosenthal, Emma Jung, W. M. Kranefeldt, Zürich: Rascher-Verlag, 1934.

[*The Integration of the Personality*, translated by Stanley Dell, New York: Farrar & Rinehart, 1939.]

"Wotan," *Neue Schweizer Rundschau*, Vol. 3.11, March 1936, pp. 657–69.

["Wotan," CW 10, ¶371–99.]

Von den Wurzeln des Bewusstseins: Studien über den Archetypus, Psychologische Abhandlungen 9, Zürich: Rascher-Verlag, 1954

"Your Negroid and Indian Behavior," *Forum*, Vol. 83.4, April 1930, pp. 193–99.

"Zeitgenössisches," *Neue Zürcher Zeitung* 155: 437.1, 443.1, 457, March 1934, n.p.

["A Rejoinder to Dr. Bally," CW 10, ¶1016–34.]

"Zu *Die Reden Gotamo Buddhos*," brochure copy for K. E. Neumann's translation of *Die Reden Gotamo Buddhos* (1956), in GW 18, ¶1575–80.

["On *The Discourses of the Buddha*," CW 18, ¶1575–80.]

"Zur gegenwärtigen Lage der Psychotherapie," *Zentralblatt für Psychotherapie und ihre Grenzgebiete*, Vol. 7.1, Leipzig: Herzel Verlag,1934, pp. 1–16.

["The State of Psychotherapy Today," CW 10, ¶330–70.]

"Zur Psychologie der Schelm-Figur," Radin, Paul, *Der göttliche Schelm*, Zürich: Rhein-Verlag, 1954, pp. 185–207.

["On the Psychology of the Trickster Figure," translated by R. F. C. Hull, in Radin, Paul, *The Trickster: A Study of American Indian Mythology*, with Karl Kerényi, New York: Philosophical Library; London: Routledge & Kegan Paul, 1956, pp. 193–211.]

["On the Psychology of the Trickster Figure," CW 9(i), ¶456–88.]

"Zur Psychologie des Geistes," *Eranos-Jahrbuch 1945*, herausgegeben von Olga Fröbe-Kapteyn, Zürich: Rhein-Verlag, 1946, pp. 385–448.

with Adler, G., Henderson, J., Jacobi, J., Jaffé, A., and von Franz, M.-L., *Man and His Symbols*, C. G. Jung, ed; after his death M.-L. von Franz, ed., with John Freeman, coordinating ed., London: Aldus Books; Garden City, NY: Doubleday, 1964.

with Pauli, Wolfgang, "Synchronizität als ein Prinzip akausaler Zusammenhänge," *Naturerklärung und Psyche*, Studien aus dem C. G. Jung-Institut Zürich 4, Zürich: Rascher-Verlag, 1952, pp. 1–107.

["Synchronicity: An Acausal Connecting Principle," *The Interpretation of Nature and the Psyche*, with Wolfgang Pauli, translated by R. F. C. Hull, New York: Pantheon; London: Routledge & Kegan Paul, 1955, pp. 5–146.]

["Synchronicity: An Acausal Connecting Principle," CW 8, ¶816–968.]

["An Astrological Experiment," CW 18, ¶1174–92.]

with Wilhelm, Richard, *Das Geheimnis der goldenen Blüte: Ein chinesisches Lebensbuch*, Zürich: Rascher-Verlag, 1929/1938.

* * *

Jung's Correspondences

C. G. Jung Briefe, Band I: 1906–1945; Band II: 1946–1955; Band III: 1956–1961, Herausgegeben von Aniela Jaffé in Zusammenarbeit mit Gerhard Adler. Olten und Freiburg im Breisgau: Walter-Verlag, 1972/1980.

C. G. Jung Letters, Vol. I: 1906–1950 and *Vol. II: 1951–1961*. Selected and edited by Gerhard Adler in collaboration with Aniela Jaffé. Trans. R. F. C. Hull, Princeton, NJ: Princeton University Press/London: Routledge, 1973, 1975.

"Letters to a Friend," James Kirsch, ed. and trans., *Psychological Perspectives*, Los Angeles C. G. Jung Institute. Part 1, Vol. 3.1, Spring 1972; Part 2, Vol. 3.2, Fall 1972.

and Freud, Sigmund, *The Freud/Jung Letters*, William McGuire, ed., translated by Ralph Manheim and R. F. C. Hull, Princeton, NJ: Princeton University Press, 1974.

and Neumann, Erich, *Analytical Psychology in Exile: The Correspondence of C. G. Jung and Erich Neumann*, Martin Liebscher, ed., translated by Heather McCartney, Philemon Series, Princeton, NJ: Princeton University Press, 2015.

and Pauli, Wolfgang, *Wolfgang Pauli und C. G. Jung: Ein Briefwechsel 1932–1958*, C. A. Meier, ed., Springer-Verlag Berlin/Heidelberg 1992.

– *Atom and Archetype: The Pauli/Jung Letters 1932–1958*, C. A. Meier, ed., translated from *Pauli und Jung* (1992) by David Roscoe, Princeton, NJ: Princeton University Press, 2001.

and White, Victor, *The Jung–White Letters*, Ann Conrad Lammers & Adrian Cunningham, eds, London & New York: Routledge, 2007.

* * *

Kirsch, James

"Balaam, a myth," *Bulletin*, Analytical Psychology Club of New York, Vol. 5, supplement, March 1943, pp. 7–10.

"C. G. Jung's Individuation as shown especially in 'Answer to Job'," typescript, n.d. (c.1961), ETH Library archive, pp. 1–19.

"Darstellung somatischer Phänomene im Traum," *Bericht über den VI. Allgemeinen Ärztlichen Kongress für Psychotherapie in Dresden 14. bis 17. April 1931*, Leipzig: Verlag von S. Hirzel, 1931, pp. 157–62.

["The Role of Instinct in Psychosomatic Medicine," *American Journal of Psychotherapy*, Vol. 3.2, 1 April 1949, pp. 253–60.]

"The Enigma of Moby-Dick," paper read to the APC of Los Angeles, March 1957, typescript, KML archive, pp. 1–20.

"Der Frankismus," typescript, n.d. (c.1934), Kirsch archive, pp. 234–40.

"From Hollywood to the Shores of the Spirit," paper read to the Analytical Psychology Club of Los Angeles, 12 November 1948, typescript, KML archive, pp. 1–24.

["Dreams of a Movie-Maker," *Spring 1950*, Analytical Psychology Club of New York, Inc., pp. 56–69.]

"Hamlet: A Drama of Haunted Man," *Harvest*, Vol. 8, London Analytical Psychology Club, 1962, pp. 24–46.

Interview with Gene F. Nameche, 15 December 1968, Los Angeles, California, typescript, C. G. Jung Biographical Archive, Countway Library of Medicine, Boston Medical Library and Harvard Medical School, Boston, Massachusetts ("Countway Interview"), pp. 1–36.

"Job," lecture broadcast on radio station KPFK, Los Angeles, April 1960, typescript, KML archive, pp. 1–18.

"Journey to the Moon," *Studien zur Analytischen Psychologie C. G. Jungs. I. Beiträge aus Theorie und Praxis, Festschrift zum 80. Geburtstag von C. G. Jung*, herausgegeben vom C. G. Jung-Institut Zürich, Zürich: Rascher-Verlag, 1955, pp. 319–35.

"Die Judenfrage in der Psychotherapie: Einige Bemerkungen zu einem Aufsatz von C. G. Jung," *Jüdische Rundschau*, Nr. 43, 29 May 1934, p. 11.

"'King Lear' as a Play of Redemption," paper read to the Analytical Psychology Club of Los Angeles, January 1961, typescript, KML archive, pp. 1–17.

"My personal contact with Jung," paper read to UCLA workshop, 24 October 1970, untitled typescript, Kirsch archive, pp. 1–15.

"The Nazi and his Significance in the Unconscious," paper read to the Analytical Psychology Club of New York, 20 November 1942, typescript, KML archive, pp. 1–31.

"Presidential Address," paper read to the Analytical Psychology Club of Los Angeles, 6 October 1944, typescript, KML archive, pp. 1–10.

"Das Problem des modernen Juden," paper read to the Psychological Club, Zurich, 4 October 1930. Typescript, Psychological Club, Zurich.

["A contribution to the problem of the present-day Jew in the light of modern psychology." Undated typescript, Psychological Club, Zurich.]

"The Problem of Dictatorship as Represented in Moby-Dick," paper read at the first Congress of the International Association of Analytical Psychology, Zurich, 11 August 1958, *Current Trends in Analytical Psychology*, Gerhard Adler, ed., London: Tavistock Publications, 1961, pp. 261–74.

"Psychology and Religion," three lectures broadcast on radio station KPFK, Los Angeles, April 1960, typescript, KML archive. Lecture #1, pp. 1–14; Lecture #2, pp. 1–16; Lecture #3, pp. 1–13.

"Psychology and the New World," paper read to the Analytical Psychology Club of Los Angeles, 12 October 1945, typescript, KML archive, pp. 1–11.

"Reconsidering Jung's So-Called Anti-Semitism," *The Arms of the Windmill: Essays in Analytical Psychology in Honor of Werner H. Engel*, New York: The Jung Foundation, 1984, pp. 5–27.

"'The Red One': A psychological interpretation of a story by Jack London," paper read at a meeting of Jungian analysts, 22 May 1954, Carmel, California, typescript, KML archive, pp. 1–25.

    ["Jack London's Quest: 'The Red One'," *Psychological Perspectives*, Vol. 11.2, Fall 1980, The C. G. Jung Institute of Los Angeles, pp. 137–54.]

    ["'The Red One': A psychological interpretation of a story by Jack London," *The Jung–Kirsch Letters*, present volume Appendix C, pp. 287–303.]

"Reflections at Age Eighty-Four," *A Modern Jew in Search of a Soul,* J. Marvin Spiegelman and Abraham Jacobson, ed., Phoenix, AZ: Falcon Press, 1986, pp. 147–55.

The Religious Aspect of the Unconscious, Guild Lecture No. 1, London: The Guild of Pastoral Psychology, 8 February 1939, KML archive.

"Religious Problems of a Young Psychologist," paper read at a meeting of Jungian analysts, Carmel, California, 7 March 1960, typescript, KML archive, pp. 1–15.

The Reluctant Prophet: An Exploration of Prophecy and Dreams, Los Angeles: Sherbourne Press, Inc., 1973.

Review of book, *"Tormented Master: A Life of Rabbi Nahman of Bratzlav*, by Arthur Green," *Quadrant*, Vol. 13.2, Fall 1980, New York: C. G. Jung Foundation for Analytical Psychology, pp. 125–27.

"The Role of Instinct in Psychosomatic Medicine," *American Journal of Psychotherapy*, Vol. 3.2, 1 April 1949, pp. 253–60.

"The Role of the Analyst in Jung's Psychotherapy," paper read at conference on Zen and Psychotherapy, Cuernavaca, Mexico, 6 August 1957, typescript, ETH Library archive, pp. 1–15.

    ["Affinities between Zen and Analytical Psychology," *Psychologia: An International Journal of Psychology in the Orient*, Vol. 3.2, 2 June 1960, Kyoto, Japan, pp. 85–91.]

"Schlusswort," article intended for *Jüdische Rundschau*, June 1934, typescript, ETH Library archive (Jung–Kirsch correspondence), pp. 1–2.

    ["Conclusion," *The Jung–Kirsch Letters*, present volume, pp. 54–6.]

"Seminar on the Pentateuch," course given at the Analytical Psychology Club of New York, 16–27 August 1943, typescript, from notes of listeners, KML archive, pp. 1–117.

Shakespeare's Royal Self, Zürich: Daimon Verlag, 1966.

"The Sleepwalking Scene in 'Macbeth'," *Harvest*, Vol. 10, London Analytical Psychology Club, 1964, pp. 80–91.

"The Story of the Seven Beggars: A contribution to the understanding of Jewish psychology," paper read to the Analytical Psychology Club of Los Angeles, 21 October 1949, typescript, KML archive, pp. 1–25.

"Then he will open the ears of men" (Hebrew title: אז יגלה אזן אנשים), paper read to a general audience in Tel Aviv, spring 1934, typescript, ETH Library archive, pp. 1–16.

["Then he will open the ears of men," *The Jung–Kirsch Letters*, present volume Appendix A, pp. 267–77.]

"Das Weltbild des Juden," paper enclosed in letter to Jung, spring 1931, typescript, ETH archive, Jung–Kirsch correspondence, pp. 1–2.

["The Jewish Image of the World," *The Jung–Kirsch Letters*, present volume pp. 15–16.]

* * *

Secondary sources

Cocks, Geoffrey, *Psychotherapy in the Third Reich: The Göring Institute*, 2nd ed., New Brunswick, NJ: Transaction Publishers, 1997.

Iselin, Hans Konrad, *Zur Entstehung von C. G. Jungs "Psychologische Typen": Der Briefwechsel zwischen C. G. Jung und Hans Schmid-Guisan im Lichte ihrer Freundschaft*, Basel: Verlag Sauerländer, 1982.

Jaffé, Aniela, *From the Life and Work of C. G. Jung*, translated by R. F. C. Hull and Murray Stein, Einsiedeln: Daimon Verlag, 1989.

Jones, Ernest, *The Life and Work of Sigmund Freud, Vol. 2: 1901–1919: Years of Maturity*, New York: Basic Books, 1955.

Jung, Emma, *Animus and Anima*, translated by Cary F. Baynes ("On the Nature of the Animus") and Hildegard Nagel ("The Anima as an Elemental Being"), New York: Spring, 1957.

Scholem, Gershom, *Major Trends in Jewish Mysticism*, New York: Schocken Books, 1941.

– *Die jüdische Mystik in ihren Hauptströmungen*, Berlin: Suhrkamp Verlag, 1957.

Stiftung C. G. Jung Küsnacht, ed., *The House of C. G. Jung: The History and Restoration of the Residence of Emma and Carl Gustav Jung-Rauschenbach*, Wilmette, IL: Chiron Publications, 2009.

INDEX

Page references in *italic* indicate illustrations. These are also listed in full at the beginning of the book, after the Contents. With regard to **footnotes**, where a subject or person is discussed only in a footnote, with at most a passing mention in the text, the page number is followed by the letter 'n' and the note number, e.g. 3n1; but where discussion is to be found in both the text and notes, only the simple page number is given, with the following exceptions: (1) where the note, but not the textual reference, continues onto the next page, both references are given; (2) where the identity is obscure in the text but clarified in a note, the note is given after the page number, but enclosed in brackets, e.g. 170[n62].

Printed in Great Britain
by Amazon